Southern
Exposure

International Development
and the Global South
in the Twenty-First Century

BARBARA P. THOMAS-SLAYTER

Kumarian
Press, Inc.

Southern Exposure: International Development and the Global South in the Twenty-First Century

Published 2003 in the United States of America by Kumarian Press, Inc.
1294 Blue Hills Avenue, Bloomfield, CT 06002 USA.

Production, design, indexing, and proofreading by ediType, Yorktown Heights, N.Y.
The text of this book is set in 10.5/13.5 Sabon. The display type is Myriad.

Printed in Canada on acid-free paper by Transcontinental Printing.
Text printed with vegetable oil–based ink.

∞ The paper used in this publication meets the minimum requirements of the American National Standard for Information Sciences–Permanence of Paper for Printed Library Materials, ANSI Z39.48–1984.

Publisher's Cataloging-in-Publication Data

Thomas-Slayter, Barbara P.
  Southern exposure : international development and the Global South in the twenty-first century / Barbara P. Thomas-Slayter.

    p. : ill. ; cm.
  Includes bibliographical references and index.

    ISBN: 1-565-49174-2 (paper)
    ISBN: 1-565-49175-0 (cloth)

  1. Globalization. 2. Economic development – Developing countries. 3. Developing countries – Politics and government. 4. Developing countries – Economic conditions. I. Title.

HN980 .T46 2003
361.9/1/091724

---

11 10 09 08 07 06 05 04 03   10 9 8 7 6 5 4 3 2 1   First Printing 2003

For Henry
with love and appreciation

And for our next generations
for whom we wish a more generous
and peaceful world

Contents

PART ONE
POLITICAL CHANGE: TRAPS, ILLUSIONS,
AND OPPORTUNITIES

PART THREE
CRITICAL ISSUES: POPULATION DYNAMICS,
FOOD SECURITY, AND ENVIRONMENTAL
DEGRADATION

PART FOUR
DESIGNING OUR FUTURE:
LOCAL ACTION AND GLOBAL CHANGE

Illustrations

TABLES

FIGURES

Preface

Southern Exposure is based on two premises: that poverty and inequality in the countries of the Global South are increasing in this era of rapid globalization and that they are among our most urgent problems today, lending themselves not only to unspeakable misery, but also providing fertile fields for anger, hostility, and violence. My approach is to examine processes of global change from the perspectives of people of the South. I hope to bring to center stage the issues faced largely by ordinary citizens rather than those of elites, those who are Western-educated, or Northerners. This is not to suggest that the fisherman in Maine is not as important as the one from the Philippines, that a taxi driver in London isn't facing problems as serious to him as those of the *matatu* driver in Kenya, or that the garment workers in San Francisco do not need many improvements in the workplace, although they likely already work in safer conditions than those provided in many of the sweatshops in Bangladesh.

Southern Exposure grows out of my involvement in the development field for more than thirty years, which has involved teaching and administration in a graduate and undergraduate program in international development at Clark University, a small, innovative New England university with a diverse student body and a strong focus on international and environmental issues. I also have a long-term association with Oxfam America, a non-governmental development and relief organization based in Boston and affiliated with Oxfam International. I have served on the board of directors of Oxfam America and have been involved, as well, with other organizations engaged in international development work. Living in four countries in Asia and Africa for over ten years has shaped many of my viewpoints. In addition, I have conducted a number of short-term research activities that have taken me to various corners of the globe. Whether interviewing members of a fishing cooperative on a remote island in the Philippines, working with children in an after-school program in Sri Lanka, meeting with elders in Nepal, or helping women in rural Kenya repair a feeder road, I have had the opportunity to observe people in a variety of settings as they go about their daily work, and I have learned from them.

When does the seed for a book first take root and how does its title emerge? For many years I have taught undergraduates in an introductory course on issues in the Third World. I have hoped that I was exposing them to experiences and perspectives of people whose lives were very different from their own but who shared many of the same concerns. I have drawn on my experience living and working in other countries, as well as ideas and viewpoints that have been challenged and expanded by the intellectual exchange of an academic community. Readings for the course have varied from academic textbooks to novels, autobiographies, journal articles, and even newspaper editorials. These classes often have a strong representation of international students from every part of the world, and I easily incorporate them into discussions, enabling them to share their perspectives on the reading materials as well as their experiences where they relate to the topic at hand. Many dimensions of exposure to the Global South have taken place in that classroom, and many students who have been in it have indicated their surprise and pleasure, as well their growth in understanding and in empathy.

Thus, I draw on an educational interpretation of the term "Southern Exposure" to suggest that Northerners — people like myself and many of my students — need more and better exposure to the ideas and experiences of the Global South. In the United States there can be a discouraging lack of information about and interest in other parts of the world, but an interest can be nurtured and even ignited. I hope, of course, that this volume, in some measure, contributes to this process.

To my mind, however, the term "Southern Exposure" has not only an educational meaning, but also a critical political and economic dimension. In particular, I see this title as referring to the exposure of the Global South to globalization processes in ways that make it vulnerable or exploited or "exposed." Exposure in this sense is detrimental to the nations of the South. We in the North have — collectively — not been very much aware of that exposure of the Global South, swept up as we have been in the high-flying economy of the 1990s. Now, however, the joy ride is over at least for the time being, and we have new, as well as continuing, worries in the forms of terrorism, escalating ethnic and religious conflicts, a devastating AIDS epidemic in Africa and elsewhere, competition in a newly multipolar world, and cultural antagonisms, not to mention an uneasy economy, that we are only beginning to understand. We are now perhaps, as a people, ready to look more closely at the nations and cultures of the Global South and to seek a "Southern Exposure." Such exposure is not only timely; it is well overdue.

Last, I have lived most of my adult life in New England, a part of the United States that has long, cold winters and short hours of daylight for several months of the year. Southern light can illuminate and brighten the most dreary of days. Using that metaphor I hope that this "Southern Exposure" can help provide illumination around the issues and problems faced by nations of the Global South in this period of very rapid global change. We have a tremendous need for empathy that crosses cultures and political boundaries, for political will to address urgent and difficult problems, and for institutions that are accountable to all of us on this globe. It is, after all, our collective journey, and we hope it is toward a more wise, just, and generous world.

Acknowledgments

The ideas, wisdom, and experience of many people have helped to shape *Southern Exposure*, and I am grateful to all of them. First and foremost are the men and women of communities in Honduras, India, Kenya, Nepal, the Philippines, and several other countries. Their observations and insights about their lives and the forces affecting them are at the core of this volume. It has been a privilege to get to know them, and I hope that this book in some way contributes to a broader understanding of their varied experiences and the challenges they face.

Over many years, colleagues from around the world have been unstinting partners in research, generously sharing their time, their ideas, and the workload. At home, it has been a privilege to work with associates at Oxfam America and to reflect — collectively — with board and staff (in many a meeting!) on the issues confronting and values shaping a non-governmental organization striving to address international equity and justice concerns.

Longtime colleagues at Clark University have, over many years, provided valued friendship and spurred thoughts about processes of political and social change. I am particularly grateful to a core of colleagues in International Development, not only for thoughts related to this book, but also for many years of congenial — even convivial — collaboration: Kristina Allen, Richard Ford, and Elizabeth Owens. To my students, I must acknowledge a particular debt of gratitude since this volume emerged out of numerous discussions and debates, whether in an undergraduate lecture hall, a graduate seminar, or a conversation over a cup of coffee. In fact, some — among them, Nina Bhatt, Andrea Esser, Njoki Mbuthi, Dale Shields, Laju Shrestha, Genese Sodikoff, and Anne-Marie Urban — have participated in extensive field research central to this volume.

Guy Bentham at Kumarian Press provided valuable comments and guidance on this manuscript, as did several unnamed but very thoughtful readers. Erin Brown and her colleagues in production were extraordinarily helpful throughout that process. To Ruth Allen, Dick Ford, Kate

Lazarus, Femy Pinto, Gwen Thomas, and Stephen Thomas, my heartfelt thanks for careful research, design of illustrations, and patient editing. Many thanks go to my extended, blended family, a source of inspiration, amusement, drama, distraction, support, and love over the years. Finally to my husband, Henry Slayter, my deep gratitude for his generous good spirits, wry humor, and untiring support. You are all very much appreciated!

Chapter 1

Understanding the "Global South"

Poverty, Wealth, and Change

To speak about "development" and the "Developing World," or the "Global South" as it is now often called, is difficult, given the contentious meanings of these terms. To understand these meanings we must begin not only by sorting out definitions, but by creating a mental picture of what it means to be poor, with few resources and few opportunities in many countries of the world at the beginning of the twenty-first century. It is not difficult to create this picture. We have a lot of help from a vast literature about village life in Bangladesh or Kenya or the struggling urban poor in India or Brazil. There are films — *Salam Bombay* to help us explore the dark side of child prostitution in Bombay, or *Valentina's Nightmare* to make vivid the horrors of the 1994 butchery in Rwanda when eight hundred thousand Tutsis were killed within a hundred days. Documentaries and news stories may reveal the strengths of the emerging powers of China or Mexico, the desperation of AIDS victims in Uganda, or the impacts of forest fires and smog on villagers in Indonesia. We have these images and we can obtain many of the facts that accompany them, but then we must somehow relate these facts, these people, and these situations to the broad context in which we all exist. We must understand the attitudes that permit them, the events that shape them, the structures that keep them in place, and the policies that sustain them.

We have had some help — even what some would consider a "wake-up call" in our efforts to understand a world apart from our own — in the form of the September 11, 2001, attack on the twin towers of New York City's World Trade Center. In the aftermath of 9/11, there has been an enormous effort to explain the causes of such terrorist attacks and how to prevent them in the future. We have gained some insights into how those who are weak, goaded by a sense of powerlessness, grievance, and perhaps hatred of a nation perceived as a Goliath, might derive some

1

satisfaction from the collapse of these symbols of American power and affluence. We have become aware of the deep frustrations and possibly humiliating choices perceived by some as they seek both to protect their way of life and to pursue an apocalyptic vision.

Securing the United States and other nations against the threat of terrorism is a high priority, but it requires more than military action. As longtime *New York Times* columnist Anthony Lewis, asserted, it will require "a profound effort by America and the West to ease the poverty and misery of the developing world.... Attacking the indecency of life in much of the Southern Hemisphere is no longer a matter of grace, of charity, of patronizing kindness. It is a matter of intense self-interest. For our own sake, we need to reduce the well of resentment."[1] Many others suggest that it is a matter of urgency that top international policy priorities become the reduction of poverty, improvements in health in developing countries, and a fair distribution of economic benefits within the global economy. In fact, one analyst puts it frankly, "If we do not promote economic growth in Muslim nations, we will, by default, promote growth in the supply of potential terrorists."[2] Others suggest that resentments have been simmering a long time among the billions of impoverished people in the world toward technologically advanced nations whose way of life — rightly or wrongly, accurately or inaccurately — is portrayed in the global media as rich and overconsuming.

Indeed, if the stubborn realities of hunger and poverty create desperate conditions and fuel despair and resentment, we need to try to understand the sources of these problems and what we as global citizens can do to address them. This is no small task, but it is the one to which this volume is dedicated. We begin in this chapter by asking some key questions: What is the "Global South"? What is the "Third World"? What is "development"? What new issues confront both South and North? What are the human dimensions of being poor and living in the developing world? How do race, ethnicity, religion, gender, and class interact in our changing global system? How can processes of an equitable globalization be focused to eliminate poverty and hunger, reduce disease, and strengthen local economies? We pose these questions in the broadest sense, but use specific illustrations from a handful of countries of the Global South to clarify them. These countries are largely drawn from among those in which the author has lived and/or worked over a number of years, particularly India, the Philippines, Kenya, Nepal, Bangladesh, Bolivia, Ethiopia, Eritrea, and Zimbabwe.

Later chapters focus on several themes. The first is political change (traps, illusions, and opportunities) examining the history of North-South relationships (chapter 2); the contemporary issues of politics and the state (chapter 3); and issues of power, conflict, and human rights (chapter 4). The second theme explores economic trends, crises, and challenges in terms of the shape of the global economy (chapter 5) and from the perspective of local livelihoods of peoples of the Global South (chapter 6). A third theme focuses on population, food, and the environment, with concerns including how these relate to development (chapter 7) and food security and rural politics (chapter 8). Last, chapter 9 considers the future: How can we create a new agenda for social change, fairness, and justice? What choices are there for addressing our common concerns and challenges? Who is speaking out in ways that might make a difference to the problems we see and the trends we have identified for the developing world in a changing global system? And so, let us begin.

What Is the Global South?

The "Global South" is one in a series of terms that has been used for at least four decades to categorize the nonindustrialized, largely agricultural, poorer nations of the world which, for the most part, have at one time been colonized by the nations of the North. It is not a particularly accurate bit of nomenclature given that not all the countries are literally in the South (and not all of the colonizers are in the North). It also includes countries with an incredible range of attributes including Mali with a gross national income (GNI) of $240 per capita, and Mexico with a GNI of $5,080, according to the World Bank's 2002 *World Development Report*.[3]

The "Global South," however, is a term that is somewhat more meaningful than the "Third World," a catch-all phrase used to refer to the less developed countries. "Third World" suggests that these countries are neither part of the "first world" of the industrialized market economies of Western Europe, North America, and the Pacific, nor part of the centrally planned economies of the Soviet Union and Eastern Europe which constituted the "second world" until 1989 and the fall of the Berlin Wall. Parallel distinctions are South-North, developing-developed, less developed countries (LDCs) and industrialized countries. Using these distinctions, new nations such as Tajikistan or Uzbekistan would be part of the Global South, but those pockets of poverty found in the North, such as coal mining districts in West Virginia, would not.

The origins of the term "third world" are interesting. The concept arose after World War II, partly out of a rejection of capitalist and socialist causes that crystalized at the Bandung Conference in Indonesia in 1955. At that conference many of the nonaligned, newly independent countries of the South met under the leadership of Jawaharlal Nehru of India and Achmad Sukarno of Indonesia, declaring that there was a third alternative to the ideologies and lifestyles of the "first world" or the "second world." What the term clearly did not mean was "third rate" or "third class." At the Bandung Conference, a psychological unity was present among the participants despite diversity in ideologies and in economic and political orientations. That unity grew out of their common colonial experience and the exploitation that many had experienced in their relations with the nations of the North.

Today, within the rapidly changing global system that exists at the turn of the century, these old perceptions of a common experience at the hands of colonial powers may be modifying the psychological unity engendered mid-century. Today new patterns of exploitation in neocolonial forms, still not fully understood, are slowly becoming identifiable. Most extraordinary is the evidence of increasing inequities in the general standard of living between the developing and industrialized countries, and within countries around the world, between an affluent few and the many impoverished. Economic statistics capture these differences in the form of per capita incomes for each nation and in figures for gross national income. Table 1.1 compares the data in those two categories for nine countries designated, according to World Bank indicators, as high income, medium income, and low income. The range of per capita income is $100 in the Democratic Republic of Congo and Ethiopia to Switzerland at $38,120. The range of GNI is from Sierra Leone at the low end with $0.6 billion to Japan at $4,337.3 billion, exceeded only by the United States at $9,645.6 billion.

Along with an annual indicator of GNI, it is useful to consider relative growth rates of national income. The figures tell an amazing story. In 1997 six countries for which there are data had declining rates of growth, including Ukraine, Morocco, and Romania. Some, such as the Democratic Republic of Congo, had no figures available at all. On the whole, however, the rate of growth for the low income countries at 5 percent was higher than that for the high income countries at 2.8 percent.

Table 1.1. Economic Indicators for Selected Nations

Nation	Gross National Income* 2000 (Billions of $)	GNI Per Capita 2000 ($)
Low Income		
Ethiopia	6.7	100
Haiti	4.0	510
Nepal	5.3	220
Middle Income		
Ecuador	15.3	1,210
Egypt	95.2	1,490
Malaysia	78.5	3,380
High Income		
Australia	394.1	20,530
Canada	647.1	21,050
Norway	151.2	33,650

Source: The World Bank, *Building Institutions for Markets: World Development Report 2002*, 232–33.

*Gross national income (GNI) is a new term for gross national product (GNP).

When you take into account, however, that the population in the wealthier countries is growing more slowly, then it is clear that the gap between richer and poorer nations, in terms of income, is actually widening.

Perhaps even more revealing is to look at these same countries in terms of key indicators for human development. The United Nations provides an annual Human Development Report offering some important indicators of overall well-being. The human development index is a composite rating based on indicators of life expectancy at birth, adult literacy rate, and gross domestic product on a per capita basis. We can review the countries illustrated in Table 1.1 from the perspective of several indicators of health and well-being. Table 1.2 indicates the range of national variation for three indicators: (1) life expectancy at birth, (2) adult literacy rate, and (3) mortality rates per 1,000 children for children under five years.

Among all nations, the country with the lowest life expectancy and the highest child mortality rates is Sierra Leone, with life expectancy for women nearly forty years and for men thirty-seven years. Its mortality rate for children under five stands at 316 per 1,000 births. Niger ranks lowest on adult literacy at 7.9 percent for women and 23 percent for men.

Table 1.2. Indicators of Human Well-Being across Selected Nations

Nation	Life Expectancy 1999	Adult Literacy 1999 (% age 15 & above)	Child Mortality for Children under 5 1999 (per 1,000)
	Female/Male	Female/Male	
Low Income			
Ethiopia	44.9/43.3	31.8/42.8	166
Haiti	55.4/49.4	46.8/51.1	118
Nepal	57.8/58.3	22.8/58.0	109
Middle Income			
Ecuador	72.8/67.6	89.1/92.8	35
Egypt	68.5/65.3	42.8/66.1	54
Malaysia	74.8/69.9	82.8/91.1	10
*High Income**			
Australia	81.7/76.0	— / —	5
Canada	81.4/75.9	— / —	6
Norway	81.3/75.4	— / —	4

Source: United Nations Development Programme, *Human Development Report: Making New Technologies Work for Human Development,* 2001, 166–69, 210–13.

*For high income countries the adult literacy rate is effectively 100 percent.

In addition, one must look at the gap between rich and poor within national boundaries. All nations show disparities between incomes of the rich and the poor, but the gap is generally greater in the less developed countries than in the industrialized nations. In Brazil, for example, the richest 10 percent of the population have approximately 48 percent of total income or consumption, while the poorest 10 percent have less than 1 percent. In Zimbabwe the richest 10 percent control 47 percent of income or consumption while the poorest 10 percent have 1.8 percent. Those nations that would be considered the most egalitarian are Norway with the richest 10 percent controlling 21 percent of income/consumption while the poorest 10 percent control just over 4 percent, or Belgium with the richest controlling 20 percent and the poorest just under 4 percent. The most egregious cases of domestic inequity for which data are available (excluding the oil-rich countries of the Middle East) are found in Latin America and Africa.[4] Thus, it is important to look not only at the growth of overall income or at income per capita; we must also look at how that income is distributed among the population — that is, who benefits from the economic growth that is taking place. High per capita incomes, such as those found in the Persian Gulf states or among the elites in Kenya, do not guarantee the absence of poverty.

Differences among Nations of the Global South

The nations of the Global South differ in some important ways. There are large and populous nations like Brazil, India, Nigeria, and Egypt, and others small in size such as Nepal, Burundi, or Belize, or small in population such as Botswana, Guyana, or Fiji. Large size usually implies diverse resources, large potential markets, and perhaps less dependence on foreign sources for materials. Large size can present its own problems, however, including administrative control, communications, and cohesion among diverse regions and ethnic groups. India now has over 1 billion people; by contrast, Gambia and Mauritius have populations of just over 1 million. Given its large size and diversity across regions, ethnic groups, and linguistic groups, many have predicted that the division of the Asian subcontinent into two states in 1947, Pakistan and India, would be followed by the break-up of India into several nation-states. Despite the range of problems it has faced, however, India has remained one, a phenomenon we explore in chapter 3.

Then, too, the countries of the Global South differ enormously in endowments including physical resources and trained citizens. Some, like Kuwait and other Persian Gulf oil states, are extremely rich; others have few raw materials and minerals. Bangladesh, for example, has fertile agricultural land and abundant water, but little else in the way of natural resources (besides an abundant labor force) that would enable it to diversify its economy. Still others may have resources as yet unknown and unexplored because of poverty or because of widespread conflict. Both Sudan and Somalia could fit into this category. In terms of human capacities, some, such as China or India, have a long tradition of education and a large network of universities. Others — Mozambique or Senegal, for example — were left by their colonizers without anything much resembling an educational system and have had to struggle to begin the process of building an educational base.

The structures of production vary as well. Most developing countries are agrarian with both subsistence and commercial agriculture, but the structures of agrarian systems and of land ownership differ greatly.

Kenya, for example, has many small farmers who are independent land-owners on farms of two to ten acres. Bangladesh has a high percentage of tenant farmers; Indonesia, the Philippines, and Bangladesh have growing numbers of landless laborers living in the rural areas and seeking a living off the land. Many Latin American countries have large plantations with wage laborers in some combination of hired labor and tenancy or sharecropping. If we think of agriculture in terms of the income categories of Table 1.1, data indicate that agriculture employs from 70 to 90 percent of the labor force in low income countries, approximately 35 to 55 percent in middle income developing countries, and in the affluent countries 2 to 5 percent.[5]

At the same time the relative importance of manufacturing and service sectors varies widely. Some of the Latin American countries, such as Brazil and Argentina, have advanced industrial sectors. India is a nuclear power, has a modern army, and possesses one of the most advanced computer programming capabilities in the world. Yet its significant manufacturing and industrial sector is small in relation to its enormous rural population, much of which is illiterate, impoverished, malnourished, and lacking the basics in clean water and access to health services.

The nations of the so-called Global South have very different historical backgrounds and social structures. The Bandung Conference in 1955 brought them together and emphasized their "common heritage" as colonized peoples. However, they represent highly diverse cultures and peoples who have inherited a wide variety of colonial institutions from the Belgians, British, Dutch, French, Germans, Portuguese, and Spanish. Some, like Sri Lanka, had more than one colonizer. Not only is Sri Lanka the home of two distinct groups, the Buddhist Sinhalese and the Hindu Tamils, Sri Lanka was colonized by the Portuguese, Dutch, and British in that order, and each of the colonizers left behind its social and institutional imprint, for better or for worse. This is indeed a complex social and political history, and Sri Lanka is not alone.

Finally, the levels of external dependence experienced by countries of the Global South vary widely. In our increasingly connected global economy, it is difficult to find specific boundaries indicating dependence or independence. Nevertheless, economic, political, and cultural autonomy clearly relate largely to a country's size and resource base. Most small nations are dependent on outside sources for a wide range of technologies and manufactured goods, and may also depend on imported educational or health care systems. For many countries of the Global

South this dependence is increasing, not decreasing — and is substantial. Large nations, like India or China, have been able in many ways to dictate the terms on which they engage the world economy. China, for example, closed itself off for a number of years in order to develop an industrial/manufacturing sector, and now is more than eager for full engagement in the global economy.

Common Characteristics of Developing Nations

If there are some key differences among the countries of the Global South, there are also some common characteristics. First and foremost is a continuing struggle for secure livelihoods amidst conditions of serious poverty for a large number of people in these nations. For many, incomes are low, access to resources is limited, housing is inadequate, health is poor, educational opportunities are insufficient, and there are high infant mortality rates along with low life expectancy. Specific health concerns focus on malnutrition, preventable disease, inadequate protein consumption, and inadequate medical care. In educational attainment, low levels of literacy, significant school dropout rates, an inadequate and irrelevant curricula, and poor facilities often characterize these countries. Figures given in Table 1.2 are illustrative of the kinds of problems faced by people in more than thirty-six countries characterized as countries of "low human development" in the United Nations Development Programme's 2001 *Human Development Report*. Figure 1.1 shows the distribution across continents of those countries most characterized by low human development indicators, as defined by the United Nations.

In addition to the attributes associated with a low standard of living, several other characteristics are common to the Global South. One is the high rate of population growth and a consequent high dependency burden. Average population growth rates of the poorer countries have been declining over the last several decades, but they remain an overwhelming concern for many countries. A few countries, particularly in Africa, have a high population growth rate, Kenya at 3.4 percent and Mozambique at 3.8 percent, for example. In countries where growth is high, so is the dependency burden — that is, the responsibility for dependents, largely young children. In many countries almost half the population is under fifteen years old. This population composition represents not only a significant responsibility, but in the immediate future, it creates demands on services for schools, transport, new jobs, and related infrastructure. If a

Figure 1.1. Countries Most Characterized by Low Life Expectancy, Low Adult Literacy, and High Child Mortality.

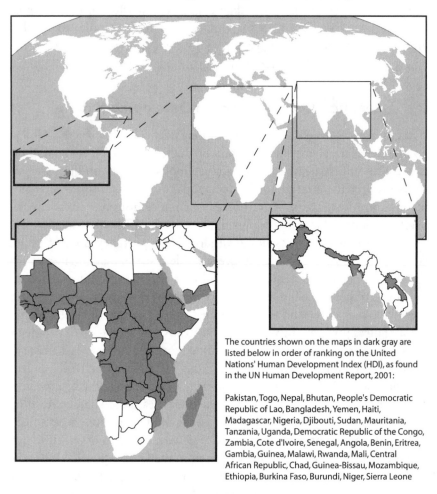

The countries shown on the maps in dark gray are listed below in order of ranking on the United Nations' Human Development Index (HDI), as found in the UN Human Development Report, 2001:

Pakistan, Togo, Nepal, Bhutan, People's Democratic Republic of Lao, Bangladesh, Yemen, Haiti, Madagascar, Nigeria, Djibouti, Sudan, Mauritania, Tanzania, Uganda, Democratic Republic of the Congo, Zambia, Cote d'Ivoire, Senegal, Angola, Benin, Eritrea, Gambia, Guinea, Malawi, Rwanda, Mali, Central African Republic, Chad, Guinea-Bissau, Mozambique, Ethiopia, Burkina Faso, Burundi, Niger, Sierra Leone

nation's gross national income (GNI) is growing at 2 percent a year and its population is growing at that rate too, then any gains are wiped out.

A common feature of countries of the Global South is high and rising levels of unemployment and underemployment. If you consider both underemployed and unemployed, much of the combined urban and rural labor force in developing countries is underutilized. If the population is growing quickly, the labor force is also growing rapidly, and jobs have to be created to keep pace with the growing labor supply. Needless to say, this problem is acute in many parts of the world with all sorts of ramifications in terms of rural-urban and international migration.

In most countries of the Global South, agriculture continues to dominate industry, manufacturing, and services in the formation of the structures of production. For many African countries agriculture constitutes more than 50 percent of the gross domestic product; for Bangladesh (at 30 percent) or Nepal (43 percent) or India (27 percent) it is high, unlike the 2 or 3 percent for the Netherlands, Japan, or Italy, which although possessing strong agricultural production, have diversified economies. Moreover, many developing economies are still highly dependent on the export of primary commodities — food, raw materials, fuels, and base metals — patterns established during the colonial era. As of 1999, primary commodities account for almost 24 percent of all developing country exports. Despite this dependence, export growth has not kept pace (excluding oil) with that of industrialized nations. The Southern nations' share of total world trade has been falling.

Another common feature is a dependence and vulnerability in international political and economic relations. The distribution of economic and political power between rich and poor nations is highly unequal. Nowhere has this vulnerability been more evident than in the Asian financial crisis of mid-1997 and 1998. Rich nations can control the patterns of international trade; can determine the terms according to which technology, capital, and aid are made available to developing countries; and now, with a flick of a key on a computer, can control financial flows in ways that may be highly detrimental to the developing world and beneficial largely to the financiers of the North. Globalization is in fact quite segmented and is creating widening inequalities between nations.

Finally, it is evident that high levels of ambivalence toward the West and Western ways characterize the people in many nations of the South. We have been sharply reminded of this fact by events of September 11, 2001. On the one hand there is a deep resentment of colonialism, imperialism, and the informal political and economic ties of neocolonialism linking colonies to the former imperial power. While not everyone goes so far as to fear cultural annihilation from the impact of the industrialized North, there are widespread and powerful themes of emancipation, self-respect, and self-determination. While these viewpoints may currently be most evident in the Islamic world, they exist widely throughout the Global South. There is, on the one hand, a distaste for the forces of global cultural homogenization: McDonald's, Nike, Coca-Cola, IBM and many other reminders of Westernization. On the other hand, there is a tremendous and widespread desire to have blue jeans, cell phones, and motorcycles, along with the science, technology, and communications capabilities permitting them. These conflicting desires to both reject and embrace Westernization characterize many people of the Global South at the turn of the century.

What Is Development?

Traditional measures of development have been largely economic. People have looked at the capacity of a national economy to generate and sustain increases in gross national income that exceed population growth rates. Economists have also regarded development in terms of changes in the structures of production and employment. As agriculture's share of production and employment has declined and that of industry, manufacturing, and services increased, development is said to be taking place. This is, of course, a narrow definition; it has become clear over time that nations could achieve growth targets in GNI without the quality of life for the majority of people improving at all. Many scholars, philosophers, policymakers, and development practitioners — not to mention ordinary citizens around the world — are aware that reductions of poverty, inequality, and unemployment, among other things, are essential ingredients in a "development process."

So what does development include? Denis Goulet, an economist-cum-philosopher, offers a thoughtful definition based on three core values: life sustenance, self-esteem, and freedom.[6] For him, life sustenance includes adequate food, shelter, health, and security and can be measured in the form of calories consumed, literacy rates, school enrollments, life expectancy, or infant mortality. These constitute a necessary but not sufficient condition for development.

Self-esteem entails a sense of self-worth and respect. The nature and form of self-esteem vary from one society and culture to another, but it entails maintaining confidence in one's own way of life and viewpoints. Freedom, Goulet's last core value, involves freedom from harmful material conditions of life, such as physical violence or intimidation, and freedom for increased choices of behavior and lifestyle. In that sense, "development" is composed of physical, ethical, and philosophical elements. Development is not value free, and it evolves within a sociopolitical context that varies with each society and culture.

It is easy but incorrect to assume that the lifestyle assuring a TV in every living room, a sports utility vehicle in the garage, and a dishwasher in the kitchen is the lifestyle to which everyone around the world aspires. While material wealth is no doubt increasingly associated with self-esteem, it does not follow that "to be richer is to be better" is a universally held value. For the Masai in Kenya and Tanzania, for example, a treasured way of life involves keeping large numbers of cattle and the freedom to move about in wide open spaces. Masai perceptions of material need differ greatly from those of small-town, or even rural, America.

So what definition of development can encompass the perspectives of the Masai in Kenya, the landless laborer in Bangladesh, the garment worker in Nicaragua, and the packer of takeout food orders in the United States? To return to Goulet, if "development" is taking place, the availability and distribution of basic life-sustaining goods — food, health, and shelter — should be increasing. For levels of living to improve, there is a concomitant need for employment and educational opportunities, and for economic and social choices to open up.

Development, to expand upon Goulet's ideas, also entails an increasing capacity of people to influence their future both individually and collectively. This concept includes economic productivity and the capacity to develop political and social institutions, as well as addressing equity issues. When people are broadly empowered to achieve influence and leverage over decisions shaping their lives, "development" is taking place. Development also needs to be sustainable and to take the future into account; otherwise the process is one of pillaging the future to accommodate the present, which is hardly "development."

Amartya Sen, an economist who won the 1998 Nobel Prize in Economics, helps us address fundamental questions about the meaning of development. He observes a world of unprecedented opulence along with remarkable deprivation, widespread hunger, extensive damage to the environment, and violation of human dignity. Two concepts that Sen analyzes are important for our discussion here: the meaning of inequality and an interpretation of the meaning of development.[7] In examining economic inequality and poverty, Sen criticizes approaches that concentrate on achievements (such as income) rather than focusing on the capacity or freedom to achieve. He wants to move attention from commodities and income to functionings and capabilities. Sen argues that development is a process of expanding freedoms. He uses the term "unfreedom" to describe such conditions as poverty, tyranny, poor economic opportunities, systematic social deprivation, neglect of public facilities, or repressive states, and he suggests that development requires the removal of the major sources of these "unfreedoms."[8] In exploring the meaning of development and in assessing the causes of inequality, Sen shies away from a focus on economic wealth. While economic growth may be valued, it is important for what it permits an individual to do, primarily to lead a more enriched, unfettered life. The expansion of freedom is both a primary end and the principal means of development. Freedom, therefore, has intrinsic value as well as instrumental value. The ends and means of development, argues Sen, call for placing the perspective of freedom at center stage.

What kind of development is, then, most desirable? Although each society must determine that for itself, the task may be increasingly difficult given the processes of globalization currently under way. How can the nations of the South best achieve their economic and social objectives, either individually or in cooperation with one another and with the countries of the North? This question remains critical. We must learn to listen to other voices, the voice of the Masai herder, the Bengali farmer, the seamstress in Nicaragua, and the young man from Iran delivering pizza in New York City.

Using Theory to Explain Processes of Economic and Social Change

The challenge of understanding processes of economic and social change has engaged theorists and activists of all descriptions from time immemorial. Scholars of ancient Greece reflected on these concerns, as did scholars, philosophers, and social reformers in England and Europe in the seventeenth, eighteenth, and nineteenth centuries. Here we focus briefly on the period of time since World War II when theorists, citizens, and policymakers, in many corners of the world, have searched for the keys to economic growth and broadly improving livelihoods, with increased equity, justice, and well-being for all peoples. These keys have been hard to find. Not only are they elusive, but the explanations about where to find them often seem diametrically opposed. Moreover, there are many explanations, confusing in their complexity and their differing assumptions, strategies, and analyses.

These theories reside in three broad categories: a neoclassical approach, the political economy school, and alternative perspectives on development, the latter including postmodernists, feminists, and those concerned about globalization and global ethics. The term "paradigm" is frequently used when discussing various theories of development and underdevelopment. A paradigm in this context is a worldview, a perspective broadly shared by a group of people on a specific topic. Paradigms focusing on development and underdevelopment have several characteristics: value assumptions about human nature and about what the good life should be, operational criteria for achieving that life, and a strategy or guide for getting there. Almost all textbooks written in the past forty years on the topic of development deal with the first two theoretical categories in some detail.[9] Critiques of the development paradigm have arisen among the postmodernist scholars. Feminist perspectives have cut across these viewpoints and are rarely included in the "development literature" despite their relevance. Finally post–Cold War theories pertinent to ethics, development, and globalization are just now emerging and do not yet constitute a definable school of thought.

A Neoclassical Approach

The neoclassical approach is the one most closely aligned with capitalism, market economies, and the economic successes of the Western world. It has other names and is sometimes called the orthodox, conventional, or traditional economic approach, or modernization theory. Its focus or *unit of analysis* is the nation-state. It regards the state as an independent actor that can make policy decisions that will guide a nation and its citizens through the processes of economic growth and development. According to this view, traditional agrarian societies are stagnant and unchanging; life is based on the seasons and has a circular rhythm. There is no notion of progress, improvement, or change. Human beings are rational, know their own interests, and can act upon them. This approach regards economic interests as paramount and views people largely as economic beings with needs to consume. The critical issue — and the one around which economics as a discipline focuses — is scarcity. Resources are scarce; there are competing needs and objectives, and the resources must be allocated among competing goals. According to this paradigm, the problems of resource allocation can be dealt with most efficiently through the marketplace which will enable the economy to operate efficiently with the greatest production given the resources available.

Three additional assumptions are central to this perspective on development. (All three are challenged by other paradigms of development.) The first is that society is harmonious. When the market is operating so as to produce the greatest output possible given the resources available, it works as if with an invisible hand managing the pieces on the chessboard to the benefit of all. This concept is derived from the work of Adam Smith who first discussed the "invisible hand" in his book *The Wealth of Nations* written in the mid-eighteenth century.[10] Second, economic changes benefit all classes in society. The benefits do not simply adhere to the affluent or to the owners of capital, or to the rulers or governing bodies of individual nations. They are enjoyed by small-scale farmers, landless laborers, and urban factory workers as well, "trickling down" to all elements within a given society. Third, changes take place in a gradual and evolutionary manner, preserving harmony and eventually benefiting all. Change does not come about in a violent or cataclysmic way.

According to this paradigm, there are, first, a host of obstacles to economic growth existing in the developing countries. They include such problems as a hot, humid, enervating climate that makes it difficult for people to work energetically. Lack of resource endowments may be another obstacle. For example, Bangladesh with its abundant water and rich soils has a strong agricultural base, but with virtually no minerals, it has difficulty establishing the requirements for industry from within its own borders. In fact, Bangladeshis, whose nation is situated largely on river delta, have to make bricks that they then break into gravel to use for road beds or for ballast for construction.

The neoclassical approach also considers the factors determined to be "missing" in any given development effort. Perhaps there is little entrepreneurship in a society; maybe there is an uneducated labor force; perhaps the infrastructure for transporting goods is inadequate. Ethiopia provides, for example, a worst-case scenario with no port (a landlocked country), a limited rail system, and poor quality roads making it difficult to move goods, food supplies, or equipment just about anywhere.

What is required for development to take place according to the neoclassical argument? The task at hand is to build capital by saving, reinvesting, and producing more profits leading to increased savings and investment. The best known proponent of the neoclassical approach to development is W. W. Rostow, an economic historian, who in 1960 published *The Stages of Economic Growth*.[11] Walt Rostow offered an economic theory of development which argued that if a poor country got the right quantity and mixture of saving, investment, and foreign aid, it would proceed along the path of economic growth down which the more developed countries had passed some decades before. He uses an analogy of an airplane on a runway waiting for takeoff.

A Political Economy Approach

A political economy approach to understanding development and under-development focuses on systems and structures, rather than individual behavior and nations. Over time this perspective has come to regard capitalism as a means for perpetuating underdevelopment. According to this viewpoint, increasing integration of the world capitalist system intensifies the economic, political, and cultural subordination of the poor countries to the rich. Capitalist institutions within the poor countries likely aggravate, rather than diminish, inequalities in the distribution of wealth and power. The consequences of the perpetuation of underdevelopment are increasing conflict and violence.

Within this broad framework is the Dependency School, originating with a group of Latin American scholars in the mid-1960s. Dependency theorists reject the neoclassical paradigm completely. They observe patterns of dominance and dependence in which the political structures and traditional economies of poor and colonized countries are reshaped to serve the needs of the dominant, imperial power rather than those of local peoples. Dependency theorists also observe the establishment of a domestic elite that works in collusion with foreign powers. Such elites, with their interest in luxury consumption or in stashing their financial gains in a safe place, do not often lead poor nations to economic growth with improved capital infrastructure and the adoption of modernizing methods of economic organization and production.

Scholars do not agree about the numbers and variations of subgroups among dependency theorists. One cluster that might be called moderate focuses on the ways in which external dependency limits the efficacy of economic and political policies. They seek ways to moderate these negative impacts. Another cluster regards reform of the system as essential. These theorists argue that the transformation of existing structures is necessary for autonomous growth. These structural transformations can make development possible. Finally, there are those for whom external dependency must be challenged and broken. For this group the fundamental problems of underdevelopment, including inadequate growth, increasing inequality, and increasing subordination, are unlikely to be solved without a complete break with the capitalist system. That is, they assert that there is no possibility for gradual improvement in Third World countries under the existing capitalist institutions. Probably the most well-known philosopher in this last school is Samir Amin, who elaborated a theory in which underdevelopment is accentuated and growth is blocked in the periphery, making autonomous development impossible.[12] For Samir Amin, a break with the world capitalist system is essential.

When these theorists seek explanations for why some nations are poor and others are affluent, they use historical analysis to explore relations of North and South. They have introduced the idea that underdevelopment and development are two sides of the same universal process.[13] "Underdevelopment is not a stage in the development of an economically, politically and culturally autonomous society." There is no unilinear transition from one type of society to another. Underdevelopment is a created condition. "Development and underdevelopment," stated Andre Gunder Frank, "are two sides of the same coin."[14]

Alternative Perspectives on Development

Postmodernist Challenges to the Development Discourse

Postmodernists offer a critique of the entire development discourse. Their viewpoint is that development per se has grown obsolete. One analyst suggests that "The last forty years can be called the age of development. This epoch is coming to an end. The time is ripe to write its obituary."[15] Their criticism of development lies neither in its technical performance, nor in the accomplishments or lack of them in terms of economic growth, but rather in something much broader. They object to modernization and development as a perception that models reality for everyone. Spreading monoculture is not desirable, and according to these theorists, that is exactly what modernization theorists propose. They universalize; they totalize; they create hierarchies based on dominance and subordination. The metaphor of development has given global hegemony to a Western concept of history, endowed with an aura of "truth." The postmodernists reject "metanarratives" and vast generalizations. Probably the most influential figure in postmodern thinking is Michel Foucault, a French theorist who philosophizes about concepts of truth, knowledge, and discourse, which he claims work together to form a structure of power in the modern era.[16] Foucault observes critical links between knowledge and power which, he maintains, form linkages that support relations of domination.

Postmodernists assert that Third World countries need alternatives to industrial, growth-oriented economies. Effort on the part of poor countries to catch up simply creates an illusion. Catching up is not possible because the industrialized nations are oriented toward transforming advanced technology and toward competitive obsolescence. Despite an effort to catch up, the gap between rich and poor countries is not only maintained but continues to widen at an accelerating pace. It is, says one scholar, a "fraud to hold up the image of the world's rich as a condition available to all. Yet this is what the economic development mythology of catching up does."[17]

In sum, postmodernists claim that the modern conceptualization of development is bankrupt. They argue that the whole paradigm of development should be abandoned and that there should be a search for alternatives to development. These alternatives should be defined by local histories, contexts, and knowledge and based upon self-defined goals that emphasize and celebrate difference, fragmentation, and otherness. Alternatives to development should cherish the uncertainty and individuality of life.

Feminist Critiques of Development Processes

The first salvos by feminists critiquing the various theories of development were launched at the beginning of the 1970s. The reasons were numerous. In the United States the women's movement was well under way, and most people were distinctly aware of the disparities between men's and women's salaries and the glass ceiling that women faced in most avenues of work. Indicators across many nations revealed women lagging behind men in terms of education, health, and life expectancy. Privatization of land in many of the former colonies of Asia and Africa put land ownership into the hands of men, but not women. Agricultural services were generally targeted toward men even though women played significant roles in food production. The list goes on and on.

A Danish economist named Ester Boserup crystallized the arguments in regard to the impact of development processes on women in a book entitled *Woman's Role in Economic Development,* first published in 1970.[18] Boserup's argument was that, in many ways, processes of modernization were proving detrimental to women, and she documented her analysis with findings from around the world. In so doing, she tackled head-on the fundamental assumptions of modernization theory. Modernization theory, as noted above, is predicated on a linear process of development. Modernization is cumulative; the process is expansionist and diffusionist, emanating from center to periphery. The idea is simply to get onto the conveyor belt and you are on your way. The neoclassical theories see women as beneficiaries of an overall process of modernization. As society moves from a subsistence to a cash economy and as technological changes are introduced, women, along with men, benefit. Ester Boserup called these assumptions into question. She demonstrated through empirical data, for example, that improved technology in farming can actually lower women's status by reducing their access to productive work.

Other feminist analyses focus on the system of patriarchy as universal, and women as an oppressed class within that system. Socialist feminists believe that sexism is an independent variable, existing through human history under every economic system. They believe that capitalism determines the particular forms of sexism in a capitalist society and that the subjugation of women constitutes a pillar of this inequitable system. Thus, for these feminists, the causes of subordination are found neither in systems of economic production nor in reproduction per se but in the way in which society chooses to value these activities.

From feminist scholars and practitioners in the South comes a focus on the linkages between gender and other forms of inequities and subordination.[19] This perspective endorses the postmodern emphasis on the local, but looks for certain universal forms of experience. Some call themselves postcolonial feminists and focus on the experiences of women of color throughout a long history of colonization, neocolonialism, and the current impacts of globalization. They use the term "recolonization" to refer to an intensifying colonization in the South and the extension of colonizing practices to the North, occurring through processes of globalization. Many feminists of the Global South define their feminism as a struggle against all forms of oppression, whether it occurs because of gender, race, ethnicity, religion, caste, or some other attribute. For them there is a global vision of freedom for all peoples from systems of domination or exploitation. They are activists; they work at the grassroots in their own communities; but they are conscious of the larger arenas in which human beings must also strive for justice and dignity.

Linking Ethics and Development in the Era of Post–Cold War Globalization

Recently some theorists have been grappling with conceptualizations of development as they relate to poverty, inequality, freedom, and the unprecedented scope and speed of globalization processes. These theorists in no way compose a school of thought, but they constitute a new generation of scholars keenly aware of the complexities and dilemmas of the contemporary world in this era of globalization. They seek explanations for the persistence of inequities, the structures and processes creating poverty, and the challenges of sustainable development and global ethics. They see the poor or oppressed not as objects to be pitied or patronized; rather such theorists perceive the resilience of the poor and oppressed, their strategic capacities and their political savvy as they cope with difficult realities. The theorists are aware that for many people the processes of economic growth have not led to reduction of poverty, increased opportunity, justice, greater equity, or human dignity. In fact, when these benefits have occurred, they have often been by-products of the economic system and a consequence of political pressure. Illustrative of such theorists are Amartya Sen, mentioned earlier in this chapter in a discussion of meanings of development; Rajni Kothari, an eminent social scientist from India, founder and director of the Center for the Study of Developing Societies and founder of the international journal, *Alternatives,* who regards poverty not as an economic problem but a function of exclusion, abandonment, and disenfranchisement; or Hans Küng, a German theologian and president of the Global Ethic Foundation, as well as author of several books pertaining to building an ethical global society, who worries that the number of losers far exceeds the number of winners in this emerging global economy.[20] Küng argues that we may be "dancing round the volcanoes" awaiting the crises that would surely clarify our need for a global ethical framework. Indeed, we urgently need to hear his voice as we seek mutual understanding between Islamic and Western perspectives, find a growing inclination in many parts of the world to resolve differences through violence and terrorism, and encounter escalating poverty and deprivation for many.

Theory and the Perspective of This Volume

Central to the theoretical perspective of this volume is a deep concern about growing exploitation and poverty, particularly in the South, exacerbated by current processes of globalization. We hope that the spirit and conviction of Sen and Kothari in regard to those who are marginalized, as well as their confidence in the capacities of the poor and the vulnerable, pervade these pages. Of course, focusing on globalization without being swayed by the political economists that we are indeed in a modern world system is impossible. But that system need not be the closed circle of the dependency theorists with the inevitability of underdevelopment as certain as night following day. Nor can it be a system in which class structures are paramount, for nowadays we see so clearly the relevance of many dimensions of humanity — religion, ethnicity, race, and gender, as well as class — among them.

Neoclassical arguments are confining because they focus on the nation-state when there are many international actors other than the state. Indeed, the inevitability of Rostow's airplane metaphor has a hollow ring in an era when the jaws of the poverty trap are nipping at the budgets and the citizens of so many countries of the Global South. Yet something is valuable in the notion of agency and the importance of policy that we can glean from the neoclassical arguments. We can't quite walk away from the problems and sulk in the certainty of some systems theorists that we never could do anything about the problems anyway. Here we can be inspired by Küng's sense of agency and his insistence that we simply must create a global ethic to provide a humane framework for this global society which is upon us, like it or not.

From the postmodernists we embrace their respect for diversity and difference as well as their emphasis on local community. We too are not fond of a universalizing blue-jeans culture, and we agree that people need to determine for themselves what their own priorities and needs may be. But we also know that this or any small community is nested in a region, in a nation, and in an international arena. Somehow each of us has to be able to reach beyond the boundaries of our local community to establish bonds and rapport with others who share our world. And with feminists, particularly those from the Global South, we recognize linked oppressions and a search for justice. We hope that their perspectives, viewpoints, and concerns are reflected throughout this volume.

Who Cares about Development Issues?

Since the last decade of the twentieth century, the United States has been, on the one hand, increasingly dominant — the only remaining super-power — and clearly the strongest economic and political power. On the other hand, the United States has also been mysteriously unable to impose its authority as a host of international actors crowd the economic and political scene, making power elusive. Our security depends on ensuring that other countries have a stake in the international system, which is extremely complicated as globalized market forces increase inequalities within a traditional nation-state system.

The nation-state seems less powerful than in times past. This fact is, in and of itself, an interesting phenomenon because new nations burst onto the international scene in the post–World War II period. From India's dramatic celebration of independence in August 1947, to celebrations of Zimbabwe's independence in 1980 and to Eritrea's in 1993 — both after long struggles — this half-century has constituted an era of expansion of the nation-state system. In 1946 there were 74 independent countries; in 1950, 89, and by 1995, the number was 192.

At the same time, after World War II, the United States was catapulted into a position of world prominence and power. Europe was in a state of collapse after the war, and power was polarized between the United States and the Soviet Union. The United States became interested in the newly emerging nations for a variety of reasons. We were, in the two decades after World War II, preoccupied with worry about the spread of revolution and of communism into newly emergent and often unstable regions. The United States and the Soviet Union disliked, feared, and distrusted each other. Both nations gave aid and intervened in the affairs of other countries for security and military reasons, hoping to reassure themselves of the loyalty of client states. The role of the United States in Vietnam epitomizes this era, but Iran, Saudi Arabia, Israel, Chile, Guatemala, and a number of other countries experienced U.S. military or political power largely for perceived U.S. security reasons. Sometimes relationships were built around a related desire to preserve sources of raw materials or to build new markets. Sometimes there were genuine concerns about social justice and enormous hardship. The outpouring of citizen support for assistance to Cambodians in 1979 or to Ethiopians in 1985, times of extreme hardship in both countries, are indicative of more altruistic motivations as well.

Now, however, the Cold War is over. The moral and ethical concerns remain. The range of problems — malnutrition, illiteracy, starvation — may be diminishing in some places, but they remain critical problems in many parts of the world. For perhaps a dozen countries the North-South economic gap is narrowing, but it continues to widen for more than 100 others. Moreover, widening income disparities are occurring within most nations as the wealthier gain through restructuring and globalization and the poorer lose as they are marginalized or left behind. The borderless world means that advantage and disadvantage do not adhere to strict boundaries. Strengths and vulnerabilities are increasingly shared. Those may be economic; they may relate to terrorism, violence, or other insecurities. They are not going away, and we serve ourselves, our communities, our nation, and our global community best if we address them.

What Issues Confront Both South and North at the Beginning of the Twenty-First Century?

The issues to be addressed by peoples of North and South are numerous. We identify twelve within the overall framework of the need to conceptualize a new North-South agenda.

A Global System

Transforming the face of the world is a globalization process cutting across all sectors of activity. BankBoston, merely a medium-size bank recently purchased by Fleet Bank, nevertheless obtained approximately 20 percent of its revenues from Brazil and Argentina, an indication of the spread and strength of Northern-based financial houses around the world. Wal-Mart is represented in fifty U.S. states, and nine countries, even China, and has over five hundred stores in Mexico.[21] In 1998, Home Depot, a chain of do-it-yourself hardware and construction supply warehouses, opened its doors in Latin America and has since expanded to eight stores — four in Chile and four in Argentina.[22] In October 2000, Starbucks opened a shop, complete with glazed donuts and banana walnut muffins, in Beijing's Forbidden City, just opposite the Palace of Heavenly Purity.[23] Oxfam, the British non-governmental relief and development organization, started in Oxford as a relief agency during World War II. There are now eleven different Oxfams around the world, and Oxfam International is a growing entity. The environmental movement from Greenpeace to the Women, Environment, and Development office in New York, to the activists protesting large-scale dam construction by the World Bank in India, knows no national boundaries. Immigrants crisscross the globe seeking employment in many parts of the world: Senegalese in New York, Sri Lankans in Rome, Iranians in Tokyo, Somalis in Stockholm. Surely the evidence is strong that globalization is well under way. If globalization is the dominant force in the world today, it also has its underside, a crossroads where globalization meets terrorism. "All the wondrous developments of the new economy — falling costs, fewer borders, easy communications — help international terrorists and criminals as much as they do businessmen."[24] This global system is a beast of many parts.

The Nation-State

While globalization is an ongoing process, the nation-state seems to be under attack from two directions. First, many are dwarfed by large-scale economic actors such as Goldman Sachs, investment bankers whose year 2000 annual earnings were $3.25 billion contributing to total assets of $290 billion.[25] Goldman Sachs alone maintains a financial value greater than the GNI of approximately 118 nations.[26] The banks and investment houses are joined in scale by the multinationals, including oil companies, such as Shell or British Petroleum, Dow Chemical, and a wide variety of transnational corporations operating across a range of sectors. Reebok shoes, Liz Claiborne clothes, Pepsi-Cola, or Procter and Gamble all have round-the-world production and sales. It is difficult for governments — either the home government or the receiving government — to monitor and control their activities.

The nation-state is also under siege from another direction. Many countries face the centrifugal tendencies generated by powerful regions; ethnic, religious, or other subgroups; and weak central governments. Since the last decade of the twentieth century, widespread breakdown of national loyalties has characterized Eastern Europe, Central Asia (formerly part of the Soviet Union), and many parts of Africa. The levels of animosity between the Hutu and the Tutsi in Rwanda, between factions fighting in southern Sudan or in Angola, or between the Serbs and the Albanians in Kosovo are grim reminders that only tenuous threads hold some nations together. So, at a time when strong governmental activities would be valuable to address a variety of problems, the state's resources and energies are sapped in new ways.

A Poverty Curtain

The "iron curtain" separating the Soviet Union from the capitalist world has disappeared, but a new curtain is rapidly gaining visibility. This one is a "poverty curtain" dividing an affluent North from an impoverished South. The buying power of many Third World countries is declining.

Jobs and working conditions become bargaining chips for firms in a world economy that has few regulations. Nike can pick up its sneaker-making operations and move them from Indonesia to Bangladesh when it finds it can pay Bangladeshis a wage that is a fraction of that of the Indonesians. Laborers on sugar plantations in the Philippines find their wages dropping as the powerful lobby of sugar beet farmers in America moves into action. Young men from China, or Honduras or Mexico or many other places, pay large sums to escape hopelessness in their home countries only to discover the despair of poverty elsewhere. The gaps between the very few rich and the very many poor are deepening the world over.

The Debt Crisis

One cannot consider the "poverty curtain" without also identifying the debt crisis as a critical issue in need of a fresh approach. The debt crisis continues to plague many nations. Between 1980 and 1995, the total external debt of low income countries rose from $55 billion to $215 billion, more than twice their export earnings.[27] The debt crisis has drained financial resources from poor countries to rich banks. It has threatened to overwhelm a number of countries that pay a high percentage of their gross national income in servicing their debt. It is a causal factor in the deepening drug trade in several parts of the world including Colombia and Bolivia. It was deeply implicated in the Asian and Latin American economic crises of 1998 and 1999. The World Bank, under pressure from non-governmental organizations, has established the Heavily Indebted Poor Countries Initiative (HIPC) in order to bring about early implementation of better terms for the indebted countries, including significant debt relief. According to the International Monetary Fund in 2001, of the forty-one countries classified as heavily indebted poor countries, only twenty-four have been approved for debt-reduction packages under the HIPC Initiative (twenty of them in Africa).[28] These packages will lift $36 billion in debt — about half of what they owe.

The Information Age

Cliches abound about the information age. Information is knowledge and knowledge is power, we are told. The comments may seem trite, but in truth transformation in communication and the capacity to control and exchange information underlie the changes in our global system. Forty years ago an international telephone call was an accomplishment usually accompanied by a long wait and a lot of static. It was rarely an edifying experience and hardly ever conducive either to enjoyment or to conducting business. Today's telephone conversations from just about anywhere in the world are sparklingly clear; faxes are in widespread use; and e-mail is often nearly simultaneous. If it is a pleasure and a luxury to be able to communicate with colleagues, friends, and family around the world, it is also a facilitator of business and financial arrangements. Acknowledging that these new levels of communication have both positive and negative repercussions, the capacity to engage in them is critical to entry into the global system. Access of countries of the South to these modern technologies varies widely, and this access is another item for the South-North agenda.

Social Polarization and Regional Imbalances

Inequities seem to be increasing everywhere. Within many nations class distinctions are growing aided and abetted by a global economic system whose restructuring seems only to aggravate social difference. Income disparities are widening, not only in well-known cases — the United States or Brazil, for example — but in many others as well. Some of the southern African countries have extreme forms of social inequities. Namibia, for example, has been described as "one country, two worlds" with a small affluent white population, a large black population living in abject poverty, and prosperous foreign-owned mining companies.[29] Others also have deep-rooted social and economic structures that reproduce poverty and perpetuate inequality. In Indonesia, Malaysia, and Thailand, which had achieved some breakthroughs in moving people out of poverty in the 1980s and early 1990s, some lower income groups are plummeting into poverty as a consequence of the Asian economic crisis of the late 1990s.

Corruption and Crime

Perhaps corruption and crime should not be lumped together. Crime is certainly a broader category than corruption; presumably corruption is always a crime, even if it is one that is tolerated or even encouraged in some situations. The mysterious disappearance of government funds, international aid that makes its way into private ministerial bank accounts, or the bloated bureaucracies mismanaging public sector business — all are a focus of any effort to address international debt and to begin to build public accountability into systems of governance. Then, too, there is the drug trade and the crime associated with trafficking, a topic that is closely linked to the debt and international trade issues noted above. Indeed, the underbelly of globalization is the underground economy and a range of activities that include smuggling, illicit logging, trading of conserved species of plants and animals, trade in contraband arms, or trafficking in people. Sometimes these illegal economic activities are linked to powerful figures in bureaucracies, the military, the police, or politics, a reminder of the dark side of our political and economic systems.

Environmental Degradation

Around the world peoples of North and South are becoming conscious of their deteriorating environments. In the North Atlantic the collapse of the Atlantic cod fishery has been declared "the ecological disaster of the century."[30] Forest fires that swept through Indonesia in late 1997 not only destroyed vast timber reserves, but polluted the atmosphere for hundreds of miles around. The collapse of irrigation schemes from salinization, the destruction of topsoils from illicit timbering, the erosion caused by farming on steep slopes, the continuing rise of CO_2 emissions, and many more flagrant abuses of the environment suggest that in the twenty-first century both South and North need to think much more deeply about our custodial responsibilities in relation to the environment.

The 1992 United Nations Conference on Environment and Development (UNCED), held in Rio de Janeiro, Brazil, captured the critical dialogue and accusations between the North, which was concerned about population growth in the South, and the South, which was concerned about relentless consumerism in the North. Statistics provide overwhelming evidence that a typical North American adult consumes far more resources than a typical Bangladeshi or Malian. For most Americans, this is a distant topic, one that somebody else is concerned about and which does not affect them very much. To many others around the world, it is yet another indication of U.S. insensitivity and disregard for global justice.

Urbanization

Perhaps the twentieth century will be remembered particularly for its incredible rates of urbanization. In 1900, approximately 150 million people, or 10 percent of the world's population, lived in cities. Toward the end of the century this figure had grown to over 2 billion. Of the ten largest cities in 2002, seven are located in the developing world. Cities serve as magnets for the rural unemployed and landless who seek new opportunities in the cities of their homeland or elsewhere in the world. Urban problems of housing, sanitation, education, transport, infrastructure, security, care for the impoverished, and cultural amenities are extraordinary.

Agrarian Reform

Although land tenure systems vary widely from country to country, it would not be inaccurate to state that many systems favor the large land-holder over small-scale farmers, favor men over women, favor owners over renters or landless laborers, and favor inherited land/wealth over open access on an egalitarian basis. In many countries good agricultural land is a scarce and coveted commodity, particularly given rapidly growing populations and inadequate alternatives for employment in manufacturing, industry, or services. Women rarely have ownership rights in land; rather, their rights come through marriage and family, and they can easily be deprived of those rights — no matter how much work they have put into the land — should those relationships change. International agribusiness, too, is a factor with which many nations must contend, whether it is the Philippines and Del Monte, Kenya and Brooke Bond, or Honduras and Dole. Such corporations control vast amounts of land and are a major influence not only in the communities in which they operate but also in policy at the national level.

HIV/AIDS

At the UN Special Session in June 2001 the international community adopted a plan of action to fight the global epidemic of HIV/AIDS. The mood was somber. Twenty years into the worst epidemic in modern times, 36 million people around the world were infected with HIV, and some 20 million had died. The UN Secretary-General Kofi Annan has called the UN's Declaration of Commitment on HIV/AIDS a blueprint from which the whole of humanity can work in building a global response to a truly global challenge. While Africa has been most severely affected by the HIV/AIDS epidemic, new regions in which HIV/AIDS is making significant inroads are Eastern Europe and China. Clearly, a massive and focused response to the AIDS pandemic is a priority for the coming decades.

Armaments

Military expenditures grew worldwide from $400 billion in 1960 to $798 billion in 2000.[31] Nowhere is the harm caused by the devotion of vast sums to armaments greater than in the developing countries. In the face of extreme poverty, famine, expanding debt, poor health, and inadequate livelihood opportunities, many nations are spending more than ever on military activities and the arms that permit them. In the 1980s the five largest recipients of U.S. weapons in sub-Saharan Africa were Liberia, Angola, Somalia, Sudan, and Zaire, all of which disintegrated into civil war. According to Demilitarization for Democracy, a Washington anti-proliferation watchdog group, by the late 1990s the United States had given military assistance to nearly every African country, training over three thousand military officers, most of whom came from nations with dictatorships or on the brink of collapse.[32] Preventing conflict and bringing about peace and security are far more complex problems than simply looking at issues of armaments, but clearly this arena needs transparency, accountability, and attention from the public. In the new century's riveting and growing concerns about widespread terrorism, wisdom in this realm is critical.

How This Book Is Organized

Chapter 2 explores the history of North-South relationships starting with the East India Company (although that is not the true beginning) and moving beyond the Cold War. The chapter identifies the ways that imperialism and colonialism have been an integral component of world capitalism, and it explores the political and economic dynamics of North-South relationships from the scramble for Africa to the collapse of the Berlin Wall.

Chapter 3 focuses on politics and the state, specifically addressing issues of the state in an era of globalization. Around the world we observe fragile nation-states despite the power of nationalist movements in the twentieth century. This chapter considers the challenges that Southern political systems face, the key issues of ethnicity and the state, and concerns about national integration and communal identification. It draws on documentation from Ethiopia, Eritrea, Zimbabwe, and India to illustrate a framework for comparative analysis.

Chapter 4 moves on from politics and the state to focus on a convergence of power politics, military repression, state terror, violations of human rights, and a resulting "international politics of refugees." It explores ethnic conflict and sectarian strife in three contemporary situations: Sri Lanka, Sudan, and Colombia. This chapter considers the new paradigm for providing assistance to refugees and explores efforts to balance the rights of migrants, asylum seekers, and refugees with those of receiving peoples. Chapter 4 also identifies some specific human rights issues including child soldiers, gender apartheid, and ethnic cleansing.

Chapter 5 focuses on the shape of the global economy and international economic institutions. In an interdependent but unequal world economy with large-scale international financial institutions (such as the IMF, World Bank, and the World Trade Organization), how does the "global citizen" make sense of monetary issues, foreign investment by multinational corporations, structural adjustments, inequitable terms of trade, and bilateral aid? The chapter delves into issues surrounding the most heavily indebted countries, Latin America's debt crisis of the 1980s, and Asia's sagging economies of the late 1990s.

Chapter 6 takes the economic issues and explores them from regional and local perspectives. It examines faltering local economic growth in the context of ballooning external debt, capital flight, and the pressures of structural adjustment. The chapter considers how these events are viewed from the perspective of countries of the South. For example, in Bolivia or Colombia, what are the links between drugs and debt, the rise of protectionism, production of coca leaves, and drug trafficking? In Bangladesh, Nicaragua, or Thailand, what is happening to the garment industry and the many women who are employed in it? How do these trends reflect changes in the global economy?

Chapter 7 focuses on the links among population issues — migration, urbanization, family size — the environment, and development, considering concepts such as the demographic transition and the demographic trap. This chapter explores the central place of women in the population/environment discussion. It identifies specific problems such as resource extraction and devastated populations and HIV/AIDS in Africa. We examine these issues in the context of deteriorating environments and pressing concerns about sustainability in both rural and urban settings.

Chapter 8 focuses on food security, family welfare, and global politics. It examines the changing attributes of two food production systems (Asia and Africa) and considers constraints on food production, women's roles in achieving food security, and specific issues such as genetically modified foods and biodiversity. While addressing questions of equity and distribution in several parts of the world, chapter 8 focuses on the concerns of sub-Saharan Africa, the only region in the world where per capita food production has declined over the past several decades. The chapter considers the structural causes of rural poverty, the "politics of famine," and the challenges in addressing this important issue.

Chapter 9 considers new voices and new choices in designing our future. There are new voices speaking out on behalf of a more just international order. Among them are voices from the South, including a host of non-governmental organizations that have emerged in the past ten years. The Narmada movement against big dams in India, the Sarvodaya movement in Sri Lanka, and the Green Belt Movement in Kenya represent new modes of organization to address common issues. Other voices include women's groups and women's academic and advocacy organizations, speaking both from the North and the South. Many other efforts exist, and all of them are aided by new forms of technology that can be put to the use of common concerns. This chapter explores ways to link human development, growth, and poverty reduction, proposing possibilities for a new North-South agenda for the twenty-first century.

The Human Dimensions of Being Poor in the Developing World

To be wealthy in the developing world is to have a lifestyle comparable to that of the wealthy anywhere in the world. To be poor is another matter. Vulnerability and insecurity are a way of life. In brief sketches we explore the lives of five real people typical of the adults (and, in one case, a teenager) in their communities in the developing world. They are all poor, which is not to say that they are culturally impoverished or poor in spirit, goodwill, friendships, or energy. But they do face inordinate hardships caused by lack of land, employment, income, educational opportunity, access to health care, and other amenities. They offer us a "face" to this Southern exposure. They help to illustrate why the issues identified above are important — to them and to us.

In Kenya

Kita Wambua lives in Kyevaluki Sublocation in Machakos District on a two-acre farm.[33] She grows maize for the household and has a few coffee bushes that bring in just a bit of cash. There are five surviving children, the eldest of whom is now twenty. Kita's biggest problem is providing school fees for her children. Mr. Wambua, who has been unwell, is unemployed, living at home, and does not seek casual work. Mrs. Wambua engages in four kinds of activities to secure additional cash income. First, she sells bananas grown on their land. About twenty bunches a year will yield a total of $30. Second, she weaves one basket a week, earning about $65 per year after costs. Third, she hires herself out as a casual laborer on other farms. In the dry season she works on the farms of others only four or five days per month. When the rains come she works there every day, earning less than $1 per day. Last, she cuts firewood to sell, for which she earns twenty cents per bundle. The household has neither a cow nor goats; there are only chickens. Mrs. Wambua worries because the land is small for the four sons who will be entitled to inherit it. Because of the high secondary school fees, she cannot afford the more advanced education that might give her sons other skills with which they could earn a living. She faces acute problems of insufficient land, inability to educate her children, and inadequate employment opportunities.

In the Philippines

Corazon and Leandro of Napo baranguay (village) on Siquijor Island struggle to raise their five small children, one of whom is blind, making a living from three parcels of virtually unplowable, rocky, and degraded rented land.[34] The harvest of maize feeds them for only two months. A myriad of income-generating activities are necessary for them to feed themselves for the rest of the year. Leandro alternates farming, fishing, and selling coconut wine from his parents' trees. Their only property is Leandro's outrigger that saves them from renting one and having to divide the catch with the owner. Corazon contributes what she can to their income by processing the fish and selling any extra to neighbors; weaving and selling mats; and caring for a neighbor's two sows from which she keeps half of the offspring. Critical to improving their situation is gaining access to better land. They hope to buy land soon by borrowing money from Corazon's siblings who live elsewhere in the country.

In Nepal

Phul Maya Thingsha is a seventeen-year-old Tamang young woman, a new daughter-in-law in a small farming household in Ghusel Village in the Middle Hills.[35] Phul Maya's in-laws were happy when she joined the household because she is industrious and strong and is an enormous help in caring for the three buffalo that they have now acquired through the Small Farmer Development Program. Rugged, steep hills, narrow trails, and isolation characterize Ghusel. Despite its relative proximity to Kathmandu (about twenty-five miles) it lacks social services and facilities for health, education, transportation, piped water, and electricity. Although it is a farming area, deteriorating soil conditions and fragmented holdings have resulted in poor yields of maize and mustard, and farmers have turned to buffalo rearing for milk to sell to the Kathmandu market. Phul Maya rises early and devotes most of her day to searching for brush and branches for fodder and fuelwood. In a typical day she will spend three hours in the morning and another three in the afternoon searching in different places for these resources. Without adequate fodder of the appropriate types, the buffaloes will produce little milk with a low fat content. So her contribution is important to the income the buffaloes generate and to the welfare of the whole family. This responsibility, however, has brought about a major change in the lives of the women of Ghusel, including Phul Maya, because the labor associated with buffalo care belongs only to them; the management of the money earned belongs to the male head of household. Moreover, at a national policy level there is little support for households and communities — and Nepal's women — in the area of natural resource access, use, and management. The government and donor agencies have generally gravitated toward large projects for roads, dams, and irrigation works with little attention to the connections between resource conservation and human livelihoods.

In Rwanda

Valentina is a young Tutsi teenager whose story of survival has been told in a Public Broadcasting Service documentary entitled *Valentina's Nightmare*. Valentina survived the brutal massacre in her village only by pretending she too was dead. She lost all her relatives, much of her health, and some of her fingers and hands from machete blows. But she is alive, and with the help of relatives is trying to restore some sense of normalcy to her adopted family and home. She is back in school, but she is sad over the loss of her family and nervous about what the future holds. She is not at all sure that her Tutsi household will, over the long run, be able to stay in their rural community or that it will be safe for them to do so.

Rwanda may be a worst-case scenario, but one does not need to look far to find situations of enormous physical insecurity and violence — in Rwanda, in southern Sudan, in Angola, in Kosovo, in Tajikistan, and in Northern Ireland, among others. Valentina's young and uncertain life is a reminder of the difficulties faced by many peoples struggling for economic opportunity and also for a place and voice within their own societies.

In Indonesia

In a remote corner of Indonesia in a town called Mojokerto, a midsized town about four hundred miles east of Jakarta, lives a rickshaw driver named Salamet whose life was transformed by the financial crisis swirling around Asia and Latin America in 1997 and 1998.[36] Salamet, twenty-seven years old and married with three children, comes from a family of agricultural laborers who have, for countless generations, struggled to survive. When Salamet was ten, his father fell to his death while pruning a palm tree. His mother remarried, and Salamet worked alongside his new stepfather lugging sacks of sand from riverbanks to sell to cement factories. The town began to thrive in Indonesia's general prosperity, and with it so did Salamet and his stepfather, Pirso, who rented cycle rickshaws in which they could carry passengers around town for a small fee. At first, they did well in their newfound business, but business slumped early in 1998 as investors began pulling out of Indonesia. The economy plummeted, and even rickshaw drivers lost business. Salamet's dilemma is clear. His mother needs medications that cost $2 a month. Mr. Salamet can afford that price; it is a sum he earns in two days. However, he may then get further behind in making his payments on his rickshaw; it could be seized and he could lose his means of livelihood. Or perhaps he would have to stop paying school fees and his son Dwi might be forced to leave the second grade and never get an education. (The Asian Development Bank estimated that 6.1 million children left school in Indonesia in the last months of 1998 because of the economic crisis.) Salamet has always been poor, but a financial crisis aggravated by speculators from the industrialized countries built up "a catastrophic bubble economy" in his country, and jeopardized the health and well-being of his family and those of many others like him. His options are few; his vulnerability great.

We need only glimpses of these lives in distant lands to recognize that the problems they face have multiple sources — some political, some economic, some rooted in long-term fears and animosities, some new, swirling in on the winds of foreign investors. What is clear is that they, in many ways, are interlocking crises and that dealing with one piece leads on to other interconnected elements. There are, among other things, many people behind the poverty curtain. In many instances it is not lack of economic change that has brought widespread impoverishment, but changes that have left a trail of displaced or dispossessed peoples. An environmental crisis reveals the eroding ability of the biosphere to support and sustain human, animal, and plant life. The denial of human rights ranges from large-scale repression and massacre to detentions to political exclusion. Militarization includes nuclear, biological, and chemical weapons of mass destruction, huge levels of military expenditures, and, increasingly, terrorism both organized and erratic. Expenditures on armaments prevent those resources from being used for other purposes; war leads to displacement and impoverishment, and often to environmental deterioration and repression of rights, and so on. To grasp a part of the puzzle is possible; to see it in its entirety is difficult.

Throughout the world we find long-lasting systematic inequalities in life chances. These inequalities, often associated with race, ethnicity, gender, religion, and caste, lead to a great range of unequal outcomes: income, wealth, power, deference, fame, privilege, and others. These categories are taking on new meanings in a changing global system. One purpose of this volume is to keep before us a sense of these inequalities, the historical patterns and trends in these social relations, and the ways they are changing with the quickening global integration occurring at the beginning of the twenty-first century.

Part One

Political Change:
Traps, Illusions,
and Opportunities

Chapter 2

Exploring North-South Relationships

From the East India Company to East Timor

Chapter 2 explores European expansionism in the forms of imperialism and colonialism, and the resulting relations between Northern and Southern states. It briefly recounts a history of the politics and economics of colonialism and its impact on culture, ideology, and social systems. The chapter explores Third World responses to imperialism and colonialism, the legacies of colonialism, and North-South relations as they have evolved in the post–Cold War era. Finally, chapter 2 considers three legacies of imperialism and colonialism haunting the twenty-first century: East Timor, Nigeria, and Afghanistan.

Imperialism is the policy, practice, or advocacy of seeking to extend the control and domination of an entity. In the broadest sense, that entity could be an individual — Genghis Khan establishing a vast empire or a roommate staking out more than his fair share of your college dorm room. It could be a company seeking to expand its control in a previously shared domain — Microsoft or General Electric or IBM at various points in their histories. It could be a political collectivity such as a tribe or a nation expanding its geographical boundaries and the numbers of people that it governs. Theories of imperialism are most often concerned with the unequal relationship that has emerged between imperialist developed countries and the dependent underdeveloped countries. We focus on this relationship in the following pages.

Modernization theory, as noted in chapter 1, justifies the historical processes of imperialism and colonial expansion by assuming that modernization is moving from the countries of Europe and North America to outlying areas where, overall, it will have beneficial consequences. For dependency theorists, the distorted structures in which the countries of the South have become trapped are the outcome of imperialist and

39

colonial ventures, and they will not simply disappear as these countries modernize. The inequities are likely to deepen.

In contemporary discussions of imperialism, development and underdevelopment, and the disparities between North and South, the great civilizations that have existed in the Global South, including powerful empires, are sometimes overlooked. In the sixteenth century, the Mogul Empire flourished in northern India, building roads, reforming taxes, patronizing the arts, and encouraging religious and artistic endeavors. One of the Mogul emperors ruling in the seventeenth century built the fabulous Taj Mahal. The Inca Empire ruled an expanse from southern Colombia to central Chile in the fifteenth century, and the Bantu civilization, culminating in the Shona Empire, centered in present-day Zimbabwe from the eleventh to the fifteenth centuries. These are just three examples of Southern "empires" and "imperialism" that have existed over the centuries. Current discussions of underdevelopment acknowledge these events and these accomplishments, but focus on the attributes of underdevelopment in the South contrasted with Northern industrialized countries. These critiques arise out of the military, economic, and political expansionism of Europe that has its beginnings in the fifteenth century. While they recognize that Third World poverty is not a new phenomenon, they focus on the ways in which it has been aggravated and deepened by exploitative imperialism and colonialism.

Imperialism: The Creation of European Empires

Europeans initiated contact with the tropical regions for strategic and economic reasons. They sought improved trade in such commodities as spices (especially pepper, cinnamon, cloves, ginger, and nutmeg), jewelry, porcelains, textiles, and gold. They sought access to raw materials and foods ranging from indigo and jute to tea, sugar, and cotton. Initially, Europeans had not gone to the sources of supply, but had purchased goods from merchants, mainly Arabs, who brought wares from China, India, and the East Indies by caravan or boat to the markets of the eastern Mediterranean.[1]

This trade began at the end of the fifteenth century; for purposes of marking it, Columbus's arrival in America in 1492 provides a convenient date. At that time Europe was largely divided into feudal realms, but new monarchies were emerging with England and France gradually expanding royal domains. Conditions were quite different in other parts of the world. Islam may have been retreating in Europe, but it was expanding throughout North Africa, Southern Asia, and into India. In China, the Ming dynasty ruled a vast territory; in South America and in Mexico the Incas and the Aztecs constituted advanced civilizations controlling large regions.

However, a number of changes were taking place in Europe that would encourage expansion beyond its borders. Medieval Europe had been relatively static in terms of economic and technological change. By the end of the fifteenth century, states were beginning to form; towns were emerging; feudalism was beginning to decay; trade and banking were flourishing, particularly in the Italian republics and later in Holland and England. Until about A.D. 1500, the Atlantic Ocean had been a barrier to travel, but gradually it became a bridge to new lands. The Portuguese, who were the first to make use of the mariner's compass, were transforming coastal navigation. They had mapped the entire coast of Africa and reached India during the last decade of the fifteenth century. By 1509 the Portuguese had created the first of Europe's commercial empires maintained by superior firearms and sea power. Trade alternated with war and plunder, but the outcome was a vast reduction in the cost of many goods. Spices, for instance, could be purchased in Lisbon for one-fifth of their cost elsewhere in Europe.[2]

Meanwhile Spain was sending explorers to the "new world," conquering the Aztec Empire in Mexico and the Inca Empire in Peru. Mines for precious metals were opened; indigenous peoples were forced into labor under a system called the *encomienda,* whereby a large grant of land to a European conquistador included the right to the labor of the native Americans who lived there. This system provided labor for both agriculture and the mines. It established the power of Spanish conquistadores but decimated the indigenous population through warfare, enforced long marches, epidemics, and forced labor. Nearly 90 percent of Central and South America's Indian population is reported to have died as a consequence. By 1560 the Spanish began to import slaves from Africa to work in the mines and fields of Central and South America. While the conquistadores and their trading partners prospered, the indigenous peoples suffered slavery, disease, and early death.

For almost a century the Spanish and the Portuguese dominated the ocean routes, with Spain claiming rights of trade with the Philippines and the Americas, while Portugal garnered these rights with Brazil, Asia, and the East Indies. By the middle of the sixteenth century rich silver deposits were discovered at Potosí in Peru, and for years half a million pounds of silver and ten thousand pounds of gold flowed annually from South America to Spain.[3] For a century Spain and Portugal retained this monopoly on oceanic trade with little competition from other European peoples.

But all this was to change as the Commercial Revolution, with its evolving long-distance trade and emerging capitalist economy, got under way in Europe. Mining, printing, shipbuilding, and manufacture of cannons and muskets all required new forms of organization, capital, and production. In addition, the new sea routes brought bulk commodities from some distance — rice or tea from Asia, timber from Russia, or sugar from the Caribbean. Commercial capitalism was in its heyday.

Eventually merchants and their respective governments came together to provide finance and security for transoceanic trade by forming trading companies. The best known of these companies were the East India Companies founded in the seventeenth century by the English, Dutch, and French. These state-supported monopolistic organizations engaged in trade in the region for which the company had a charter. They searched for markets for domestic products and raw materials for the commercial activities at home. They brought home gold, silver, and other precious metals when possible. By the eighteenth century these companies were encroaching on the monopolies held for more than a century by the Spanish and the Portuguese. In fact, this period of Spanish and Portuguese dominance has been called the first phase of the nearly five hundred years of European expansion. It came to a close at the end of the eighteenth century with the rise of British dominance that lasted nearly a century. The eighteenth century saw the emergence of a worldwide imperial system of commerce. There were commodities — cotton, sugar, and tobacco — from Central and South America; ivory, gold, and palm oil from Africa; cotton, spices, and tea from Asia; timber, furs, and grain from North America, all in a global trading network. Slaves provided cheap labor where needed; profits accrued to Europeans in this worldwide imperial system.

It is almost impossible to comprehend the magnitude of the slave trade, but historians estimate that 11.7 million Africans were exported in the Atlantic trade, 7.4 million North across the Sahara, and 3.8 million in the Indian Ocean trade for a total of 22.9 million.[4] The horrendous story of the slave trade and the cruel and humiliating treatment they experienced on this side of the Atlantic has been documented in story, film, and song. What may be less well known is the devastating impact on African societies caused by this loss of young people: breakdown of social structures, unsettled conditions, disrupted farming cycles, violence, and consequent social collapse. This was Africa's introduction to capitalism and the world economy.

The British maintained imperial control around the world by virtue of a loosely administered system of trade and bureaucratic regulation. "The sun never sets on the British Empire," so it was said, and indeed that seems to have been the case for most of the nineteenth century. In fact, in the course of the nineteenth century there was a revolution in transportation and a reduction in long-distance transport costs by about 90 percent. The iron-hulled, propeller-driven steamships made possible massive transport of raw materials. Economies from Latin America to India to Australia were increasingly organized around production of primary commodities for export to the metropolitan center. For example, British tea imports grew from forty-two tons in 1700 to twenty-five thousand tons in 1850.[5] Britain's economic wealth and political power, based on extensive trade, grew spectacularly in the nineteenth century. The other European countries were in no position to compete.

Meanwhile, Queen Victoria ascended to the British throne in 1837 and ruled for sixty-four years. In the first years of her reign, England was immersed in an Industrial Revolution as well as an Agrarian Revolution, developing into an industrialized country through coal mining, iron and steel production, shipbuilding, and textiles. The economy was based on free enterprise and free trade. The British navy was the most powerful in the world, and British prestige and influence were widespread. It was, in addition, an era of British expansionism. The British were interested in trade and investment and also felt some sort of mission to "civilize" the world through spreading Christianity, a deeply felt obligation making the missionaries never far behind the traders and the soldiers in the movement of British nationals abroad.

After 1870 this situation was beginning to change. First, the Industrial Revolution was spreading to the continent. The numerous German states became united into the German Empire in 1871, and Germany gradually became more nationalistic under the leadership of Otto von Bismarck. Not only Germany, but also France, Belgium, and Italy were beginning to industrialize and were developing rivalries among their various trading groups abroad. The Americans and Japanese were involved too. In the last two decades of the nineteenth century and the first of the twentieth, nearly 20 percent of the world's territory was annexed by the imperial powers.[6] While acquisition of colonies may not have been a primary objective, all these countries had strong commercial interests abroad and wanted to protect opportunities for their trading companies.

The scramble for Africa resulted in a massive French empire in the north and west. When France started contemplating linking Algeria with Senegal by rail and establishing tariffs in a French-speaking West African arena, the British became anxious. Meanwhile in another part of Africa in the 1870s, both the British and the French were becoming worried about Egypt and the possibility that its government, then bankrupt, would collapse. The British and French intervened to protect their investments, and by 1882 the British were controlling Egypt. It was not long before the British government decided it had to protect the source of the Nile in Uganda from takeover by a rival power. Thus that nation's interests in East Africa gradually expanded. Britain's engagement did not reflect a genuine concern about East Africa, but rather a concern about its own strategic positioning within a newly developing, large power context. Egypt's security was linked to India's security, and India was the so-called "jewel in the imperial crown." The enormous wealth created by British trade was very much dependent on the reliability of that commerce.

Before the century was out, the Europeans, sitting in the governing halls of Europe, had "carved up Africa." Portugal colonized Angola and Mozambique; Belgium was in the Congo; the Germans in South-West Africa, Cameroon, and Tanganyika (later combined with Zanzibar to create Tanzania); the British in Ghana, Nigeria, and other parts of West Africa as well as the east; and the Italians in Libya, Eritrea, and part of Somalia. Germany and Britain, for example, had completed the partition of East Africa with the Imperial British East Africa Company and the German East Africa Company acknowledging each other's respective spheres of influence.

Kenya's situation at the end of the nineteenth century is illustrative. Kenya, first known as the East Africa Protectorate, was formally acquired by Great Britain in 1895. By 1896 the government had begun building a railway between the coast (Mombasa) and Lake Victoria in order to facilitate settlement, farming, and movement of agricultural produce, and trade. This venture took six years to complete, employing thirty-two thousand Indian railway workers brought into the Protectorate from India for the purpose, along with five thousand Indian clerks and craftsmen. It cost $16 million and was considered a most costly undertaking. Determined to make this territory pay its own way, the government established the Crown Lands Ordinance legalizing the sale or lease of "unoccupied land" in the Protectorate, thus making it possible to populate the area with Europeans. In this way, East Africa was brought into the global community on terms favorable not to its own people but to the interests of the Europeans who made their way there at the end of the nineteenth century. Kenya, and the rest of East Africa as well, illustrates the single-minded determination with which imperial powers sought control over various colonies. In East Africa, as in other regions, the decisions to "take over" and to establish strategic alliances and control paved the way for the colonization that was to follow.

A History of Colonialism

The term "colony" or "colonial" may refer to a group of beings living together, such as a colony of ants or a settlers' colony. In a political context, however, the term "colonialism" refers to a system in which a state maintains political jurisdiction and control over a territory some distance from it for purposes of economic exploitation, or political or strategic interests. European nations established two types of colonies. In the temperate zones of both North and South, large numbers of people from the home country established settlements that eventually replicated the country of origin. This was not the case for tropical colonies that, despite frequent long-term residence, were, for the most part, not regarded as permanent homes for Europeans.

Colonial Economies

Systems of production varied around the world by region and by colonial power. The common thread, however, was that they were established to benefit the distant imperial powers, whatever the cost to local communities and their residents. In Latin America the *encomiendas* gave way to *latifundios*. These were large grants of land or estates, *haciendas*, for agricultural production. The pattern of settlement involved using Indians as laborers who were settled on the land and advanced money and goods, thereby creating a debt peonage. What emerged was a feudal system of vast rural estates owned by descendants of the Spanish conquistadores who prospered while dominating laborers who were surviving at a subsistence level. These laborers were completely dependent on the owner of the estate, who wielded political, economic, and legal power over them.

Colonialism ended officially in Latin America during the first part of the nineteenth century, and nation-states were established. Nevertheless, increasingly an international export economy dominated Latin American economies, creating new forms of dependency. Brazil, Colombia, and Ecuador sent tobacco, sugar, coffee, and cocoa into the markets of Great Britain and the cities of Europe; from Mexico, Chile, Peru, and Bolivia went industrial minerals, and Argentina and Uruguay exported agricultural food products, grown in their temperate climates, to European markets. European investment capital also dominated these economies until the twentieth century when U.S. companies began to gain control of the region's sources of raw materials, manufacturing, and trading.

In Asia large-scale colonial settlement began in the nineteenth century. Whereas the Spanish, Portuguese, and the various East Indian companies had largely engaged in trade throughout the seventeenth and eighteenth centuries, by the nineteenth century they were establishing estates for production of plantation crops. In India and Sri Lanka (then Ceylon) the British established coffee and tea estates and rubber plantations. In Indonesia the Dutch introduced sugar and coffee plantations; and in Malaya (now Malaysia) the English were engaged in growing palm oil, rubber, hemp, and sugar. These plantations became export enclaves established to produce agricultural and raw materials for European countries.

In addition to producing commodities for Europe, the colonies were developed as markets for European manufactured goods. A consequence was the precipitous decline in indigenous manufacturing and the replacement of locally made goods by foreign imports. One of the most dramatic examples of the effect of colonial policies in Asia is Bangladesh (then part of India and known as East Bengal). It was a prosperous region through the late eighteenth century with a diverse agricultural base and a thriving silk and cotton industry. East Bengal's agriculture was converted into producing raw materials for export, including indigo, safflower, jute, and tea. The local textile industry nearly disappeared in the face of an influx of textiles manufactured in Great Britain.[7] Thus, organized largely for commerce and booty in the eighteenth century, by the mid-nineteenth century the British had become rulers with an organized bureaucracy and a community of agricultural settlers, not just traders involved in business and commerce. In India, for example, they had acquired territorial responsibilities and had as objectives collecting revenues, establishing law and order, and assuring property rights.

Throughout their colonies the British introduced ideas of private property. They codified and legalized private rights to land and thus transformed both the ownership of land and its distribution. In India, for example, men traditionally had rights in land, but not exclusive ownership. There were village rights, and customary rights, lineage rights, and hierarchical levels of owners and managers had various rights to rule and rights to extract agricultural surpluses and to collect taxes, but not to own the land absolutely. The privatization of land under the British occurred in different ways, but largely with the consequence that customary rights were weakened for those lowest in the hierarchies of land rights. At the same time land ownership tended to concentrate among the elites. In addition, ownership and distribution of land gradually became linked to rural indebtedness to moneylenders and to landowners.[8] According to some scholars, the British formed a system in which the foreigner, the landlord, and the moneylender took the economic surplus away from the peasantry and failed to invest it in anything leading to growth. Exploitative landlordism did not originate in the British era, but British imperial rule certainly accelerated and intensified it.

In Africa patterns of colonial land settlement followed two trajectories. The first approach, generally associated with British colonialism, involved settlers established on large estates using Africans as cheap labor to produce crops for exports. The second model, generally associated with French colonialism and found largely in parts of West Africa and Uganda, encouraged African peasants to grow cash crops on their own land. In this second model, foreign firms largely handled the transport, processing, and marketing of crops. In the settler economies (the first model) Africans were not allowed to grow cash crops on their own land because that would compete with the products of the settler farmers. Various taxes (hut and poll taxes) were imposed on African households, and these taxes had to be paid in cash. Because the Africans were not permitted to grow and sell significant cash crops, such as coffee, they were forced to seek wage labor in order to have the cash to pay their taxes.

In many instances, African communities were moved off of prime agricultural land and placed on reserves less suitable for agriculture. Records from the District Office of Murang'a District (then Fort Hall District) in Kenya are illustrative. The data from 1926 reveal the inequitable allocation of land between European settlers and the African (Kikuyu) population, both of whom were supporting themselves through agriculture. The settlers and the Kikuyu population of Murang'a District had about the same amount of land to farm, but the settlers had less than 1 percent of the population to support by farming and the Kikuyu had more than 99 percent, as Table 2.1 reveals.

Table 2.1. Murang'a District, Kenya, Colonial Era Land Distribution, 1926

Type of Land	Amount of Land	Population Living on Land
European farmland	500 square miles	385 people
Native reserves	580 square miles	143,924 people
Forest reserves	130 square miles	0

Source: Colonial Reports, *Fort Hall (Murang'a) Handing Over Report* (Nairobi: Government of Kenya Archives, Microfilm, 1926).

In effect, the African communities were pushed back on marginal land supporting ever larger numbers of people on land increasingly eroded and unproductive. Food production declined. The communally managed land systems gave way before the onslaught of estate agriculture and the confiscation of commonly held land. Africans became cheap producers of raw materials and foodstuffs, working on tea, coffee, sisal, and pineapple plantations, as was the intent of a settler-run economy. The settlers frequently organized themselves politically in order to discourage any moves for African freehold farming and to oppose granting lands to any other groups, such as Asians.

In Kenya, for example, the British Protectorate government was primarily interested in rapid economic development by a colony that could "pay its own way." The government wanted the region to be self-supporting. The settlers, on the other hand, wanted to assure their sources of land and labor, to be able to rely on an African population amenable to European supervision, and to affirm European racial superiority. The system of production was oriented completely toward an export economy based on European hegemony both within the colony and within the global system.

The economic consequences of colonialism for peoples of the Global South were enormous. First, the world was shaped into a pattern of dominating and dominated countries. International specialization benefited primarily the industrialized countries that exchanged manufactured goods for the raw materials, foods, and other primary goods of the colonies. That is, the economies were all oriented toward the outside, toward producing for foreign markets in ways that benefited people elsewhere. Second, they were often dual economies with an export enclave and a large subsistence sector. The two sectors were linked in that the export enclave, usually in the form of a plantation or mining community, was dependent upon the creation of a poorly paid labor force managing on subsistence wages. Third, in many instances land was expropriated, the concept of private property introduced, and the best lands reserved for foreign settlers. Fourth, space was organized to serve the colonizers in ways that benefited them and restricted growth elsewhere. For instance, infrastructure, roads, transport, and communications were constructed so as to serve settler areas rather than the general population. Last, access to economic opportunity was restricted. Sometimes it was restricted along class lines, forging a new elite beholden to the foreign power. Sometimes it was restricted along racial and ethnic lines. The outcome of these arrangements was that any benefits to flow from the new production system went to a very few people who held power within the colony and to the imperial power abroad.

Colonial Politics and Governance

Colonial powers, first of all, established territories with fixed political boundaries where none had existed before. In some instances — Southeast Asia, for example — these boundaries were contiguous with cultural and ethnic boundaries, but often they were not. Second, within each territory, the colonial power established political order and an administrative hierarchy to sustain it. The structure was centralized and authoritarian and undergirded by force, exploitation, and repression in varying degrees, but sufficient to maintain the colonial power. Authority emanated from the chambers of Europe and made its way through governors and provincial and district commissioners, down eventually to those local leaders who had been integrated into the colonial administrative system. Underlying the colonial system of governance was a premise of inequality "inherent in the colonizers' conception of their own superiority, and their consequent arrogation to themselves of the right to determine the fate of the governed."[9]

The most important objectives of the colonial governments were to establish a system of control that would enable them to maintain law and order, to collect taxes, and to make the colonial economy profitable. To achieve these objectives many governments virtually dismantled the traditional systems of governance. In Africa, colonial powers at times utilized tribal structures to deal with specific issues or problems, but over time, the powers gradually usurped the authority of indigenous institutions and created new institutions that they dominated. The British developed a system of indirect rule in which they relied on indigenous authorities often appointed by them. It was economical from the point of view of the colonial government, and it appealed to the indigenous leaders themselves. The French had a high level of assimilation of local people in administration and in higher education. French colonies elected representatives to the National Assembly in Paris. Among the British colonies racial exclusiveness prevailed, and there was no thought that the colonized might "someday be like us."

The European imperialists encountered diverse peoples in most regions of the world. Sometimes there were numerous languages, religions, races, and ethnic groups. Often there were two major groups existing in a somewhat delicate relationship. The arrival of the imperial power transformed that relationship, and the colonizers often used the change to their advantage. Sri Lanka, for example, was colonized by the Portuguese in the sixteenth century, by the Dutch in the seventeenth and eighteenth centuries, and by the British in the nineteenth and twentieth centuries. The British found a dominant Sinhalese culture with a population approximately 80 percent Buddhist Sinhalese ruled by Sinhalese kings. Approximately 20 percent of the population was Tamil and Hindu. It was not long before the new colonial power was utilizing its authority to build relationships among the Tamil community and in the process to undercut the Sinhalese rulers. Slowly the Tamils built up a cadre of educated citizens, many of whom served in the imperial bureaucracy. Resentments began to fester among the Sinhalese as they perceived undue influence, power, and position going to the rival Tamil community. Not more than ten years after Sri Lanka's independence, the Sinhalese were looking for ways to redress the situation. They did so by demanding that the official language of the country be made Sinhalese and by insisting that a variety of other benefits be directed specifically toward the Sinhalese community. Now, nearly half a century later, there is an ongoing civil war between the Sinhalese and the Tamils in Sri Lanka (see chapter 4) as the Tamils seek autonomy in the northern region populated largely by Tamils and the government seeks to maintain a unitary government. While the origins of this dispute are not exclusively in the colonial experience, they have been greatly exacerbated by the policies of the British colonial power toward these two ethnic and religious communities.

In Africa we can find many such examples. Rwanda is perhaps the most poignant. There are several perspectives on the origins of the conflict between the two major tribal/ethnic groups in Rwanda: the Hutu and the Tutsi. Each has persuasive arguments and its supports and detractors. The most widely accepted interpretation is that the agriculturalist Hutu migrated to Rwanda and Burundi from Central Africa in the early part of the last millennium; the cattle-rearing Tutsi came to the region during the fifteenth and sixteenth centuries in successive migrations from the north. Over the centuries these two groups integrated substantially and eventually shared many of the same characteristics. At the end of the nineteenth century, Europeans, specifically Germans and Belgians, conquered Rwanda, elevating the Tutsi aristocracy to increased control over the region. Establishing a variety of ways to assure a flow of taxes and resources to the Europeans, the colonial authorities conferred power and privilege on those who worked in their administration, spoke French, and became Catholic. Favoring the Tutsi, the Europeans built a system of rigid ethnic classification, introduced required identity papers that stated one's ethnicity, and reserved education and jobs in both administration and army almost exclusively for the Tutsi. Under colonial rule, social relationships in Rwanda became more uniform, rigid, unequal, and exploitative.[10] Thus it is not surprising that decolonization and independence were accompanied by social revolution and the overthrow of the Tutsi establishment, all roots of the violence of 1994.

Sri Lanka and Rwanda are only two among many such examples of colonized regions exploited in such a way that ethnicity slowly became an increasingly salient factor in the economics and politics of the locality. Sometimes the imperial power favored some over others, according to ethnicity, religion, or race. Sometimes colonialists employed indirect rule in ways to build animosities of one group toward another. Whatever the specifics, it was often the case that the colonial experience increased sensitivities among different ethnic groups and, in many instances, escalated tensions to a serious level.

Over time one problem in particular characterized the affairs of local governance: an increasing hiatus in authority structures. Slowly indigenous authorities lost their effectiveness as they lost control over land, over warfare, over the maintenance of law and peace, and over the nature of their society. In many parts of Africa, schools, missions, a settler-oriented cash economy, and government introduced an outside world with new modes of access through education and wage employment. Propelled by a variety of economic and social circumstances, many young people oriented themselves toward this modern lifestyle, a lifestyle for which their elders had little enthusiasm and over which they had virtually no control. The problem — a changing younger generation, often dissatisfied and sometimes confused, accompanied by the deterioration of indigenous authorities and the inadequacy of new ones — characterized many local communities during the colonial period throughout Africa and elsewhere.

Colonial Impacts on Ideologies, Values, and Social Systems

Attitudes toward Local Cultures

Perhaps the most invidious influence of colonialism has been the imposition of the language of the imperialist on the people of the colony. In many Third World countries the language of the colonial power is the one that is used officially for communication across the country; the indigenous languages are used primarily in the home and local community. Language, as Ngugi wa Thiong'o points out in *Decolonising the Mind*, has a dual purpose: it is a means of communication and a carrier of culture.[11] Experiences are handed over from one generation to the next and become the basis for values and for a distinctive culture and history. It becomes the "spiritual eyeglasses through which a people come to view themselves and their place in the universe." Colonialism imposed control not only on economic production but also on social production. It dominated not only through military consequences and political rule, but through domination of the mental universe of the colonized, determining how people perceived themselves and their relationship to the world. African children encountering literature in colonial schools and universities were asked to experience their world from the perspective of European interpretations and experience. This approach, of course, effectively banished them to the periphery, because literature, history, and geography were all taught in a Eurocentric way.

Along with language came the culture of the colonizers. Perhaps the most powerful tool of cultural disruption was Christianity. Eager for converts and convinced of their righteous superiority and access to truth, missionaries undermined traditional belief systems and sowed seeds of discontent. Nowhere is this phenomenon captured more vividly than in Ngugi's *The River Between*.[12] The central figures of Ngugi's classic tale are caught up in a conflict between the Kikuyu community and the Church of Scotland. At issue in the novel is female circumcision that had long been practiced by the Kikuyus as a ritual marking the transformation of a teenage girl to womanhood. Missionaries from the Church of Scotland forbid its practice among their congregation. The story revolves around two Kikuyu factions, one adhering to the tenets of the Church of Scotland and the other to traditional Kikuyu values; the young lovers were caught in the maelstrom. It was not an easy situation to sort out either in the story or in real life. The churches demanded loyalty and denigrated the spirituality of the traditional religion. At the same time, the missionaries provided schools, and along with them some of the tools for beginning to address the injustices of a settler economy.

Colonialism and Women

It is risky to generalize about the impact of colonialism on women given the diverse cultures and historical periods to be examined. However, four generalizations are possible. First, the colonial powers generally brought their own assumptions about women's roles with them, and these assumptions affected policies and attitudes toward women in the colonized regions. Indeed, in Victorian England and other European societies of the time, the views on women's roles were quite restricted, often more so than in some societies of Asia and Africa. In sub-Saharan Africa, for example, these assumptions caused colonial administrators to overlook the roles of rural African women in food production. In France, Germany, or Great Britain, where there were male farming systems, women did not have primary responsibility for cultivation of food crops. In Africa they did. This fact was ignored in the development of agricultural policies by colonial administrators, to the detriment of household farming in rural African communities. Another example concerns ideological assumptions about the uniqueness and sacredness of the patriarchal nuclear family. Some administrators and many missionaries did not grasp the complexity of and rationale for the extended and often polygamous family systems in Africa.

Second, colonial governments were quite prepared to use women to serve the economic and political interests of the imperial power. For example, the introduction of commercialized agriculture contributed to the aggrandizement of the Europeans and to the loss of the colonized women's economic power. This happened throughout the colonies through the privatization of land, in which women were not only ineligible for land ownership but lost their traditional rights to use land. In Africa, women's agricultural labor on the reserves subsidized male wage labor on plantations and in mines. Men were not paid living wages to support a family. Women and children stayed behind in rural communities where they were supported by the labor of women in agriculture, trade, and small-scale income-generating activities. When new technologies were introduced, men were the recipients of the new knowledge. So, for example, in Uganda men learned new processes for growing cotton, despite the fact that women had been the producers of cotton. Thus, throughout the colonies women were "used" to support European priorities in a variety of ways.

Third, there has been a tendency to lump Third World women in a single category and to view them as passive victims of "strange" social customs. These customs might vary from the extreme foot-binding practiced for centuries in China to child brides in many parts of the world, or to polygamous households. Third World women have been perceived as the "gendered other." The nuances of class, ethnicity, and other forms of identity were lost in this homogenizing way of viewing women and women's roles. Indeed, it is possible for some women to benefit by virtue of a privileged position in a colonial context, perhaps through affluence or being a member of a favored ethnic group. There may, nevertheless, be long-term deprivation and loss of status for the majority of women in that society.

Last, theorists examining the colonial period vary widely in their views on the perceived impacts of the colonial process on women. Their perspectives conform to the larger outlines of development theories. Modernizationists, for example, determine that colonization will ultimately be beneficial as it brings new knowledge and technology to the colonized, including women. If there is a problem, it is one of diffusion. The benefits may be slow in "trickling down" to women. Perhaps the critical question is how do women who have been colonized perceive their interests. Do they identify with other women? Do they identify with men who have also been colonized? Where do their interests lie? Sen and Grown speak to this question effectively in their book *Development, Crises, and Alternative Visions*.[13] Their vision focuses on both poverty and gender subordination and seeks a world where inequalities based on class, gender, and race are challenged and banished in every country. Another group of women examining colonialism and women has been identified as "postcolonial feminists." Postcolonial feminism arises from the experiences of women of color, including both women of the South and minorities situated in the North. It focuses on the ideologies and practices of racism, colonialism, and neocolonialism and the ways in which they contribute to the oppression of women of color.[14] Of particular interest here is their emphasis on globalization as a continuation of five centuries of imperialism and colonialism and its reliance on exploitation of women. They use the term "recolonization" to describe the intensification of colonization in the South and its extension to the North. They bring together notions of exploitation, globalization, and the politics of location in ways that make us reflect on the continuing impact of the colonial experience.

Third World Responses: Nationalism and Nationalist Identities

It should be no surprise that the experience of colonialism, which would affect people so profoundly and in so many ways distort and harm their way of life, would generate a strong response. And so it did, in the form of nationalist movements. People involved in these movements sought to establish pride in their own identity, removal of foreign rulers, and, ultimately, political self-determination. In many instances those national leaders who led the struggles for independence were themselves deeply influenced by the foreign cultures they were opposing. Mohandas Gandhi, the spiritual and political leader of India in the 1930s and 1940s, and known for *satyagraha* or nonviolent struggle against oppressors, was a lawyer trained in London who had participated in the movement for racial justice in South Africa before returning to his homeland. Jawaharlal Nehru, India's first prime minister and Gandhi's close colleague in the struggles for independence, was trained at Oxford. Jomo Kenyatta, leader of Kenya's independence struggle and that nation's first prime minister, spent many years in London working and studying anthropology at University College in London. Ho Chi Minh, Vietnamese revolutionary and nationalist who led the Vietminh in decades of struggle against French and U.S. imperialism, spent many years studying and working in Paris. Leopold Senghor, the first president of Senegal, was as comfortable in the literary salons of Paris as in Dakar.

These leaders, and the movements they headed, sought political independence from the imperial powers. They sought it as nations, an identity that had been carved for them by the colonialists. Before imperialism and colonial settlements, most Asian societies had been organized around feudal or princely kingdoms, shifting dynasties, bureaucracies, and empires. In Africa and also in the Americas prior to the eighteenth century, people had been loyal to tribe or to ethnic community. These loyalties were transformed by the imperial powers who put their stamp of the nation-state on the colonies. The nation was, of course, relatively new to Europe as well, having been formalized in the last part of the nineteenth century.

One important characteristic of these nationalist movements was a focus on identity. There was bitter criticism of the intent of colonialism as cultural annihilation. In addition, the West's focus on the individual was abhorrent to many who viewed the West as hedonistic and materialistic, excluding any sense of community. Freeing people from colonial dominance became a central objective and was often attached to powerful symbols. For example, in India Gandhi used as symbols of Indian identity the spinning wheel and *khadi* cloth, a very simple cotton cloth woven in India's villages on hand looms. Those visual symbols of simple rural life became central to the expression of Indian nationalism and identity. In French West Africa in the 1950s and 1960s this search took the form of a movement for negritude, the concept that black is beautiful and a source of pride and dignity. This movement marks the beginning of black consciousness, a deliberate effort to overcome the centuries of exploitation and humiliation. In 1955, representatives of twenty-nine Asian and African countries met in Bandung, Indonesia, to discuss common problems such as decolonization, nonalignment, and trade relations. It was the first time people from a large bloc of developing countries had met to discuss issues important to them in a forum not dominated by Northern institutions. Today a powerful theme in the non-Western narrative continues to be the urgency of regaining the self-respect that was lost through the imperial and colonial experience.

Nationalism proved to be an effective way to unite an oppressed people against the oppressor. Nationalist movements sought to dismantle the yoke of oppression for all the colonized. They did not focus on reorganizing society beyond obtaining power for the disenfranchised. However, some nationalist movements were also revolutionary in that they were determined to restructure society as well. China, for example, experienced a movement that combined both nationalist and revolutionary elements. It sought to rid itself of foreign domination, including

Japanese occupation. It also sought under the leadership of Mao Tse-tung and the Chinese Communist Party to reshape politics as well as class and social relations within the society; China succeeded in this endeavor in 1949.

After World War II, the momentum of nationalist movements around the globe was enormous. Throughout the Third World, people sought to achieve dignity, material progress, and autonomy by ridding themselves of the imperialist oppressors. With incredible speed in the fifteen years following the end of the war, many nations achieved that objective. India was the first in August 1947, but by the early 1960s nearly twenty African nations had acquired independence, some of them in intense struggles for their freedom. The Dutch recognized Indonesian independence in 1949. Algeria and Vietnam engaged in long wars against the French for their freedom. Not until 1954 when the French suffered a major defeat at Dien Bien Phu did they abandon their efforts to govern Vietnam, but then a divided Vietnam was joined by the United States in a struggle for control of that country. The war between North and South Vietnam, with China aiding the North and the United States fighting with the South, dragged on fifteen years. In Algeria the French finally departed in 1961.

The peoples of these new nations, from Pakistan and India to Kenya and Ghana and Jamaica and Trinidad, were filled with pride and hope as they launched a new era as independent, self-governing states. The United Nations General Assembly reflected these numerous changes. In 1960 there were ninety-nine member states in the UN General Assembly. In 1965 there were 117. In the course of that five-year period, eighteen newly established nations had been added. Only a few nationalist struggles remained. Zimbabwe (then Southern Rhodesia) became independent in 1980, Belize in 1981, and a few others have achieved independent status since then, including Eritrea in 1993 and East Timor in 2002.

North-South Politics in the Cold War Era

In the years immediately following World War II, there were many new, optimistic nations of the South. Europe, on the other hand, was exhausted, devastated by the long war years. Plans for the postwar period had been launched at various Allied wartime conferences held between 1941 and 1945. The Atlantic Charter issued jointly by U.S. president Roosevelt and British prime minister Winston Churchill promised sovereign rights and self-government to all those who had been denied them. It promised freedom of speech, freedom of religion, freedom from want, and freedom from fear of physical aggression, the "Four Freedoms" that President Roosevelt had originally described in his State of the Union message in January 1941. At Yalta, a Crimean summer resort on the Black Sea, they discussed the possibilities of an international organization, the United Nations. In July 1944, the governments of Britain and the United States convened a conference at Bretton Woods, New Hampshire, to develop plans for two institutions to manage the postwar world economy: The International Monetary Fund (IMF) and the International Bank for Reconstruction and Development (World Bank), institutions that, for better or for worse, continue to define the postwar era.

The colonial systems organized around the world were in a state of collapse as peoples of the South demanded independence. The colonial countries, no longer great powers and decimated as a result of the war, were in no position to resist, had they wished to do so. Moreover, the reimposition of colonial rule would have violated the very principles for which they were presumably fighting — freedom, justice, self-determination. Together the outpouring of nationalist feelings in the Global South and the weakened state of the European powers led to a transfer of power that, for the most part, was relatively peaceful.

The political climate, however, was tense. In the aftermath of World War II, two powers were dominant: the Soviet Union and the United States. They squared off as opponents in what has become known as the "Cold War." Each power feared the military strength of the other. Each abhorred the philosophical underpinnings of the other. The Russians, drawing on their beliefs in Marxism/Leninism, viewed capitalism as a decadent way of life, unprincipled and to be destroyed as rapidly as possible. The Americans perceived communism to be intent on destroying the state and all those who were not prepared to accept communism as a way of life. Both could observe that the Third World countries were becoming more numerous and outspoken, and both perceived new political and strategic relevance in the countries of the South.

In this recognition, each pursued several strategies relevant to Third World countries. First they sought to acquire loyal followers among the newly formed Third World states. That is, they sought client states who would agree to support their position vis-à-vis the other superpower in public fora such as the UN General Assembly. Second, they engaged in proxy wars, providing military support to other nations that would wage their skirmishes for them. So, for example, through the 1960s and part of the 1970s, the United States provided military support to Haile Selassie of Ethiopia in exchange for an anti-Soviet stance. Ethiopia was locked in sporadic conflict with its neighbor, Somalia, bordering it to the east. Somalia, in turn, received military support from the Soviet Union in return for its pro-Marxist, pro-Soviet stance on a variety of issues. Such scenarios were played out around the globe as the United States and the Soviet Union became increasingly competitive with one another. These struggles were undergirded, at least from the American perspective, by the "domino theory." Americans widely believed that if one country became communist, those adjacent would follow as the "rot" set in. Thus, it was necessary to prevent any country from falling to communist subversives, lest others immediately follow. This philosophy justified to Americans the U.S. roles in both the Korean War and the Vietnam War.

Some newly independent countries managed to exploit this super-power rivalry effectively. They, in effect, invited the superpowers to bid for their support by upping the ante for foreign aid, whether food, general aid, or military support. Egypt, when seeking support for con-struction of the Aswan dam, effectively played off the United States and the Soviet Union in this manner. Others used "weapons of the weak" where by stalling on decisions, foot dragging, or other subtle means they could achieve their objectives and possibly undermine those of their pa-tron state. The outcome was that aid, in the form of both capital and technical assistance, increased to Third World countries. From the U.S. point of view, the hope was that this aid would bring about economic growth that would, in turn, bring political stability and more friendly attitudes toward the West. During the 1950s and 1960s foreign aid in-creased substantially as a result of the Cold War. Pakistan, South Korea, and Taiwan received significant levels of aid from the United States, whereas the Soviet Union provided support for India, North Korea, and China. However, both superpowers learned that aid does not necessarily bring allies among Third World nations. Relationships, even in a bipolar world, were complex, and loyalties shifted with the political, historical, and geographic terrain.

The Berlin Wall and New Global Dynamics

Tensions between the United States and the Soviet Union began to ease throughout the 1980s with Prime Minister Gorbachev's introduction of *glasnost,* or "openness," a policy of permitting open discussion of political, economic, and social issues and an effort to democratize the Soviet Union. In a dramatic moment at the end of 1989, the Berlin Wall separating West Berlin from the Soviet-dominated sector of East Berlin was torn down and Germany was reunited. It was a momentous occasion symbolizing the end of the Cold War. With the Soviet Union's dissolution in 1991, a number of new states emerged from the southern regions of that former state. These newly independent states, part of a precarious new global dynamic, have been marked by severe interethnic and political conflicts as they have faced the challenges of exercising sovereignty and building state structures and capacities. In fact, there has been a tendency in the region for leaders to focus on consolidating their own personal power rather than building broadly democratic political institutions. Several of the region's leaders have established themselves as "president for life" with no attention to procedures for facilitating political change.

The states of Central Asia are resource rich with plentiful oil and gas reserves, but characterized by highly volatile and unpredictable social tensions and fragile politics. Water management is an issue for the entire region, but particularly for those states in which agricultural crops that require a lot of water are widely grown. Crops such as cotton were introduced by Russian colonists who shaped economies that were export-oriented, servicing the rest of the Soviet Union. Now these states all have Russian minority populations to complicate the ethnic mix. This population has often expected preferential treatment. These states also have Muslim populations with the full range of Islamic perspectives. The Islamic fundamentalism sweeping across that region from the Middle East and South Asia is a concern to the leadership of all these countries and to many beyond. Decolonization in Central Asia, as one analyst points out, "is becoming increasingly reminiscent of what occurred in parts of sub-Saharan Africa, where a number of states have spent the past forty years stepping backwards from the levels of development that characterized their country and its population at the time of independence or in the first decade after independence was achieved."[15]

These Central Asian countries — Tajikistan, Kyrgyzstan, Uzbekistan, Kazakhstan, and Turkmenistan — constitute a region with which both North American and European nations have wished to engage economically and politically. As a consequence, in the last ten years, Central Asia has become a new focus for international aid from the more affluent countries. Given the competition for an already scarce resource — bilateral and multilateral aid — it is no surprise that Africa has found its proportion of international aid declining as interest in supporting Central Asian countries has grown. Resources that might have been allocated to addressing Africa's problems have been targeted for these new countries with their rich resources and delicate politics, leaving African countries with ever expanding needs. For example, the food shortages faced by both Southern Africa and the Horn of Africa at the beginning of the twenty-first century are legion. The requirements for mounting an international effort against AIDS in Africa are also extraordinary. These competing issues and concerns must be analyzed in the context of colonial structures that shaped the present-day world and current globalization processes that are creating new alignments and opportunities in whirlwind fashion.

Legacies of Imperialism and Colonialism: An Overview

European imperialism spread relentlessly throughout much of the world from the fifteenth through the twentieth century. It resulted in colonial settlements in the eighteenth, nineteenth, and twentieth centuries in large parts of Asia, Africa, and Latin America. The imperialism (largely for trade and plunder) and the settlements (largely for raw materials and agricultural commodities) left an imprint with both positive and negative elements. Certainly infrastructure — roads, ports, railroads — in many parts of the world was improved. New technologies in communications, transport, and energy provision were introduced. On balance, however, colonial powers left a legacy of rigid and inappropriate economic and political structures, a legacy with which most Third World countries, now independent, are still coping. This legacy might be summarized briefly in seven points.

Organizing the Use of Space

Wherever they went, the colonial powers organized space to suit themselves. The infrastructure established was intended to serve the needs of traders or European settlers, not the indigenous peoples. Roads and railways, for example, went to settler communities, not to communal areas. Cities, too, were organized for the benefit of elites, chief among them the European administrators, merchants, and farmers.

National boundaries conformed to colonial imperatives and not to national borders or ethnic or cultural divisions. Throughout Africa this fact alone has created extraordinary tensions. Some ethnic groups are divided in cumbersome ways. Somalis find themselves divided among five states. The Masai are located in both Kenya and Tanzania. Others are unified in states with communities with which they have never been friendly or with some who have routinely exploited them. The Luos, Kalenjens, and Kikuyu share Kenya's common national boundary, but may not be sure, beyond that, what they have in common. The Ogoni of Nigeria fear enormous exploitation from the large ethnic groups of Nigeria who have taken advantage of the former's small numbers, staggering poverty, and huge oil fields. The Shona and Ndebele are bound together in the state of Zimbabwe, even though the Ndebele are more closely related to tribal communities in South Africa. And so it goes. The consequence of the colonial experience is that the nation-state has been superimposed illogically on the African landscape. This circumstance is also found in other parts of the world. The Indian subcontinent, governed by Britain as "the jewel in the British crown," split upon independence into Muslim Pakistan and Hindu India. Then Pakistan further divided in 1971 as economic and political differences between Bengali-speaking, rice- and fish-eating Bengalis and Urdu-speaking, wheat- and meat-eating Punjabis became too great a strain for the divided nation of Pakistan. In sum, at every scale of land management and use across local, regional, and national dimensions, the colonial powers organized space to serve their own imperatives. At its worst, it became the geography of apartheid.

Orienting Economic Systems to Serve the Colonizers

The colonial powers organized systems of production to meet the needs of Europeans in the colonies and the strategic and commercial interests of the colonizing nation. Imperial powers in Africa and elsewhere impoverished the subsistence economy by confiscating land, confining some agricultural communities to reserves, demanding forced labor, and imposing taxes to force people to work for settlers. The position of local farmers became increasingly unfavorable vis-à-vis the Europeans who appropriated much of the surplus in rents, taxes, and fees. Over time, dependence of Africans on purchased goods increased, and they became engaged in market processes. In sum, a largely subsistence agricultural community and low-wage labor force were serving the needs of large European farmers in a well-capitalized sector. While the specifics may vary by region and continent, the intent and outcomes have been similar: the interests and needs of indigenous populations were ignored or destroyed in the face of the colonizers' demands for their land and their labor.

Manipulating Indigenous Institutions of Governance

Efforts on the part of colonial powers to establish themselves at the top of the pyramid of power among colonized peoples took several forms. Sometimes they ignored the traditional patterns of authority — clan, council of elders, age groups, or others. In such cases they established their own leaders who often held little stature within the local community and therefore had little authority. Such steps created difficult and confusing situations for community members. Sometimes colonial powers simply became an imperial overlay using the existing systems of governance to their own advantage. Such, for example, occurred in India with the use of Indian *zamindars* or tax collectors and *jagirdars* or territorial administrators. Sometimes they manipulated one ethnic group to the disadvantage of another, moving its members into distinctly more powerful positions than those held by any other group. Such tactics left in their wake a variety of malfunctioning institutions at local, regional, and national levels.

Creating Elites and Inequities

Throughout the colonies there was a concentration of economic and political power, first in the hands of the Europeans and second in the hands of those who supported the colonial regime. This is not to suggest that there were not enormous differences in wealth and thus power in some regions prior to European colonization. The Mogul Empire in India or the emperors of Ethiopia's Central Highlands provide examples of great wealth amid much poverty. Nevertheless, the power structures of colonialism put into place new avenues for gaining wealth, status, and prestige, all geared to a small minority chosen by the imperial authorities. The limited educational opportunities created very narrow access to the top of the pyramid, available only to a limited and privileged few.

Using Formal Education to Promote Colonial Interests

Education was used to promote the ends of the colonial power. In Africa it was largely provided by missionaries who competed among themselves in ways often quite self-serving and destructive to the local communities they intended to serve. Competition among religious denominations to gain members was often quite fierce. In addition, church-related educational systems constituted a source of major conflict with traditional African sociocultural institutions. At the time of independence very few Africans had attained higher education despite more than a half century of a colonial presence. In India and other parts of Asia where there were long traditions of literacy and scholarship, members of elite communities were educated in the institutions of the colonizing country. These opportunities tended to solidify the relationship between the upper classes of the colonized country and the colonizer, deepening the gap between elites and ordinary people within the colonized setting. These educational systems also provided staff for middle to upper levels of the bureaucracy as required by the colonial power.

Creating External Economic Dependence

With the colonies producing largely for export to the colonizing power, external economic dependence was assured. Roads, railways, irrigation systems — all valuable in their own right — were nevertheless designed to support the export economy. One consequence is that the colonies, now as independent nations, have had difficulty developing appropriate internal economic structures that serve the needs of large numbers of local residents. Banishing the bonds of political dominance has proved somewhat easier than eliminating economic dependence. Those structures are very much in place and still a matter of sore concern as the formerly colonized countries struggle to attain equity in the global economic system.

Involving the Colonized People in Proxy Wars and Great Power Competition

Over the centuries many colonized peoples have been trapped in the competition among imperial and colonizing regimes for power, influence, and fortune. Such competition can be seen, for example, in the histories of East Africa or Central Africa as the British, the Germans, the French, and the Belgians maneuvered for access and control over land, peoples, and trade routes. It has led to proxy wars in which the great powers have manipulated colonized areas or client states to fight their battles for them. For example, Ethiopia, backed by the United States, fought with Somalia, backed by the Soviet Union, for control over the Ogaden region of the Horn of Africa. This competition has also left some regions plundered and devastated by virtue of their strategic location, a fate that it seems no country has suffered more than Afghanistan.

What is the balance sheet for colonialism? While it may be tempting to give a wholesale indictment of colonialism, it would be both foolish and unrealistic to suggest that it had only negative features. To be sure, the driving force was the economic, political, and strategic gain of the European powers. In the process, however, they strengthened infrastructure and introduced new technologies. In some instances, they provided concepts of justice and freedom that had a leavening influence on notably harsh systems. Nevertheless, in the final analysis, colonialism left behind a host of economic and political structures skewed toward the needs, interests, and concerns of people in distant lands. It increased existing inequities, created new forms of inequalities, reorganized relationships among colonized peoples to suit imperial whims, and left a tangle of problems that countries made independent half a century ago are still unraveling.

Colonial Legacies Haunting the Twenty-First Century: East Timor, Nigeria, and Afghanistan

The political, social, and economic complexities created by the colonial experience can be found in every corner of the world. Probably the pathos engendered can be found everywhere as well. We have selected three colonial experiences — one from Asia, one from Africa, and one from the Middle East — to provide glimpses of ways in which the legacies identified in the previous section have taken hold in specific settings. In each case the imperial power or colonizer was different: in East Timor the Portuguese had been a presence from the late sixteenth century. Nigeria was colonized by the British; Afghanistan has endured British, Russian, and American invasions and control. In one case, East Timor suffered a subsequent power grab from a neighbor, Indonesia, thereby greatly increasing the brutal impacts of conflict, colonization, war, and resistance.

East Timor: Tiny and Tough

East Timor, a small nation with a population under 1 million, is just now coming out from under the spiraling circumstances launched 400 years ago with the arrival of the Portuguese and firmly established in a structural arrangement between the Portuguese and the Dutch 250 years ago. East Timor (about the size of Massachusetts) is situated on the eastern half of Timor Island, located between the Indonesian archipelago and Australia. Controlled by the Portuguese for nearly two centuries, in the mid-eighteenth century the Dutch assumed control of West Timor as part of the Dutch East Indies, now Indonesia, while Portugal retained control of roughly half the island, now called East Timor, and ruled the area until the 1970s.

At that time, Portugal, in the midst of its own civil war, began a withdrawal from its colonies of Mozambique, Angola, and East Timor. Several East Timorese political parties emerged, each with different perspectives on the future of the region: one with socialist inclinations favoring immediate independence, one favoring integration with Indonesia, and one for maintaining ties with Portugal with a slow transition to independence. Elections were held in 1975 and won by Fretilin, the party urging immediate independence. Shortly thereafter Indonesian forces invaded East Timor, and seven months later the Indonesian government declared East Timor the twenty-seventh province of the Republic of Indonesia. The East Timorese immediately launched a resistance to Indonesian occupation, and these struggles lasted until 1999. During this period approximately one-third of the East Timorese population was killed.

The extraordinary bloodshed and consequent efforts to bring about peace led to the award of the Nobel Peace Prize of 1996 to two leaders of the East Timorese Resistance. Finally, in 1998, the Indonesian government bowed to international and domestic pressure and agreed to hold and abide by a referendum in East Timor to determine whether it should become independent or remain part of Indonesia. In the referendum held on August 30, 1999, under UN observation, the East Timorese voted overwhelmingly for independence. However, the Indonesian militias did not accept the results of the vote, took control of East Timor, and widespread violence ensued. Eventually, a multinational peacekeeping force organized by the UN Security Council provided security for the East Timorese, well after another three thousand East Timorese had been killed, and established an international peacekeeping force and a civilian authority to govern East Timor as a UN-administered protectorate.

In May 2002 East Timor became a fully independent nation under the leadership of newly elected president Xanana Gusmão, long the key resistance leader for the East Timorese. Gusmão had spent years in an

Indonesian jail for his role in the resistance movement, and had become known as the "Timorese Mandela."[16] The East Timorese strong sense of loyalty and identity has, no doubt, been strengthened by the imperialistic behavior of the Indonesian government and military. Indeed, East Timor is a nation that has been forged through centuries of colonial influence, violence, and oppression as well as lengthy struggles against oppression.

Nigeria: African Giant and Colonial Jigsaw Puzzle

Nigeria, like the other parts of West Africa, was initially incorporated into a world economic system through the slave trade. The horrific record of this trade and its lasting consequences, which are well known, did not abate until the middle of the nineteenth century. Toward the end of that century, the increasingly industrialized economies of Europe, and especially Britain and France, were turning to West Africa to obtain a variety of resources and to establish markets. The Berlin Conference, organized by the major European powers in 1884, set the framework for colonial territorial divisions in Africa, "carving up" Africa according to the whims and preferences of the imperial powers. No Africans were involved in that conference. While this event may largely have been a paper exercise, it did lead to the economic and political activities that determined British hegemony over the area that is modern-day Nigeria.

Nigeria, the largest state in West Africa with a population of 120 million, illustrates the complexities of dealing in a postcolonial world with the boundaries and borders established by the colonial power. Nigeria comprises over 250 ethnic groups, of which three constitute 66 percent of the total population: the Igbo in the southeast, the Yoruba in the southwest, and the Hausa/Fulani in the north. While the British established English as the national language of governance, only a small minority of Nigerians were actually educated in English at the time of Nigeria's independence in 1960. Thus the newly independent government included Igbo, Hausa, and Yoruba as official languages of government. Moreover, education is offered in thirteen "state" languages, and at least fifty-four other languages are widely used. This linguistic complexity poses many questions, often with considerable financial implications. As we move into the information age of the twenty-first century they become vivid indeed. For example, in how many languages should national television and radio broadcasting be transmitted? What are the languages to be used in the nation's universities, in the military, or by the legislative body?

In the case of Nigeria religious diversity is also at issue. The Yoruba are Christian (about 20 percent of the population) and the Hausa/Fulani are Muslim (29 percent of the population). Moreover, these distinct groups enjoy very different cultures. The Hausa/Fulani are highly centralized, hierarchical and deferential to authority, whereas the Igbo are considered egalitarian and given to debate and challenge. All these issues — linguistic, religious, culture, and style, along with economic differentiation — came into play in the early years of the Nigerian state.

At first the democratically elected government struggled to meet the challenge of balancing the interests and needs of its highly diverse population. However, by 1962 good spirits and goodwill were eroding in disputes over the national census. The Igbo, who had taken advantage of colonial educational opportunities, enjoyed positions in government well beyond their proportion of the population. The more numerous Hausa/Fulani had resisted British influence and increasingly came to fear that they would be disadvantaged within a system controlled by the Igbos and possibly the Yorubas. Moreover, the eastern region had massive oil resources. Both internal competition over their control and external envy over their presence contributed to increasing tensions. Two military coups in 1966 eventually triggered the civil war in which Nigeria's Eastern Province seceded from the Nigerian federation and declared itself the independent Republic of Biafra. A brutal three-year civil war ensued. Biafra was defeated in January 1970, and the end of the war has been followed by three decades of military rule and authoritarianism.[17] Many of Nigeria's leaders have been characterized by extreme corruption that has led to spiraling rounds of public alienation and protest followed by government repression.

Military rule ended with the death of General Abacha in 1998 and the election of President Obasanjo in 1999. Nigeria remains, however, a fragile democracy and rapidly seems to be becoming a battleground for political opportunists willing to stoke the fires of violence among their supporters. Alignments may focus around religious, ethnic, class, and regional differences. Since 1999, more than ten thousand Nigerians have died in violent outbursts that have affected every part of the country. The underlying problem is access to scarce resources, whether those are land, jobs, political power, or basics such as water or transport. This situation is aggravated by a large, angry, frustrated underclass of unemployed youth, many of whom have migrated to the urban areas and are ripe to participate in the cycles of violence. Conditions in Nigeria are also aggravated by a widespread certainty on the part of many Nigerians that corruption is rampant and that leaders of all types have profited to the detriment of the general population. Thus, any president of Nigeria has an enormous challenge in wielding this potentially strong state into a functioning entity. The legacies of colonialism underlie these political, social, and economic challenges.

Afghanistan: Imperial Crossroads as Buffer and Battlefield

For centuries Afghanistan has been both a meeting place and a battlefield for the peoples surrounding it. The country is located at a crossroads connecting Iran, central Asia, the Arabian Sea, and India. Sometimes Afghanistan has served as a buffer between competing empires and ideologies. At other times it has served as a corridor through which armies have marched, and sometimes it has been a battlefield on which they have fought.[18] Repeated experience with imperial conquerors as well as efforts to colonize the country have helped shape a fierce sense of independence and pride widely regarded as characteristic of the Afghans.

Afghanistan is a feudal society organized around many tribes and clans with a long history of alliances, militancy, and strife. About sixty different Pashtun-speaking tribes together compose 38 percent of the Afghan population. They are a people known to be independent and combative, well armed, loosely organized, given to blood feuds, and strict adherents to their interpretation of Muslim law. Over the centuries it seems that the only force uniting them has been a common outside enemy. Other key groups with an ethnic and regional definition are the Hazaras, the Uzbeks, Turkmen, and the Tajiks. Recently women have been what one analyst calls "the vanished gender."[19] Afghanistan has among the highest infant, child, and maternal mortality rates and the lowest literacy and life expectancy rates in the world. It also is one of two or three countries with the lowest levels of per capita food availability.

In the last half of the nineteenth century, Russia and Great Britain maneuvered for influence in Central Asia. The British acquired their Pashtun subjects in 1849, but they did not settle the border between India and Afghanistan until 1893 when the Durand Line was agreed upon. The problem with the Durand Line was that the Pashtuns live on both sides of the frontier that now divides Afghanistan and Pakistan. Afghan Pashtuns fought the British in three wars, and more than fifty punitive expeditions were fought between the British and the Pashtuns between 1839 and the partition of India in 1947.[20] At that time Pakistan inherited the Pashtuns east of the Durand Line and determined to keep the same Tribal Territories arrangement. Even so, there are rumblings among the Pashtuns for an independent Pashtunistan on the frontier including Pashtuns from both sides of the border.

At one time Afghanistan was on the front line of the Cold War, and eventually it emerged as a buffer state between the United States and Soviet-led alliance systems, successors of the British and Russian empires. In the late 1970s, the Soviet Union invaded Afghanistan. The United States supported the rebellion against the Soviet Union indirectly, providing assistance to the *mujaheddin* (Afghan warlords), working with the government of Pakistan and providing support for the Taliban. One million people died during the Soviet Union's ten-year occupation ending in 1989. After providing billions of dollars worth of arms and ammunition to the *mujaheddin,* the United States abandoned Afghanistan, figuring the Cold War and the confrontation were over. It gave its allies in the region, Pakistan and Saudi Arabia, a free hand in the Afghan civil war that ensued. Meanwhile the Islamic Movement of Taliban, a quasi-religious, military, and political organization of extremist Islamic believers led by mullahs (religious leaders from the city of Kandahar) emerged as a possibility for bringing some peace and stability among the *mujaheddin.* The Taliban thus presented itself as an Islamic solution to the problems of a failed state, but only three years later civil war erupted, pitting the Pushtun population in the south and east against the ethnic minorities of the north — Tajik, Uzbek, Hazara, and Turkmen.

The terrorist attacks on September 11, 2001, killed more than two thousand people and instantly transformed the Taliban's relationship to the rest of the world. The Taliban had sheltered Osama bin Laden, the suspected mastermind of the attack, and his followers, providing them with sites in Afghanistan for training and planning their operations. When the Taliban proved unwilling to turn bin Laden over to international authorities, their leaders made themselves vulnerable to attack by U.S. forces. This attack took place in late 2001; the Taliban forces were eventually defeated and an interim government was established under Hamid Karzhai, a charismatic Pashtun facing tremendous challenges.

What are these challenges with which Afghanistan enters the twenty-first century and how do they relate to the extensive imperial thrusts they have experienced? Afghanistan's economic situation is horrendous. War has destroyed most of the infrastructure and populated the countryside with land mines. Moreover, Afghanistan's primary economic activities revolve around smuggling and the drug trade. It produces most of the world's opium, and almost all of that comes from what were Taliban-controlled areas. Afghan opium was exported to the West through Pakistan in the 1980s, but there are now multiple export routes through Iran, the Persian Gulf states, and Central Asia.

Smuggling of consumer goods has also expanded enormously in the last ten years. Afghan and Pakistani truckers smuggle goods across territories that include Russia, the Caucasus, Central Asia, Iran, and Pakistan. Some have suggested that before September 11, the value of smuggling to and from the rest of the region may have been as high as $5 billion. The smuggling has crippled legitimate local industries that cannot compete with smuggled, foreign-made, duty-free consumer goods. The illegal economy is expanding given that the formal one is virtually nonexistent. With a devastated infrastructure, extreme poverty, and education and health care limited, fighting and smuggling are the major forms of employment.

Scholars have suggested that Afghanistan is now at the core of a region that includes conflicts not only in that country, but also in Tajikistan, Uzbekistan, Kyrgyzstan, Pakistan, and Kashmir. At the heart of the regional standoff is the battle for the vast oil and gas riches of landlocked Central Asia. There is also competition between the regional states and Western oil companies about who will get to build the pipelines needed to transport energy to markets in Europe and Asia.[21]

The challenges ahead for Afghanistan grow out of its geopolitical positioning and imperial/colonial entanglements. The government needs an army that can maintain law and order, contain regional warlords, control the drug industry, and maintain loyalty to the center without threatening some agreed-upon level of regional autonomy. This is a tall order in a region that has known little peace in decades and in which the elements of civil society are in shreds. Afghanistan also must address the intricacies of interethnic relations in a multiethnic state, the relationship between the state and clan, tribal and feudal structures, and appropriate paths for economic development in this conservative Islamic society. These challenges would be daunting for all but the hardiest among us.

Southern Perspectives on Northern Expansionism

Over many decades scholars, writers, and political analysts from the South have portrayed for their own communities, and for readers in the

North, the disruption, perils, humiliations, and impoverishment created by the imperial and colonial experience. We turn now to these people for their insights and for illustrations that can help us understand the ways in which these relationships and this past provide a legacy that shapes our individual options and our common future.

Frantz Fanon, a West Indian educated as a psychiatrist in France, practiced medicine in Algeria. Fanon wrote *The Wretched of the Earth* in 1961, conveying with intensity the anger and outrage of those who have been colonized as well as the bitterness of the anticolonial struggles. He affirmed violence as a "cleansing force" for those who have suffered colonial violence.[22] Fanon influenced not only the theoretical underpinnings of national and independence movements around the world but also their emotional fervor and organizational momentum.

In 1972 Walter Rodney, a Guyanese carrying out research on Africa, lamented "Europe has underdeveloped Africa...."[23] One African who heard and responded to these thoughts is Ngugi wa Thiong'o, a Kenyan literary figure who has analyzed the colonial experience in both fiction and nonfiction. Ngugi's early novels, such as *Weep Not, Child* and *The River Between* portray the dilemmas, the loss of identity, and the generational and racial conflicts of the colonial period, as Europeans took over lands, limited rights, and dominated cultures.[24]

Ngugi's *Decolonising the Mind* focuses on the politics of language and his fear that European imperialism will destroy his culture and his language, Kikuyu, as a reflection of and vehicle for that culture. Ngugi provides an eloquent cry against the cultural hegemony of the West. He explores the African reality in which a cultural bomb has been dropped by imperial forces to "annihilate a people's belief in their names, in their languages, in their environment, in their heritage of struggle, in their unity, in their capacities and ultimately in themselves."[25] His novels, along with those of Chinua Achebe, Wole Soyinka, Kamala Markandaya, Buchi Emecheta, or Wilson Katiyo — to mention just a few of the many literary figures of the South — deal with the tensions between the colonizers and the colonized; the loss of pride, identity, and place; and the anger and upheaval arising from the invasions of person and space.

V. S. Naipaul, a Trinidadian and winner of the 2001 Nobel Prize in Literature, has written numerous novels focusing on place, identity, and displacement. His characters are often uprooted, frequently from one continent to another, caught between past loyalties and present temptations, between the modern world and the traditional one. They are troubled by the strange amid familiarity, a looming chaos and ever present corruption. His classic *A Bend in the River* (1980) captures the pathos of the life of an Indian who lives in a town at the bend of a great river in a newly independent country in Central Africa. It speaks to the confusion, the corruption, the danger, and the seduction as two worlds collide in a place caught between the dangerously alluring modern world and its own tenacious past and traditions.[26] In Naipaul's most recent novel, *Half a Life* (2001), the central character, Willie, struggles in India, England, and Mozambique to cope with his heritage and to figure out just who he is, a process increasingly complicated today for many individuals around the world.

From all over Africa has come a searching and compelling outpouring of story, poetry, and novel examining the implications of the colonial experience. Some have looked beyond, at the period of independence, as people struggle to come to terms with the political and social consequences of colonialism. Coetzee's *Disgrace* (1999), for example, examines the bitterness and pathos as blacks and whites struggle to deal with the past in the course of learning to accommodate one another in a newly independent South Africa.[27] Another South African novelist, Nadine Gordimer, has explored the social and political tensions around race relations in both colonial and independent periods of that nation's history.

Literature from South Asia is replete with examples of works focusing on the colonial experience, from Kamala Markandaya's *Nectar in a Sieve* to Michael Ondaatje's *Running in the Family*.[28] Writing recently of colonialism and neocolonialism in India and other places, Indian scholar/activist Vandana Shiva has become a fiery advocate for the environment, for women's rights in managing resources, and for sustainable use of the global commons.[29] She has been a formidable opponent of the exploitation and wastefulness of industrial economies and of the negative consequences of globalization.

Other critics examine relations of power focusing on the ideologies by which the West has asserted itself in global economic and political affairs. Asoka Bandarage, a Sri Lankan scholar, links imperialism, militarism, and violence in what she considers an ongoing psychological colonization reinforcing a white supremacy based on Western education, Christianity, the colonial state, and the capitalist economic system. For her, "Control of Third World resources and suppression of social revolutions are the major imperatives of western imperialism during the postwar, neocolonial era as they had been during the era of classical colonialism."[30]

Many scholars argue that the hegemony of the West can be traced to the colonial encounter and the creation of the "captive mind" that values the culture of the colonizer over that of the colonized.[31] Some want to replace Western models with local ones. Others focus on the simple inclusion of new voices, ending the Western monologue. Many are concerned about the "lack of penetration of third world thought into the first world."[32] This gap remains a significant issue for scholars of the South and for those of both South and North who seek to expand their understanding of processes of global change. These ideas are expressed in the form of literature, essay, song, and poem, as well as formal treatises. These perceptions from the South can and must shape our understanding of the processes of social change creating development and underdevelopment.

Summary Observations

This chapter has attempted to place the North-South relationship in its historical context. It has reviewed the broad outlines of imperialism and colonialism to convey their impact neither on the North nor on the international economy, but instead on the colonized peoples. It has explored the colonial legacy and its effects on ideologies, values, and social systems. The chapter has reflected on the exuberance of the newly independent states of the immediate post–World War II era as well as the changes in global dynamics with the demise of the Soviet Union. Last, it has provided glimpses of three formerly colonized states — East Timor, Nigeria, and Afghanistan — and the burdens they still carry as a consequence of their colonial experience. This chapter concluded with some perspectives of Southern scholars, writers, and analysts about the colonial experience. The next chapter focuses specifically on the nature of the state and politics in the Global South and the varied challenges it faces at the beginning of the twenty-first century.

Chapter 3

Politics and the State

Concepts, Political Realities, and Challenges

Sorting out the divergent tendencies we observe in the politics of the Global South is not easy. On the one hand, there are forces of international integration such as the African Union (AU) or the Southeast Asia Regional Organization (SEARO). On the other hand, disintegrating forces are at work in many places such as Somalia, Sri Lanka, and Colombia. Do we grasp onto the hope inspired by Nelson Mandela who led the struggle against white supremacy and then relinquished power in a post-apartheid South Africa? Are we overwhelmed by the horror of atrocities in Rwanda when the Hutus and the Tutsi turned upon one another? Do we cling to the hope for a peaceful coexistence of Palestine and Israel, or do we become cynical and numb with yet another bout of terror, hatred, and bitterness? Do we commend and indeed celebrate India's fifty years of independence, or do we mark the occasion with somber reflections upon the continued struggle over Kashmir, the assassinations of two prime ministers, and the flaring of vitriolic caste animosities in Bihar or Gujarat?

These markedly different situations, as well as our varied responses to them, suggest the value of a new methodological approach for understanding politics and states in the Global South at the beginning of the twenty-first century. This approach has been identified as the "new comparative political economy."[1] It relies on comparative historical analyses of a small number of cases instead of single case studies or large quantitative comparisons. Generalizations are difficult to create and to sustain across many units and vast regions, but analysis of some specific cases enables us to see more clearly the processes at work and the complexity of both international and microlevel forces affecting people everywhere. The perspective of this chapter derives from analysis of contemporary political processes, grounded in everyday political realities. It is divided into three major sections addressing key concepts, political realities, and challenges.

The first section clarifies some terms for thinking about politics in the Global South, including *nation, nationalism,* and *national identities.* It reflects upon the state and its key attributes, and introduces five key concepts useful for exploring politics in the Global South. They are

- the *paradox of simultaneity:* a situation in which a nation has highly contradictory conditions and tendencies existing side by side;
- *dependency and autonomy:* the complex, fluid, and ambiguous relationship between dependency and autonomy for all states, but particularly for those of the Global South;
- *belonging:* the confusion and sometimes disagreement over who belongs — issues of communalism, ethnicity, representation, fragmentation, and consensus building;
- *porous boundaries:* the porous boundaries of politics, and particularly the permeable nature of most political systems in the Global South; and
- *rules of the game:* clientelist politics, in which the substance of politics is found in patrimonial and patron-client relations elaborated in a myriad of networks not readily identified as "political."

The second section explores specific political realities in Ethiopia, Eritrea, Zimbabwe, and India. We have selected these nations as our cases for comparative historical analysis in order to reflect on the five concepts and the political challenges. Ethiopia and Eritrea provide examples of identity politics (both ethnic and religious), militarism, and revolutionary transformation that characterize many countries around the world. Although all countries of the Horn of Africa — Somalia, Sudan, Djibouti, Ethiopia, and Eritrea — are replete with illustrations of the five concepts noted above, we focus particularly on the latter two countries. Analysis of Zimbabwe permits exploration of a region of Africa where the legacy of racism and colonialism is strong but where communal affiliations are being contained and a national allegiance is under construction. Here questions about the boundaries of politics and the rules of the game in clientelist politics abound. Zimbabwe is also immersed in both regional and international politics in ways often detrimental to its ordinary citizens. Last we explore the multiple realities of India and that nation's march to modernity. We consider the extraordinary inconsistencies of

India's status as one of the most technologically and militarily advanced nations in the world, and, at the same time, one of the poorest with a vast population of illiterate, impoverished citizens. Nowhere is the paradox of simultaneity more apparent.

Around the world, national economies are integrating into a vast global system. Simultaneously, political fragmentation exists within many nations whose elements are competing, if not fighting, warily over distribution of national resources. It is useful to consider these four nation-states — Ethiopia, Eritrea, Zimbabwe, and India — and how they cope with crises of legitimacy, capacity, and control within their political systems. For these states we reflect on who belongs, the relationships between dependency and autonomy, the porous nature of their political systems, the "rules of the game," and their extraordinary political realities shaped by contradictory inclinations and conditions.

The final section identifies continuing challenges for states of the Global South. It clarifies the work to be done by all states and their leaders, characterizing it as

- *state building:* strengthening governing institutions and building the infrastructure that enables the government to carry out its work;
- *nation building:* developing consensus around common issues and an identity with both the existence and the ongoing purposes of the state;
- *participation:* finding ways that the voices of all people can be heard and that the government can be rendered accountable;
- *economic growth and distribution:* strengthening the economic base in ways that both enhance the nation's productivity and management of its resources while assuring some level of fairness in resource access and control;
- *managing globalization:* seizing the opportunities and diminishing the harm of globalization processes.

We link these challenges to the concepts posed at the outset of this chapter. In particular, these include problems of building consensus in the context of communalism, managing intra-elite conflict, building capacity when there are largely fragile institutions, defining and understanding the "rules of the game," and mitigating dependencies while strengthening autonomy. We draw on the four countries examined — Ethiopia, Eritrea, Zimbabwe, and India — for illustrative purposes.

A Comparative Political Perspective

Definitions

First, it is useful to clarify the ways in which the terms *state, nation,* and *nation-state* are used. A formal definition of a *state* is that it is an administrative and legal order with binding authority over all action taking place in the area of its jurisdiction. It is at one and the same time administrative, coercive, and legitimizing. Often we use the terms *state* and *nation* in a way that suggests that they are one and the same. We might talk about the states that are currently members of the United Nations, or we could also remark that there are 191 nations that are members of the United Nations. The two terms are sometimes combined for emphasis or clarity in the double noun *nation-state*. Sometimes, however, the term *nation* is used differently. It refers to a population with its own language, cultural traditions, and historical aspirations that may or may not claim sovereignty over a particular territory. Palestine might be called a *nation,* but the Palestinians do not yet have the formal apparatus of a *state*. The Armenians might consider themselves a *nation* though they are scattered throughout the world. Native Americans often use the term *nation* in ways that identify their particular origins and tradition that may or may not coincide with a geographic area.

Nationalism involves a desire for self-determination, a pride in one's own identity, and a resistance to authority of outsiders. The nation, and the nationalism it evokes, may readily be recognized as identical to the "state" as in the case of French or Japanese nationalism. It is possible, however, to have a national identity and to be, at the same time, only part of a state. An example of this situation would be the Native Americans in the United States or the French Canadians. It is also possible to be a state with many nationalities contained within it. The Soviet Union, as a state, comprised many nationalities. Thus, the *state* and the *nation* may be coterminous, or they may not.

Nationalism locates the source of individual identity for a nation within a "people" who constitute the foundation of its sovereignty. The nation, the salient political structure of modern society, has become the focal point for loyalty and the basis of collective solidarity. Nationalism is probably the defining attribute of politics in our contemporary world. The social structures associated with nations, states, and nationalism constitute "a towering presence in the life of every conscious individual."[2] Nationalism also provides a primary focal point around which people cluster in the economic and political struggles encountered in the process of globalization. A critical problem arises, of course, when nations, states, regions, ethnic loyalties, or religions do not coincide; when boundaries are porous or ambiguous; or when competition among peoples across these variables reaches high levels of intensity. The flood of Albanian refugees from the Kosovo region of Serbia in early 1999 is poignant testimony to the upheavals associated with conflicting perceptions of nationality and associated rights, and the violence that can ensue. The thirty-year determination of Eritreans to separate from Ethiopia to form their own state provides another example of intense nationalism and the relevance of the conceptual lens of *belonging*.

The twentieth century was characterized by numerous *national movements,* that is, movements of bodies of people to achieve self-determination and to throw out foreign rulers, colonialists, or oppressors. Many well-known and highly revered nationalist leaders led the struggle against foreign powers in order to bring independence to their people. Names from around the world are familiar to all of us, among them Mao Tse-tung in China, Jawaharlal Nehru in India, Jomo Kenyatta in Kenya, Nelson Mandela in South Africa, Ho Chi Minh in Vietnam, and Fidel Castro in Cuba. Throughout the Global South people have struggled for freedom and the right to manage their own affairs, with most of these struggles having taken place between 1920 and 1980. John Isbister, observing this phenomenon in his book *Promises Not Kept,* laments the promises broken by the leaders who rose to power on promises for social change long since forgotten by those who made them, and by the international community that has largely contrived to use the resources of the South to benefit the North.[3] The promises of the early years of nationalist fervor have dissipated, often with few results, and people around the world continue to experience enormous frustration and hardship as they deal with life-threatening conditions and brutal poverty.

Key Concepts

We turn to five concepts that can help us understand political processes in the Global South at the beginning of the twenty-first century.

The Paradox of Simultaneity

This phrase refers to events, conditions, or trends occurring at the same time that we would not normally expect to find together. Western philosophy and scientific thought are grounded in notions of progress and linearity. With effort, good ideas, careful policy, and determination, the individual or the society can improve, moving in a direct way from point A to point B. The latter position is expected to be an improvement over the former position.

However, political life in the Global South, as elsewhere, is routinely characterized by nonlinear ambiguity. There are simultaneous processes that would appear to be directly contradictory to one another and yet which coexist in varying degrees of ease and/or tension. Nations can be both modern and undeveloped at the same time. Kenya's rural women still use the hoe and the knife for farming, while twenty miles away in Nairobi the Internet cafes flourish. In India, the bullock cart coexists with an immense national manufacturing capacity in motorcycles. In Bangalore, the hub of India's computer industry, the barefoot, illiterate messenger in traditional garb brings tea to the elegantly suited and shod software engineer.

Moreover, it often makes sense to operate simultaneously according to the systems and logic of both traditional and modern ways. Both are at one and the same time legitimate and useful. For example, the prosperous Kenyan businessman who is engaged in complex international negotiations for imports and exports also engages in complex relations as a patron to assorted kinsmen of his ethnic community. He has a "foot in both worlds" and keeps both planted with skill and ease. He is negotiating this world of simultaneity in modern and traditional ways.

At another level there are simultaneous processes of international integration and national disintegration. Many nations are experiencing — at one and the same time — integration of economies and disintegration of societies. Nigeria, for example, has experienced the centrifugal tendencies of its several regions that have wanted to pull apart in disassociation with one another, while, nevertheless, as a nation, evolving ever closer links with the global economy through international oil companies. In fact, inept and fragile political systems are often dealing with both integration and disintegration at precisely the same time.

Simultaneous and contradictory processes lead to a mix of Western norms with those values intrinsic to other cultures and social systems. They lead to new patterns of economic behavior, new political formations, and new cultural mixes. Some of the most startling of these juxtapositions are found among the countries of the Middle East where traditional Islamic values coincide with — and face the intrusion of — Western industrialization as well as Western cultural mores and more open political processes. At the beginning of the twenty-first century this cultural conundrum must be central to consideration of political and globalization processes.

Dependency and Autonomy

Much analysis about the Global South dismisses as insignificant the authority and control these countries have over their own agenda. This authority and control is often called "agency," or a capacity to act instrumentally on one's own behalf. Traditional modernization or development theory has, in effect, diminished the notion of decision making and control by making development more or less automatic, if you just pull a few things together. The prices must be right; savings plan determined; the infrastructure in place; then the automatic takeoff is more or less under way. Dependency theory has the same effect, though the analysis differs. Control is in the hands of the powerful, industrialized North, and Southern nations are simply in a reactive mode. Postmodernism, which laments the lack of agency or decision-making power on the part of communities of the South, nevertheless trivializes it and renders the capacity for meaningful action negligible.

All nations exist in an interdependent world, and within this context, some have more autonomy than others. This autonomy may vary by location, size of population, resource base, trade and aid relationships, or other factors. Within a broad set of parameters, ranging from great dependency to substantial autonomy, there is a wide range of positions and possibilities. Securing these possibilities is what national leadership is all about. The capacities for independent action, for authority, and for agency should not be diminished. Opportunities must be recognized and nurtured for states of the Global South to leverage political power within their own national systems as well as the international systems in which they are embedded.

Who Belongs?

Throughout most of the Global South, the question of "who belongs" is increasingly important. Ethnicity can be a defining attribute. Ethnic claims are based on a perception of common origins, as well as shared history, norms, language, dreams, and other ties and attributes that link a person to a given set of people. An ethnic group may be spatially defined as well. The consciousness of special identity encourages people to organize in order to advance their common interests. Nevertheless, ethnicity and the sense of belonging to a particular group of people are not immutable. They may change both individually and collectively over time. Moreover, an individual with parents from two different ethnic groups may claim loyalty to one, both, or neither. Ethnicity is the product of a "continuing historical process, always simultaneously old and new, grounded in the past and perpetually in creation."[4]

Ethnicity is often a political as well as a cultural phenomenon. Some suggest that in Africa ethnicity is the single most important variable around which individuals, households, and communities collect for common action.[5] Analysts of contemporary Africa emphasize that ethnic awareness, vis-à-vis other groups, is a consequence of the colonial period in which governance was often achieved through promotion of ethnic rivalries. In the postindependence period, ethnic groups, like others, place claims upon the state. They compete among themselves and with other groups for state-controlled resources. One analyst notes that the "re-tribalization of the public sphere has sharpened the tension between civic or state citizenship and ethnic citizenship."[6]

In addition to interethnic rivalry, there can be intraethnic competition within any given ethnic group. Clans, factions, and schisms within ethnic groups occur constantly. The levels of cohesion and fluidity vary according to personalities, issues, and the situation. The Somalis, for example, are a clearly defined ethnic group and perceive themselves as distinct from non-Somalis. Yet clan loyalties within the Somali community have led to the breakup of Somalia with little likelihood of the reemergence of a united Somali nation in the foreseeable future.

Religion also constitutes a pole around which critical and exclusive loyalties are established. Within Christianity, Islam, Judaism, and Hinduism can be found groups with quasi-religious and political agendas. One analyst suggests that "the 21st century will be regarded by future historians as a century in which religion replaced ideology as the prime animating and destructive force in human affairs."[7] Certainly one need not look far to find that there may be validity in that assertion: Protestants and Catholics in Northern Ireland, rival Islamic fundamentalist sects in Algeria, Arabs and Jews in the Middle East, Muslims and Hindus in Kashmir, Hindus and Buddhists in Sri Lanka, and Christians and Muslims in the Philippines or Nigeria. Across the South Christianity has been growing, particularly radical Protestant sects and a form of Roman Catholicism that is quite traditional and even reactionary. In Asia, Africa, and Latin America, these churches have been winning support and commitment, partly because of the ways they deal with oppression and deprivation. Alongside these rapidly growing churches have been some extremist Christian movements such as the Lord's Resistance Army in Uganda. No religion, however, has a monopoly on terrifying forms of extremism, whether it is Shiite mullahs of Iran sending young men to martyrdom in human wave assaults against the Iraqi army in the 1980s or butchery committed by Hindu fanatics against Indian Muslim communities in Bombay. Who belongs and how these groups and their perceptions relate to states, nations, and governance are of critical importance.

The Porous Boundaries of Politics

Everywhere politics permeates all aspects of human behavior. Yet, in some places institutions are clearly established for purposes of governance and can be identified as such. The local town council, for example, has the function of town policymaking, adjudication, and regulation. Political parties endeavor to influence public policy. We can differentiate between formal political bodies and those that are established for other purposes, such as churches, hospitals, or recreation. In many parts of the world, the boundaries are not clear. There is no well-defined separation between the political realm and social, economic, religious, or cultural arenas. To complicate matters further, many political groups operate outside government control and across borders. Such could be said for just about every guerrilla group, militia, or armed liberation front from Sri Lanka to Colombia, Sudan, and Angola.

Thus, when investigating politics, one must be attentive not only to organizations and relationships that are clearly political, but to others as well. In India, for example, caste affiliation must be investigated for its relationship to electoral processes, locally and at state and national levels. In Brazil, women's organizations and the women's movement have become increasingly visible in political life over the past thirty years and have been active in influencing political change and democratization. Throughout Central America and certainly throughout much of Africa, the church, as an institution, plays an important political, as well as religious, social, and cultural role.

Kenya provides a useful example of the linkage between religion and politics. Clerics from the major religious denominations in Kenya, including the Anglican Church of the Province of Kenya, the Presbyterian Church of East Africa, and the Methodist Church, speak out formally on controversial topics relevant to national political and economic conditions. The clerics are openly critical of increasing inequities within Kenyan society, and they do not hesitate to criticize government policies. Such actions by leading clerics are applauded by Kenyan citizens who perceive that religious leaders are speaking out on behalf of ordinary people in the face of government intransigence and malfeasance. Of all Kenyan organizations, the churches come closest to forming the kind of political network that can have some power within the polity at large. Throughout both rural and urban Kenya, churches are vital institutions, assuming a leadership role as a voice of public conscience. In addition, Kenya currently has a religio-political movement, Mungiki, which has become a focal point for "globalization from below," leading a crusade for the rights of the poor in the face of domestic corruption, while also sometimes being coopted by the state and encouraging political tribalism.[8] All these voices are vital to new social formations emerging in Kenya, a nation that illustrates the need for sensitivity to the porous nature of political boundaries.

The Rules of the Game in Patrimonial and Clientelist Politics

A patrimonial system is based on traditional, patriarchal domination. It features traditional status and authority, and the personal loyalty of staff, retainers, subjects, or followers. There are patterns of elite coalitions revolving around a patrimonial leader or leaders, determining their loyalties on the basis of confidence in personal leadership and on the rewards and benefits that will result from a particular association. The means for forming these linkages are numerous. Patronage and rewards of office are, of course, central. Personal charisma and common ideological concerns are also important. There is reciprocal obligation, but it may not be of a strictly personal nature. It may involve access to resources at the center and delivery of benefits, resources, and services to followers, while support, usually political, moves upward to the benefactor. Followers may be at the periphery, literally part of a rural constituency, or they may be members of elite factions engaged in an unending process of merging, separating, and shifting coalitions around the center.

In the political systems operative in many nations of the Global South, ethnic loyalties and organizations play a significant role in advancing the material and other interests of their members. They often do so through patron-client relationships that are a common phenomenon in the politics of many states. In some instances, leaders functioning as "ethnic entrepreneurs" whip up ethnic hostilities in inflammatory ways for their own political purposes, playing on and using ethnic distinctions to create conflict sometimes leading to "ethnic cleansing."[9] We have observed this phenomenon, for example, in Rwanda and in Sri Lanka. Ethnically based communal solidarity, as found at varying levels of political and social organization, may be a potent and feared force. The convergence of ethnic, regional, and/or administrative lines has important implications for politics and for community mobilization as discussions of Ethiopia, Zimbabwe, and India demonstrate.

Within this structure there may be, and often are, highly personal, informal agreements between leader and follower or patron and client, in which there is private, though not public, accountability. These personal sets of obligations lead to clientelist states in which bonds of reciprocal obligation align dependent subordinates with individual political or administrative leaders in informal structures that are more or less cohesive. Clientelist politics can coexist with "modern" political parties and governing bureaucracies, serving as the dominant organizational mode within these structures. Thus, the patrimonial model of the state — emphasizing as it does personal loyalties, informal power structures, networks, and factions, with linkages from the locality to the center through clientelist relations — constitutes a useful tool for analyzing political processes in the Global South.

Political Realities:
The Horn of Africa, Zimbabwe, and India

The Horn of Africa: Untangling Ethiopia and Eritrea

Conflicts over boundaries, concerns over who belongs, fragmentation, communalism — these issues are bubbling all over Africa, and nowhere more so than in the Horn of Africa. They shape politics through two often diametrically opposed values: self-determination and territorial integrity. Self-determination involves the right of a people to choose by whom they are governed and to which political entity they belong. Territorial integrity refers to existing national boundaries. It presupposes that a government has a right to defend its boundaries and that no other state is justified in disrespecting those boundaries. In Africa, the colonial powers of Europe drew up the boundaries, often in a most illogical way with no relation to the realities of African geography or the preferences of existing communities. Thus, these two principles — self-determination and territorial integrity — can come head to head. These principles are central to politics and political conflict in the Horn of Africa.

The Horn has long been considered a troubled region. It consists of five states: Ethiopia, Eritrea, Sudan, Somalia, and the city-state of Djibouti. Strategically the region is important as it commands the Red Sea and the northwestern Indian Ocean and is near Middle Eastern oil. As a consequence it has been the object of international competition. In the last half of the twentieth century the region served as a platform for East-West competition between the superpowers, the Soviet Union and the United States. Now in the early years of the twenty-first century, a broad cross-section of international players is engaged there.

Within the region of the Horn protege regimes, sponsored and supported by states outside the area, as well as ethnic complexity have complicated political affairs. The longstanding Ethiopian-Eritrean conflict subsided with Eritrea's independence in 1993, but continues to flare up over specific land rights and over decisions regarding the long border shared by the two states. The civil war between Northern and Southern Sudan has lasted nearly half a century with intermittent respite from fighting and shows no sign of abating. The Somalis, on the one hand, are rent by clan warfare that has destroyed the national social fabric, and on the other hand, are characterized by irredentism, the desire to join the Somali communities of Kenya, Djibouti, Ethiopia, as well as the current subunits of the former Somalia, into a greater Somali state. On a cultural level, the Christian Ethiopians have a deep-seated fear of Islamic encirclement. Religious loyalties — Christianity, Islam, animism — provide a backdrop for the various conflicts occurring in the region today. In sum, the Horn of Africa is an exceedingly complex region.

Ethiopia is a pluralistic state and society historically dominated by a cultural minority, the Amhara-Tigre peoples from the high central plateaus, with a large number of culturally subordinate groups in peripheral regions. Twice the size of France with a population over 60 million in 1999, Ethiopia has major inequities in terms of wealth, power, and privilege as well as sharp differences among various religious, ethnic, linguistic, and economic groups.[10] Historically, Ethiopia is an empire emanating from the Central Highlands that has absorbed adjacent communities, assimilating them by conversion and coercion. In the twentieth century, the most famous emperor of Ethiopia was Haile Selassie, who ruled from 1930 to 1974 and did much to modernize Ethiopia while also allying himself closely with the United States and other Western powers that provided capital for economic development.[11]

Haile Selassie placed high on a continuum of modernizing leaders; however, there were problems. First, the emperor concentrated on building the structures and apparatus of the state. His key objectives were to establish firm control over all regions, to collect tax revenues, to encourage economic growth, and to acquire the tribute due to him as emperor. He was not concerned about exploitation of subordinate populations, nor were questions surrounding the process of nation building his priorities. He did not have policies designed to foster national political integration and equitable development. Indeed, he was committed to royal absolutism even while introducing the constitution and encouraging modernization. Throughout his reign, it was evident that the Amharas and Tigreans were favored with a wide range of opportunities and benefits. This observation led to continuing unrest among some of the subordinate groups within Ethiopia, particularly the Oromo.

Of special importance in this discussion of the Horn's boundaries, colonial impacts, questions about who belongs, and issues of self-determination and territorial integrity is the long war between the peoples of Eritrea and Ethiopia. Eritrea is an area about the size of South Korea, bordered on the north by the Red Sea and on the south by Ethiopia, with a population of 3.5 million (1999) representing nine ethnic groups. Italian occupation of the region began in 1882, and Italian colonialism in what is now Eritrea lasted through the end of World War II. Both Italian colonialism and Amharic-Tigrean repression toward peripheral groups have shaped a sense of Eritrean separateness. In addition, they have led many of the peoples of the Eritrean region to seek their independence. At the end of World War II, Eritrea became a UN protectorate under the supervision of Ethiopia. In 1962 Haile Selassie seized the opportunity to secure valuable access to the Red Sea and to end Ethiopia's landlocked status by formally annexing Eritrea. That act launched a war of attrition between Ethiopia and Eritrea that lasted about thirty years and, along with severe droughts, became a near-overwhelming burden for both peoples.

By the early 1970s, drought, famine, and warfare had taken an enormous toll on both Ethiopia and Eritrea. In Ethiopia there were high levels of landlessness among peasant farmers. Moreover, elites, increasingly educated and aware of democratic principles beyond their borders, were becoming disaffected and began questioning government strategies, policies, and corruption. Finally, in 1974, a Marxist-led revolution removed Emperor Haile Selassie from power, and established a new government under the leadership of Mengistu Haile Merriam.

The new government faced various economic and political crises arising from multiple sources. The most important were a major famine in the early and mid-1980s, aggravated by drought and long-term environmental misuse, civil war with Eritrean forces, and a variety of government pricing policies favoring large commercial farms but detrimental to small-scale farmers. Forces in opposition to the government of Mengistu grew under the military leadership of Meles Zenawi, now prime minister of Ethiopia, and Isaias Afwerki, now president of Eritrea, who won the war in 1991. Two years later, as a peaceful outcome of the struggle against Mengistu, Eritrea became independent.

Overall, the struggle of Eritrea to obtain independence from Ethiopia was extremely costly. Nearly 400,000 refugees fled the border regions; many went to Sudan, but Eritreans also comprise a sizeable diaspora spread throughout Europe and North America. More than 150,000 Eritreans lost their lives, and Ethiopia's losses were also enormous. Some estimate that $60 billion was spent on the war. Since independence, border disputes have erupted and relations between the two nations have been tense. At present, a UN Peacekeeping Force monitors the border, and despite diverging interests and historic grievances, there is peace. Ethiopia and Eritrea are developing very different and asymmetrical visions of the role of each state in the Horn of Africa. Ethiopia perceives itself as the regional power; Eritrea, on the other hand, was forged out of the struggles for political, economic, and social survival vis-à-vis the privileged Amhara rulers of Ethiopia and does not wish to see Ethiopia gain hegemony within the region.[12] Boundaries and these issues of self-determination versus territorial integrity remain at the heart of politics in the Horn of Africa and continue to be central to relations between Ethiopia and Eritrea.

It is not only Ethiopia and Eritrea where ethnic and religious complexities, patron-client politics, elite exploitation, and competition over resources have led to conflict in the Horn of Africa. The conflict between Northern and Southern Sudan is rooted in deep-seated animosities involving land and resource access set in a context of religious, ethnic, and cultural differences shaped by national and international power struggles. The Somalia-Ethiopia relationship is characterized by long-term tensions as both claim vast and overlapping portions of the Ogaden,

Ethiopia's easternmost region that, as the map is drawn, juts into Somalia. Somalia claims that the Ogaden is critical to the historic patterns of pastoralist migration of the Somali people.

As if these conflicts are not enough, outsiders have muddled in the affairs of the Horn. The United States and the Soviet Union, the two postwar superpowers, became involved in the relationships in the region of the Horn in order to pursue their own international interests. From the 1950s through the early 1970s, Ethiopia was a client state of the United States, receiving an enormous amount of military aid, while Somalia was a client state of the Soviet Union. Then in the early 1970s the dancing partners changed. With the ascendance to power of a Marxist government, Ethiopia became a protege of the Soviet Union with support from Cuba as well, while the United States established a relationship with Somalia. These relationships have declined in importance since the end of the Cold War, leaving many to feel that Africa was useful to the superpowers only in the context of proxy wars and has been abandoned since 1989. Certainly the nations of the Horn of Africa have been subject to the push and pull of contradictory and competing forces, regional as well as international, not just in recent years, but for generations.

Southern Africa: Zimbabwe and the Politics of Land

As a region, Southern Africa has some similarities to and some critical differences from the Horn of Africa. Southern Africa has had several long and grueling struggles against European colonists (Portuguese, German, British, Afrikaner), an experience not shared widely in the Horn. Both Southern Africa and the Horn of Africa have endured long guerrilla struggles between "brothers" to secure access to power and resources. Among these are the Eritrean-Ethiopian War, the civil war in Sudan, and postindependence conflicts in Angola and Mozambique. South Africa's giddy euphoria over the release of Nelson Mandela from prison or the solemn pride as independence was declared in Zimbabwe compare with the widespread jubilation in Ethiopia with the downfall of the Haile Selassie regime. Both regions have enormous poverty, unemployment, hunger, and many disaffected young people. The Southern Africa region must contend with two particularly significant crises. The first is the continuing control over large portions of agricultural land by white farmers who represent a very small percentage of any one nation's population. The second is the AIDS pandemic, one of the most horrific crises of the late twentieth and early twenty-first centuries. Southern African nations are among the most AIDS-ravaged in the world.

Zimbabwe is our focal point for Southern Africa. Like Ethiopia, Zimbabwe is a landlocked country, but it faces a set of issues quite different from those of Ethiopia. A country of nearly 12.6 million people, Zimbabwe is composed largely of two distinct ethnic groups: the Shona and the Ndebele. Zimbabwe has two salient problems: first, an affluent, foreign-owned sector that dominates the economy and is determined to maintain the economic status quo; and second, a large, poor, and land-hungry farming population.[13] Its economy is largely in the hands of non-Zimbabweans or settlers with foreign interests controlling approximately two-thirds of business and industry. Zimbabwe has a well-entrenched settler population with about five thousand white farmers producing 75 percent of total food crops. Unlike a number of other African countries, Zimbabwe is not a mono-commodity exporter. Nevertheless, ninety years of settler colonialism disrupted rural social and economic life. Peasant populations have been dislocated and crowded into communal areas that have been set aside for collective ownership on the part of particular tribal groups. In general, these are the poorest lands, and commercial farmers who are largely of European descent hold the better agricultural lands. Land pressures and a rapidly increasing population have led to ecological deterioration and a decline in food production in many of these communal areas, or Tribal Trust Lands as they are called. President Robert Mugabe has promised that land taken by whites during the colonial era will be returned to black Zimbabweans, but so far relatively few have been resettled on such lands.

The majority of Zimbabwe's citizens, 89 percent, belong to the Shona community, and most of the remainder are Ndebele. The Shonas are a Bantu people, primarily agriculturalists, who have lived in the area of present-day Zimbabwe for centuries. By the early nineteenth century, the Ndebele people, pastoralist herders who are related to the Zulus of South Africa, had begun moving from the drier regions around Bulawayo into the regions preferred by the Shona. They also began exacting tribute from the Shonas and exerting power over them in other ways.

By the end of the nineteenth century whites were moving into the area that is now Zimbabwe under the leadership of Cecil Rhodes, a British colonialist, entrepreneur, and government administrator. For a period, Rhodes's British South African Company ran the region under charter from the British Crown, but in 1923, the company surrendered its authority to a settler government. The white settlers had voted for the status of self-governing colony rather than union with South Africa. In the first decades, in this area now called Southern Rhodesia, these settlers established large farms producing tobacco, corn, and other staple food crops. They depended heavily on preventing competition from the African farmers and on securing a cheap labor force from among the Africans. They employed several strategies to assure their economic and political dominance: (1) separation of races by clearly demarcated land alienation and reservation; (2) discriminatory marketing regulations; and (3) development of infrastructural, institutional, and financial mechanisms that supported the white economy.[14]

The Land Apportionment Act of 1930 divided land into racial blocks giving whites exclusive rights to better portions and shifting blacks to reserves. Approximately one-third of the arable land went to Europeans, who constituted 6 percent of the population, and by 1961 almost all the best land was in the hands of the white farmers while the black Africans got the low-rainfall, arid, hilly land. The Land Tenure Act of 1970 finalized the division of land between Europeans and Africans with Tribal Trust Lands designated as African areas. These Tribal Trust Lands were vastly inferior to the land retained by the Europeans, and they were inhabited by far more people than they could readily accommodate in agricultural livelihoods. Grain Marketing and Maize Control Acts controlled prices of staple food crops and subsidized white farmers. The Master and Servant Act introduced pass laws controlling the movements of the African population. Large investments were primarily in infrastructure such as railways and white farmers' agricultural support services. Most of the mining, manufacturing, finance, and transport were owned by foreign capital, largely British and South African. A direct consequence of foreign ownership of the economy has been a large capital outflow for many years.

It is not difficult to understand how serious conflict would emerge between a small white population largely in control of the economy and a large African population that is disenfranchised and impoverished. In 1959 a state of emergency was declared throughout both Northern (now Zambia) and Southern Rhodesia, which was to remain in force until Southern Rhodesia became independent as Zimbabwe twenty-one years later. In 1962 the Rhodesian Front was formed with the explicit intent of preventing black rule. Meanwhile Africans formed the Zimbabwe African People's Union (ZAPU) under Joshua Nkomo with largely

Ndebele support and the Zimbabwe African National Union (ZANU) under Robert Mugabe and other colleagues with largely Shona support to organize Africans against the Rhodesian Front. Both ZANU and ZAPU created liberation armies and learned some of the skills of gaining political support among the local population in order to provide a base for operations. The struggle for independence lasted fifteen years, and the terms of settlement and transfer of power were finally negotiated at meetings in Great Britain.

In 1980 elections were held with more than two hundred observers from thirty countries, and Robert Mugabe was elected president. In an address to the nation, he appealed for reconciliation, inclusiveness, and cooperation, saying:"Let us deepen our sense of belonging and engender a common interest that knows no race, color, or creed. Let us truly become Zimbabweans with a single loyalty. Long live our freedom." In his final report, the British election commissioner stated, "I have no doubt whatever that the result of the election (Mugabe's victory) accurately reflects the opinions of the electorate. It was the authentic voice of the African people."[15] And he went on to proclaim, "In the end, the essential triumph has been that of the people of Zimbabwe themselves.... Their faith in the processes of peace has exceeded their courage in war."

As a newly independent nation in Southern Africa, Zimbabwe had to deal with a hostile South Africa still in the throes of apartheid. A major objective of the white South African government was to prevent Zimbabwe from becoming a stronghold for the African National Congress, the key party in South Africa's struggle for independence. It sought to neutralize and even to control Zimbabwe. Some of this effort was extremely hostile. South Africa ended Zimbabwe's preferential tariff agreements, sent the Zimbabwe migrant labor force home, and carried out sabotage of Zimbabwe's air force and the oil pipeline from Beira (in Mozambique) to Mutare in Zimbabwe. For its part, the goal of Zimbabwe was to lessen, but not to eliminate, dependence on South Africa.

While Zimbabwe itself was not swept into superpower politics in the way that Ethiopia and other countries of the Horn of Africa have been, it nevertheless has felt the pressures associated with the Cold War. The United States was a strong donor to Zimbabwe in the early years of independence. However, when Zimbabwe abstained in a UN vote condemning the Soviet Union for shooting down a South Korean airliner that had strayed over its space, the United States cut its aid to Zimbabwe.

Similarly when Zimbabwe criticized the U.S. invasion of Grenada in 1983, the United States again acted swiftly to cut aid. Thus, Zimbabwe found itself not only immersed in the conflicts of the region, but also swayed by global politics as they were being played out in Africa by the superpowers.

Nearly twenty years after independence, land is still the most critical issue for African farmers. Until recently, whites in Zimbabwe, now less than 2 percent of the population, owned about one-third of the arable land and almost all of the good land.[16] The government has made many promises about land reform and giving land to the landless, but with little follow-through; not much land has changed hands. With elections scheduled for early 2002, President Mugabe sought public support by encouraging his followers to go ahead and seize land without worrying about compensation for the owners. In 2001 there were numerous farm seizures by poor farmers, particularly veterans of the independence struggle. Squatters took over a number of white-owned farms, and the political situation became increasingly tense. Zimbabwe's High Court declared farm seizures illegal but the government ignored its declaration. Meanwhile, the government had become increasingly authoritarian, jailing members of the opposition and proposing to keep international reporters out of the country. It was no surprise that President Mugabe won the election, and not long afterwards he "backed off" on some of the land seizures. Of the forty-five hundred white commercial farmers who had owned the large farms producing tobacco and wheat, there are now about six hundred farming mostly on smaller holdings.[17] Some farms are to be returned to their owners and the squatters are to be sent elsewhere. Many of the impoverished resettled farmers are struggling to survive without needed inputs. Thus the land issue continues to create a chaotic and painful situation for all involved and undoubtedly remains a future political football.

It is widely believed that the president and his supporters are growing rich and that these riches derive from several sources. Much of the 8.7 million acres of land acquired by the government since 1980 is reputed to have gone to Mugabe and his supporters.[18] A second source of wealth is said to be the minerals in the region of eastern Congo where President Mugabe has deployed Zimbabwean armed forces, along with those of six other African countries. Ostensibly these forces have been supporting the Congo government against rebel groups and regional rivals. Set to withdraw in late 2002 under the UN's Lusaka Peace

Accord, the troops were unwilling to depart lest they lose their control over local resources, including diamonds, copper, and cobalt. According to a report prepared under Security Council direction, the armed forces of Rwanda, Uganda, and Zimbabwe are "leaving behind networks of corrupt businesspeople and criminals to exploit the nation's natural riches."[19] Meanwhile, poverty, hunger, unemployment, and related hardships continue unabated amid the politics of land and the competition over resources in Zimbabwe, and, more broadly, throughout southern Africa.

South Asia: The Complex Tapestry of India

On August 15, 1997, India celebrated fifty years of independence. The occasion was preceded by months of soul searching about India's accomplishments and failures, progress and regression. Opinions varied widely. For one analyst India was characterized by "fragmentary modernization or uneven development" while for another there were exciting and diverse currents and trends.[20] Should India's peoples celebrate their "grand tapestry of castes, languages, regions and faiths which have survived together these five decades, or should they lament the secessionist movements in Kashmir or the caste wars in Bihar?"[21] Should they take pride in their parliamentary democracy, or despair over levels of corruption and demagoguery that permeate Indian politics? Should they take satisfaction from their skilled and well-equipped military force and their accomplishments in the field of computer software and technology? Or should they focus on the vast numbers of illiterate and impoverished, still working with the bullock cart and the treadle sewing machine? It is clear that India, as well as its shortcomings and progress, cannot readily be pigeonholed. India offers us cause for optimism and cause for pessimism, cause for admiration, and cause for concern. It also offers, in the words of one *New York Times* columnist, "excitement, zest, and infinite variety."[22]

The data tell us something about India's accomplishments. Table 3.1 reveals a comparison: India just after independence and India in 1999. The differences are striking.

The comparisons across five categories reveal the enormous progress that India has made during the past half century. For example, illiteracy dropped from 81.7 percent in 1950 to 43.5 percent in five decades; life expectancy at birth increased from thirty-two years to nearly sixty-three for the same period. What the figures do not show are the absolute

Table 3.1. India: Key Development Indicators for 1950 and 1999

	Population	Infant Mortality (per 1,000)	Life Expectancy (at birth)	Illiteracy	GNI per capita ($)
1950–51	350 million	146	32.1	81.7%	$60
1999	1.016 billion	70	62.9	43.5%	$460

Source: *New York Times*, August 14, 1997; UNDP, *Human Development Report*, 2000.

numbers that are affected by high rates of population growth. India, for example, has more illiterate people now than the nation did in 1950, but that figure is indeed a smaller percentage of the total population in 1999 than it was in 1950. In 1950 there were 164 million Indians who lived below the poverty line, or 50 percent of the total population; in the mid-1990s there were 312 million poor people, or approximately 33 percent of the population.[23] Even though the per capita income is more than seven times greater in 1999 than in 1950, many Indians have insufficient money to own a bicycle, a radio, or a pair of shoes. Even though India produces enough grain for its population and has banished widespread famine, many people have insufficient food and poor nutrition. Thus, the irony characterizing India is evident. The paradox of simultaneity, discussed earlier in this chapter, is evident everywhere in India.

We can begin to understand some of these conditions and inconsistencies if we look briefly at India's past. For centuries India has been a land of farmers living in thousands of villages on land that belonged to the state, be it a princely kingdom, empire, or other form of governance. Between the early sixteenth century and the mid-nineteenth century, peasants in the more northern regions were governed by the administration of the Mogul Empire. This was a far-flung empire, and an administrator in a peripheral area was given control over a large territory or *jagir* that was cultivated by local farmers.

British influence first came to India in the seventeenth century through the East India Company, a British trading company that arranged agreements with local rulers for trade in silk, jewels, spices, indigo, and other commodities. As the Mogul Empire began to lose control, the East India Company began to establish itself, slowly extending its role and gradually gaining territory and influence in India. Eventually the British government assumed control over the territories that had been managed by the company. In 1876 Queen Victoria added to her titles that of Empress of India. From that point onwards, in fact, the British government directly ruled about 60 percent of India, while the remainder was ruled indirectly as princely states under maharajas. Direct rule, however, was with and through Indian political structures. Thus was launched a collaboration between the British government and the upper classes in India.

There were several important consequences of British colonialism, particularly in the period from the mid-nineteenth century on. The British dramatically changed land ownership patterns by instituting land privatization, making land a commodity that could be bought and sold. As a result, a new class of wealthy landlords was created. The change in land ownership patterns brought increased inequities, land speculation, usury, and an indebted peasantry.[24] A second consequence was the devastating impact on India's artisanal sector. The small-scale home industries in India could not compete with mass-produced goods from Great Britain. Particularly hard hit were domestic textiles that had to compete with Britain's modern textile mills. Increasingly India became a supplier of raw materials — cotton, indigo, opium, tea, jute — for export. A third consequence concerned infrastructure. By the early twentieth century a modern infrastructure — dams, roads, seaports, telegraph system, railroad lines — was well under way. British commercial capital aided the process of the industrial revolution in India particularly with communications and transport infrastructure, but it was Indian entrepreneurs using Indian capital who built the steel mills and catapulted India into the role of an industrial power.

Britain left significant political legacies, some beneficial and others worrisome. The British established the principle of equality under the law; facilitated administrative unification; developed English as a common language of cross-regional governance and commerce; and encouraged familiarity with scientific, technical, and educational opportunities and outlooks in other parts of the world. The British did not attempt to mitigate the rigidities of the caste system and thus "looked the other way" in regard to the harsh treatment of untouchables within the social stratification system of India. They did, however, ban *sutti*, a Hindu custom practiced by some in which a widow is cast upon the funeral pyre of her husband and burned to death.

In some ways, the British used communal differences to suit their own political purposes, and these actions often aggravated communal antagonisms. For example, they frequently chose to employ high-caste Hindus in top administrative positions, selecting them over the Muslim administrative support system they were replacing. Muslims and Hindus worked together during the 1920s and 1930s, particularly under the leadership of Mohandas Gandhi, who led a peaceful noncooperation movement in opposition to colonial rule. However, in the 1940s, the competition for power and position in postcolonial India came to a fevered pitch as the Muslim League under the leadership of Mohammed Ali Jinnah demanded a separate homeland for Muslim-majority regions of India. The Hindu Congress Party resisted partition, but eventually negotiations among the British colonial government, the Muslim League, and the Congress Party led to a separation of the two peoples. Muslim areas were established in the northeast and the northwest to become an independent Pakistan with Mohammed Ali Jinnah as president. Jawaharlal Nehru became prime minister of India with a stirring address that seems as compelling now as it did on August 14, 1947:

> Long years ago we made a tryst with destiny, and now the time comes when we shall redeem our pledge, not wholly or in full measure, but very substantially. At the stroke of the midnight hour, when the world sleeps, India will awake to life and freedom. A moment comes, which comes but rarely in history, when we step out from the old to the new, when an age ends, and when the soul of a nation, long suppressed, finds utterance. It is fitting that at this solemn moment, we take the pledge of dedication to the service of India and her people and to the still larger cause of humanity.... Peace is said to be indivisible, so is freedom, so is prosperity now, and also is disaster in this one world that can no longer be split into isolated fragments.[25]

The immediate impact of independence and partition, however, was an enormous migration of 10 million terrified Hindus and Muslims attempting to cross the border in opposite directions seeking their new homeland. More than 1 million were killed in deadly religious riots and mass migrations in which the looting and pillage that ensued are legendary.[26] While many Muslims left India at that time, India remains a nation with a significant Islamic minority. Fourteen percent of India's population, or approximately 140 million, are Muslim.

As the leader of newly independent India, Jawaharlal Nehru played an important international role in the post–World War II years. He was a key participant in the Bandung Conference held in Indonesia in 1955 in which the nonaligned powers, largely countries that had been colonized and were newly independent, determined that there was a "Third Way." They did not need to support the capitalism of the so-called First World or the socialist/Marxist approaches of the "Second World." They could identify their own path for socioeconomic change and development, "a third way that takes the best from all existing systems — the Russian, the American and others — and seeks to create something suited to one's own history and philosophy."[27]

Partition and independence for India and Pakistan were, of course, not the end of the difficulties. From the start the two nations have quarreled over the fate of Kashmir, whose Hindu ruler had determined that the largely Muslim population would remain part of India. Since then India and Pakistan have fought two wars (1948 and 1965) over Kashmir, and the situation is still not resolved. In addition, the two wings of Pakistan were not logical partners. While the Punjabis in the West and the Bengalis in the East had Islam in common, they differed on just about everything else from preferred foods, to language, lifestyle, dress, and favorite poets. Over time, animosities and distrust grew as the Bengalis in East Pakistan believed that greater resources were being allocated to West Pakistan and that they were being denied important rights and privileges. These hostilities culminated in a war in 1971 in which India intervened on behalf of East Pakistan, leading to the creation of a newly independent state, Bangladesh, out of the old East Pakistan. This too was not without significant cost, as more than 1 million died in that struggle.

From the outset, politics in India has been beset by a violence that has also affected its top leadership. Gandhi was assassinated by a right-wing Hindu fundamentalist immediately after independence in January 1948; two prime ministers have been assassinated: Indira Gandhi in 1984 and Rajiv Gandhi in 1991. All of these assassinations have been linked to extremism around communal, sectarian issues. Besides the Muslim-Hindu-Sikh configurations, there is the defining system of social stratification in Hinduism, the caste system. It is impossible to understand India without at least acknowledging the role that caste plays in that society. The caste system that is central to Hinduism, the religion of approximately 80 percent of India's population, permits no social mobility. That is, one is born into a caste and remains in that caste. Education and wealth cannot formally change one's social standing, and opportunities to obtain both are often denied on the basis of caste.

There are four main caste groups — the Brahmans, defined as priests or teachers; the Kshatriyas, warriors and civil servants; the Vaisya, who are traders, and the Shudra or farmers and artisans. In reality, there are many caste subdivisions. Lowest of all in this hierarchy are the scheduled castes or "untouchables," Harijans, "Children of God" as Gandhi called them. Each caste has an occupation associated with it on a hereditary basis, although not all persons of that caste necessarily earn their living by that occupation. There are various customs, manners, and marriage regulations associated with each caste. Untouchability was officially abolished by the 1950 constitution, but it remains very much present in contemporary Indian life. Attacks and counterattacks have been carried out by caste-related militias in incidents that frequently inflame the public. The continuing caste violence in Bihar, India's poorest state, and in other states as well, reveals the relevance of these concerns at the beginning of the twenty-first century.

Indian society is changing, if very slowly. New political alignments are emerging at the state level and are beginning the process of remaking India's political map. Long dominated by the leadership of the moderate and centrist Congress Party that brought independence to India, the national government has been controlled since early 1998 by the Bharatiya Janata Party of the Hindu right with its vision of a resurgent, politicized Hinduism as an essential part of Indian identity. Today India is haunted by both its communal and its caste legacies. Muslim/Hindu antagonisms are never far below the surface. Crowds are quick to destroy or defile the sacred places of the "other's" religion, causing agony, anger, and ammunition for the next round of hostile actions. There are repeated flash points and surges of Hindu-Muslim violence, particularly across the northern tier of Indian states.

Finally, relations with Pakistan remain extremely volatile, particularly over the region of Kashmir that both claim but which India controls. India believes that Pakistan is aiding militants, insurgents who have waged a thirteen-year secession struggle in Kashmir. Early in 1998, tensions between India and Pakistan exploded over the acquisition of nuclear power, first by India, then in an assertive quid-pro-quo move by Pakistan. Declared willingness on the part of both the Pakistani president and the Indian prime minister to recognize nuclear parity and move beyond the military competition has come to naught. The border remains extremely tense. In early 2002, even as diplomatic efforts continued in an attempt to avert the fourth war between India and Pakistan, soldiers on the Indian side of the border sowed thousands of acres of farmland with land mines in what seemed to be preparation for a long stand-off between the two nuclear-armed rivals. In fact, India has been laying mines along virtually the entire length of its eighteen-hundred-mile border with Pakistan.[28] Clearly, the politics of Kashmir still stand firmly planted between these two nations and, at present, deny the possibility of a lasting friendship. The politics of Kashmir — of religious and ethnic identity, porous boundaries, and an unwieldy blend of dependence and autonomy — epitomize the volatile and fragile politics of South Asia.

Linking the Case Examples to the Key Concepts

These nations — Ethiopia and Eritrea in the Horn of Africa, Zimbabwe in Southern Africa, and India in South Asia — readily illustrate the five concepts for analyzing politics in the Global South delineated in the first part of this chapter. The ambiguous and simultaneous but contradictory processes, the paradox of simultaneity, can be observed in India where Cyber Towers rises from the campus of a software technology park in Hyderabad, a sleek Internet-connected symbol of the new India that is feverishly courting foreign investment, selling its wares in the global marketplace, and creating wealth at an astonishing rate. In a village less than fifty miles away, there is one telephone that almost never functions, and women and children work in the fields for less than $.50 a day.[29] In Eritrea revolutionary forces encouraged women to participate in the liberation struggle. They spent years on the front lines, but now must cope with an exceedingly patriarchal social structure in which they are expected to be subordinate and subservient and in which their political participation may be welcomed officially but is rejected in practice.

In terms of "dependency and autonomy," tiny Eritrea is determined to defy the International Monetary Fund and the World Bank by not seeking financial support from those institutions that they believe would make it become dependent. Yet this impoverished state — autonomous and independent in some ways — is highly dependent in others. It depends on remittances from the diaspora of Eritreans living abroad and sorely needs investments from that group to jump start its economy. Ethiopia may be the regional hegemonic state, but it is nevertheless often dependent on food aid to relieve the horrendous combinations of drought and famine that afflict it periodically. Zimbabwe's government defiantly maintains its authority on land issues, yet finds much of its economy, including important agricultural commodities, in the hands of foreign investors.

Everywhere there are questions about "who belongs." Hindu revivalism in India makes Muslims, Sikhs, and Christians wonder about the long-term viability of India's secular state and their roles in it. Ethiopia, Eritrea, or Zimbabwe may talk about the "politics of inclusion," but they often practice the "politics of exclusion." Opponents are eliminated; rivals are jailed. Eritreans living in Ethiopia are sent home. Whites living in Zimbabwe are forced off their farms. Religious factions, communalism, race, caste, gender — the various markers of social groupings — are cause for exclusion from the rights, benefits, and privileges that "membership" normally accords.

Porous boundaries exist everywhere both in a political sense and in terms of actual state boundaries — Ethiopia and Eritrea, or Pakistan and India. Is Eritrea's Peoples' Front for Democracy and Justice (PFDJ) a political party, a movement, or a government? No one is quite sure. Was the ill-fated understanding between the presidents of Eritrea and Ethiopia about the shared border a matter of political blunder, institutional failure, or the falling-out of friends? Where do caste-based political parties fit into the political structures of India's system of governance? How do we understand politics and the state in these three countries, let alone others of the South, when the institutions of governance are sometimes unrecognizable and borders and boundaries are exceedingly vague? Being cognizant of the porous political boundaries is a first step in unraveling their complex political relationships.

Finally, the patron-client structure is central to the "rules of the game" in the politics of all these nations. No one can deny that Robert Mugabe asserted his authority as president, father of independence, and patrimonial figure in the months preceding the 2002 elections. He established the "rules," and the "game" had to be played his way. In Eritrea citizens have expressed alarm as the president has imprisoned key political figures and journalists who simply raised questions about policies and requested discussions or reported differences of opinion. It appears that the camaraderie engendered by the liberation struggles has given way to authoritarianism and desire to exercise power and control. In India the growing chasm between rich and poor is shaped by the rules of the game and by a power structure determined in no small measure by who belongs.

These are but a few of the examples that could be used to demonstrate the relevance of these five attributes in analyzing the state and politics of nations of the Global South. We turn now to an exploration of the continuing political challenges that these nations must address.

The Continuing Challenges

The first part of this chapter offered an approach for comparative analysis of states, provided some definitions for political analysis, and suggested five concepts useful for understanding the politics of the Global South. The second part introduced historical perspectives on four states — Ethiopia, Eritrea, Zimbabwe, and India. In this last section we propose a brief examination of five challenges faced by all nations, but we cast them particularly in terms of the concerns of countries of the Global South. These challenges are (1) state building, (2) nation building, (3) participation, (4) growth and distribution of resources, and (5) seizing the opportunities and diminishing the harm of globalization.

State Building

The state, as noted at the outset of this chapter, is an administrative and legal order with binding authority over all action taking place in the area of its jurisdiction. It has administrative responsibilities, and it must also enforce laws, ensure that rights are honored, and secure public order. State building is concerned about the regulatory and extractive functions of government. The state focuses on such matters as building transportation and communication systems, and strengthening the bureaucracy so that it can collect taxes and deliver services. Terms often used to refer to state building are "penetration" and "integration." The state must have the "capacity" to carry out its business in an efficient and effective manner. If the roads are so limited or poorly maintained that victims of famine cannot be reached with relief food supplies, then the government is not very effective. If government is unable to collect property, income, or sales taxes or other kinds of taxes from its population, then it is strapped for funds to carry out its work. If it has insufficient funds, it cannot have the staff to carry out administrative functions and support services. Thus, it is not effective.

The World Development Report for 1997, *The State in a Changing World,* asserts that "development without an effective state is impossible."[30] The state must play a central role in regulating the economy, securing peace and public order, and protecting the rights and material welfare of citizens. One concern at the beginning of the twenty-first century is the capacity of many states, particularly in Africa, to accomplish these objectives. A whole cadre of observers, scholars, and policymakers is vocal in the collective lament that many African states are irresponsible and unaccountable to their citizens, with the consequence that violence, poverty, and disease are increasing. Some of these governments — such as those of Zimbabwe, Ethiopia, and Eritrea — are clearly authoritarian. For others, there is a low level of political capacity at the center; there are problems of authority, and problems of accruing sufficient power to carry out responsibilities. In some the legitimacy of the state or its leaders is in question. They are no longer perceived as having the authority or the right to make decisions on behalf of the public and to expect compliance. Authority that is socially recognized and legitimated no longer exists. Still others are now being called "failed states." Among them are Somalia or Congo, states where there is a nearly complete breakdown of capacity to govern and the "right" or widely accepted authority to do so.

A relevant paradigm is "the political instrumentalization of disorder," a concept in which political actors seek to maximize their personal returns on the state of confusion, uncertainty, and chaos that characterizes many polities.[31] There are personalized political contests played out through neopatrimonial clientelism. In such situations disorder can be a resource, and there is no incentive to move toward a more institutionalized ordering of society. Certainly the brief summary of Zimbabwean politics reflects this paradigm, and it would be possible to discern its elements in many other countries as well. Other analysts are not quite so disheartened and assert that community-based, grassroots planning and action are central to the process of building accountability and wresting African politics from the disorder so aptly described by various critics. They look at local successes in countries such as Ghana or Botswana as examples of emerging, effective institutional infrastructure. Clearly positive illustrations exist, but their presence does not diminish the widespread need for building the apparatus of effective and accountable government in many nations of the Global South.

Nation Building

The term "nation," as discussed earlier, means many things to many people. In this volume, we have defined "nation" in terms of a common sense of identity, loyalty, and shared commitment that a given group of people may have. The term connotes a political entity, though not necessarily one that is geographically defined. In an era in which the state is the primary unit of political action, a sense of loyalty to the state or to the nation-state — that is, nationalism — is the most commonplace use of the term. Such loyalty is a valuable asset for political leaders and may be absolutely necessary for good and effective governance. Pakistan, as originally constructed, illustrates the difference between nation and state. When Pakistan was carved out of the Indian subcontinent in 1947, the Pakistanis worked very hard to develop a sense of nationhood on the part of both the West and the East Pakistanis. It was clear to all that there was a new state called the Islamic State of Pakistan. What was not clear was that anyone felt any loyalty or commitment to it. The Bengalis and Punjabis of East and West hardly knew each other at all. The events surrounding the formation of the new state were conducive to distrust, fear, and concern rather than to trust and loyalty. The leaders from both wings worked hard to develop a cadre of young adults similarly educated for future leadership, to inculcate pride in the national anthem and the flag, and to generate enthusiasm for this new nation called Pakistan. Despite these and other efforts, it was extremely difficult to generate enthusiasm for and a sense of national loyalty toward this new entity.

By the late 1960s, the government of Pakistan was quite clearly focused on maintaining order and staying in power. Its emphasis was neither on development nor on equity between the two disparate parts of the country, but on survival of those who were running the country. Under such circumstances it was very difficult to build a widespread popular consensus, particularly given the two very different regions of the country. Pakistan was precipitated into a national crisis that ended in civil war and separation because there was no sense of legitimacy of the shared entity, no loyalty to this "nation" and no consensus around the transfer of power from one group to another. Without such a consensus, it became necessary to govern by force and coercion. Coercive means are costly and in this instance, so very costly, that they led to the breakup of the state. Approximately twenty-five years after its formation, Pakistan fell apart. East Pakistan became Bangladesh, and what was formerly West Pakistan became simply Pakistan.

The challenges of nation building are legion throughout the Global South. We have observed Eritrea's thirty-year struggle for liberation from Ethiopia. We see the impacts of civil war in Nigeria, the residue of Hindu-Muslim conflicts in India, and the devastation of East Timor's fight for liberation from Indonesia. We recognize the difficulties encountered by Pakistan struggling to keep together two disparate entities, East and West Pakistan, with a thousand miles of India between them. Malaysia delicately balances the interests of its citizens of Malay, Chinese, and Indian origin; the government of the Philippines grapples with its dissident Muslim population in the southern islands. This challenge of nation building is extraordinary and promises to be one of the most complex that we — all global citizens — face in the twenty-first century.

Participation

Participation is about power and about finding ways to enable individuals and groups to participate in decision making relevant to the issues and conditions of the community in which they live. There are, of course, different kinds of participation. In actuality, participation can be for purposes of transforming a present system or simply for maintaining the status quo. Much behavior that passes for participation is in fact intended to maintain the system, giving no more than lip service to the notions of change or accountability. Sometimes, for example, the term "participation" may refer to what is really one-way communication of information from a government or agency to members of the community. Such a situation can easily be manipulated by local leaders for purposes of building patronage and usually promotes dependence rather than self-reliance. Another way in which the term "participation" is used refers to a reactive form of activity usually controlled by outsiders. Such "participation" may involve donations of labor, money, or other resources to a community project, but initiative for the activity lies with an outside party. This type of participation is commonplace with non-governmental organizations that are engaging in local development activities and working with communities on small-scale infrastructural projects. Active participation arises within a community; community members themselves are the agents of change though they may act in concert with outside sources of funds, technical expertise, or other resources. There is a strengthening of local institutions and an effort to increase accountability within the systems of governance.

Policies toward participation affect the capacities of governments to further their state- and nation-building objectives. For example, there appears to be a clear understanding on the part of India's leadership that if India is to survive intact, it must accommodate diversity and encourage broad participation in the political system. For the most part,

Indian unity has been fostered by combining public commitment to the notion of the secular state and public affirmation of the principles of accommodation to diversity, sustained by the flexibility and tolerance characteristic of much of Hindu philosophy. Early attempts to impose Hindi as the official language for the subcontinent as a whole met with enormous hostility, particularly from the Tamil community in the South, and the effort was abandoned. Communal tensions in India flare up regularly, but the context in which these tensions occur is one of accommodation of difference, and recognition of that difference within the political system. While the Bharatiya Janata Party now in control of the central government would like to move India toward the identity of a Hindu, not secular, state, the party has not yet managed to do so. The capacity of the government of India to sustain and nourish this complex linguistic, cultural, religious, and racial mixture that we know as India may depend on these notions of accommodation and inclusion. There needs to be room for the engagement and participation of all.

By contrast, in Pakistan, the breaking point between East and West came when the political participation of the Bengalis was disavowed, even though their majority votes had elected a Bengali as prime minister of the unified Pakistan. The West Pakistanis did not allow Sheikh Mujibur Rahman, the Bengali who had won the election, to take office. The Bengalis of East Pakistan figured there was no room for them in a Pakistan dominated by the peoples of the West. They could not envision a future in which accommodation and inclusion would be principles whereby they could become fully engaged and could fully participate. War between East and West Pakistan ensued.

In addition to national policy and the actions of the state, there is the realm of civil society, those organizations and institutions existing outside the public sector and outside the market. These organizations are not profit-making concerns, but are involved in a range of activities from conservation, such as the Sierra Club, to childhood enhancement such as the Girl Scouts or hospitals or educational institutions. It is commonplace today to view the organizations of civil society as a collection of private organizations and institutions that somehow work for the collective good in the face of an incompetent and predatory state and that, in due course, may seek state accountability to local citizens.[32] Some scholars, however, warn to the contrary. The organizations of civil society may at best be an uncertain counter to communal or class-based patronage systems. At worst, civil society can deteriorate into the violence and brutality of the religious riots of India, ethnocide of Rwanda, the warlords of Afghanistan, the paramilitaries of Sierra Leone, or the fratricide of Ethiopia and Eritrea.

Unbundling the concept of civil society and reconsidering our notions about politics and civil society is a good idea. What new social formations are emerging? How might they facilitate community mobilization, and how do they relate to existing forms of organization? What sorts of realignments of powerful interests and identities might be taking place? Do they have the potential to bring new voice to the poor and disenfranchised? How can communities mobilize to alter the terms of exchange by which they relate to the world beyond? How do subordinate groups and classes become empowered? What are the bases of community organization and mobilization? All of these are important questions to be asking in terms of the nations of the Global South. When a government closes off avenues for encompassing diversity, for constructive participation in the polity, and for assuring its own accountability, frustration is likely to grow and give voice to despair.

Growth and Distribution of Resources

Government and politics set the framework and provide much of the infrastructure for building an economically productive society. Government also shapes the distribution of goods, services, and benefits. The question is: Who gets what in the new nation? How are resources shared? How are benefits, goods, and services divided? These questions may be asked with a particular ethnic group in mind, or a particular region, caste, or class. When the East Pakistanis made the calculations and found the preponderance of development funds in the budget were going to West Pakistan rather than East, despite their greater population, they were not happy. When Luos in Western Kenya looked closely to determine where Kenya's educational funds were going and found their region was being excluded, they, too, were not happy. When the Tamils of Sri Lanka found they were not getting access to the resources, benefits, and opportunities available through the Sri Lankan state, their protests led ultimately to a quest for autonomy. Exclusion may be real; it may only be perceived, but both perceptions and reality count in the processes of building a nation and a state.

In many countries, clientelist politics, such as those described at the outset of this chapter, are the primary method by which individuals and communities try to alter the distribution of goods, services, and opportunities and try to diminish the inequities that characterize their situation. If someone from your tribe or ethnic community is in a powerful position, you hope that person will pass benefits and largesse to you and your community. Chances are the individual will. While clientelist politics may offer some flexibility for distribution of resources, it is nevertheless based on inequitable relationships, reciprocity between unequals, and benefits and services to be rendered selectively to individuals or to specific communities. Many others are completely left out. The cases we have examined in some detail are replete with examples in which clientelism benefits a few followers and enhances the power, status, and prestige of the patrimonial leader. This system of mutuality between national leaders and selected individuals and local communities may aid some people and some communities, but it does not alter fundamental power relationships. Developing systems that are widely regarded as fair and accountable to a broad cross section of the population can go a long way toward strengthening the nations of the Global South. Most are very far from meeting that objective.

Seizing the Opportunities and Diminishing the Harm of Globalization

The four customary challenges — state building, nation building, participation, and growth/distribution — are the ones most commonly regarded as responsibilities of the state. These, however, must be carried out in the context of rapid globalization, and thus, we include as the last item the capacity to deal with globalization processes in ways that do not undermine the state and its capacity to meet its objectives. Processes of globalization offer both threats and opportunities to every state whether north, south, east, or west. For the new nation, the politically fragile nation, or the economically undeveloped nation, the vulnerabilities may be more apparent than the benefits. Certainly the history of globalization is fraught with disadvantage and dislocation for the countries of the Global South. In the colonial era they were plundered and used primarily for the benefit of the empires and advancement of the North. This new era of globalization has many similarities. The multinationals are setting up McDonald's restaurants, Pepsi bottling plants, and car assembly operations for purposes other than generosity. They anticipate a profit, and it is incumbent upon the host government to assure that the benefits of the arrangements do not flow only in one direction — out of the country hosting them. This can be very difficult to accomplish (a) because of the power of the groups with which they are negotiating, and (b) because of the tendency of many governments to assure benefits to the incumbents, leaving ordinary citizens not only unprotected but bearing the costs of their leaders' transactions.

Moreover, the authority of the state is being accosted from other directions including CNN and other news media, the Internet, and non-governmental organizations whose numbers proliferated in the 1990s. Multilateral institutions such as the United Nations or the International Monetary Fund impose demands, regulations, and obligations. All these international actors alter the scope of state authority. Governments may feel they have precious little control over transborder movements or even activities within their own boundaries. Technological changes have made it difficult for states to control movements of all kinds of things, whether they are material — cocaine, diamonds, weapons, or financial flows — or ideas — those pertaining to a Hollywood culture, fundamentalism, democracy, or human rights. Even the question of who is present and who is to be counted poses difficulties. Citizens, permanent residents, visitors, guest workers, refugees, and undocumented immigrants all may be resident within the boundaries of any given state, each category with its own set of rights and needs. In sum, the permeability of politics and borders makes the tasks of governance all the more complicated. These issues have been around a long time. What is new is the rapidity with which these changes are taking place and the scale of their impacts. Globalization may be undermining state authority; it certainly is changing the scope of state control. Sovereignty — both in reality and in perception — is fragile. The responsibilities it confers are central to strengthening governance in the Global South.

Chapter 4

Conflict, Human Rights, and the Politics of Refugees

Challenges to Security in the Global South

For nearly half a century — the end of World War II to 1989 — the possibility of a nuclear war between the superpowers, the Soviet Union and the United States, shaped international relations and security questions. With the reforms launched by the Soviet Union's Mikhail Gorbachev in 1985, the symbolic as well as real fall of the Berlin Wall in 1989, and the breakup of the Soviet Union into independent nations, confrontation no longer seems likely. Threats now emanate from two other sources: deadly conflicts within troubled states and terrorism perpetrated by both state and nonstate actors. Civilian populations suffer severe consequences from these contemporary conflicts. At the beginning of the twentieth century the estimated ratio of soldiers to civilian casualties in conflict situations was nine to one; today that figure has reversed and the ratio of soldier to civilian casualties is one to nine.[1] This reality by itself captures the enormous changes in security issues facing the world's population at the beginning of the twenty-first century.

In addition, there is a diffusion of power beyond the two post–World War II superpowers to other international actors. Japan is a significant international economic actor; China now has a seat in the United Nations Security Council and has become a member of the World Trade Organization. India and Pakistan are now nuclear powers. These and other emerging nations are creating a multipolar world, leaving behind the bipolar world of the Cold War years. The United States may appear to be the only superpower, but if it is one, it faces many limitations. One analyst refers to all these changes as "Tectonic forces leading to breakup, breakdown and blow-up."[2]

Chapter 4 explores several topics related to conflict and to humanitarian issues in the Global South. It briefly identifies the various sources

111

of conflict, in the form of religious nationalism, crises of legitimacy and authority, and both state and nonstate terrorism. It notes the changing technology of warfare, and the politics and economics of arms sales as they relate to the unfinished agenda of development. The chapter then examines three areas of conflict. In Sri Lanka conflict derives from combined ethnic and religious differences exacerbated by colonial policies. In Colombia the roots of conflict reside in class, poverty, and competition for resources and benefits within the state system. In Sudan differences in religious identity, conflict over resources, and the colonial experience provide the context for a prolonged civil war. The chapter links the problems faced by these nations with challenges to the state identified at the end of chapter 3. Refugees, an all too frequent consequence of such conflicts, are next addressed, along with the changing institutional approaches to managing refugee problems. Finally, we identify three human rights issues: child soldiers, using the Sierra Leone case; gender apartheid as experienced by the women of Afghanistan; and ethnic cleansing, drawing upon the Rwandan example.

The demise of colonial structures, the end of the Cold War, and the fragility of many new state systems have contributed to a burgeoning of local conflicts in the Global South. A key factor is that people with different identities and loyalties find themselves within a state system in which they are competing with other groups for scarce resources. While this situation is not unusual, tensions may be exacerbated by a lack of structures for sharing power and resources equitably, and by little inclination for doing so. Conflicts that were kept under wraps during the ideological standoff between the Soviet Union and the United States have emerged into the open. The breakup of the Soviet Union has further complicated the politics of Central Asia, creating new states out of former Soviet regions. Both Afghanistan and Somalia provide illustrations of the "failed state" in which the structures of power, authority, and legitimacy are so weak that they are overwhelmed by warlords who take over and compete with one another.

A key factor in contemporary conflicts is the breakdown of state authority in Africa and the rise of rebel groups and factions, often based on ethnic identities, that are competing for control of mineral resources. This competition has often been characterized by cruelty, violence, and extreme exploitation. Sierra Leone and Congo are two regions in which terrorism and turmoil have been overwhelming in recent years. The horror stories of child soldiers, drugs, gems, and mutilated civilians from the hinterlands of Sierra Leone and Liberia are legion. In Congo, the war has claimed more than 2.5 million lives since 1998, and the struggles over land and resources show no signs of abating. There are conflicts among networks, militias, and governments over resources — gold, diamonds, oil, cocaine. Some struggles, of course, contain elements of all these categories.

In sum, conflicts in the Global South today take several forms. There are the conflicts between states, frequently laced with ethnic, religious, or identity struggles. There are conflicts within states as people compete for scarce resources. There are revolutionary movements to end exploitation of the poor and build a new society, including such examples as the Shining Path in Peru or the New People's Army on Mindanao in the Philippines. There are the religious fundamentalists who wish to create a new religious state or infuse an old one with religious values. Among these are the Hindu fundamentalists in India or the former Taliban in Afghanistan. There are various anticolonial movements such as those found in East Timor or Eritrea, both now newly independent.

Religious Nationalism

Religious fundamentalists attribute infallibility to a particular religious dogma in its literature, its teachings, its morals, and its interpretation of the historical record. In many cases religious fundamentalists are identified with national objectives. No one part of the world has a monopoly on it. We see Islamic militants opposed to Israel or the United States, and equally opposed to some of their own more secular leaders, such as the Palestinian leader Yasir Arafat or Egypt's Hosni Mubarak. Hindu fundamentalists struggle against Islamic and Christian influences and also oppose those who would ameliorate the harsh confines of the caste system. In early 1999, the contrasting viewpoints of secularists and religious fundamentalists in Turkey came to focus on whether a newly elected female member of parliament could wear her head scarf while taking her oath of office.

At its most extreme, religious fundamentalism takes the form of "satanization" in which all forces opposing the particular religious group are considered forces of evil. Underlying much of the support for religious fundamentalism is a genuine concern for what is regarded as moral decline, fostered by Western culture, but experienced globally. In the United States such a perspective has undergirded the violence of some of the extreme antiabortion activists as well as that of some members of the Christian militia.

Many issues arise in an analysis of religious nationalism. Can religious states be sufficiently tolerant to permit minority rights within the state? Will minority groups face, at the very least, discrimination and, at the most, persecution and death? Given the Holocaust experienced by European Jews during World War II, the tremendous loss of life of both Hindus and Muslims at the time of the partition of India, the continuing tensions between Muslim/Malay and Chinese Indonesians, or the long-term conflict between Tamils and Sinhalese in Sri Lanka — to mention a few situations of religious conflict — these concerns are not insignificant.

Crises of Legitimacy and Authority

Many new nations emerged in the years just after World War II. It was a heady and exciting time. For vast numbers of people around the world, there was hope and promise of freedom, development, self-respect, and a new way of life. For some, these promises have materialized, but for many, even most, they have not. In some instances, small factions of elites and their supporters have garnered the benefits of control over the structures of the state. In others, particular ethnic groups or particular regions or communities have been neglected by the authorities or have perceived themselves to be omitted from common resources and benefits. In some instances there is an extreme reaction, as in East Pakistan when the Bengalis "voted with their feet" (as discussed in the preceding chapter) and chose to end the union with the West, thereby creating Bangladesh. There are other such instances of civil war and creation of new states. There are also numerous instances of a successful insurgency relieving a regime of its power, as, for example, when the regime of Mobutu Sese Seku, long the central powerful figure in Zaire (now Congo), was ousted by the forces led by Laurent Kabila. There are many more examples of smoldering hostilities, mounting instability, and diminishing identification with the political system as we have seen in several states of West Africa.

One of the causes of these crises of legitimacy and authority on the part of some states in the Global South is that they were artificial creations from colonial times, assembled from diverse peoples who did not have a long history of association and little inclination to create one. In theory, members of a nation share loyalty to a group that has defining traits such as language, history, or ethnicity. Problems arise when the boundaries of the state do not coincide with the boundaries of the various national groups residing within it. Sometimes a state incorporates several nations within its boundaries; sometimes its boundaries actually separate members of the same identity group. The process of building loyalties to a new entity is fraught with difficulty. It is also a very important process, identified at the end of chapter 3, as the challenge of nation building.

Legitimacy and authority are linked. If a government is based on popular consent and people perceive that the government has the right to govern, then it has legitimacy. If it is based on coercion — that is, the imposition of force in order to obtain compliance — then the government will likely be perceived as illegitimate, unjust, and unworthy of support. Many governments walk on a tightrope: excessive coercion may enable the government to introduce and sustain complex policies including a big effort for development, but it can lead to outbursts of pent-up frustration, as in China in 1989. Too little capacity to enforce rules and the will of the government can lead to chaos and breakdown as in Liberia or Sierra Leone. And, of course, the "failed state" such as Somalia offers a worst-case scenario.

Terrorism: State and Nonstate

Terrorism is defined as acts of violence committed against innocent persons or noncombatants that are intended to demoralize targeted groups, overcome opposition, and achieve political ends through fear, destruction, and intimidation. Terrorism has been around for a long, long time. What is new about terrorism at the beginning of the twenty-first century is that terrorists are operating in an international arena. No longer are there only isolated and local acts of violence. There are commercial airline hijackings such as the destruction of Pan Am 103 over Lockerbie, Scotland; the bombings of the United States embassies in Kenya and Tanzania in August 1998; and the destruction of the two towers of the World Trade Center and related events of September 11, 2001. Moreover, in the current era, terrorists can obtain highly destructive explosives and weapons with which to attack even civilian targets. Biological and chemical terrorism are real threats, as the October 2001 anthrax scare in the United States has indicated. And, as we enter the twenty-first century, a new and potentially devastating form of terrorism is emerging. This is cyber-terror, the capacity to penetrate computer systems and telecommunications systems and cause pandemonium or breakdown in such systems as air traffic control, power grids, or telephone systems.

State-sponsored terrorism can take several different forms. Some states, such as Iran, Iraq, Libya, and Afghanistan, have sponsored terrorism, largely directed against the United States. They do so by providing sanctuary, training, and operational support for known terrorists. They may also plan and carry out activities such as those perpetrated by the preindependence South African government against both Zimbabwe and Mozambique. Still others have a record for terrorizing their own citizens in what have become infamous instances of "the disappeared." In Chile and Argentina, for example, recent governments have had infamous track records of violently eliminating citizens who disagreed with state policy. The international uproar over Chile's General Pinochet, and his possible extradition from Great Britain to Spain on charges of mass murder, was based on his presumed role in state terrorism.

Nonstate actors, usually groups trying to gain control of their governments or gain independence from the state for a particular group or region, carry out subversive or nonstate terrorism. The IRA in Northern Ireland has a multidecade track record of terrorist activities against the British government. Guests in the Japanese ambassador's residence in Peru were taken hostage in December 1996 and held hostage for over four months by extremists of the Tupac Amaru Revolutionary Movement (MRTA). Terrorists associated with the Liberation Tigers of Tamil Eelam, the Tamil independence movement of northern Sri Lanka, were responsible for the assassination of Rajiv Gandhi when he was on a tour to Madras in 1991. Since 1989, the Kashmiri insurgency has taken more than twenty thousand lives, of which at least half have been civilians.[3] Terrorist methods are also used by those who wish to advance a particular agenda without actually seeking state power, such as transforming a bureaucracy, assassinating a particular leader, or assuring religious hegemony. No continent is free from terrorist activity that may have local, regional, national, or international import, as the United States learned most abruptly one sunny late-summer morning in September 2001.

Arms Control and Development: Unfinished Agendas

Military expenditures doubled worldwide between 1960 and 2000 from $400 billion in 1960 to $800 billion.[4] Nowhere is the harm caused by allocation of vast sums to armaments greater than in the developing countries. In the face of extreme poverty, famine, expanding debt, poor health, and inadequate livelihood opportunities, many nations are spending more than ever on military activities and the arms that permit them. In the 1980s the five largest recipients of U.S. weapons in sub-Saharan Africa were Liberia, Angola, Somalia, Sudan, and Zaire (Congo), all of which are impoverished nations that have disintegrated into civil war. According to one military watchdog group, by the late 1990s the United States had given military assistance to nearly every African country, training over three thousand military officers, of whom nearly three-fourths were from dictatorships or nations on the brink of collapse.[5] The United States remains the largest arms supplier in the world, together with Britain, Russia, China, and France providing 84 percent of the total.[6] Three regions — the Middle East, East Asia, and Western Europe — are the dominant arms-importing regions.

It is difficult to overestimate the extent of the arms trade. Officially the overall global arms trade is declining, but the official figures greatly underestimate the size of the arms market, excluding, as they do, the black market and unreported sales that in many countries are far more than the legal sales. The figures also exclude weapons obtained by barter — for instance oil, or some other commodity, for weapons. South Africa has recently sought to upgrade its military hardware with about $5 billion in purchase of warships, submarines, helicopters, and jets from Britain, Germany, Sweden, and Italy. In turn South Africa exports artillery pieces to the Middle East and assault rifles, mortars, and armored cars to other African nations.[7] Any type of weapon (except for nuclear, biological, and chemical weapons, or long-range missiles) is available in the market, according to the Center for Defense Information, which indicates that suppliers are offering state-of-the-art electronics, optics, and munitions to potential buyers.[8]

One particularly devastating technology of warfare that has riddled much of the Global South is the antipersonnel mine, commonly known as land mines. An estimated 100 million mines are deployed across sixty-four nations, injuring over 26,000 people per year. Africa has more land mines in the ground than any other continent, with anywhere from 18 million to 30 million in eighteen countries. Angola alone has 9 million to 20 million land mines. In 1996, eighty-five nations introduced a resolution at the UN to ban the use, stockpiling, production, and transfer of antipersonnel land mines. The United States has refused to support this ban, stating that it cannot yet abandon the use of mines in Korea. In

1997 Jody Williams and her colleagues of the International Campaign to Ban Landmines won the Nobel Peace Prize for their work both to ban the use of antipersonnel mines and to clear them.

Another weapon of war central to a discussion of conflict and human rights in the Global South is gender-based violence. Gender-based violence includes rape, prostitution, sexual mutilation, sexual humiliation, and trafficking, and it is used as a tactical weapon. An attack not only on the individuals involved, but also on family and culture, gender-based violence is intended to humiliate and weaken the morale of the target group or to terrorize a population and force people to flee. Gender violence works like other forms of torture; the attacks, particularly rape, often have a tragic ripple effect extending beyond the pain and degradation of the rape itself because rape victims are often ostracized by their communities.[9] Sexual abuse and exploitation are not new tools of war, but they are increasingly widespread with the shift to conflicts within state borders. The increased involvement of civilians results in a great increase in civilian casualties. A European Community investigative team estimated that twenty thousand Muslim women were raped in Bosnia between April 1992 and January 1993 as part of a deliberate and official strategy to humiliate their culture and destroy their morale.[10] In its 1992 report entitled *Rape and Sexual Abuse,* Amnesty International provides the first instance in which an international human rights group has identified the sexual abuse of women as a distinctive form of illegitimate state action.[11] In times of war when the social boundaries and norms are disrupted, sexual abuse has been, and will undoubtedly again be, a vicious military weapon.

Ethnic and Sectarian Struggles, Insurgencies, and Guerrilla Movements

One tool for understanding these conflicts is to examine the various meanings and interpretations of ethnicity and the ways in which ethnic loyalties are linked to growing numbers of conflicts at the beginning of the twenty-first century. Chapter 3 provides a clarification of ethnicity in its presentation of concepts useful for understanding politics in the Global South. Many ethnic groups have been forged in the competitive environment of modern nation-states and have been bound together by material interests. Such competition arises with the striving of ethnic groups for scarce but valued goods and resources. This has been the situation in many states formed in the post–World War II period. They have been struggling to develop, and the resources to generate an adequate standard of living and livelihood security for all have simply not been available. One ethnic group may be perceived to be benefiting while another is languishing. Such a situation is greatly aggravated when ethnicity and geography converge. That is, the ethnic group occupies a particular, easily defined space such as the Tamils in the northern portion of Sri Lanka, or the Kurds in defined regions of Iraq and Turkey.

Many issues arise vis-à-vis specific ethnic groups and the state; analysts must ask under what conditions diverse ethnic groups can be incorporated into one centrally governed political system. What are the specific processes for enabling such a system to work? Should we contemplate increasing separatism on the assumption that it is extremely difficult to develop systems for negotiation and compromise among groups? There is no single answer; the questions are important. Many states have found ways to build loyalties among members with diverse ethnic backgrounds. Among them are Malaysia, Belgium, and Guyana. Nevertheless, as one Sudanese scholar states,

> Virtually every African conflict today has some ethno-regional dimension to it. Even those conflicts that may appear to be free of ethnic concerns involve factions and alliances built around ethnic loyalties. Ethnicity is both a source of conflict and a tool used by political entrepreneurs to promote their ambitions.[12]

In the following section we explore three case examples of states undergoing long-term conflict: Sri Lanka, Colombia, and Sudan. Sri Lanka experiences ethnic conflict and turmoil that has torn the island apart for three decades. For Sudan, religious identity is dominant, and issues of resource access and control loom large. For Colombia, long-term egregious inequities, class distinctions, pressures for livelihoods, opportunities within the illicit global economy, and severe manipulation of the polity for personal gain are apparent. In all three situations, global politics and economics frame the causes and consequences of the conflicts. The following discussion clarifies the origins of these particular conflicts, their manifestations, and possible outcomes in order to help us understand more broadly the causes, nature, and implications of contemporary intrastate conflicts.

Sri Lanka: Strife in the Pearl of the Indian Ocean

Sri Lanka is a story of national disintegration of two peoples, each feeling increasingly threatened by the other, and each driven to take action that can only reinforce the other's fears in an unending spiral of violence and retaliations. Sri Lanka's 19 million people consist of Sinhalese, who are primarily Buddhist and represent 75 percent of the population, and Tamils, who are largely Hindu, composing 18 percent of the people. While the Sinhalese constitute the majority population of Sri Lanka, they consider themselves a minority in the context of the larger Tamil population that includes 55 million Tamils just across the eighteen-mile-wide Palk Straits separating Sri Lanka and India's state of Tamil Nadu.

Sri Lanka has a history in which pressures of colonialism exacerbated the relations between two heretofore relatively harmonious peoples, the Tamils and the Sinhalese. The British colonialists favored the Tamils and placed them in a disproportionate number of top positions in the civil service. After independence, the Sinhalese majority sought to redress this situation in ways that, in fact, created discriminatory policies against Tamils. In 1956, SWRD Bandaranaike became prime minister on a platform that touted Sinhalese nationalism and established Sinhala as the country's official language, thus disadvantaging the Tamil-educated citizens in terms of higher education and employment. Bandaranaike was assassinated in 1958 by a radical Buddhist monk for agreeing to negotiate with the Tamils to meet some of their demands.

From that point onwards, communal tension festered. The government exacerbated these tensions by embarking on a program to develop areas in the north and east of the island, resettling thousands of Sinhalese families in areas the Tamils considered their homeland. In 1969 the Privy Council in London directed the Supreme Court in Sri Lanka to review the constitutionality of the Official Language Act. The Sri Lankan government responded by abolishing appeals to the Privy Council, thus ending for the Tamil people their only avenue to seek justice through independent judiciary decision. Meanwhile, the Sinhalese established a revolutionary organization thereby sharpening the divide between the two communities, and the main Tamil opposition group formed the organization that was the precursor of the militant Liberation Tigers of Tamil Eelam (LTTE). The LTTE continues to be the major Tamil military force today. Throughout the 1970s, the government continued with affronts to the Tamil community, such as restricted entry of Tamil students to universities, as well as police brutality at a Tamil literary conference, and the government-ordered burning of the Tamil library in the northern city of Jaffna in 1974. Along with these problems were economic and class issues as the economy sagged during that decade. By the late 1970s, Tamil political parties were calling for the establishment of an independent, sovereign, secular, socialist state of Tamil Eelam to include all the geographically contiguous areas that had been the traditional homeland of the Tamil-speaking people in the northeastern part of the country. At the same time, the Tamil Eelam movement split into a number of factions, some of which aggressively opposed each other.

By the early 1980s, Sri Lanka had erupted into full-scale communal violence. Hundreds of Tamils were killed and over a hundred thousand fled to South India. The Sri Lankan prime minister sought support from the Indian prime minister, Rajiv Gandhi, to assist with negotiations in the context of great violence and severe human rights violations. The Sri Lankan government moved to provide greater autonomy and a devolution of power to the Tamil communities, including official status for the Tamil language, but these concessions led to a backlash among the Sinhalese population. Meanwhile India sent an Indian peacekeeping force to help disarm the rebels. Relations with India became very complicated. At one point Indian planes were airlifting relief supplies to the Tamils in the North; at another point they were fighting against the Tamil Tigers. Negotiations and peace talks were on-again, off-again. India finally withdrew forces from Sri Lanka in May 1990, and a year later the Indian prime minister Rajiv Gandhi was assassinated in Madras, allegedly by a Tamil Tiger suicide guerrilla.

Attempts to bring about resolution have so far been unsuccessful. Terrorist activities by the Tamil Liberation Tigers have aimed at fuel depots, trains, plans, boats, and buses as well as important Buddhist shrines. Assassinations of key public officials — both Sinhalese and moderate Tamils — have been part of the Tigers' agenda, and suicide bombers have been a trademark of their tactics. More than sixty-two thousand people have been killed since the conflict began.[13] The Tamils continue to seek self-determination, a homeland of their own in the north and the east. The government maintains a fierce offensive stance with its Special Task Force commando unit deployed to capture strategic positions and destroy the Tiger forces and their base of support. In February 1998, Sri Lanka celebrated its fiftieth anniversary of independence, but the conflict continued.

Then, unexpectedly, early in 2002, the election of a new Sri Lankan government, with a strong public endorsement for a peace strategy, permitted the signing of a cease-fire agreement with the LTTE.[14] Velupillai Prabhakaran, who has led the Tamil independence struggle, made his first public appearance in ten years. The first face-to-face peace talks in seven years between the government and rebels, brokered by Norwegian diplomats, began in mid-2002. Tremendous anxiety and continuing mistrust underlie the hope of a negotiated settlement. While ruling out a separate state for Tamils, the new government of Ranil Wickremesinghe is willing to discuss much greater autonomy for Tamil regions within a democratic Sri Lanka. So far Velupillai Prabhakaran has not committed himself to such arrangements. The negotiators expect to work over two to three years on the details of a compromise. Hopefully, Sri Lanka will figure a way to honor and encourage ethnic and religious pride in the context of pluralism and secularism.

Could this conflict have been avoided? It would appear that more judicious, inclusive policies could have gone a long way to eliminate Tamil hostilities. Tamil resentment has been inflamed for at least two generations by the Sinhala-only policy and a variety of other insults and deprivations. Sri Lanka illustrates how specific policies can lead to a situation in which ethnic and religious identities become salient and exclusive. It also demonstrates the ways in which ethnic entrepreneurs can seize a fragile relationship between different ethnic groups and exploit it for their own purposes. On both sides — Sinhalese and Tamil — ethnicity has been politicized to the detriment, but hopefully not to the demise, of the nation.

Sudan: Africa's Longest-Running Civil War

Sudan, the largest country in Africa, is a nation of great racial, ethnic, cultural, and religious diversity. This diversity, along with competition over potential resources, underlies the civil war that has been ongoing in Sudan intermittently for the last forty-four years. It ranks as Africa's longest-running civil war. In the northern part of the country are Muslims (approximately 70 percent of the population) of African-Arab descent who emphasize their links with the Arab and Islamic worlds. In the south are people of black, sub-Saharan African descent, primarily Nilotic tribes, Animist or Christian, who identify with the nations and cultures of sub-Saharan Africa. The south has resisted the universalizing religious culture of the north. In addition, there are key resource issues.

The government of Sudan has earned an estimated $500 million annually from oil since it began export in 1999; the large reserves are located in southern Sudan. Companies from China, Canada, and Malaysia, as well as Sudan's national petroleum company, have created a petroleum consortium for oil production and for construction of a thousand-mile pipeline.[15]

For decades the region known as Sudan was caught up in the geopolitical conflicts arising among Turkish, Egyptian, French, and British forces as the power of the Ottoman Empire waned and that of the European nations waxed. At the end of the nineteenth century, British-led Anglo-Egyptian forces ended slavery and nominally unified Sudan. A decision by colonial authorities to administer the north and south separately reinforced Arab culture and Islam in the north, encouraged southern development along indigenous African lines, and introduced Christian missionary education and elements of Western civilization for purposes of modernization in the south. Interaction between the two sets of people was strongly discouraged.[16]

War broke out between the north and the south just a few months before independence was declared in January 1956. Armed conflict between the government in Khartoum and various liberation movements in the south has been intermittent ever since. The north has perceived its responsibilities and interests in the Arabization and Islamization of the south; the south has perceived such action as Arab hegemony and has sought, first, some sort of political federation and later independence through an armed struggle. In the south, the Sudan People's Liberation Movement (SPLM) rejects an Islamic state and the imposition of Islamic law and seeks a secular, democratic, and pluralistic Sudan.

The key issue for Sudan is the relationship between religion and the state. Religion has become central to defining one's status within the system as well as access to the benefits and resources of the state. The residents of the south do not wish to have the cultural values of the north imposed upon them. One southern faction claims that it wants to preserve the unity of Sudan in a secular pluralistic state. This position is being challenged by a breakaway faction in the south calling for separation. Thus, the principal cleavage remains north-south, but internal differences in both north and south are fragmenting political and military agendas. Many believe that most southerners would opt for separation if given the choice.[17]

To date an estimated 2 million people have been killed in the fighting and resulting famines. Raids by both government and the southern militia, drought, bombing by government forces, disruption of food aid, and decimation of villages and towns have forced thousands to flee and have greatly increased the numbers of internally displaced refugees. Relief agencies orchestrated by the United Nations High Commission for Refugees (UNHCR) have mounted a major refugee and humanitarian relief program in the south, and there is no end in sight. This relief operation established in 1989 in response to both drought and violence, Operation Lifeline Sudan (OLS), involves more than thirty non-governmental organizations and operates in both government and rebel-controlled areas.

Can Sudan — both north and south — create full equality, human rights, and a sense of national identity for all within the framework of a single political system? Or are the different visions of north and south such that partition is the only realistic answer to this longstanding conflict? The Sudanese people have been entrenched in a chronic conflict that has devastated the country since independence. These circumstances pose the question: Is a common identity for Sudan, given its great diversity, deep conflicts, and complicated claims, desirable or even feasible, or are separate identities and political partition the more realistic course of action?[18]

Colombia: Insurgencies and the Cocaine Connection

Colombia is in the unique situation of being Latin America's oldest democracy while also being afflicted with the longest-running civil conflict in the hemisphere. Colombia has suffered from civil war for fifty years, a conflict exacerbated by the dramatic expansion of the drug trade. Colombia is the single most important country in Latin America in terms of exporting cocaine and heroin to North America. The Colombian drug dealers, known as the "Medellín Cartel" and their drug-insurgency nexus have created transnational trade networks making them the core of the Latin American drug trade. The Medellín cartel allegedly accounts for about 80 percent of the cocaine exported to North America.

Four circumstances have put Colombia into the preeminent position in the Latin American drug trade.[19] First, it is strategically located between the coca-producing nations of Peru and Bolivia and the routes through the Caribbean and Central America that lead to North American and European markets. Second, the country's vast forests can conceal clandestine processing laboratories and airstrips. Third, Colombians have demonstrated entrepreneurial skills that are useful in organizing the trafficking of drugs. Fourth, some Colombians residing in the United States have been willing to serve as the final distribution points in the trafficking network.

During the 1980s the confrontation between the drug barons and the government escalated into a brutal war with drug dealers and guerrillas on one side and the government on the other. The drug barons and their guerrilla allies eventually formed a virtual counterstate, controlling large portions of the countryside. While there have been a number of different guerrilla factions, today there are two major guerrilla forces: the Revolutionary Armed Forces of Colombia (FARC), established in 1966 and possessing well-documented ties to narcotraffickers, and the National Liberation Army (ELN). They, along with the Colombian security forces and paramilitary groups, are battling for territorial control. The objective of FARC is to bring down the government, and to that end it has long staged armed attacks against Colombian political and military targets. The largest paramilitary organization is the United Self-Defense Forces of Colombia (ACCU). This group is financed by large landowners to combat the rebels and is reputed to be responsible for killing hundreds of civilians.

To date, more than thirty thousand Colombians have lost their lives to violence, and more than 1 million have fled their communities and are internally displaced persons.[20] Murders, kidnappings, torture, forced displacement, air bombardments, destruction of basic infrastructure — all are commonplace, including kidnappings of passengers on commercial flights. For its part, the government has supported paramilitary groups whose violence and human rights abuses are well established. The paramilitary groups are responsible for about 70 percent of all human rights violations.[21] These violations include threats to intimidate civilians and to raise money. For example, letters demanding payment of a "war tax" and a threat to mark the victim as a "military target" if he fails to pay are typical. Both the guerrilla groups and the paramilitary groups use kidnapping as a major source of revenue and torture, threatening and terrorizing at will.

Negotiations between the rebel forces and government representatives were launched in April 1999, aborted several times, then launched again in January 2002, with third-party assistance from ten countries, the Catholic Church, and the United Nations. Key items on the agenda were (1) creating agricultural alternatives to growing coca, (2) introducing political reforms to increase democratic processes, (3) strengthening the justice system and attacking corruption, and (4) combating right-wing paramilitary groups that have massacred thousands of suspected guerrilla supporters. From the start of peace talks, violence in Colombia increased dramatically as armed actors struggled for the upper hand, straining already fragile negotiations. The cycle continues: negotiations are launched; violence escalates; negotiations break down.

Aid for Colombia comes in several forms — economic, military, and humanitarian. Aid from the United States to Colombia began to rise in 1990 with the first Bush administration's "Andean strategy," a five-year, $2.2 billion plan to try to stop cocaine production and transport. Anti-drug aid granted to the Colombian military and police tripled in two years while military sales jumped from $21 million to $75 million over the same period. Recent efforts on the part of U.S. policymakers in regard to Colombia have been somewhat contradictory. The U.S. Congress approved major support, known as Plan Colombia, for a counternarcotics effort, including training and equipment for the Colombian army. While the money has been designated for use against drug growers and traffickers, much of the equipment is likely to be used against the leftist guerrillas, some of whom are involved in protecting coca crops and landing strips in southern Colombia. Since both leftist guerrillas and rightist paramilitary militias are involved in the drug trade, it is difficult to combat these operations. Humanitarian aid has also come to Colombia for helping the internally displaced persons. The European Commission, for example, has provided substantial sums for food, health, sanitation, and infrastructure over the past five years.

Meanwhile there are plans to build Colombia's economy in other ways. In the 1980s efforts to diversify the economy encouraged movement away from coffee, the dominant legal export, to coal, oil, flowers, and an increasing array of manufactured goods. Flowers are a $550 million industry for the nation and support more than 120,000 direct and indirect jobs.[22] Almost all of Colombia's flowers are grown for export, and more than 80 percent of exported flowers go to the United States.

Despite these efforts, Colombia remains at the core of the Latin American drug trade, a position that it continues to occupy in this new century.[23] The drug barons — the *narcotraficantes* — have prospered and have plowed some of their wealth back into their communities in the form of new business, housing, charities, and public facilities. They are gradually becoming "respectable." They are also at the heart of a drug-insurgency connection that continues to be very powerful in Colombian politics. These politics are part and parcel of a political system that is corrupt and elitist, as well as fundamentally undemocratic, with the military dominating a nominally civilian government.

Gathering Lessons from These Conflicts

These three countries constitute a small sampling of the many situations around the world in which there are ethnic or sectarian conflicts and/or insurgency and guerrilla movements. Lessons that might be useful in examining other situations can be drawn from this brief review.

1. Conflict may become a way of life. In Sudan, Colombia, and Sri Lanka, for example, virtually a generation of young adults knows no other environment than one in which fear, hatred, violence, and insecurity mark their days. Living with anger and fear may become natural. It is the way things are. Such attitudes can become deeply entrenched, making trust, collaboration, and reconciliation very difficult to achieve.

2. In these three cases, power plays emerged among elites competing for limited resources, and these actions generally disadvantage or harm the rest of the population. There is competition between FARC and the ELN in Colombia, among the various Tamil splinter groups in Sri Lanka, and among the southern Sudanese factions. In the process of these struggles for the upper hand, small farmers and peasants are victimized, their livelihoods destroyed, their relief food supplies confiscated, their rights violated. Further, demagogues can easily exploit such situations, inciting one group to harm another or to deny access to rights and privileges, as occurred in all these cases. The "instrumentalization of disorder," discussed in chapter 3, reveals elite political actors maximizing their personal returns, crippling the state's capacities to meet its responsibilities, and destroying any semblance of community life.

3. In the cases of Sri Lanka, Sudan, and Colombia international ramifications relate to our changing global system. Not only were several of these conflicts exacerbated by colonial relationships, but their outcomes were and are being shaped in part by international responses. In the case of Sri Lanka, India intervened sometimes on behalf of the Sri Lankan government and sometimes with humanitarian assistance to help Tamil victims of the conflict. Sudan's conflict exists within the larger context of international oil politics and a broad Islamic hegemony stirring

the region. Colombia, of course, is enmeshed in the global drug econ-omy. Moreover, global communications have transformed international awareness of, and responses toward, these conflicts. People around the world can watch events unfolding, whether images are of fleeing refugees or despairing victims of drought and violence.[24]

4. Systematic social and cultural discrimination, as well as political or economic repression, heighten the likelihood of violence and conflict. It was too late for the Tamils, for example, when twenty-five years after declaring Sinhala to be the only official language, the government of Sri Lanka decided to reconsider that policy. There is evidence worldwide that denying people respect for their customs and language, as well as access to the resources and benefits of the state, may lead to horrendous and long-term conflict and violence, both planned and spontaneous. The task of nation building — of a just and respectful inclusiveness — may be only one of several challenges states face, but it undergirds the capacities for people to live together.

Addressing the root causes of violence involves creating the condi-tions under which security, well-being, and justice for all can flourish. It requires that nations be attentive to the relationships among human rights, economic well-being, political engagement, and peace. It involves addressing the problems of the productive capacities and market power of the poor. If there are significant threats to survival, if people feel vulnerable and increasingly desperate, or if basic standards of justice and fairness are not applied equitably, then the risks of violence and humanitarian catastrophe grow.

Balancing Rights: Migrants, Asylum Seekers, Refugees, Receiving Peoples

Twentieth-Century Refugees

People may flee their homes for a variety of reasons. They may be sub-ject to violence; they may have experienced a flood or an earthquake or perhaps an economic or political disaster. Three broad categories of situations link refugees and human rights concerns. Some refugees are activists who have engaged in some politically significant activity that has alarmed the state, which then seeks to destroy the activity or the person. One of the most famous political refugees of the 1990s was Salman Rushdie, the Pakistani novelist whose book *The Satanic Verses* so offended the religious patriarchy of Iran that they, in effect, put out a death warrant or *fatwa* for him. Rushdie went into hiding in 1989 when he was condemned to death by the Ayatollah Khomeini and remained in hiding until 1998 when the *fatwa* was lifted.

Another category of refugees consists of those who are targeted by other groups or by the government and singled out for abuse by virtue of belonging to a particular group — the Kurds in Iraq or the Jews in Germany before and during World War II. Still a third category consists of those who are victims, displaced by societal violence that is not necessarily directed at them as individuals but which makes life virtually impossible. Those fleeing the violent struggles between the guerrilla forces and the government/paramilitary forces in Colombia constitute an example, as do the Ethiopians fleeing the war between Eritrea and Ethiopia. What makes refugees distinctive is that their flight is involuntary as opposed to voluntary movement, and the causes are political rather than economic, though in practice, these two often merge. Ultimately "the definition of a refugee is a person whose presence abroad is attributable to a well-founded fear of violence as might be established by impartial experts with adequate information. The movement of refugees beyond national borders may be the result of flight to avoid harm or the result of expulsion, also a form of violence."[25]

The twentieth century was characterized by marked flows of refugees. World War II saw, of course, a massive exodus from Europe to other continents. Then at the end of the war with decolonization and the emergence of many new states, there were massive new flows of refugees from China, between India and Pakistan, from Vietnam, and from Cuba among others. These refugee movements were often accompanied by widespread violence, killing, and enormous suffering and deprivation. With the 1960s came the decolonization struggles in Africa, and suddenly many countries were host to refugees who had little opportunity to return and little opportunity to find a permanent haven. Thus some refugee camps have become virtually permanent fixtures, new villages in the countries of asylum.

There are estimates that from the mid-1970s there have been between 10 million and 15 million refugees in the world at any one time. In addition, there is an equivalent number of internally displaced persons, so the total is around 30 million. According to the United Nations High Commission for Refugees (UNHCR), population displacements in 1995 alone totaled 27 million, of whom 14.5 million had crossed an international border. Refugees in excess of ten thousand exist in some seventy countries around the world.[26] These large numbers create an enormous responsibility for the UNHCR and for other organizations, including both bilateral agencies and non-governmental organizations, as well as governments, that are assisting refugees. Since its founding in 1951, the UNHCR has grown from a staff of thirty-four individuals with a budget of $300,000 to its end-of-the-century 277 offices in 120 countries, a staff of more than five thousand, and a budget of nearly $9 million, serving approximately 22 million people around the world.[27]

Changing Approaches to Refugee Problems

With changes in the numbers and the internationalization of the refugee problem, many nations are exhibiting a declining commitment to the principle of granting asylum and are attempting to contain displaced people within their own homeland. The task is perceived as one of preventing and resolving refugee problems and the forces that create them. This is quite different from the traditional approach in which humanitarian organizations acted on behalf of persecuted or distressed people only after they had actually become displaced or crossed a border. This latter perspective has been called an exile-oriented approach in which the emphasis is on the right of people to leave their country of origin to seek asylum. It places responsibility on the receiving country for solving the problems of the refugees. It is clearly reactive and exile-oriented.

Increasingly this approach is regarded as inadequate. Many of the nations that are hosting large numbers of refugees are themselves poor societies with fragile economies, delicate political systems, and major social problems. Eastern Congo's infrastructure, for example, was overwhelmed by the masses of Hutus who fled Rwanda when the Tutsi-led forces took over the Rwanda government in mid-1994. Macedonia and Albania were ill-prepared to deal with the large numbers of Kosovo Albanians trudging across their borders to safety in 1999. They too are poor countries with delicate political and social systems.

The new approach is based on a different conceptualization of notions of sovereignty, acknowledging that events taking place inside a country may constitute a threat to international peace and security beyond that nation's borders. People are aware that national boundaries are increasingly permeable, and there is a widespread concern that refugee problems are transnational and must be resolved through actions coordinated among the relevant countries. In fact, many countries are weary from refugee problems and both concerned and hesitant about providing the open-ended asylum that they have graciously provided in the past. Kenya, for example, is quite anxious to keep the Sudanese and Somali refugees along its northern borders contained within refugee camps. There is, consequently, a growing involvement of the UNHCR in countries from which refugees originate as well as those countries in which they have settled temporarily. The new approach has a homeland orientation. Whereas the traditional approach emphasized the right to leave one's own country and to seek asylum elsewhere, this new perspective focuses attention on the right to return to one's homeland and on the "right to remain" or the "right not to be displaced." Experience shows that dealing with crises before refugees are forced to flee is far better than dealing with the problems of returning them from a land of asylum. Frequently refugees return to a devastating situation: homes taken over or razed; roads, bridges, schools, and other public buildings destroyed; the physical infrastructure in a state of collapse, and even, in many instances, land mines. The people of the host country are left to deal with an environment that may have been devastated through land degradation and deforestation as large numbers struggled to stay alive, cook, and keep warm.

International Migrants

Separate from the question of refugees are issues surrounding international migration. Refugees have left their country because of violence, human rights abuses, armed conflict, or political terrorism, but many people also move for different reasons — economic or educational — that may be either permanent or short-term. The UNHCR estimates that approximately 120 million people live outside their country of birth or citizenship.[28]

The movement of people is a global phenomenon with the ILO estimating that one hundred states are countries of major inward or outward migration. Some flows are transglobal; others are regional. Filipinas for example, often go to Japan, Hong Kong, Singapore, or Thailand for employment; Somalis frequently head to the Middle East; Haitians may go to the Dominican Republic. Why do people migrate? Disparities in wealth, opportunity, and security underlie many, if not most, decisions to emigrate. Disparities among countries are increasing. The knowledge about these disparities is also increasing, and global communications networks make this knowledge widely available. Moreover improvements in mass transport allow people to move easily and quickly from one part of the globe to another. While most industrial nations keep an open-door policy for those immigrants who bring special skills or have family connections, they have made it very difficult for unskilled labor to enter. The economic reasons are apparent: there has been a decline of traditional labor-intensive industries and an increase in capital-intensive technologies requiring limited numbers of highly skilled workers. At the same time recent decades have seen considerable downsizing of industry and a growth in domestic unemployment levels.

As immigration has become tighter, a new business has popped up in the form of professional agents or entrepreneurs whose job is trafficking in those who seek to migrate. Whether it is Mexicans who wish to cross the border into Texas, Tamils who seek to leave Sri Lanka for London, or Chinese who want to make their way to New York, migrant trafficking is a growing and global practice often carried out under abusive, coercive, and dangerous circumstances. The ILO suggests that there are as many as 30 million illegal immigrants throughout the world.

As this discussion reveals, distinguishing between refugees and economic migrants is often difficult. The distinction between a refugee and a migrant is based on the description of a refugee as someone who has a well-founded fear of persecution in his or her country of origin. Perhaps there is a generalized violence and disorder from which they flee, but in some countries this does not qualify them for political asylum, even though they might not be able to return without putting their lives at risk. In addition, where violence and political chaos are present, there is often economic collapse. With high unemployment and no livelihood security, people may wish to migrate to escape impossible and unpromising living conditions. They would be hard pressed to sort out the political and economic determinants of that decision. This dilemma has often been resolved by providing such refugee/migrants with a legal arrangement entitled "humanitarian status" that provides temporary residence rights.

In the midst of all these concerns about migrants and refugees, one should keep in mind the people of the receiving states. It is a challenge to manage refugee and migratory movements in ways that promote the well-being of those people, sustaining their human rights, while also addressing the concerns of the receiving communities. The latter may see new pressures on their resources, their employment opportunities, and their social structures, all of which are aggravated by outside agencies, such as the UNHCR, that are providing assistance to the newcomer. This situation too can be fraught with tension.

Refugee Warrior Communities

Refugees are people who flee conflict and violence and seek safety and a normal and peaceful life. There are, however, those who flee in order to be able to carry on a conflict from a safe haven beyond the borders of the conflicted state. With a sanctuary for the warriors and relief assistance for the refugees, a symbiotic relationship can develop as has been observed with the contras in Nicaragua, the Khmer rebels on the Thai Kampuchean border, or the Rwandans in eastern Zaire. There is now a highly developed international refugee support system that can and has sustained large civilian populations for years. When the camps are close to or part of the front, war can become the dominant reality for the entire exiled population. Armed militants appear as protectors of the community, and close links are forged between the refugees and the warriors.[29] The presence of the refugee-warrior situation blurs the distinction between humanitarian and political activity and poses many dilemmas for agencies offering external assistance. The politicization and sometimes militarization of the relief camps mean that it is practically impossible for repatriation to occur, so the refugees remain in camps that become semipermanent. In addition, solidarity may continue between those who have fled and those who remain at home, permitting support and cover for the militant operatives who move back and forth across the frontier.

Aid in Conflict Settings

The first complex humanitarian emergency of the post–World War II period occurred in 1967–70 during the Nigerian civil war when there was an unprecedented international relief airlift run by non-governmental organizations to assist civilian victims in Biafra, the eastern state that eventually declared secession but failed to obtain its independence. A post-Biafra comprehensive study revealed the likelihood that the humanitarian effort may have contributed to unnecessarily prolonging the war and to the death of nearly 1 million civilians.[30] One organization, Médecins sans Frontières (MSF–Doctors without Borders) concluded that it and others had been used by the leaders of the Biafran secession in ways that may have added to the suffering and starvation of the very people they were trying to help.[31]

One concern is that resources provided by aid agencies are highly valued and scarce and may be manipulated, taxed, stolen, or otherwise regarded as booty of war by warring parties. Thus, an aid effort may simply aggravate the war by encouraging conflict over the aid spoils. In Sudan, for example, there has been constant struggle to assure that food aid gets to the civilian population that is suffering from drought and civil war, rather than to the militias that are engaged in fighting.[32] The difficulties are compounded by the ready emergence of bandits and thugs to whom violence and the spoils of war become a way of life. They join militias, marauding and plundering, often savagely as has been observed in many situations, most recently in Kosovo or Uganda. During the Somali crisis of the early 1990s, it was reported that 80 percent of the huge quantities of food piling upon Somali docks was being stolen by the country's warlords to fuel their military campaigns, thus preventing the delivery of urgently needed relief to those who were starving.[33]

Apart from avoiding the negative influences, aid in conflict situations should provide assistance to people in areas of violent conflict in ways that help those people disengage from the conflict and develop alternative systems for overcoming the problems they face.[34] How can aid agencies and aid workers encourage local capacities for peace? Non-governmental organizations and other aid agencies may be able to provide safe space for discussion and working on joint problems. They may also provide a forum for discussion as well as incentives for disengaging from conflict. These efforts are made infinitely more complicated by the fact that many wars are deeply embedded in people's daily lives and in the social fabric, making disengagement not impossible, but very difficult.

The range of needs that must be addressed in order to foster recovery in a postconflict situation may be enormous. They may include extensive efforts to demine the countryside, reestablish irrigation systems, assist the government to function again, and build the necessary basic infrastructure for transport, commerce, health, and education. Speaking in 2001, for example, a Somali educator emphasized that no nurses had been trained in any part of the former Somalia since the mid-1980s. This is a simple indicator of the lack of trained professionals in many regions emerging from serious conflict. Important too are the social and political tasks of reconciliation of a people reluctant to trust one another again, yet needing to live side-by-side in situations that can easily lead to fear, anger, and hatred.

Human Rights, Conflict, and Development

Development and Displacement: Unraveling the Issues

What are the links between trends in development opportunities and the global phenomenon of increasing refugee populations? One clue might come from the UNDP's 1998 Human Development Report that ranks countries on the basis of a Human Development Index (HDI), a composite measure of income, life expectancy, and educational attainment.[35] None of the twenty-five countries at the top of this index are, at this point, the country of origin for large numbers of refugees. Most refugees come from countries ranking low on the HDI index. Yet it is also apparent that not all countries with a low rank are "sending" refugees. Tanzania, Senegal, and Malawi are among the twenty-five poorest countries, yet people are not leaving those countries in large numbers.

Poverty, unemployment, inequality, inadequate health and education, and competition for scarce resources may play a part in creating the conditions that trigger refugee movements, but they, alone, are not the causes. Instead there appears to be a correlation between extreme poverty and refugee movements but not a direct causal relationship. Poverty, scarcity, and inequality may provoke conflict and violence leading to population displacements, but they can also be the consequence of conflict with the destruction of infrastructure, the loss of investment, and the departure of the most skilled citizens for more settled and promising situations. In most instances the conflict that has led to the refugees' situation has not been started by people trying to overcome poverty, scarcity, and inequality, but by leaders who perceive that their manipulation of the population under those conditions can enhance their power. Thus, conflict, violence, and warfare in which many may participate often serve the interests of only a few.

Human Rights and the Protection of Special Groups

According to the 1948 Universal Declaration of Human Rights, all human beings have a right to life, liberty, and security of person.[36] They have a right not to be subject to torture, slavery, or arbitrary exile. They have rights to own property, to move freely within the borders of their country, and to be protected against arbitrary interference in their privacy and family life. In many instances, people's human rights are abused not only on the basis of their individual characteristics or activities, but also because of the social group to which they belong. There is an established body of law which recognizes that people who wish to preserve a distinct identity should not be subjected to forced assimilation, segregation, or discrimination. The International Covenant on Civil and Political Rights states that such minorities "shall not be denied the right... to enjoy their own culture, to profess and practice their own religion or to use their own language." Similarly, the International Convention on Genocide forbids any activities that are undertaken with "intent to destroy, in whole or in part, a national, ethnic, racial or religious group."

There is, therefore, a strong public record on behalf of individual human rights and on behalf of supporting the individual identities of groups who wish to preserve them. In light of this body of international law and understanding, a brief look at three situations in which there is denial of rights is instructive. The first is the use of child soldiers — that is, children who are forced to become combatants or to serve adult soldiers in a variety of ways. The second is gender-based discrimination as exemplified by the women of Afghanistan whose rights were broadly denied by the Afghan regime of the Taliban. The third is ethnic cleansing, a term that has been widely used in the last decade to describe efforts to undermine, remove, and destroy a particular ethnic group. We draw for this last situation the experience of the Hutus and Tutsis in Rwanda.

The Protection of Children

Sadly, children in many parts of the world are victims of war. They may flee with their families under war-ravaged circumstances; they may become separated from those who will care for them; they are subject to the dangers of land mines and unexploded shells or grenades with which they come into contact; and they are subject to the atrocities that leave lifelong wounds that are very slow to heal. Overall, they suffer a disruption of the family support system that is essential to enable a child to thrive and develop.

One particular group deserves notice: child soldiers. Increasingly children are participating in war as combatants. Children as young as eight years of age are being forcibly recruited, coerced, and induced to become combatants.[37] These children are recruited in a variety of ways including conscription, kidnapping, and arbitrary seizure from the streets or even from schools, orphanages, and refugee camps. Sierra Leone is illustrative of a most egregious and vicious situation for children in combat. For nearly ten years children made up between 40 and 50 percent of the insurgents' total force strength of around fifteen thousand and composed a fifth, or five thousand, of the government's Civil Defense Forces. They served as soldiers, human shields, spies, porters, and sex slaves.[38] Only with the deployment by the United Nations and British forces in May 2000 did the fighting stop and the children's intensive military involvement diminish.

Child soldiers have fought or are fighting in at least seven countries in Africa besides Sierra Leone. The total number of child soldiers throughout the world is estimated at three hundred thousand. If Goodwin's interviews with child soldiers in Sierra Leone, as depicted in the *New York Times Magazine* in February 1999, are any indication, their casual, menacing approach to killing is not only frightening; it assures the enormous difficulties ahead of reintegrating into society a generation of children for whom killing is their only skill and violence is a way of life.

Gender-Based Discrimination: Women and the Taliban in Afghanistan

Known throughout the world for its extremist Islamic stance, repressive rules, and terrorist involvements, the Taliban, which ruled Afghanistan between 1996 and 2001, may be best known for the extreme restrictions placed on women, restrictions that are regarded by many as the equivalent of gender apartheid. When the Taliban took control in 1996 it imposed strict edicts that banished women from the work force, closed schools to girls, and expelled women from universities. These edicts also prohibited women from leaving their homes unless accompanied by a close male relative, and required women to wear the burka, a garment completely covering the body head to toe. They denied women and girls health services because they could not be examined by male physicians and because women were not allowed to work. Religious police enforced these edicts, and punishment for violation of the Taliban decrees was severe, including beating, flogging, and even death. In effect, women were virtually housebound and denied the rights to education, health care, freedom of movement, and participation in public life that most societies guarantee for all their citizens. Prior to the Taliban's rule, women in Kabul were well represented in schools, in the university, as civilian government workers, and in the medical profession. Under international pressure the Taliban, while in power, modified a few of these restrictions.[39] Girls continued to be barred from education but a modest effort occurred with religious education in *madrassas,* religious schools, for girls. Under pressure, a small number of women were able to return to work in hospitals or wards reserved for women.

Yet not until the fall of the Taliban regime were girls able to attend school and women permitted to go about their daily business outside the home. Even now, with politics fragile and insecurity great, with a government still insecure, and the *mujaheddin* (Afghan warlords) positioning themselves for advantage in a coming power struggle, Afghan women are unsure about their roles, their rights, and their freedoms in the emerging structures. These women know how vulnerable they could be in the event of a reversal of attitudes or a resurgence of intolerance toward women in public places. Women's rights are human rights, yet it is amazing how little the international community, and specifically those organizations concerned about human rights, could do in the face of a regime that intended to perpetrate discrimination and violence toward women.

Ethnic Cleansing: Hutus and Tutsis in Rwanda

Rwanda is a name that in many people's minds has become a surrogate term for gross human rights violations in the form of ethnic cleansing. While violence designed to destroy a community of people is not new, the term "ethnic cleansing" appears to have emerged in the 1990s out of conflicts in the former Yugoslavia as well as in Rwanda. East Africa's Rwanda is a tiny, green, landlocked country characterized by steep, terraced slopes covered with tea, bananas, and eucalyptus. In 1994, it was home to 5 million people and had one of the highest population densities in Africa as well as an annual population growth rate of over 3 percent through 1990.[40] Its citizens belong primarily to two different ethnic groups, the Hutu and the Tutsi. In a three-and-a-half-month period beginning in April 1994, a Rwandan genocide claimed lives of eight hundred thousand. Why?

The Hutu and Tutsi people have a legacy of competition and political animosity that was greatly exacerbated during Belgium's colonial rule by favoritism toward the minority group, the Tutsi. Rwanda became independent in July 1962, and the Tutsi slowly lost their political and social power to the majority Hutu. In postindependence Rwanda, years of Hutu-Tutsi conflict created a community of Tutsi refugees, many of whom established themselves in Uganda and formed a core of opposition to the Hutu regime in Rwanda. In the 1980s other problems emerged. Pressures on limited agricultural land mounted; per capita food production declined dramatically; prices for Rwanda's principal export crop, coffee, fell; a structural adjustment program arranged with the IMF froze salaries and devalued the currency by approximately 80 percent.

A new situation was created in late 1990 when the Tutsi-led Rwandan Patriotic Front (RPF), supported by Uganda, invaded Rwanda. Hutu leaders reacted, and extremists among them conceived a genocidal plot that was unleashed by the plane crash that killed the presidents of Rwanda and Burundi. The genocide should not have come as a surprise. Nevertheless, while the UN Security Council members and the U.S. government dithered, as many as eight hundred thousand Rwandan Tutsis were killed by the Hutu militia, the *interahamwe*, before an invading force of Tutsi-led exiles organizing themselves in neighboring Uganda routed the Rwandan government and sent 2 million Hutus fleeing into Zaire, Tanzania, and Burundi. Interspersed among the refugees were armed Hutu militia who had committed the genocide. They took control of the refugee camps, confiscating supplies intended for humanitarian relief and engaging in insurgency activities against the new government in Rwanda.[41] It is believed that dysentery, cholera, and dehydration killed at least fifty thousand refugees in eastern Zaire in the month of July 1994 alone. As news of this suffering spread, an outpouring of humanitarian assistance managed to prevent mass starvation, but the circumstances and overall loss of life were staggering.

What have we learned from this tragedy? It is widely believed that early intervention in Rwanda could have made a difference. The Commander of the UN Assistance Mission for Rwanda (UNAMIR) asserted that there was a window of opportunity in which a force of five thousand could have prevented massive violence, assisted in the return of refugees and displaced persons, protected the flow of humanitarian aid, and provided a secure environment to enable talks to begin between Hutus and Tutsis.[42] The absence of external constraints clearly permitted genocide to occur.

Key Issues for the Twenty-First Century

Several destabilizing forces have a strong impact on the topics covered in this chapter. One of the most important is the ever-widening gap between the "industrialized North" and the "developing South." There is increasing economic inequality as well as persisting competition among and within nation-states. Increasing levels of poverty, whether at a state, household, or individual level, in the context of the interpenetration of national and transnational economic processes, is a destabilizing factor lending itself to massive refugee movements as well as increased levels of hostility and frustration. Colombia, Sudan, and Sri Lanka are merely illustrative of the kinds of conflicts to be found in many corners of the world. Bitterness, anger, and fear are the harvest of such situations.

A second set of challenges for the twenty-first century is a growing populism. There are peoples' movements that are seeking critical changes in existing structures. They may be activists seeking fair trade measures from the World Trade Organization, Hindu fundamentalists seeking to redefine the state, or the Palestinian Intifada seeking its own state. They may be environmental advocates, abortion rights activists, or pro-life activists. Sometimes these social movements are militant in presenting their claims; other times they are peaceful. These claims, whether they are perceived as just or unjust, may present important ethical and security issues — sometimes even life-threatening concerns — to the broader public. For the state, a central challenge is to channel this populism and to build the kind of participation that is not destructive of the larger polity. Increasingly this challenge is for the international arena — the global system — as well.

A third set of issues pertains to the enormous changes in power relationships taking place at the end of the twentieth and beginning of the twenty-first centuries. Localized and regional conflicts have become a significant security concern for the world. These conflicts, often in the form of ethnic and other sectarian violence, seem to be proliferating. New peacemaking and peacekeeping instruments are essential if we are to have a peaceful world. The United Nations needs a new strategy to prevent and/or diminish the distress emerging in these situations. We know from experience that the international community does not yet have the structures in place to respond effectively to looming disaster or genocide.

A fourth set of issues pertains to arms build-up and the arms trade. We need a focus on the means for achieving peace, not simply those for waging war. The United States is spending vast sums for advanced weaponry as well as a national ballistic missile defense while cutting foreign assistance and reducing arms-control and disarmament initiatives. Given the complexities of achieving peace and security in most parts of the world, these military expenditures fall short of the subtle diplomatic and other policy instruments required.[43] There is, moreover, a boomerang effect to the arms trade. In 1995 the U.S. defense secretary noted that the last five times the United States had sent significant numbers of troops into areas of conflict — in Panama, Iraq-Kuwait, Somalia, Haiti, and Bosnia — U.S. forces faced adversaries that had previously received U.S. weapons, military technology, and/or training.[44]

Finally, across the globe people are increasingly recognizing a core of common humanitarian values. This recognition and understanding must be strengthened. Efforts to diminish the severity of domestic and international conflicts that create humanitarian emergencies are necessary but not sufficient. They must be undergirded by determination to build the norms and political will, as well as the international capacity, to assure that the human rights of all the world's citizens are protected. In his recent book *A Global Ethic for Global Politics and Economics*, Hans Küng examines the structural revolution in the world economy, stressing that globalization is unavoidable, ambivalent or highly varied in its consequences, and unpredictable, bringing with it a variety of unintended side effects.[45] He asserts that we need common values around shared rights and responsibilities that can form the cornerstone of an ethical global civil society. Collaboration between people of different cultures and interests will be easier when we are motivated by shared commitments.

Part Two

Economic Relationships, Trends, Crises, and Challenges

Chapter 5

The Shape of the Global Economy

The Global Economy at the Beginning
of the Twenty-First Century: A Snapshot

What does a snapshot of our global economy at the beginning of the twenty-first century reveal? Is it the fax machine now housed in every office and in many homes around the world? Is it millions of individuals and thousands of groups communicating with one another via the Internet? Is it Coke or Cadbury, Shell Oil or British Petroleum, Marlboro or Colgate-Palmolive, or the countless other multinationals that dominate international trade and investment? Or should we look at the big investment houses of Goldman Sachs or Morgan Stanley Dean Witter for the "real" picture of the global economy? Perhaps a more accurate reflection would be found in the workshops and factories of Hong Kong, Dhaka, or Jakarta producing Nike sneakers, Liz Claiborne clothing, or Motorola's computer chips. Perhaps it can be found in the cane fields of the Philippines or the banana plantations of Honduras amid the laborers cutting sugar cane or bananas. Cellular phones, skyscrapers, sweatshops, banana plantations, and motorcycle traffic jams — all these images are accurate; they reflect both the amazing economic change and technical accomplishments at the beginning of the twenty-first century and the enormous economic dislocation, poverty, and marginalization existing at the same time.

This chapter explores the global economy largely from a "big picture" perspective, providing an overview (or a bird's-eye view) of key global economic trends and concerns at the beginning of the twenty-first century. It first identifies the "global connection" and six issues relevant to any analysis of contemporary global economics. It then considers the key actors in the global economy, starting with the three major international financial institutions — the World Bank, the International Monetary Fund, and the World Trade Organization — and moving on to an overview of multinational corporations and finance capital and global

145

investors. The chapter then takes up the "multinational scorecard" and specific issues concerning the roles and impacts of multinationals in the global economy. Next, chapter 6 explores trade issues for Southern countries with a particular focus on primary commodity exports and the move toward regional trade organizations. Chapter 6 then reviews the boom in international banking with emphasis on the debt crisis, the Asian financial crisis of the 1990s, and the Heavily Indebted Poor Countries (HIPC) Initiative.

What Is the Global Connection?

The global economy is rearranging, linking, and even uniting us in new ways. The key is the marketplace — global capitalism — and the ways in which the technology of the information age has transformed it. An industrial system of multinational production exists along with a global market for finance capital and a new social and economic reality for all of us, rich or poor. The interconnections involve cross-national joint ownership of enterprises and collaborations in multiple sites: Schindler, a Swiss company, has controlling ownership of Elevadores Atlas in Brazil from which it produces for Brazil and exports to other Latin American countries and to Africa. Matsushita, a Japanese cell phone maker, joins with Psion (British), Motorola (American), Nokia (Finnish), and Ericsson (Swedish) in a new partnership, Symbian, to refine an operating system for the next generation of small mobile phones and palm-top computers.[1]

Capital has "wings"; labor is fixed in one place. Power resides with those who control the capital and can choose their labor market. Finance capital has no concern for national identity or political and social consequences, and it moves to new locations where labor is plentiful, regulations and constraints are few, and no one is paying much attention to levels of exploitation. Thus, industries have shifted their manufacturing and assembling operations Southward where there may be tremendous need for employment and little regard for workers' wages or rights or working conditions. All of this activity has been accompanied by downsizing of firms — worldwide — as all forms of technology, especially the computer chip, have permitted machines to take on much of the work of people. In the current global market a system of outsourcing has evolved whereby small firms provide parts, components, and pieces to the multinationals. With this system, the small firm — not the multinational — absorbs the risk of failure or loss.

Central to this transformed economic system is a level of mobility unimaginable even at mid-century. This mobility involves both people and goods. A businessman may routinely conduct business on three continents in a single week. Long-term employment opportunities are affected by these changes in mobility as well. One Boston-based non-governmental organization has on its staff a New Zealander who directs its office in Lima, Peru, and an Englishman who directs the office in Phnom Penh, Cambodia. Such mobility allows people to move in all directions, but it occurs on a large scale for purposes of both education and employment as large numbers of young adults from Southern countries search for new opportunities abroad, particularly in the North.

Goods, too, are moving about at unaccustomed levels and rates. The oranges on the breakfast table in Philadelphia may just recently have been on the tree in Mexico, and the avocados served at a restaurant in London may have been plucked in Kenya only a day or two earlier. Fresh-cut roses from Colombia are flown to a Boston florist who has them delivered to wedding festivities or a sick patient all within a matter of a few days. The ease of mobility is one key element of the global economy, and without it this international marketplace would not be flourishing as it is today.

Finally, the speed with which change is taking place is extraordinary. The accelerating pace of change can be seen in every field of human activity. At the beginning of the twentieth century, agriculture dominated economic activity. However, with industrialization over the last one hundred years, we have moved from the horse and buggy or poky automobiles to high-speed jet planes crossing oceans with several hundred passengers at a time, quite a change from the experimental flight of the Wright brothers in 1903. Meanwhile, the speed of communication is accelerating rapidly. The international telephone call in 1950 might have taken a day or two to place and after connected the parties probably could not hear each other very well anyway. Now with satellite connections, such calls are virtually instantaneous and usually with excellent connections. Electronic mail is even easier. There are 560 million Internet users functioning in more than 30 languages.[2] With the Internet and television bringing daily reports of events around the world, we are well on our way to becoming a global community. This speed of communication and easy access to information for decision making is transforming the ways in which we all work in the global economy.

Emerging Issues

Given the rapidly expanding global economy, certain critical issues require attention from both citizens and policymakers as we struggle to make sense of this changing world and bring order, fairness, and understanding to it. While there are probably dozens of issues from which to choose, we focus here on those that are largely economic in origin and offer five for further reflection.

Vulnerability of Poor Nations to the Economic Activities and Policies of Rich Countries

The gap between poor and rich countries is enormous. The centers of capitalist enterprise, the international institutions of trade and finance, and the rules and regulations governing them are dominated by the nations and institutions of the North. A number of factors reinforce this subordination. They include the monopoly that Northern enterprise has on technology, knowledge, and patents as well as the vast amounts of capital that flow out of the banking and investment institutions of the North around the world. Transnational corporations are able to take advantage of vast pools of impoverished and underemployed labor in the Third World, forming a disconnect between productivity and wage rates. In this, as in other matters, the old adage applies: "He who pays the piper calls the tune." Further, protracted problems of indebtedness, poverty, adverse terms of trade, and deteriorating social conditions affect many nations of the South.

Inequities between Rich and Poor, within Nations, and between Nations

With quickening global economic integration has come a widening income disparity between the rich and the poor within nations as well as between rich and poor countries. Some are able to take advantage of the opportunities presented by globalization processes, but many more are squeezed out of jobs or find that the fast movement of capital and opportunity around the globe is leaving them behind. Some characterize the process as one of increasing immiseration, a condition in which peasants and a cheap labor force are increasingly exploited while the dominant classes benefit, all with the help of the state.[3] One analyst has labeled the dichotomy between rich and poor nations a poverty curtain replacing the iron curtain of the Cold War era.[4] Certainly the statistics bear out this conceptualization of the problem. Figures for 2000 indicate that the low income countries have an average per capita gross national income of $520 whereas the high income countries' GNI per capita is $25,510.[5]

Tensions between States and Markets

With the march of economic activities across national boundaries, a tension between the requirements of the state and the requirements of the market has emerged. Governments want to be able to control economic activities within the boundaries of the state, but finance capital moves in and out virtually at will, and the large multinational corporation can easily shift its operations and its bookkeeping to suit its preferred profit margin. Governments have watched their power over the national economy shrink over the past several decades as the international marketplace has become increasingly dominant. In effect, governments may be trapped. They want the investment and value of corporate production with the various benefits that may ensue, yet they may also find that the corporation is difficult to manage, intrusive in domestic affairs, and unduly competitive with local businesses. There are many tales of corporate use of international economic clout to meet political objectives that may not coincide with those of the people or the government — or both — of the host country. In addition, offshore banking, as well as offshore incorporation, allows widespread evasion of national taxes. Recently a big U.S.-based accounting firm was formally established in Bermuda as a Luxembourg corporation owned by a Bermudan corporation even though it does more than half of its business in the United States. It will be American when it comes to paying Luxembourg taxes and Luxembourgian (or whatever nationality works best) when it comes to paying U.S. taxes.[6] Thus, in a variety of ways both the opportunity and the inclination for multinational business and banking to erode national sovereignty are increasing. Meanwhile, at another level, the international financial institutions, key actors in the global economy, are pressuring poorer nations in order to hold them accountable for efficient and honest government in light of major international loans. This is all to the good, but often very difficult requirements are imposed upon them. Thus the state has become beleaguered from several angles.

Global Problems Crossing National Boundaries

Many problems must be addressed by more than one nation because they do not occur within national boundaries. These often link economic and environmental issues in critical ways. The ocean fisheries, for example, must be protected by all nations whose people earn a living from the particular site or from catching the given species. Regulations about hunting whales must include Norwegians, Americans, Japanese, and other relevant nationalities. The collapse of the Atlantic cod fishery is a vital matter for Canada, Spain, Portugal, Panama, South Korea, Cuba, the United States, Norway, Denmark, and Japan, among others. Air pollution is another problem that knows no boundaries. When forest fires in Indonesia were burning late in 1998, residents in Singapore, the Philippines, and Thailand had to deal with smoky skies and adverse respiratory reactions. Water pollution in the form of runoff of manure, fertilizer, and pesticides from farms, or salinity from irrigation schemes can occur in India from waters flowing from Pakistan, or in Bangladesh from waters flowing from India. There are countless places around the world where water sources are shared by more than one country and require joint management of the resource and of the economic activities pertaining to it. Global cooperation is needed beyond the nation-state as societies struggle to identify their current needs and interests and their responsibilities to future generations.

The "Other Face" of Globalization

When we talk about "the economy," we usually mean the activities captured, summarized, and recorded in national statistical data as gross national income, or GNI. This definition leaves a lot out, namely the underground economy, the black market, and all that is illicit. The very same forces that are fostering the legitimate global economy are nourishing globally integrated crime primarily in drugs, sex trafficking, contraband arms trafficking, smuggling, illicit logging, money laundering and the movement of illicit funds, trading in protected species of plants and animals, and illegal immigration. A recent estimate places the value of such business at roughly 8 percent of the global economy and suggests that crime has become a global growth industry.[7] All the illegal economic activities require investigation and management. They distort resource allocations, damage human beings, undermine government policies, and contribute to economic instability. Their negative impacts entail both economic and social costs. This "other face" of globalization cannot be considered, however, without looking at the broad questions of extreme poverty. These illegal economic activities — a spin-off of the globalizing economy — must be examined in the context of all the other issues identified. They relate to the growing vulnerability of the South, the inequities between nations, widespread poverty within and between countries, the limitations on the power of state governments, and the ephemeral boundaries between states. It will take global cooperation to solve them.

Key Actors in the Global Economy

International Financial Institutions (IFIs)

There are many international financial institutions, but the term "IFI" normally refers to the "big three": The International Bank for Reconstruction and Development (World Bank), the International Monetary Fund (IMF), and the World Trade Organization (WTO), formally called GATT, the General Agreement on Tariffs and Trade. Two of those organizations originated at the end of World War II at a conference of forty-four nations in Bretton Woods, New Hampshire. Their immediate focus was the reconstruction of war-devastated European nations, but their purpose was also to ensure stable currencies and free trade. In a most fundamental way they were designed by the capitalist powers of the North and reflect their interests and concerns. Over time that interest has evolved into managing the expansion of a global capitalist economy and the gradual integration of all nations into this system. Voting in the IFIs is proportional to fees assessed, which means that five Northern powers (United States, Britain, Germany, France, and Japan) control more than 40 percent of the votes in the World Bank and the IMF, with the United States as the largest contributor.[8]

The World Bank

The first World Bank loans were for reconstruction in Europe; however, as the U.S. Marshall Plan got under way in Europe, the Bank shifted its focus to developing countries and to providing loans for large-scale infrastructure projects. Today Bank documents characterize its central purpose as promoting economic and social progress in developing nations by helping raise productivity so that their people may live a better and fuller life. Four offshoots of the World Bank are the International Development Association (IDA), the International Finance Corporation (IFC), the Multilateral Investment Guarantee Agency (MIGA), and the International Center for Settlement of Investment Disputes (ICSID). The latter two are not considered aid institutions. The IDA provides long-term loans to the very poorest countries, giving them a ten-year grace period before repayment of principal must begin with no interest charges. The IFC helps promote and assists productive private enterprises in developing countries by providing financial, legal, and technical advice. The MIGA promotes foreign direct investment in developing countries by providing investment guaranties against political risk. The ICSID provides conciliation and arbitration facilities for investment disputes between states and foreign investors.

All 184 current member governments contribute a small amount of money called "paid-in capital," guaranteeing that they will pay a larger amount of "callable capital" should the bank fail to collect on its loans. The bank then borrows money on the capital markets at a low rate of interest and lends to member governments at a low rate. Voting rights are dictated by members' subscriptions, with the largest contributors enjoying a comfortable majority of votes. The United States, Japan, and the European Union together control 55 percent of all votes. All decisions are made by the board of executive directors, which is controlled by the five largest shareholders. The World Bank president has always been an American citizen, and the head of the IMF has always been a European citizen.

In its early years, the Bank focused on large-scale infrastructural projects in developing countries. Then, under the leadership of Robert McNamara who was World Bank president from 1968 to 1980, the Bank began to emphasize basic needs, the agricultural sector, and eliminating poverty. More recently it has been engaged in structural adjustment loans with a heavy emphasis on "conditionality" — a term establishing IMF requirements whereby a country receives a loan only if it agrees to the reforms prescribed by the Bank and the IMF. Then by the early 1990s, the Bank became aware that sustained economic growth was not taking place even in countries following the conditions of structural adjustment. The Bank then began to emphasize good governance including accountability, transparency, and reduced levels of corruption.

There has been considerable public opposition to World Bank policies in recent years. Much of it has centered around environmental concerns, particularly Bank support for huge dams and other large-scale projects that have had a destructive impact on the environment, displacing thousands of poor people and causing profound human and ecological damage. The Sardar Sarovar dam in the Narmada River Valley in India came to symbolize this form of destructive development with massive financing. People from around the world joined Indian environmentalists and locally resident tribal peoples to protest large-scale, capital-intensive, economically wasteful development, widely regarded as inappropriate and inequitable for Indian conditions.[9]

Other critiques of Bank activities have emerged around structural adjustment issues. A campaign entitled "Fifty Years Is Enough, the Case against the World Bank and the International Monetary Fund" was launched by a coalition of non-governmental organizations to protest the policies of the World Bank and the IMF. The NGOs argue that these policies are designed to facilitate the repayment of debt and the steady transfer of wealth out of Third World countries to the bankers of the industrial countries. This transfer of wealth has had devastating consequences for the poor majority. A book entitled *Fifty Years Is Enough* draws evidence from thirteen countries to show that the policies advocated by the World Bank and the IMF are not working for the vast majority of poor people around the world.[10]

Still another avenue of criticism has emerged from women's groups who assert that Bank policies ignore the situation of women, and have, at best, sustained the status quo of unequal gender relations, while, at worst, deepening gender disparities. A coalition of non-governmental organizations has formed a group called "Women's Eyes on the World Bank" that is monitoring Bank activities in relation to gender.[11] This coalition asserts that the World Bank lacks a clear conceptual and operational framework for integrating gender equity into all Bank operations. There is little doubt that integration of gender analysis into the design of Bank programs has been slow, and even where gender analysis and participatory processes are conducted, the absence of accountability mechanisms often results in a failure to translate into strategies within the lending program to remove gender inequities and ensure that men and women benefit equally from development.

Another arena of opposition concerns the Bank's apparent indifference to the rights of indigenous peoples. This issue arises in several regions, one of which is Tibet. The World Bank had offered the government of China a development loan of $160 million, which would have helped resettle sixty thousand poor Han Chinese farmers in an area designated a Tibetan and Mongolian Autonomous Area. Critics perceived the proposed resettlement as part of a broader campaign by the Chinese authorities to weaken Tibetan national identity and argued that the loan would violate World Bank guidelines specifying that indigenous ethnic minorities should not suffer adverse effects from Bank-financed projects.[12] The Bank defended the resettlement plan as an integral part of its efforts to reduce poverty in China that has cut the number of rural poor from 280 million to 80 million in about ten years. Eventually, in July 2000, under increasing international pressure, the World Bank canceled the loan.

The International Monetary Fund

The IMF was set up to monitor the stability of the international financial system, encourage international monetary cooperation, promote stability in exchange rates, and help governments with short-term balance-of-payments problems. The IMF is located in Washington, D.C., and its Board of Governors, composed of the finance ministers of the 184 member governments or the heads of central banks, meet annually. A member government is assessed a quota or contribution based on the size of its economy and its population, that is, its weight in the global economy. This weight also determines its voting power and borrowing capacity. The latter is called a "drawing." Currently the United States controls about 17 percent of the votes.[13] By approaching the IMF, a member country facing a financial crisis has access to the Fund's resources and advice. The total size of the IMF's quotas has increased from about $9 billion at its inception to over $200 billion today.[14]

After the 1982 debt crisis, the IMF took on the major function of providing loans to countries desperate for financial support. These loans are based on a recipient government's adherence to IMF conditionalities or requirements for the receipt of the loan. Because it is at the apex of the conditionality system, the Fund has become the gatekeeper to debt relief, donor assistance, and various forms of financial packages. The conditionalities include directives that are intended to liberalize trade by reducing import tariffs and nontariff barriers, to devalue currency, to privatize state-owned enterprises, to reduce social service expenditures, to trim wages, and to introduce a variety of other austerity measures. The IMF has been widely criticized for the harsh measures imposed through its structural adjustment program. Critics argue that the IMF is guided by short-term economic objectives including low inflation rates, regular flow of debt payments, and small budget deficits. The economic reforms upon which these objectives depend — privatization, trade and investment liberalization, prioritizing export production, and austerity in social service budgets — have a harsh impact on poor people and favor the interests of large Northern banks and corporations. This economic liberalization in the developing countries has been undertaken not in the context of multilateral trade negotiations, but under IMF–World Bank structural adjustment programs which have forced the pace for many developing countries, causing great hardship for most of their populations. One consequence is that many poor developing countries are now far more open to trade than rich industrialized countries. The IMF's Trade Restrictiveness Test combines the major types of trade barriers, including the average level of tariff protection, the coverage of nontariff barriers, and export taxes. According to this index Haiti and Chile are four times as "open" as the United States or Japan.[15]

The IMF is not insensitive to the criticisms that have been leveled against its policies. In 1999 it replaced the Enhanced Structural Adjustment Facility with the Poverty Reduction and Growth Facility, shifting its emphasis to poverty reduction in the poorest countries. The intent is to individualize programs, to enable the country to be more fully in charge of the planning process, and to gain broad citizen support within the country receiving the loan. While the IMF documents, such as the Poverty Strategy Reduction Paper, are certainly more democratic, sensitive, and even more humble, transformations of large bureaucracies are notoriously slow, and whether reality will match rhetoric remains to be seen.

The World Trade Organization

In 1947 the General Agreement on Tariffs and Trade (GATT) was established to reduce trade barriers through multilateral negotiations. Since 1947 negotiators from approximately 125 member nations have met to liberalize world trade in multiyear conferences called "rounds." In 1995 GATT was renamed the World Trade Organization (WTO). China, eager to join the WTO/GATT for a number of years, finally was invited to join in December 2001.

Several principles are important to the operations of the WTO. First, all members accept all of its rules unconditionally, Unlike GATT, the WTO does not offer its members the option to choose which of its rules to enforce. Second, the rules extend far beyond tariffs and nontariff barriers to include intellectual property rights, investment, and other trade-related matters. WTO has a dispute settlement system and operates on a global scale. The most recent GATT Round was the Uruguay Round completed in 1993 that reduced average tariffs worldwide from just over 6 percent to just under 4 percent. It did not address problems of workers' rights, a topic that WTO has been reluctant to take up subsequently because there is strong opposition from Southern governments. Among these issues is concern about child labor. There are also numerous issues surrounding environmental standards used in production processes. A new round, now a WTO round, was launched in November 2001 at Doha, Qatar, and has been identified as the "development round."

There are many concerns about the ways in which the WTO functions although it is, in fact, regarded as a more democratic institution than either the IMF or the World Bank. Those two institutions operate on the basis of "one dollar, one vote," whereas the WTO is based on a system of "one country, one vote."[16] Nevertheless, poor countries may suffer severe underrepresentation with no more than one delegate, whereas rich countries not only have delegates, but also have busloads of lawyers, advisors, and other professional staff. Transparency is an issue, as is democratic process. GATT negotiators always met behind closed doors in Geneva, Switzerland. Critics have argued that neither GATT, nor its successor WTO, has appropriate mechanisms for public accountability in the form of participation of non-governmental organizations, publication of documents, or public hearings. The reality is that WTO meetings and decisions are very much dominated by the interests of the rich industrialized countries.

A second concern arises particularly from the struggles of many Southern countries to diversify their economies. They may need some leeway beyond that offered by the WTO to protect domestic industries. Other nations are chafing at the need for clarification of worker rights and maintenance of environmental standards. The WTO has established a committee on trade and environment, but this committee has made little progress in dealing with these issues. Some critics suggest that programs to build capacity and protect the environment should be negotiated as core elements of trade agreements.[17] In sum, there is much controversy surrounding WTO policies, processes, and activities.

Multinational Corporations

A multinational is a firm with foreign subsidiaries that extend the production and marketing of the firm beyond the boundaries of any one country. Multinationals are not involved only in exports; they send a package of technology, capital, managerial talent, and marketing skill abroad to carry out production in foreign countries. In many cases different stages of production are carried out in different countries. Multinationals have been in existence since the 1890s — Singer Corporation, American Bell, and Standard Oil, for example — but they have become powerful actors in the global arena only in the last forty years. Multinationals integrate production and marketing on an international scale. They can dominate markets because of size, access to financial resources, and control over technologies. Mobile and flexible, they make decisions with the interests of the firm as their primary objective, with little concern for the particular country, the environment, or the needs of international workers.

Many changes of the last several decades have encouraged the growth of multinationals as international economic actors. Technology and organizational sophistication have made expansion possible. Development of communications, transportation, and new techniques of management have permitted the centralization of decision making with the integration of far-flung production and marketing operations. Telecommunications, the computer, and all the opportunities emerging in this information age have facilitated the global work of the multinationals. The silicon chip inscribing electronic circuitry in a tiny space has been central to this economic transformation. Today's multinational world is populated by mergers of giants such as Exxon and Mobil, by names familiar in nearly every household — McDonald's, Coke, or Disney — and by cutting-edge high-tech firms such as Intel, king of computer chips; Microsoft, whose software encircles the world; and Cisco Systems, which makes the black boxes that tie the Internet together. At one and the same time corporations are consolidating and diversifying across national boundaries. Toyota Motor Corporation, Japan's largest car maker, for example, is increasing its stakes in the telecommunications industry. Toshiba, a large Japanese electronics firm, joined with the Swedish appliance giant Electrolux to bring out a new line of home appliances under the brand name "Electrolux by Toshiba" in order to expand sales in Japan. German, French, Italian, and U.S. telecommunications firms are engaged in endless maneuvering around alliances, hostile challenges, threats, bids, breakups, and takeovers.

In 1971 280 of the 500 largest multinationals were U.S.-based. By 1991 Europe topped the list with 168; the United States had 157 and Japan 119, with multinationals emerging in Korea, Taiwan, and Thailand.[18] According to the UN Conference on Trade and Development, some 40,000 transnational corporations and their foreign affiliates control two-thirds of global trade in goods and services. Most trade, however, is controlled by a few hundred giant corporations that are larger economically than most nations.[19] The growth of transnational corporate investments and the steady dispersal of the elements of production across many nations has transformed the system of trade so that much of it is generated within the multinational companies themselves, exporting and importing among their own foreign-based subsidiaries.

Finance Capital and Global Investors

A dramatic development took place in the 1970s and 1980s: an explosion in commercial banking as a source of finance for developing countries. In fact, the banks in the United States, Europe, and Japan replaced the multinational corporations as the major source of private foreign capital for developing countries. In 1970 investments by multinationals in developing countries were $3.5 billion while new bank loans totaled $2.7 billion. By the end of the decade bank loan disbursements of $48 billion had surpassed corporate flows of $13.5 billion. Interest income had become the dominant form of earnings for the industrialized nations from the developing countries. Thus there was a fundamental restructuring of financial relations between North and South. The movement of stocks, bonds, and currencies in global exchange markets has accelerated dramatically. The volume of financial trading across national borders is extraordinary, and it is largely transacted by approximately fifty of the world's largest banks and a handful of brokerage houses who invest on behalf of their clients.

Multinationals in North-South Relations

The Multinational Scorecard

What are the pros and cons of the multinational as a form of economic organization? This question is very difficult to answer in the aggregate. Multinationals may increase economic efficiency and stimulate growth or they may stifle growth locally, eliminate competition, and decrease efficiency. It all depends — on the country, the commodity or product, the multinational, the market. What we do know is that conflicts arise between the multinational and the host country in three areas: (1) matters of economic control, (2) matters of national political process, and (3) approaches to growth, welfare, and efficiency.

Why should multinational corporations pose a problem for developing countries? One reason is that they tend to dominate key industries, raw materials, or the primary commodity on which a country depends for foreign exchange — copper in Zambia, for example, or bauxite in Jamaica. Second, multinationals often represent a significant percentage of the largest and most powerful firms in economies of the South. Given their prominence in key industries, they inevitably have an impact on the Southern nation's economy. This fact leads to concerns that decisions crucial for economic growth and development are being made by firms whose decision-making centers are elsewhere and whose purposes have little to do with the well-being of that particular country.

All of this poses several dilemmas for the host government. On the one hand, the government wants to be able to regulate multinationals so as to maximize national benefits. On the other hand, they do not want to frighten away potential investors. The multinational may control resources that the country wants for development — oil drilling technology, for example — but the host government may not be able to draw up or enforce laws that will adequately regulate the foreign investment. Or, as is sometimes the case, the government may see ways to profit from an investment for which the costs are borne by a marginalized community without much influence over domestic power structures. For example, in Nigeria successive central governments have collaborated with Shell Oil regarding investments that have devastated the landscape and livelihoods of the Ogoni people, as discussed in chapter 7. Thus, the host government and the recipient community must look very closely at the type of business being established and what it brings to the developing country. We may be quite sure that the MNC will not be seeking access unless there is a clear advantage to doing so.

In what ways can a multinational have a favorable economic impact on a poor country? It can fill resource gaps by bringing in investment capital. It may contribute to foreign exchange earnings by generating exports. It may bring in new technology that improves the efficiency of production, and it may improve the quality of labor by training workers. The MNC will certainly create jobs, and it may even have a beneficial impact on overall welfare by providing housing, education, or health benefits for employees.

At the same time another set of arguments holds that the multinational is most likely to exploit the host country and perpetuate dependence. Multinationals do not bring in as much investment capital as supposed because they borrow on the local market, often competing successfully against local entrepreneurs for limited funds. Then, too, outflows of capital are high. Profits get returned to the home office and, in the process, gains may be disguised to avoid local taxes. Transfer pricing through intracompany trade may deprive the host country of tax revenues. The technology that is imported is often suitable for a capital-rich, labor-scarce economy, not the reverse, and may come at a very high cost. Thus the multinational may distort growth and create enclaves using capital-intensive technology while employing relatively few local citizens, absorbing local capital while destroying local business, and, in the long run, hindering local development.

Many countries of the South have taken firm steps toward careful management of multinationals operating within their boundaries. Three conditions can help these nations strategically. First, a governments' bargaining position improves vis-à-vis the investor who has a lot of money and infrastructure tied up in industry, mining, or manufacturing. Second, there is increasing competition for investment opportunities among the multinationals of the North — from Japan, the United States, and Europe. And, third, of course, the North continues to be dependent on some very important raw materials from the South, ranging from oil, to bauxite or copper, to the coffee propelling most of us to work every day.

Some governments have nationalized key industries. Others have created legislation and new structures to increase government control and host-country shares of proceeds. Still others have limited the sectors in which foreign investments are permitted. For example, in some countries, transport or public utilities are not sectors in which foreign multinationals may invest. Some have established state-owned corporations in basic industries such as petroleum or transportation. Others set limits on the amount of equity foreigners may hold in local companies. Many governments are getting very savvy about the ways they deal with multinationals. For example, they may give special tax advantages or exemptions from land use or labor regulations in order to provide incentives for investment in a particular arena.

These observations pertain to official policy. They do not address how elites may be benefiting privately from the presence of the multinationals. They do not address questions of redistribution of national income. They do not ask whether more astute management of multinationals by host governments will result in widespread benefits across many sectors of society or simply remain to benefit the privileged few. Billionaire families —

such as the Riadys of Indonesia in banking and real estate, the Tatas of India now diversified in eighty companies, or Kim Woo Choong's Daewoo Group from South Korea, with many billions in annual revenues — prosper, but others may not only fail to flourish, their well-being may actually decline.

Eyes on the Issues

If we return to the issues posed at the outset of this chapter, we can see that the multinationals are shaping them vigorously in several ways.

A Relentless Effort to Capture Markets

At the beginning of the twenty-first century, economic emphasis is on international markets, and in this realm, the multinational is a key player. Almost daily one reads of major corporate openings in new countries, mergers among the giants, and multinational takeovers. No company has been more symbolic of America's expanding global influence and the multinationals' relentless search for new markets than McDonald's, whose first restaurant opened in 1955 and whose 25,000th restaurant opened June 1999.[20] McDonald's operates in 115 countries on six continents and now has the McVeggie, a nonmeat hamburger, with an eye to capturing not only vegetarians but also the vast non–beef eating market of India.

Indeed, no market has been more intriguing to the multinationals than China's with its lure of more than 1 billion consumers. Not until 1978 at the end of China's Cultural Revolution did China begin in a very limited way to open its markets to foreign products. Investments in China are now coming from around the world, particularly from Hong Kong, Taiwan, South Korea, Japan, France, the Netherlands, Sweden, and the United States. In a recent year, foreign direct investment (FDI) amounted to approximately US $70 billion or 7 percent of GDP.[21] Now foreigners may even build retail stores in China, as the Japanese Yaohan Department Store Company did with 55 percent interest in a joint venture with a Chinese company.[22] Even though road and rail service are poor, tariffs are high on imports, laws are enforced inconsistently, negotiations and relationships are delicate, and political uncertainties exist, many corporations are still eager to take advantage of the welcome China has extended to foreign business and the enthusiasm with which the Chinese — even ordinary Chinese — have greeted foreign products. Coca-Cola built its first plant in Shanghai in 1927. It was absent between 1949 and 1979. when it reentered the Chinese market, and it now has more than twenty-eight bottling plants around the country. Coca-Cola has about 10 percent of the total nonalcoholic beverage market in China and 35 percent of the carbonated soft drink sales.[23] Johnson and Johnson not only has joint-venture factories in China but it also has wholly owned operations. Procter and Gamble opened its first shampoo plant in the southern city of Guangzhou in 1988 and now manufactures a broad cross-section of health and skin care products. Avon has "Avon ladies" selling cosmetics, and Nike manufactures sneakers in China through more than a dozen subcontractors, though largely for an export market. Adidas, Jansport, and Puma are there as well. Dell Computer Corporation, Motorola, and French telecom giant Alcatel are involved in electronics and communications. Foreign automobile manufacturers, including Volkswagen and Ford, are also producing cars in China. Not all has been rosy, however. Complexities are many and Occidental Petroleum Corporation stands as an illustration of the difficulties of investing in China. In the mid-1980s, Occidental initiated a joint venture in a coal mine in central China on which it lost up to $50 million before pulling out in 1991.[24]

While companies have been eager to gain a foothold in the vast Chinese market, they have also engaged in cutthroat competition to increase market share in other parts of the world. For example, in Venezuela in 1996, Coca-Cola scored a coup by securing a joint venture contract with the bottling firm that had been associated with its arch-rival, Pepsi, for five decades. Coke's market share in Venezuela jumped from 10 percent to 55 percent.[25] Such competition exists not only in foods, beverages, and personal care products but in high tech and other industries as well.

Who Wins? Who Loses?

The winners are quite evident. According to data released by the Internal Revenue Service in June 2003, average income of the wealthiest four hundred taxpayers in the United States in 2000 was more than $150 million, and their share of income more than doubled in the period between 1992 and 2000.[26] Others are affected quite differently, and none more so than laborers in the textile sweatshops around the world. Saipan provides an example. Saipan is the largest of fourteen volcanic islands making up the Commonwealth of Northern Mariana Islands and thus has been a United States Trust Territory since the end of World War II. Residents of Saipan are U.S. citizens.

The garment industry got established on Saipan in the early 1980s as a result of U.S. federal legislation permitting manufacturers on Saipan to export clothing to the mainland duty free and largely without quotas. It was not long before a variety of manufacturers had factories located on Saipan: Arrow, Liz Claiborne, The Gap, Montgomery Ward, Geoffrey Beene, Eddie Bauer, and Levi's, to name some of the prominent ones.[27] To support this effort (that in 1993 involved an estimated $279 million worth of wholesale clothing shipped to the United States) are approximately forty thousand foreign laborers, many of whom come from the Philippines, China, and Bangladesh. Since the islands are exempt from the U.S. minimum wage, the Commonwealth sets its own minimum wage that only in 1999 moved from $2.15 (the rate since 1984) to $3.05 an hour.[28] Moreover, most laborers live in cramped barracks under difficult conditions. Often, recruiters lure laborers with false promises that they are being taken to America and will be paid top wages. Some have paid several thousand dollars as recruitment fees and land, not on the shores of the mainland United States, but in Saipan where they live and work in appalling conditions, a finding of the U.S. Occupational Safety and Health Administration.[29] These miserable exploitative conditions are reminiscent of indentured servitude. Recently former and current garment workers, labor unions, and human rights groups filed lawsuits against U.S. clothing companies and their contractors in Saipan. They alleged that the companies violated the anti-peonage and indentured servitude laws of the United States and broke international laws based on human rights and falsely advertised their produces as "made in the USA." A total of twenty-six U.S.-based retailers and manufacturers have been sued. Eighteen, including Calvin Klein, Gymboree, and J. Crew, have settled; others have yet to do so.

Another exploited group that is not prospering in the face of globalization and the onslaught of powerful multinationals is small farming households around the world. Brazil's small tobacco farmers provide an illustration. Brazil is the leading exporter of tobacco, and four companies dominate its tobacco market. Before the era of global competition there were a number of other, smaller tobacco companies, but they have been swallowed up by conglomerates that now set the prices among themselves, rather than buying leaves on the free market. This has brought much hardship to the 160,000 tobacco growers.[30] The tobacco companies have legal advantages and tax incentives to help them compete in the world economy. In 1998, Souza Cruz, which controls 84 percent of the Brazilian cigarette market, increased profits by 40 percent, despite substantial inflation and cost increases for the growers, while prices obtained by the growers for their tobacco remained stagnant. In effect, the farmers have no bargaining power; there is no "free" market, and the farmers absorb all the risk. Farmers will likely be pushed off the land that they are selling in desperation to make up for continued losses. Large companies will purchase the land, and the farmers who stay behind will work as laborers on land that formerly belonged to them.

This scenario is occurring in many places around the world because governments do not protect small farmers who are often deeply in debt and seek investment from foreign firms. The multinational brings its clout to the bargaining table, and in the process the smallholder suffers. Examples include Kenya where small farmers sell out to large-scale commercial flower or horticulture firms such as Brooke Bond. Another is Costa Rica where the emphasis on nontraditional agricultural exports (NTAE) is forcing some farmers to sell out to Ticofruit in order to pay off debts encountered while trying to make the move into these new commodities.

The Information Age Bonanza

The computer age and electronic potentials create unimaginable opportunities for worldwide economic control in almost all spheres. As companies continue with their global merging, eliminating small players and gathering market share, we need to look particularly at what is happening in information technology. The telecommunications field, for example, is undergoing significant globalization. Mexico's largest phone company is now part owner of an energy and fiber-optic company based in Tulsa, Oklahoma, and the two companies are offering long-distance service in the United States and Mexico. Cellular phone technology is rapidly making telecommunications mobile. Already cellular phones have the ability to transmit e-mail and faxes, and soon they will be able to pull data off the Internet and carry video and graphics as well, according to Nokia, the world's number-one mobile phone vendor.[31] At the end of 2001, Nokia had eighteen production facilities in 10 countries, research and development offices in 15 countries, and sales in over 130 countries.

On the one hand there is tremendous innovation in this field, and we all benefit from the convenience and adaptability of these new technologies. On the other hand, there are emerging controls and monopolies that may, in the long run, diminish the creative inventiveness of the technology field. Several examples from communications and related fields are of great interest. The Internet has spawned alliances and battles among music industry titans of the United States, Britain, and Japan that are scrambling to control the distribution of music over the Internet. The British-Dutch publisher, Reed Elsevier, and its Dutch competitor, Wolters Kluwer, merged to create a global publisher of professional and trade journals. The companies with combined 1996 sales of $6.6 billion are now making the large investments needed for the change from print publishing to electronic publishing. The company may thrive, but the outcome may not necessarily be beneficial to the general public for whom an open and competitive system, not fettered by information-age oligopolies, is more likely to be advantageous. All of these high-tech information-age questions may seem remote to many countries of the Global South struggling with far more basic problems of poverty, health, livelihoods, and food security. Nevertheless, they do shape the nature and structure of our evolving global system and determine who will reap the benefits in years ahead.

Trade and the Global South

Commodity Exports

More than fifty developing countries depend on three or fewer commodities for more than half of their export earnings.[32] Dependency is most pronounced in sub-Saharan Africa where seventeen countries rely on non-oil primary commodities for three-fourths or more of their export earnings. In Burundi, coffee alone accounts for up to 80 percent of export earnings. In Burkina Faso, cotton accounts for half the export earnings, and Ghana relies on cocoa for about one-fourth its earnings. Improved earnings from commodities could make a substantial contribution to development, but there are many obstacles to achieving this objective. Trade may be a key to economic betterment, but poor countries have little control within the global economy. World prices for most primary commodities show an unmistakable downward trend. As Table 5.1 reveals, prices for nineteen major export commodities were more than 20 percent lower in real terms in 2000 than in 1980. For eight of these commodities, the decline exceeded 50 percent. It is not difficult

Table 5.1. Price Decreases for Primary Commodities, Real Terms, 1980–2000

0–10%	10.1–20%	20.1–30%	30.1–40%	40.1–50%	50.1–60%	60.1–70%	70.1–80%
Banana	Iron ore	Phosphate	Copper	Coconut	Lead	Coffee	Cocoa
Tea		rock	Groundnut	oil	Palm oil	Rice	Sugar
		Fertilizer	oil	Cotton	Rubber		Tin
		Aluminum	Fishmeal	Maize			
			Soybean	Wheat			

Source: IMF, *International Financial Statistics Yearbook*, various issues. Oxfam International, *Rigged Rules and Double Standards: Trade, Globalization and the Fight against Poverty* (Brussels: Oxfam International, 2002), 151.

to imagine the implications both for individual nations and individual households.

Uganda, for example, exported roughly the same amount of coffee in 2001 as it did in 1995, but earned one-fourth of the export revenue. In Ethiopia, one small farmer laments, "Five to seven years ago, I was producing seven sacks of red cherry (unprocessed coffee) and this was enough to buy clothes, medicines, services and to solve so many problems. But now even if I sell four times as much, it is impossible to cover all my expenses."[33]

Trade restrictions and the constraints of structural adjustment have compounded problems with primary commodities. Several factors are important. First, there is little opportunity for countries of the South to participate in the processing, transportation, marketing, and distribution of their primary commodities. Most commodities are exported from developing countries in unprocessed form, which means that the value added by processing remains in industrialized countries. Ghana provides an illustration. A major world producer of cocoa, Ghana has often found itself in a situation in which the price of chocolate on the world market is going up while the price of the cocoa bean is going down. The consumer may be paying more for Lady Godiva or Swiss chocolates but Cadbury's and Nestles are reaping the benefit. Profit results from the processing and refining of the cocoa bean, but it is extremely difficult for a Ghanaian firm to break into that aspect of production. Developing countries account for more than 90 percent of cocoa-bean production, less than half of cocoa-butter production, one-third of cocoa powder, and 4 percent of chocolate. Because each stage of processing adds value, developing countries, even though they may dominate the early stages of cocoa production, receive only a small share of the final value. Germany grinds more cocoa than Côte d'Ivoire, the world's largest producer, and Great Britain grinds far more than Ghana.[34] Data from UNCTAD's *The Least Developed Countries Report 2002* reveal that

> the commodity-exporting LDCs are failing to capture more value added through quality improvement, product differentiation and local processing.... [I]n fact there is clear evidence that there has been a collapse of commodity processing in LDCs over the last twenty years. In terms of domestic processing, instead of moving up the value chain, the LDCs are sliding down it. This has actually occurred in both commodity-exporting LDCs and those exporting manufactures and services.[35]

Second, prices are likely to be volatile. If the bottom drops out of the coffee market or the copper market, there are no protections for the small producer. Zambia earns approximately 90 percent of export earnings from one commodity, copper. A boom in copper prices may be beneficial, but a bust, such as Zambia experienced in the mid-1970s, provided a real shock to the economic system. Stabilized commodity prices could help the development process, but consumers don't want stabilization when prices are declining and producers are opposed when they are rising. Hence securing commodity stabilization agreements is very difficult.

Third, there are various tariff and nontariff barriers against exports from developing countries, especially with processed products. Tariffs are taxes on imports of products into a country. They increase the price of imported goods on the domestic market and therefore protect domestic producers. They also provide revenues for governments. Nontariff barriers include quantitative restrictions such as import quotas, seasonal import restrictions, rules of origin, and a wide range of product standards. They can be just as effective as tariffs in restricting exports from developing countries. Processed foods are particularly subject to tariffs and tariff escalation, which is of particular concern to developing countries. Rice can go into the European Union countries free of duty, but it faces a stiff tariff when it is imported as processed rice or rice products. Wood products, palm oil, and other primary commodities face similar treatment. Kenya is one of the world's leading coffee exporters, yet for decades, a camper on safari in Kenya wanting easily prepared instant coffee had to purchase a British import, with the value added in the United Kingdom.

Terms of Trade, the Composition of Trade, and Comparative Advantage

These concepts are important to understand when trying to unravel issues surrounding trade and developing countries. For the vast number of developing countries, terms of trade are frequently deteriorating vis-à-vis the industrialized countries. The value of primary commodities on which they rely to earn money for imports does not manage to keep up with the cost of importing manufactured goods they require from the North. There is a downward trend in real commodity prices in terms of their capacity to buy manufactured goods. Over time a greater amount of a nation's agricultural exports is needed to purchase the same amount of manufactured imports. Thus, the bales of jute which might at one time have purchased a truck for Bangladesh are now inadequate, purchasing only the equivalent of a couple of tires. If Bangladesh could diversify its exports, perhaps it would not matter how many bales of jute were required, but its choices are limited. Furthermore, the neoliberal model of comparative advantage tends to keep it in the same relative position. If Honduras produces wonderful fruit, it should keep producing fruit, sell it abroad, and buy the things it needs. Fruit, however, may not provide the level of income that Honduras needs if it is to build a transportation infrastructure, educational system, medical establishment, and telecommunications industry. Hence, it may not be very appreciative of the concept of relying on its current comparative advantage, and may wish to diversify its economy so as to have more trading options. Of the fifteen poorest commodity-exporting countries, thirteen have experienced a significant deterioration in their terms of trade over the past forty years.

At issue with a number of commodities is a conflict between the United States' philosophical support for free trade and its actual inclination to subsidize U.S. farmers heavily. In the 1980s a farm bill as high as $430 billion in some years led to — among other things — heavily subsidized sugar and rice to be exported at artificially low prices, and causing production in the Philippines and Jamaica to drop substantially. U.S. support for its sugar beet farmers was not up for discussion. (American farmers were under duress, and 250,000 American farmers went out of business in the 1980s.) The U.S. Congress catered to corporate interests, protected farmers and home industries, while preaching the ideology of free trade to other nations and demanding strict adherence to it in the IMF-imposed structural adjustment policies, all the while failing to "walk the talk." Winner of the 2001 Nobel Prize in Economics, Joseph Stiglitz asserts,

> The attack on American-style globalization . . . is fed by a perception of American hypocrisy and the unfairness of the new global regime. The Uruguay Round forced developing countries to open up their markets to the products of the developed countries, while leaving in place protection and subsidies for many of the goods produced by the developed world. . . . [36]

Newly Industrializing Countries

Some countries have managed to diversify their economies by employing a strategy of export-oriented industrialization (EOI). They emphasize production for export, often getting started with manufacture of clothing and footwear. Four countries or city-states that have followed EOI policies and become known as the NICs or newly industrializing countries are Taiwan, South Korea, Hong Kong, and Singapore. The NICs' successful export-led growth has occurred in the context of land reform (South Korea and Taiwan), integration of rural and urban domestic markets, and relatively easy access to the large U.S. market offered to allies against communism in the 1960s and 1970s. Both the Taiwan and South Korean economies were able to utilize the Vietnam War as a stimulus to economic development through U.S. purchases and contracts. Throughout the 1960s and 1970s the world market favored the NICs. They were thriving in an era of few global trade rules and faced almost none of today's pressures to open their borders to capital flows. They combined an EOI approach with high levels of tariff and nontariff barriers, public ownership of large segments of banking and industry, export subsidies, and restriction on capital flows, including foreign direct investment. Such policies are either precluded by today's trade rules or discouraged by IMF and World Bank policies or sanctions.[37]

Regional Economic Organizations

Regional economic organizations have been established in several parts of the world in order to promote trade among neighbors. They constitute an important, if sometimes controversial, tool of economic growth and exchange.

The North American Free Trade Agreement (NAFTA) that was getting under way at the beginning of the 1990s creates a pact among Canada, Mexico, and the United States to eliminate various taxes and regulations, allowing goods and services to be sold more freely across all three nations. It does not involve common tariffs and other trade barriers toward the rest of the world, nor a common foreign policy or effort to combine currencies or other policies. NAFTA covers goods and services produced in the United States, Canada, and Mexico that must be assembled partly or entirely from North American components in order to qualify for tariff-free treatment. The nationality of a factory's owner is not at issue. Taking effect on January 1, 1994, NAFTA phases out tariffs over a five- to fifteen-year period. It dismantles Mexico's virtual ban on American banks and allows American securities firms into the Mexican market. (Mexican banks were already allowed to buy American banks.) Mexico is able to retain its ban on foreign ownership of oil and natural gas reserves, but American drilling companies would be allowed to share in some of the profits from striking oil in Mexico.

Some troublesome issues have been dealt with in side agreements, including penalties for not enforcing environmental laws, investigations concerning labor abuses, arbitration for charges of discriminatory treatment on investments, and procedures for determining issues pertaining to consumer safety on such things as pesticide use. The North American Development Bank was established to work both on behalf of communities hurt by the pact and on environmental clean-up projects along the U.S.-Mexico border.[38]

NAFTA inspired avid supporters and vehement critics. The avid supporters said that NAFTA would produce an economic renaissance. More judicious in their comments were three hundred economists ranging from conservative to liberal who signed a letter to President Clinton supporting the North American Free Trade Agreement.[39] In general, these economists agreed that the impact on the U.S. economy would be small and the impact on Mexico would strengthen the hand of a pro-American, pro–free market government in Mexico and help Mexico's citizens. Further, it might also reduce pressures on illegal immigration. Critics said that NAFTA would destroy jobs, cut wages, and damage the environment. Others suggested that NAFTA would favor big business and the owners of multinationals while causing job loss for domestic U.S. laborers as U.S. companies cut back on employment and relocate south of the border.

What in fact has happened? Over the past decade, concern has been growing that corporate rights, as defined through NAFTA, are impinging on development and environment policies. For example, regulations forbidding expropriation have been manipulated by corporations to hamper the Canadian government from protecting the public vis-à-vis a toxic petroleum additive, and the Mexican government from maintaining minimum international standards of public protection on a hazardous waste disposal site.

The impact of heavily subsidized corn exports from the United States to Mexico that undercut the maize production of small farmers there is an increasingly tense issue. According to the Institute for Agriculture and Trade Policy in Minneapolis, American corn sells in Mexico for 25 percent less than its cost.[40] Mexican farmers through their farmer organizations are advocating a renegotiation of NAFTA, indicating that Mexico has lowered its import barriers and agricultural products are flooding in from the United States and destroying their livelihoods. American farmers get 20 percent of their income from subsidies; American subsidies are at record levels, and in 2002, Congress passed a farm bill that included a $40 billion increase in subsidies to large grain and cotton farmers.[41] No wonder Mexico's small farmers are protesting.

Other regional organizations are not as fully and formally developed as NAFTA, but progress is occurring in many parts of the globe. The Asian Pacific Economic Cooperation group (APEC) hopes to settle issues leading to free trade by the year 2020. The potential of this region is enormous, as we observe in the discussion in chapter 8 of the emerging East Asian agro-food system and the reorganization of relations of production and consumption among these nations. In Latin America there is MERCOSUR, and in the Caribbean, CARIBCOM. Africa has the East African Community (EAC), the Southern Africa Development Community (SADC), and the Economic Organization of West African States (ECOWAS). All of these economic organizations have the potential for strengthening regional relationships and providing a counterbalance to the economic North-South divide, the poverty curtain described in chapter 1.

The Boom in International Banking, the Debt Crisis, and the Financial Crisis of the 1990s

As noted at the outset of this chapter, commercial banks have become a major source of finance for developing countries, and, in turn, interest has become the dominant form of earnings for the industrialized nations from the developing countries. Why did this happen? Why did commercial banks become enthusiastic about lending to developing countries? The answer can be found in the oil crises of 1973 and 1979. In 1973–74 the Organization of Petroleum Exporting Countries (OPEC) raised oil prices fourfold, with a second sharp rise following five years later. Oil, of course, is the critical source of energy in industrial societies, and the industrialized economies of the North were highly dependent on imported oil. The impact of these price increases on the industrialized countries was electrifying, leading to rationed gas and, over time, massive efforts to become less dependent and more self-sufficient in terms of oil supply. The Third World countries, however, suffered the most hardship. Suddenly they were faced with astronomic bills for the oil they were importing to support their fragile efforts to industrialize. As Nyerere of Tanzania emphasized, "for the amount of money with which we used to buy thirteen barrels of oil, we now only get one."[42]

Meanwhile, OPEC's actions led to vastly increased foreign currency earnings for the major oil-producing states, and these returns were finding their way into the money markets of the industrialized countries. The commercial banks in the United States, Europe, and Japan recycled the petrodollars to finance development in Third World countries. The industrialized countries were not growing rapidly, while the Third World countries were eager for development funds. The banks were eager to find new lending opportunities for these monies coming in from the oil-producing states and calculated the risks, profits, and opportunities accordingly. First, they diversified risks over a large number of borrowers. Second, they devised schemes such as rolling over a grant or refinancing so that a nation could get a new loan to repay an old one. Third, they assumed that their governments would bail them out if necessary. The largest lenders were the big banks in the United States and the United Kingdom, and the major recipients were the biggest economies among the developing countries, particularly Mexico, Brazil, South Korea, Argentina, Venezuela, Indonesia, and the Philippines. By the early 1980s, Mexico and Brazil not only had twice as much debt as the third in rank, South Korea, but they held a high proportion in commercial bank debt and were paying high rates of interest. That is, they were paying over 10 percent in interest whereas countries borrowing from the World Bank would be paying just over 3 percent. Meanwhile, the banks holding the debt were extended well beyond their total assets and were highly vulnerable. By 1980 all developing countries were facing financial difficulties, including deteriorating terms of trade and rising interest rates.

What Happened in Latin America?

For about fifteen years from 1960 through 1974, Latin American countries had enjoyed accelerated economic growth based on expanding private and public investment. Then in the mid-1970s, the oil crisis changed the situation and economic growth slowed down. These nations, however, continued to have easy access to international credit because of the recycled petrodollars that were coming their way. By 1980 in Latin America, debt had reached $400 billion and was increasing by more than 20 percent a year. Debt servicing — the interest paid on the loan — was about half the value of exports; most of the debt was short-term, owed to commercial banks that had variable floating interest rates.[43]

Under these conditions, debt interest and amortization took most of these countries' foreign exchange, leaving little for development. The banks continued to lend to these indebted countries, but primarily to enable them to maintain their debt service payments through bridge loans — that is, new loans to enable them to repay the principal owed and interest required on the old loans. Thus the debt continued to rise but there was little investment in the economy to build a productive capacity and to break the cycle.[44] Moreover, there was a sharp increase in private credit sources versus official sources such as governments and multilateral agencies, and a sharp rise in short-term obligations maturing in less than one year. The only way to break the cycle was through cutting imports or increasing exports or both. Meanwhile, in the early 1980s there was a global economic downturn with "stagflation" — inflation without growth — in the North. Demand for commodity exports fell, and prices plummeted as well.

In 1982 Mexico announced that it could not cover the servicing on its $100 billion owed to foreign banks. Given the widespread exposure of the foreign banks, there was a threat of global financial collapse. A chain reaction ensued as major banks realized the extent of their vulnerability and cut back loans in all of Latin America so that they were making them primarily for the purpose of helping the debtor countries meet interest payments as they became due. Given low levels of trade and depressed exports, this made a very difficult situation for the Latin American countries. All tried to cut back on imports while increasing exports.

Mexico slashed imports and introduced conditions of great austerity: cutting inflation dramatically, selling off state industries, denationalizing banks, and opening up to foreign investment. Mexico, Brazil, and Argentina ultimately sought cooperation and not confrontation in finding approaches to deal with the crisis and to renegotiate the debt. By 1989 Mexico signed a favorable agreement with its creditors for debt reduction and new loans with repayment obligations to be spread over the long term (fourteen years) rather than short term.

What Was Happening in Other Regions?

In 1982 when the debt crisis broke, the developing countries owed $700 billion. In 1999 the long-term debt of 137 developing countries or countries in transition reached $2.47 trillion, over four and one-half times greater than at the onset of the debt crisis.[45] Debt and debt servicing have risen more rapidly for sub-Saharan African countries since 1982 than for other regions. If debtor countries cannot rely on trade surpluses and have low capital investment, they simply cannot grow sufficiently to repay the loan and service the debt. They are in a vicious cycle of economic stagnation and poverty. Debt rescheduling becomes a way of life that can rapidly escalate the amount owed. Perhaps more important, lives of ordinary people deteriorate noticeably. Real personal income declines dramatically. Cuts in food subsidies, health services, and other social investment affect the poor most acutely.

Thus in the poor countries, the outflow of debt repayment continued to deepen the crisis of poverty. In fact, at one point, an estimated two dollars of every three dollars in aid from the World Bank's concessional facility, the IDA, was coming back to the World Bank in the form of debt payments.[46] The implications are clear. In Zambia, for example, the government spent $37 million on primary school education between 1990 and 1993, a period of crisis in the educational system caused by chronic underfunding, while at the same time it spent $1.3 billion on debt repayments.[47]

In an article in *Foreign Affairs* in 1987, one analyst asserted, "The combination of slow worldwide growth, lagging purchasing power of commodity exports, and debt servicing burdens spells a sobering and perhaps bleak outlook for commodity exporters in general, and for the heavily indebted among the developing countries in particular."[48] In 1998, sub-Saharan Africa paid $1.41 to creditors for every $1 received in grants. Until the HIPC Initiative, it seems that not a lot had changed in the intervening eleven years.

The Heavily Indebted Poor Countries (HIPC) Initiative

The Heavily Indebted Poor Countries (HIPC) Initiative, established in 1996, and doubled in 1999 through the Enhanced HIPC Initiative, arranges comprehensive debt relief for heavily indebted countries that are already eligible for International Development Association assistance. To be eligible a country must face an unsustainable debt burden, beyond available debt-relief mechanisms, as well as other vulnerabilities such as limited diversity in products available for export, low foreign currency reserves, and limited resources. Forty-one poor countries are considered the most heavily indebted, of which 80 percent are in Africa. Some pay 60 percent of their annual budget in debt service, which leaves little to invest in development programs.

A country seeking debt relief through the HIPC Initiative must arrange with the IMF for a Structural Adjustment Loan in which it will agree to meet the various targets required of it. The IMF will provide a new ten-year, 0.5 percent interest loan for which the recipient must adhere to the macroeconomic program for three years. The plan includes various structural reforms as well as evidence of a portion of the budget spent on primary health and education. By spring 2002, twenty-seven countries were receiving debt relief through the HIPC Initiative, of which twenty-three were in sub-Saharan Africa. Eventually it is anticipated that some thirty-four countries will receive at least partial debt relief under the HIPC Initiative.

There are shortcomings to the HIPC Initiative, but it is a move in the right direction. For the present its conditions are quite rigid and strict, and many countries needing help are not likely to become eligible. Some critics suggest that the IFI staff administering HIPC "live in a world of statistics and bureaucratic definitions rather than one in which hunger, deprivation, and death have real meaning."[49] Sources of funding remain an issue. The World Bank has led the way by offering to contribute $500 million from its resources (that would have gone to IDA) into a Multilateral Debt Facility, but additional contributions appear to be more problematic.

Some discussion occurred around the concept of a Year of Jubilee in which the third millennium could have opened by forgiving all debt incurred by the poorest countries. While there were many critics of this proposal, its attraction lay in the evidence of the preceding eighteen years indicating that the poorest countries were unable to pay off their debts under the current debt reduction arrangements and policy prescriptions.[50] Clearly something new needed to be tried to enable countries to get on with the important work of development. The proposal had the endorsement of Pope John Paul II who in his pastoral letter, "The Coming of the Third Millennium," appealed for a rapid solution to the question of international debt — reducing it substantially, if not canceling it outright, given the consequences for the economies of so many nations and the living conditions of so many people.[51] While the proposed debt forgiveness was never a guest at the celebrations for the new century, out of this effort the Jubilee 2000 Movement was formed. This coalition of many organizations has sustained public pressure and advocacy on the topic of debt relief.

Finally two related and important points are useful to identify. First is the need for economic and political reforms in many debtor countries. Second is the continuing need for a new inflow of capital. No long-term solution to the debt question is possible without a mixture of economic and political reform in the debtor countries and additional fresh capital, both of which are needed to assure economic growth. Perhaps, in welcoming the new century, a global community could introduce a new type of conditionality requiring commitment to equitable development and commitment to decreased military spending.

The Asian Financial Crisis of the 1990s

A financial upheaval which began in Thailand in mid-1997 and swept through much of Asia was labeled by President Clinton in his State of the Union address, January 1999, as "the most serious financial crisis in half a century." The 1990s had seen a convergence of the interests of the American investor and the needs and opportunities for investment and development across Asia. In 1980, fewer than 1 percent of pension fund assets in the United States were invested abroad, but by 1997 that figure had risen to 17 percent.[52] As part of the globalization process, Asian Third World markets became known as "emerging markets" and became increasingly attractive not only to pension funds, but to banks from the United States, Europe, and Japan and major brokerage companies. They poured money into the emerging markets of Asia between 1990 and 1995. In fact, a flood of capital poured into five countries: Indonesia, Malaysia, the Philippines, South Korea, and Thailand. All reports were bullish in those years, despite evidence of slowing exports, bad loans, and overexpansion. By 1996, a year before the crisis began, capital was beginning to flee from Thailand for banks in Switzerland, London, and New York. However, not until 1997 was there a net outflow from the five Asian countries that had been the recipients of the flood of capital investment. At that point the three excesses became evident: excess borrowing, excess investment, and excess capacity with factories and equipment kept idle because of lower-than-expected demand.[53]

With Thailand's economy in a financial self-destruct mode, it was not long before the currencies fell in the other Asian countries that had situations similar to Thailand's. Indonesia and South Korea accepted bailouts. In both cases the United States contributed (which it had been unwilling to do with the earlier case of Thailand), and in both cases critics noted that the bailout bolstered the Western banks, hurting the countries they are lending to, and benefiting the foreigners who lent to them.[54] Meanwhile tens of thousands of investors were liquidating their holdings in emerging markets. The impacts were felt as far away as Russia, Brazil, and Argentina.

A report of the World Bank released in December 1998 concluded that global investors who lent money to developing nations with abandon, and Asian officials who were eager to absorb the cash, bore significant blame for the financial crisis. The report also indicated that the Bank, the IMF, and the U.S. government bore responsibility for mishandling it. They had urged the stressed nations of Thailand, Indonesia, and South Korea to raise interest rates in order to reassure investors and stabilize currencies, but the strategy backfired, stabilizing the currencies at the cost of plunging the countries into deep recessions with substantial unemployment. Thousands of small businesses were sent into bankruptcy.[55]

What exactly happened? The heart of the problem seemed to be the surge of capital flows. Investors speculated on stocks and real estate and built up large "bubble" economies. American bankers and money managers poured billions of dollars into these so-called emerging markets. Then when the crisis hit, American officials insisted on tough measures like budget cuts and high interest rates that many argue made things worse.[56]

The downturn had enormous social implications. There was an explosive mix of soaring unemployment, spreading poverty, and rising social instability. In Indonesia violent clashes occurred between soldiers and students and between Christians and Muslims. In Malaysia demonstrators protested against Prime Minister Mahathir Mohamad for imprisonment of and trumped-up charges against his deputy prime minister. In Thailand an overvalued currency led to alarming trade deficits, crisis, and panic that affected nearly everyone. A 1998 report by the International Labor Organization of the UN specified that the "social costs of the Asian economic crisis are far higher than initial estimates and are dramatically worsening."[57]

Rethinking Global Economic Structures

Countries all over the world have become enmeshed in the international economy with all the complications that the dominance of finance and technology now pose for it. In a sense, the financial markets are driving the global economy. In a typical day, the total amount of money changing hands in the world's foreign exchange markets alone is $1.5 trillion, an eightfold increase since 1986 and equal to total world trade for four months.[58] American, European, and Japanese banks, brokerages, insurance companies, and hedge funds have sought financial liberalization and open financial markets in order to facilitate investments in new opportunities around the world. Globalization now gives just about everyone who owns some stocks, has a retirement fund, or has some life insurance a financial stake in activities almost anywhere.

The U.S. government has promoted financial liberation, directing its efforts at Asia largely because Asia is perceived to be a lucrative market for American banks and investment firms. Yet, some countries are too small to absorb surges in capital inflows, or might be devastated by a sudden outflow of money or simply not have the capital controls, the banking regulations, or the legal system to manage large amounts of foreign capital. To some analysts, this does not matter if the "market is working," but one must also ask — working for whom? The West, says Stiglitz, has "driven the globalization agenda, ensuring that it garners a disproportionate share of the benefits, at the expense of the developing world."[59]

More broadly, the industrialized North, and in particular the United States, has been strongly committed to a free-market ideology with its free flow of capital and the notion that both are central to achieving economic growth and prosperity. Yet, this commitment has been largely one-sided. Through their control over international financial institutions, the United States and other industrialized countries have forced the developing countries to open their markets to products from the industrialized nations while tightly controlling the entry of products, such as textiles and agricultural commodities, from developing countries. They have provided billions in subsidies to farmers in the North, making it very difficult for farmers in the South to compete. If we are honest with ourselves, we must recognize that the protesters of Seattle, Genoa, and other places — along with the organizations working tirelessly to demonstrate the unfairness of the "rules of the game" established by the World Bank, the IMF, and the WTO — are the ones who are now forcing greater public accountability on the part of these institutions. Increasingly we see that IFIs largely serve the financial and business interests of the North and are often arrogant and self-serving.

Many suggest that the underlying problem is found in the financial structures created at Bretton Woods half a century ago. These structures are no longer functional in today's global economy with its high-speed exchanges of information and explosion of investment capital circulating throughout the world with dizzying speed wherever the owner finds the highest return. Few are clear on the next steps that might stabililze markets while fostering economic growth and equitable development. The public outcry against globalization, observed at Seattle and Genoa, is accompanied by fundamental concerns about a variety of specific economic issues: commodity prices, controls on currency movements, fair labor practices, rights to engage in collective bargaining, and transparency in business and trade transactions. These require reform of global financial structures. The new round of trade negotiations at Doha, Qatar, launched in November 2001 reflects a beginning in redressing some of the imbalances of the past and focusing more squarely on the concerns of the developing countries. Certainly efforts to rethink the overwhelming international debt accrued by many countries is another important step. Without some form of debt relief, many countries are mired in repaying the interest on past loans, some of which simply benefited the private coffers of dictators pledged to support the West during the Cold War. They cannot initiate a process of economic growth. Debt simply reinforces the cycles of economic stagnation and broadens poverty. For the least developed countries the situation has been identified as a poverty trap in which there is significant commodity dependence, the build-up of an unsustainable external debt, and the emergence of an aid/debt service system, sometimes labeled the "debt game."[60]

The continuing vulnerability of the Global South to reliance on primary commodities; the increased vulnerability of low-wage, labor-intensive ghettoes; the new vulnerabilities to international financial capital flows; and the deepening vulnerabilities to the power of Northern governments and institutions to shape their economies and polities are cause for concern for people of the Global South. They are also cause for concern for people of the North who are beginning to recognize the links between acute poverty, social upheaval, anger and hostility toward Northern nations and institutions, and the urgent need for social and economic justice.

Chapter 6

Economic Realities
and Local Perspectives

Rural Livelihoods, Debt and Drugs,
and Globalizing Industries

Most of the time those of us who reside in the Global North look at economic issues from our own perspective. We are delighted that the price of a pound of coffee has been declining; we welcome inexpensive shirts and blouses stitched beyond our borders; we are thrilled that raspberries from Guatemala are available in our supermarkets; and we love receiving roses on Valentine's Day. We don't think much about the implications of these items for the cultivators and factory laborers who have made these products available to us. This chapter focuses on the implications of globalization for ordinary citizens in the Global South. The first part presents some comparative statistics about income and lifestyles across the globe. The second part provides glimpses of rural livelihoods in four different communities in Kenya, the Philippines, Nepal, and Honduras. These communities are typical of broad swaths of the country in which they are located, and all have been touched by globalization processes. Third, we examine a specific and wrenching case: Bolivian peasants engaged in coca production whose lives are enmeshed in the global drug and debt crisis. This case demonstrates the complexities of globalization, its impacts at all scales of political economy from local to global, and the vulnerability of poor farming households to the vagaries of outside forces. The last part considers globalizing industries from the perspective of their impact on selected developing countries and on the men and women who live and work there, whether smallholders, contract farmers, factory workers, wage laborers, or consumers. This chapter should help clarify the conditions, the context, opportunities, and obstacles

181

experienced by ordinary people in the Global South as they go about securing their livelihoods.

Defining the Problem:
Stagnant or Worsening Economic Conditions

In 1998, 3.5 billion (58 percent) of the Earth's 6 billion people lived in the world's sixty-three poorest countries.[1] Thirty-seven of these sixty-three poorest nations are in Africa. The 3.5 billion people produced an average per capita GNI of $520. If one lops off 10 percent from the number of income-deprived people to represent local elites, then there are roughly 3.2 billion income-deprived people — still more than 50 percent of the world's population — living in a state of stagnant or worsening economic and social development. To illustrate these discrepancies more dramatically, Figure 6.1 shows change in per capita GNI from 1970 to 2000 for the world's fifty-two richest and sixty-three poorest nations. It suggests that while the world's wealthy are leaping forward aggressively in their accumulation of income and treasure, the world's poor are locked into economic stagnation.

Per capita GNI is not the only indicator that poverty is deepening. In a major review of global poverty, the International Fund for Agricultural Development (IFAD) found a continuing expansion of those living in absolute poverty. In 1965, 511 million people worldwide lived in a state of total deprivation; by 1988 the number had risen to 712 million, with African nations bearing much of the burden of the increase.[2] For a local example, in Kenya, the number of people living below the poverty line in rural areas increased from 3.5 million to 10 million from 1965 to 1988, a threefold increase in absolute numbers. A follow-up study notes a continuing rise from 11.5 million absolute poor in 1994 to 12.6 million Kenyans in 1997.[3] Still another measure, this time from the World Bank, demonstrated that for sub-Saharan Africa, those living on less than $1 a day increased from 180 million to 219 million between 1987 and 1993. This figure represents almost a third of sub-Saharan Africa's 700 million people.[4] The United Nations Development Programme (UNDP) notes that the number worldwide living on less than $1 a day was 1.3 billion in 1993, an increase of 100 million from 1987.[5]

Throughout the 1990s the lavish wealth accumulating in the industrialized countries was not reflected in the countries of the South where

Figure 6.1. Per Capita GNI 1970–2000:
A Growing Gap between Rich and Poor

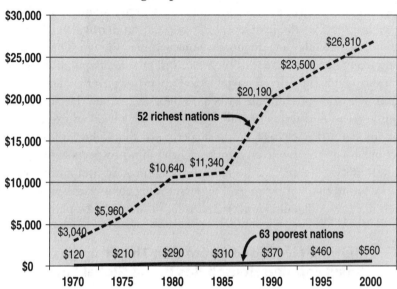

Source: Figures are based on World Bank, *World Development Reports* and the *2002 World Development Indicators,* using Atlas method in current U.S. dollars. Note that the Bank's inclusion of the richest and poorest nations varies from year to year. In 2000, "poorest" was defined as the nations with PC/GNI below $760, and "richest" as those with PC/GNI higher than $9,361.

extreme poverty declined slowly. Although the percentage of poor living on less than $1 a day fell to 23 percent, the number of poor people remained roughly constant as the population increased.[6]

Lest one think the situation is totally bleak, important and substantial gains were achieved during these years. For example, UNDP's *Human Development Report 1997* cites gains in health and education in developing countries since 1960:

- Infant mortality has declined 50 percent.

- Malnutrition rates have dropped by one-third.

- Percentage of pupils in primary schools has increased from half to three-quarters of school-age children.

- Rural people with access to safe water has risen from 10 percent to 75 percent.[7]

These important social gains do not offset the more basic fact that more people are poor now than two and three decades ago. While rising population densities and growing land scarcity among poor nations are clearly part of the problem, high population density and shrinking land access in Malaysia, Singapore, South Korea, Taiwan, Thailand, and Hong Kong have not impeded their gains in income. Population growth, by itself, is not the critical variable to explain impoverishment. Causes of impoverishment continue to be complex and varied. Declining commodity prices and terms of trade, the rapid expansion of external debt in many countries, changes in the structure of that debt with increasing portions owed to private creditors, and the dim prospects for improved capital inflows are all of concern. A brief glimpse of four rural communities around the world can lend understanding to how and why income levels are low, stagnant, or even declining in many developing nations.

Multiple Livelihood Strategies: The Struggles of Small Farming Households in the Global South

Four illustrations — from Kenya, the Philippines, Nepal, and Honduras — clarify some of the issues facing rural households as well as the changes in livelihood systems experienced by rural communities in the South as they are drawn more firmly into a global economic and political system. These examples reveal the following:

- Households and communities, however remote, are being incorporated into the cash economy and affected by structures far beyond their immediate setting.

- There is increasing socioeconomic differentiation at the local level and declining access to resources for many of the world's poorest households.

- Most families engage in multiple livelihood strategies. That is, not many survive on agriculture alone; it is simply too risky and unproductive.

- Migration is an important strategy around the world for poor households, and it takes widely different forms depending on the region and social and economic circumstances.

- As a consequence family and household structures are changing significantly.

Mbusyani, Kenya: From Cattle to Coffee[8]

Mbusyani is located in a largely semiarid region of Machakos District in Kenya where over 90 percent of the population is engaged in rain-fed farming and modest livestock keeping. At the core of changes in Mbusyani lie new modes of livelihood, specifically a shift from cattle keeping to coffee growing. One hundred years ago, the region was sparsely settled. The 1890s brought major changes in land use among the Akamba, a Bantu-speaking agropastoralist people who had lived there for several generations. At one time these lands were considered suitable for cattle and were grazed by large herds belonging to the resident Akamba. Decades of government regulations limited the land available for herds, enforced destocking and privatized land that had previously been common grazing land. No longer do farming families keep large herds of cattle. Instead, almost all struggle to earn a cash income from coffee grown on land only marginally suitable for its production. The privatization of land, the loss of communal lands, the increasing number of land sales, the pressures to get jobs and earn money, and a growing gap between rich and poor are all aspects of this transformation. It entails significant modifications in responsibilities for both men and women as they struggle to secure a livelihood for their families.

Thus, the Akamba people of Machakos District, including Mbusyani, are undergoing a transformation from a cattle-keeping, agropastoral society to one of agriculturalists heavily reliant on a cash crop and well integrated into the cash economy. Local residents face changing sets of norms and expectations; gender roles are becoming more fluid as men migrate for jobs and as women join the ranks of the educated. These communities contain many fragmented families as husbands, sons, and daughters, though particularly men, seek employment elsewhere. Many note a gnawing concern about the numbers of children growing up within those communities for whom there will be no land, and for whom they fear there will be no jobs. Yet people are aware of new opportunities as well as challenges. Their attitudes reflect, among other things, changes in both generational and gender perspectives on rights, obligations, and accepted behavior patterns.

Inexorably these communities are being drawn into and affected by the broader political and economic systems in which they exist. No longer are these relatively isolated and self-contained communities that are able to feed themselves and manage their own affairs without concern about the outside world. Government intrusion began in the colonial era. Economic as well as political intrusion now comes from far beyond the capital city. Ironically, as they move from cattle to coffee, the vast majority of households are being integrated into those larger systems on terms that are disadvantageous. Many are becoming more dependent and less self-reliant than in times past. The impact on food production and resource sustainability has largely been a negative one. Most households have marginal livelihoods and continuing economic and ecological difficulties.

Over time, the people of Mbusyani have adopted numerous ecological, social, and economic strategies to cope with economic and ecological problems. These include various environmental strategies such as bench terracing, tree planting, dam construction, afforestation, and water conservation. Economic strategies include household decisions to produce untried commodities such as tobacco, and a variety of different household and interhousehold income-generating activities. Buoyed by resources from family members working outside, some households prosper. Others, unable to gain a toehold in the cash economy, find the merest household expenditure an overwhelming burden. These households must deal on a daily basis with the exigencies of desperate poverty in an economy that increasingly functions through the medium of cash. Local residents may become, on the one hand, creative at finding solutions to problems and, on the other, mired in low-level and often ineffective patterns of economic activity. Particularly evident is the growing differentiation among households. Households vary substantially in the constraints they face and in the opportunities they perceive.

Siquijor, the Philippines: Resources and Livelihoods in an Island Community[9]

The Philippines, once a nation rich in natural resources and fertile land, is now beset by a rapidly growing population, severe environmental degradation, and marginal economic growth. Over half of the Filipino people reside in rural areas with 51 percent of these families living below the poverty line. In many ways, Siquijor, an island in the Central Visayas, is characteristic of much of the rural Philippines. Far from the nation's central power and economic structure in Manila, it is marginalized in its access to politics and the national economy, and it has one of the lowest per capita incomes in the country. Yet, despite the poverty and isolation, Siquijor has often been a focus of attention from outsiders. Exploitation of its once-rich fishing grounds by Japanese fishermen began before World War II. Manganese was commercially mined from the 1930s through the 1970s. Most recently, the island's white beaches have become a focus for tourism development.

Over the past century, pressure from outsiders and from the local population has taken a toll on the delicate and limited island ecology. Overwhelming evidence of environmental degradation is found in the loss of most of Siquijor's primary forest and declines in soil fertility and stability. Evidence is also found in the declining quantity and variety in the fisheries.[10] Under these conditions, residents have long been unable to support themselves solely on the fruits of their labor on the land and sea.

There are few economic alternatives for the residents of Siquijor. Local and regional entrepreneurs run a limited number of small-scale businesses, such as tourism or cement-block making. Local and regional middlemen export livestock, meat from the coconut palm, and small quantities of products extracted from the remaining secondary forest and the sea, such as seashells, seaweed, and vines. Islanders have participated in an export economy since the 1750s, but they have been limited by the fact that the island's resource base does not offer anything unique to fill a special niche in regional markets.

Islanders have thus built their livelihoods on a mix of activities and resource bases such as agriculture, fishing, home-based income-generating activities, local off-farm employment, and out-migration. Many women, for example, are involved in small-scale enterprises such as making nipa shingles, weaving mats, and raising hogs to supplement income from farming. This mixed economic strategy maximizes income, avoids exhausting any one resource, and reduces risk. Yet, keeping such a wide range of options open requires residents to make difficult choices about allocating scarce household resources. Given the nature of the market economy, families must often make these choices along the lines of gender and age. Both women's and men's flexibility to allocate their labor and other resources generally declines with their socioeconomic status; that is, poorer households have fewer choices and more constraints than do richer ones. Sometimes they are forced to make logical short-term decisions about managing resources, decisions that are not necessarily appropriate for the long-term sustainability of the resource base or of their families. For example, in this community, many households engage in dynamite fishing, sinking homemade explosives in glass bottles under the surface of the water to blast fish to the surface where they are scooped up into baskets. Dynamiting has both environmental and health consequences. It has led to depletion of some of the fish stocks and has indiscriminately destroyed parts of the ecosystem. It is also responsible for deaths and maiming of fishermen. Villagers are well aware of the long-term consequences of dynamite fishing, yet they are under pressure to meet their livelihood requirements, and so the process continues.

Ghusel, Nepal: Land, Livestock, and Livelihoods[11]

Ghusel is a community in Lalitpur District, Nepal, that has been undergoing changes in gender, caste, and ethnic dynamics as it has made a shift from subsistence agriculture to livestock rearing. Ghusel's shift from traditional subsistence farming to the wider economy has, on the one hand, assured food security to many households previously vulnerable to hunger, and, on the other hand, created new inequalities in gender roles and ethnic/caste relations. Over 93 percent of Nepal's 24 million people depend on the agricultural sector to earn their livelihood.[12] Ghusel Village Development Committee is characteristic of much of the middle hill region of Nepal.

During the last half of the twentieth century, Nepal's policies favored timber extraction. These policies, combined with rapid rural population growth, have resulted in widespread forest clearance. The inevitable by-products of deforestation include soil erosion, loss of farmlands, and serious flooding in the lowlands. Flooding results from upstream deforestation caused by overgrazing and lopping for fuelwood. Nepal is caught in a spiral of decline. Especially vulnerable are the men and women residing in the middle hills who rely on forests for fuelwood and fodder.

Ghusel, a community of seventeen hundred residents in Lalitpur District, presents a microcosm of the escalating problem of diminishing forest resources in Nepal. Ghusel's economy has made a shift to livestock production, thereby enlarging the demand for fodder and fuelwood. Livestock raising for sale of milk is complementary to agricultural production as there is a strong correlation between agricultural yield and available manure. Water buffalo have become the key source of income and investment in Ghusel. Thus Ghusel, as in many Nepalese communities in the middle hills, possesses a highly integrated and interlinked production system with productivity of agriculture greatly dependent on the presence and productivity of livestock.

Ghusel lies a brisk five-hour trek from the nearest road. Despite the community's proximity to Kathmandu, it lacks social services and facilities for health, education, transportation, water, and electricity. Households are dispersed; transport is difficult; development efforts and services are minimal; and access to goods within the community is negligible. Ghusel boasts one maize mill, one tea shop (that sells items such as sugar, snack foods, matches, and tobacco), and two primary schools.

Ghusel's 220 families, with an average landholding of 1.15 hectares per household, practice permanent cultivation of food crops and livestock production. Buffalo have become the key source of income and investment in Ghusel. This activity has been facilitated by the Small Farmers Development Program (SFDP), a nationwide poverty alleviation program. The National Dairy Corporation has worked with the dairy farmers to form local milk associations and has provided an assured milk market. The community of Ghusel is now integrated into the cash economy through milk sales in the Kathmandu market. The shift in means for earning income has brought financial benefits to many residents as well as new opportunities for cooperation among households through the dairy cooperatives. These organizations are successfully bringing farmers together to collect, transport, and sell their milk collectively. They work across the boundaries of class, caste, and ethnicity on a common set of objectives.

These interventions, however, have had negative consequences for (1) women with respect to greatly increased livestock care, (2) the distribution of benefits by gender as well as ethnicity and caste, and (3) the management of lands for fodder and fuelwood to which viable livestock production is intrinsically linked. Women experience significantly increased workload, diminished mobility, and little involvement in household resource allocation decisions. The credit program disproportionately benefits the wealthier Brahmin community, despite its mandate to reach the poor in the community, composed primarily of its Tamang residents. The ongoing extraction of government forest resources without replanting or sustainable management of forests threatens the livelihoods of local residents. The current high rates of forest resource extraction affect the larger ecology of Ghusel and exacerbate soil erosion, landslides, and disappearance of certain fodder types. Without major readjustments, this livelihood system is unsustainable.

Choluteca, Honduras: Resources, Rural Livelihoods, and Poverty[13]

Honduras has entered the twenty-first century with a burdensome legacy of economic inequities and environmental degradation. The widespread commercialization of the agricultural sector of Honduras has presented multiple constraints, as well as short-term opportunities, for the subsistence farmers, small producers, and other men and women who derive their sustenance primarily within the rural landscape. Failed attempts at equitable land reform, severe land degradation and deforestation, as well as high levels of population growth and unemployment all characterize the myriad economic, social, and environmental problems facing these communities.

Choluteca in southern Honduras, a region bordering the Pacific between Nicaragua and El Salvador, has many characteristics typical of other rural areas in Honduras's southern highlands. Once located in subtropical humid forest of the lower Choluteca River watershed, these communities now cultivate semiarid lands. Traditional agricultural practices of slash and burn and intercropping of basic grains prevail, while land shortages have reduced drastically the accompanying system of shifting cultivation involving extended fallow periods. Drought conditions are quite common, and during the dry months, unemployment reaches levels as high as 60 percent. Most families depend upon the off-farm income earned outside the community during this time period.

Variations in population sizes, altitudes, crop diversity, distances from Choluteca town, physical infrastructure, and access to government services all affect the changing livelihood systems of the women and men who live there. Emerging from the current structures of population and resources distribution in Choluteca and the other parts of southern Honduras is "a class of semi-proletarianized households without access to sufficient land and off-farm employment."[14] Since the mid-1950s, national and international development efforts in the region have consistently promoted and nurtured the expansion of nontraditional exports, including cotton, sugar, cattle, and, more recently, melon and shrimp. As a result, the consolidation of land into large landholdings has pushed many *campesinos* onto marginal lands or into wage labor.

Because of its predominantly mountainous landscape, the amount of land suitable for cultivation in Honduras is limited. Overall population growth has placed pressure on the land and the country's resource base, but the uneven distribution of that population and land ownership patterns more fully explain the far-reaching expansion of small farmers and their families onto the fragile hillsides. Men, women, and children living in the rural communities of the uplands of southern Honduras confront growing uncertainties and formidable obstacles as they struggle to carve their livelihoods out of the region's steep hillsides. Growing pressures on the marginally productive uplands have led to an increase in both seasonal and permanent migration to the export-agriculture zones and urban areas. Southern Honduras is one of the primary *zonas expulsoras* (zones of origin of the migrants) because of its relatively high population densities, degraded land, and limited access to government services.

The problems facing the rural populations of the uplands of southern Honduras, are, therefore, two-tiered. First, people must manage their households and resources within a restricted space on the fragile, low producing slopes to the north of the lowlands that are immersed in export agricultural production and controlled by the landed elite. Second, within the upland communities, access to and control over local natural resources and income-generating opportunities are further limited along lines of gender, class, and age. The first tier, composed of the inequities generated by the expanding large-scale capitalist political economy, provides the framework in which these communities are situated. The second tier is more specifically linked to the daily livelihood strategies of individuals and households inside of these communities.

As we can observe from the illustrations above — Mbusyani, Siquijor, Ghusel, and Choluteca — most households engage in multiple livelihood strategies. They may cultivate maize and beans primarily for consumption, but perhaps are able to sell bananas or some vegetables on the local market. The adult males and females may both engage in wage labor, working locally on the land of more affluent households. They may also seek nonfarm sources of income, such as owning a shop, fishing, working seasonally in the export zone, making baskets or pots, or knitting. Historically exchange work relationships have been an important way to increase access to labor resources during peak agricultural responsibilities. Often, a household member will head to the nearest town or city in search of work, and will try to send some funds home to help support the household left behind. Frequently the wages they are able to earn are insufficient to support that family member in the city, let alone provide much for those in the rural household. Many households engage in all of the above at a low level of return. Both the quantity and the quality of the assets they control are poor, and the consequence is low productivity and low returns.

This strategy of livelihood diversification enables rural families to construct a diverse portfolio of activities and social support capabilities in their struggle for survival and in order to improve their standards of living.[15] This strategy is used, of course, by households functioning at very different levels. From Tanzania to Mexico to Indonesia, evidence reveals that nonfarm incomes are critical to improving the overall well-being of rural households and constitute a critical strategy not only for survival but also for improvement of the quality of life.[16] Further, researchers have asked which people, among members of rural households, are able to gain access to the most remunerative nonagricultural employment. It is no surprise that educational level is a key factor in determining who has access to these opportunities.

Households develop an array of short-term coping strategies in order to deal with crises. They also have long-term objectives designed to strengthen their asset pool, income, and social position and to increase future claims on resources through marriage or patronage ties. There is a continuum in which households use strategies to minimize risk in normal times by diversifying income, increasing production, and investing in assets and exchange relationships.[17] At a time of crisis, these strategies may be gradually abandoned as the household mobilizes resources to respond to the crisis, perhaps by liquidating savings, selling assets, reallocating labor, or claiming loans and gifts from relatives or patrons. Crises often occur simultaneously or successively rather than in isolation. For example, a drought that precipitates a poor harvest may lead to malnutrition, illness, and loss of work capacity that threatens food production, livelihood, and health all at once. It may be hard to find a causal link between the death of the family's cow and later illness of a child, but certainly a low level of nutrition can be part and parcel of a vicious circle spiraling downward. It is difficult to figure out where to break the circle. Despite efforts to diversify livelihood systems, poor households are vulnerable to shocks and stresses whether they are caused by weather, politics, economic policies, or medical contingencies.

Some have suggested that sequential stages exist in which coping strategies are apparent: austerity, reduced consumption, temporary migration, divestment and asset disposal, and crisis migration, obviously moving along a continuum toward more severe responses.[18] What is apparent from observations in the communities above is that many households exist in a constant state of crisis in which the first three responses — austerity, reduced consumption, and temporary migration — are always in play. There is not so much a conscious effort to anticipate a particular problem as there is a constant need to contain risks and prevent collapse.

Structural changes arise with the growth of capitalism. They include increases in wage labor, migration of male family members, a decline in various forms of vertical ties to patrons, and the overall context of declining terms of trade for many Third World countries. They have aggravated the environmental and economic difficulties facing many poor families in the last several decades. Poor households grapple with increased risks and insecurities, which ebb and flow with the seasons, with recurring environmental disasters, and with the vagaries and whims of the international political economy. In the Global South the impacts on poor households are acute.

Enmeshed in the Global Politics of Poverty, Debt, and Drugs: Bolivian Peasants

One of the most complex situations in which poor households in the Global South can become involved is production or processing of agricultural commodities leading to illegal drugs largely for sale in Northern markets. These households are pummeled by conflicting policies and programs. Crops such as poppies for heroin or coca for cocaine may be the most lucrative a farmer can grow in a situation in which returns from other agricultural commodities are dismal. Farmers may be encouraged to grow these crops by various entrepreneurs in the business or by governments struggling with enormous international debt. They may also be discouraged or forbidden from growing and processing these crops by their own governments often responding to international pressures from foreign governments. These small farmers are caught up in a vicious circle of poverty, debt, and drugs played out at all scales of international and domestic politics and economics. From Afghanistan to Myanmar, to Thailand, Colombia, or Peru, the poverty/drug/debt nexus is evident. However, nowhere is it more acute than in Bolivia, where we turn for an exploration of small farmers enmeshed in the politics of drugs and debt.

Bolivia, a landlocked country of 8 million people located in the Andes, is the poorest country in South America, ranking ninety-fourth in gross national income among the 173 nations ranked by the United Nations.[19] Historically, Bolivia has been disadvantageously integrated into the international economy through the export of primary products. This pattern began with the Spanish conquest and the overthrow of the Inca Empire through the export of silver, and later with the export of tin and other minerals.[20] Today cocaine is the most recent of Bolivia's export commodities. In the last twenty years, the cultivation of coca and the processing and distribution of cocaine sulfate and cocaine hydrochloride, which are illegal derivatives of the coca plant, have linked the smallest Bolivian coca cultivator with the processes of globalization and the vagaries of social and economic demands far beyond his or her borders.

Traditionally, coca has been an important part of the Andean culture. The coca leaf is widely believed to have spiritual, social, and medicinal values, and it is used as a stimulant, as well as a protection against hunger, cold, and the effects of altitude. It may be chewed in a wad (similar to chewing gum in the United States or betel leaves in South Asia) or consumed as a tea or in combination with herbs as remedy for various ailments. It also has value as an object of trade, and peasants sometimes use coca as a means of exchange instead of currency. Historically, smallholders or *cocaleros* have grown coca on individual family plots, not on large estates. It is grown legally and consumed in a variety of ways; it is not used in the powerfully destructive form of cocaine. Thus, the coca leaf is integral to the way of life in Bolivia.

Cocaine as a commodity in international trade has boomed in the last twenty years. The Andean region of South America is the heart of the international cocaine trade. Because it is popular, particularly in the Northern Hemisphere, cocaine generates profits that are extremely important to the Bolivian economy. In the mid-1990s, about 90 percent of cocaine-based production took place in Peru and Bolivia, while the remaining 10 percent was produced in Colombia.[21] Major Colombian drug trafficking groups import hundreds of tons of cocaine base from Peru and Bolivia, convert it into cocaine HCl at clandestine drug laboratories in Colombia, and export this product to the United States and Europe.

Analysts associate cocaine's increased production in Bolivia with the downward spiraling economic processes of the 1980s leading to the debt crisis, which hit Bolivia severely, and the consequent implementation of neoliberal economic agendas and structural adjustment programs. Pressures from the World Bank and IMF implementing the Structural

Adjustment Programs had a dramatic impact on the Bolivian economy in the 1980s. These policies coincided with a tremendous fall in the price of tin and led to the closing of inefficient state mining enterprises in which twenty-two thousand out of twenty-eight thousand mine workers employed in the state sector lost their jobs. In these last two decades Bolivia has faced an economic crisis characterized by negligible economic growth rates, hyperinflation, increasing unemployment, and agricultural stagnation. This worsening poverty has been accompanied by the expansion of coca production and the drug trade. In the early 1990s drug trafficking was bringing between $300 million and $500 million into the Bolivian economy each year, compared with legal exports of $1 billion.[22] Studies suggest that, at that time, the total value of the industry was $1.5 billion, of which $600 million stayed in the Bolivian economy, with three hundred thousand people participating in some aspect of the coca-cocaine production chain.[23]

This economic crisis was compounded by widespread drought in the early 1990s leading to food shortages and deepening poverty. Bolivia was already heavily dependent on imported grain, and the quantities needed began to grow dramatically, all in the context of the collapse of the value of the boliviano, hyperinflation, and monetary instability. As happens around the world, poor, relatively unskilled, and newly unemployed workers generally flood rapidly into the informal sector, taking up petty trade and other casual work. In this instance a number of the unemployed mine workers migrated to the Chapare region of Bolivia and established themselves as small coca leaf farmers, working also as day laborers in the coca paste processing pits, a newly emerging, labor-intensive cottage industry.

Their perception that they could make some money was based not only on the reality of the Bolivian economy, but a growing consumption of cocaine in the Northern Hemisphere. The new reality in the United States and Europe during that same period of time was an escalating demand for cocaine and other drugs. Cocaine use increased dramatically with the development of the process to convert cocaine powder into crack cocaine. Given that crack could satisfy an addict for $20, the crack epidemic created a great demand for coca.[24] The coincidence of deteriorating economic conditions in Bolivia and increasing drug consumption in the North was central to a booming coca/cocaine production and trade in Bolivia.

Suddenly Bolivia was leveraged into a dominant position in the coca-cocaine economy. A global struggle emerged over how to deal with the drug trade. The U.S. government, concerned about increasing drug consumption in the United States, wanted a supply-side approach, cutting off the production of cocaine at its source. Others preferred different approaches, and the Bolivian government (along with other governments of nations producing drugs) was quick to point out that without the demand of the North, there would be no cocaine trade. The issue became an important political football used by competing groups to promote their agendas. The *cocaleros* were in the midst of a fierce conflict pitting the small farmers, *narcotraficantes* (drug traffickers), the Bolivian government, the Bolivian military, and the U.S. government — each with its own perceptions, interests, and perspectives on the drug trade — against one another.

The United States has put tremendous pressure on the Bolivian government to eradicate the coca fields, thus taking a supply-side stance in its struggle against the increasing amount of cocaine entering its borders. In turn, the Bolivian military has sought vastly increased military assistance from the United States, particularly since it had suffered substantial cuts during the period of financial retrenchment. The Bolivian government has not hesitated to use the coca-cocaine issue to negotiate increased economic assistance from the U.S. government to compensate for measures the United States demanded to destroy the coca-cocaine production capacity. Such compensation has been regarded as just, given U.S. demands for the liquidation of the coca economy. Bolivian and U.S. drug enforcement agents have launched numerous campaigns to destroy the productive capacity of the *cocaleros* but they have met with little long-term success. Despite new international and Bolivian state policies, strategies, and public programs launched to target producers, traffickers, and corrupted officials, the illicit coca-cocaine sector has inserted itself ever more deeply into the fabric of the Bolivian national economy.[25] In fact, coca leaf is the most valuable cash crop for peasants, and its two illegal products — cocaine paste and cocaine hydrochloride — are among the country's most important exports.

The U.S. and the Bolivian governments have widely differing perceptions of the seriousness of the cocaine traffic and the responsibilities for addressing it. In fact, in the early 1990s the U.S. efforts to halt the flow of cocaine from Bolivia caused widespread hostility and a perception on the part of Bolivians that they had lost their sovereignty. Aggressive air interdiction campaigns forced traffickers to transport the cocaine base via land and water to ever more remote and inaccessible destinations, far from the drug interdiction forces. This decentralization to hundreds of smaller Latin American trafficking organizations posed a new challenge to governments and the drug law enforcement authorities. It also pushed drug production ever further back into the remote corners of the jungle.

In 1995, the U.S. official priority for controlling drugs shifted from interdiction to eradication. Eradication of drug crops has a long history, and in the Andes region it has been singularly unsuccessful. The intent has been to diminish supply, drive prices for cocaine up, and thereby decrease its use. However, this approach has not proved workable. When eradication is effective in one area, production increases somewhere else. This may be another plot for a single farmer, more remote than the stand just eradicated. Typically, coca growers who are paid to dig up their bushes and grow pineapples, bananas, or another crop eradicate the coca field under question and then proceed to cultivate a second one deeper in the jungle. Peasants could receive twenty-five hundred dollars for every 2.5 acres of land they cleared of coca, but there were no guarantees they would stop planting. The approach clearly was not achieving the objective of cutting back substantially on coca production and the cocaine trade. This approach can also lead to movement of production to other countries. For example, it is well known that the increase of eradication in Peru led to skyrocketing cultivation in Colombia. According to FAO reports between 1990 and 1999, eradication campaigns reduced Bolivia's coca fields by more than half from 50,300 hectares to approximately 21,800.[26] Yet, these figures do not take into account the clandestine clearing of new fields and the overall regional increases in acreage identified by other sources.

In the context of a globalized struggle over how to control illegal drugs, the Bolivian government has tried to pursue two policies. The first is "coca for development," designed to increase foreign support for the expansion and diversification of the Bolivian economy.[27] The second is "coca diplomacy," designed to promote a market for legal products derived from coca.[28] In 1998, President Banzer established the Dignity Plan in which the government signed agreements with communities across Chapare, the region from which 90 percent of Bolivia's coca comes, for credit, roads, and technical assistance for growing alternative legal crops in exchange for a commitment never to grow coca again. Any communities refusing to sign or breaking their agreements would face forced eradication of the crop, possible arrest, and perhaps forced relocation. By mid-1999, seventy-five agreements covering seven thousand growers had been signed.[29] Many of the communities are composed of former miners and small cultivators of maize and potatoes for whom growing tropical fruits and vegetables is not a familiar activity. It is estimated that about nine thousand families in the Chapare are now growing legal crops, compared with five thousand in the early 1990s. But that still leaves ten thousand who primarily grow coca, and coca, of course, continues to pay better than any other agricultural commodity. Maize doesn't have a stable price and coffee prices have dropped. Coca leaf prices have soared from eight dollars for twenty-five pounds in early 1997 to eighteen dollars in early 1999 to forty dollars by late 2000. No wonder farmers are enticed into its production. One farmer lamented, "My children's hunger cannot wait for the price of corn, coffee, and cacao to recover."[30] As a consequence, given this level of economic desperation, it is exceedingly difficult for anti-drug officials to keep farmers from resorting to coca production. Official figures for 2001 indicate that the government of Bolivia has achieved significant results in reducing coca cultivation by more than 70 percent since 1996.[31] Informal estimates are less confident of this result, noting that recent changes in the government and disturbances throughout the country have slowed down eradication and permitted farmers to replant illicit coca. The latter, of course, are eager to do so for all the reasons noted above.

Today the coca/cocaine economy in Bolivia produces about a third of the world's coca leaves, the raw material for cocaine, and ranks second to Peru in coca production. After Colombia, it is the largest exporter of pure cocaine to Europe and the United States. Bolivia has become increasingly important as a transit country, primarily for cocaine base of Peruvian origin. The UN has recently suggested that between 100,000 and 460,000 Bolivians work in all aspects of the coca-cocaine trade, including some 200,000 to 250,000 cultivators. Whatever the figures, it is clear that efforts to reduce illicit coca production have not been matched by similar efforts to find viable alternatives for all those employed in coca.[32] Peasants in the Bolivian highlands remain vulnerable to the global forces of cocaine politics and economics and continue to eke out a living as best they can.

To return briefly to the discussion of small farmers, livelihood diversification, and short-term coping strategies, Bolivian *cocaleros* are clearly among the most vulnerable citizens of our global economy. They are buffeted, as perhaps few other small farmers are, by global forces of the drug trade, by the demands and actions of powerful nations in other parts of the world, and by the changing winds of their own government's policies. They must function in a new world that is not of their own making, and to do so they grasp whatever opportunities they can.

Southern Perspectives on Globalizing Industries

Many citizens in the Global South are caught up in global industries of various sorts. Unlike the situation for the Bolivian *cocaleros,* these opportunities are most often legal and encouraged by governments of both North and South. They may, nevertheless, be oppressive and exploitative. We turn now to two other arenas — textile and garment production, and nontraditional agricultural exports — for the insights they yield about "economic realities from a Southern perspective." For textiles, we explore both the secondhand clothing market in Africa and the sweatshops scattered around the world producing garments for Northern customers. The nontraditional agricultural exports under discussion include flowers grown in Colombia and horticultural products from Kenya and the Dominican Republic.

Garment Flows: North to South and South to North

The Secondhand Clothing Market in Africa

Most people who think about globalization and North-South relations from the perspective of textiles and clothing manufacture have in mind the vast flow of manufactured apparel from Third World countries to the West. Any student in a U.S. university, on any given day, may be wearing shoes manufactured in Brazil, a shirt made in Sri Lanka, a jacket from China, and jeans stitched up on Saipan. Many students have joined demonstrations protesting the sweatshop conditions under which many, if not most, of these clothes are produced. They may be completely unaware that there is a vast trade in clothing moving in the opposite direction — from the closets and racks of the United States or Europe to the shops and open-air bazaars of many countries of the Global South, especially Africa.

Textile and garment production have long linked North and South. The nineteenth-century cotton grown in India or Bangladesh found its way to the mills of England and made a return trip in the form of cotton cloth. More recently, the phenomenon has taken a very different twist. With structural adjustment and neocapitalist policies, governments that once regulated imports very tightly are permitting goods to enter their borders. Among those goods widely found in most African countries are vast quantities of secondhand clothing.

According to one researcher, "Worldwide second-hand clothing exports increased sixfold between 1980 and 1995, from a value of $207 million in 1980 to $1,410 million in 1996. Sub-Saharan African countries are among the world's largest importers, with consumption of second-hand clothing exceeding that of all other regions."[33] The United States is the world's largest exporter with Germany, the Netherlands, the United Kingdom, Belgium, and Luxembourg also engaged at significant levels. Much of it is moved by charitable organizations such as the Salvation Army or Goodwill via companies that operate sorting plants that sort and compress the clothing into bales to ship to importers in the receiving countries. Generally these businesses are wholesalers who provision small-scale traders and retailers.

What are the implications of this liberalization of imports and vastly expanded trade in secondhand clothing? Several outcomes are observable across Africa. The first has been a drastic impact upon local textile production. When African governments became independent, mostly in the early 1960s, many initiated a domestic textile and clothing industry. There was, for example, Rivtex in Kenya or Juaping Textiles and Printex in Ghana. Such firms operated in a highly protected, near-monopolistic situation. Citizens purchased their fabrics and clothing from them because there were high duties and tight controls on such commodities imported from outside the country. These were, in the classic sense of the term, highly protected industries often characterized by high prices and low quality. When African governments were forced to liberalize their economies, it wasn't long before the textile industry was feeling the crunch. Imports from Southeast Asia were coming in, and the second-hand clothing market was booming. Naturally the impact on domestic textile firms was disastrous. In Zimbabwe alone, four textile firms were liquidated after failing to pay back loans accumulated since the advent of the Structural Adjustment Program.[34] In other African countries, textile firms met a similar fate. They could not survive in the face of this competition.

How does the typical African consumer feel about opportunities afforded him or her in the secondhand clothing market? Typically responses are exuberant. There is ample choice; prices are affordable; and one can be stylish as well. In short, there is widespread enthusiasm. With popular support for importing secondhand clothing running at high levels, governments have not been inclined to cut back on these imports. In both rural and urban outdoor markets in Zambia, the secondhand clothing sections are now larger than the food sections. Purchase of secondhand clothing crosses all social segments of society, and two-thirds of the most affluent households surveyed meet some of their clothing needs in this market. The least well-off meet most of their needs in this way.[35] Indeed, Zambians have a sense of agency and creativity as they select and give meaning to the clothes they acquire through this market. This exuberance, however, takes place within the context of complex center-periphery relations, concerns about dependency, and broad development policy dilemmas confronting many countries of the African continent. We know that in the short term the African consumer benefits. We know that the wholesalers, retailers, and traders are profiting as well. The long-term impacts on African economies — on industry, on economic growth, on job opportunities — are less clear.

Garment Production for Northern Markets

Since the 1970s, the world has experienced a notable expansion of export-oriented industrialization in Third World countries, a large portion of it pertaining to the garment industry. For many Third World countries, the development of a garment export industry has been a central component of a modernizing strategy. In recent years the global commodity chain shaping apparel production has become globally dispersed. Upgrading within this industry has been associated with the shift from assembly of goods (using imported inputs) to full-package production of clothing items, an approach now widely used in East Asia and often called the East Asian model of textile and apparel production for export.[36] East Asian manufacturers have become intermediaries between buyers in the United States — from JCPenney or Reebok, to Liz Claiborne or The Limited — and hundreds of apparel factories in Asia.

Governments have endeavored to attract foreign entrepreneurs, providing various incentives such as concessions on land use and site selection, limited taxation and cheap labor. In fact, in many instances, the government seems to be in league with foreign investors trying to assure a cooperative labor force even in the face of unfair practices and unhealthy working conditions. They do not want to raise the minimum wage or even to enforce routine labor laws too vigorously lest the firms depart for another setting, causing valued jobs to disappear.

The apparel industry is at one and the same time traditional and antiquated while also very modern with global sourcing networks managed with the most advanced transportation, communication, and information technologies available. Many economists view this industry as an important and effective "hook" whereby a poor and developing economy is linked into global markets. Once linked, it can find avenues for strengthening economic opportunities. Others have tried to look closely at both the benefits and costs of this export-oriented industry. Social analysts have focused on three sets of questions: (a) the conditions under which most garment workers are employed, (b) the impact on social relations, and (c) the impact on women. Given that the vast majority of employees in the garment industry in Third World countries are women, considering the realities of this economic transformation from their perspective is of particular interest.

There has been widespread documentation of "sweatshop conditions" pervasive throughout the export garment industry in the Third World. Organizations such as the National Labor Committee, a New York–based labor rights group, have raised public awareness of the elements of "the sweatshop global economy." They — and others — have documented low wages, long hours, unventilated factories, unpotable drinking water, monitored or limited bathroom privileges, locked doors, illegal firings, mandatory overtime, and other abusive conditions. They have publicized evidence to demonstrate that some of the worst offenders in their view (Chentex in Nicaragua, for example, or Charter in El Salvador) have contracts with such widely known firms as Eddie Bauer, Wal-Mart, and even the U.S. Army. The context is truly international. For example, at a Nicaraguan factory owned by a Hong Kong manufacturer thirty-five thousand pairs of jeans are sewn per day, yet employees earn about twenty cents per pair of jeans that may sell for thirty dollars in the United States.[37]

Given the tenacity of the anti-sweatshop movement, some firms have tried to respond. For example, in El Salvador, The Gap has established an Independent Monitoring Group to meet with workers, hear complaints, investigate problems, make spot checks, and look over the books.[38] The successes of this group are limited, however, and the circumstances are complex. There are seventy thousand garment workers in El Salvador, 80 percent of whom are women earning very low wages. The government is fearful that firms will negotiate contracts with Honduras and Nicaragua where wages are lower and the populations are poorer. The minimum wage in El Salvador covers less than half of the basic needs of a family of four; the two-income factory worker household in Nicaragua — each putting in sixty to seventy hours per week — still cannot afford more than a hut with a dirt floor.[39] Nicaragua and El Salvador are illustrative. China, Saipan, Thailand, Indonesia, Vietnam, and many other places offer further evidence of "the race to the bottom" in which globalization promotes a destructive competition in which workers, communities, and entire countries are forced to cut labor, social, and environmental costs to attract mobile capital.[40]

Obviously, for most women engaged in factory work within the garment industry, the paycheck — however small — is welcome even if it is accompanied by a life of unremitting drudgery. Beyond this, there are other effects on social relations within the household and on women themselves. Women in Bangladesh are illustrative. Twenty-five years ago in Bangladesh, the manufacturing of garments, as a formal export-oriented industry, was minuscule. Today, Bangladesh has over thirty-three hundred garment factories employing over 1.6 million workers, of whom 83 percent are women. It is one of the major exporters of ready-made garments in the world market. Of Bangladesh's total exports, 76 percent are garment-related.[41] In 2001 Bangladesh claimed a $4.3 billion apparel industry, an incredible asset to an impoverished nation offering some of the world's cheapest labor.[42] Bangladesh exports approximately sixty-three types of garments. Raw materials for these garments — mainly fabrics — come from other countries. Approximately half the clothing exports go to America, where a quota system on imported clothing favors Bangladesh through the end of 2004.

The extensive employment of women in the garment industry stems from push factors including the small size of landholdings, the high proportion of rural households that do not own their own land, the displacement of women's rural labor through the introduction of mechanized devices in postharvest operations, along with an increase in female-headed households. There are also pull factors, especially the nature of new jobs opening up in the garment industry.[43] Bangladesh is an Islamic country, and a factory job — in a protected, largely female environment — is one of the few socially acceptable ways for women to earn a living. Even so, there is protest on the part of conservative elements in Bangladesh society over this departure from traditional female roles. In the garment factories, women earn, on average, thirty-five dollars per month, earnings actually higher than the average per capita monthly income.

Unfortunately, all of the garment factories in Bangladesh are inadequately supervised and are "among the worst sweatshops ever to taunt the human conscience."[44] Frantic production schedules, decrepit buildings, frequent fires, long hours, a callous disregard for safety on the part of employers — all characterize Bangladesh's garment industry. Nevertheless, despite the harsh working conditions and the meager pay, the jobs are highly coveted by Bangladeshi women.

Formerly limited to seeking wages through domestic employment or unskilled labor of various sorts, largely agricultural, Bangladeshi women now have a better and more remunerative opportunity. Some suggest that this opportunity has created a new class of industrial women workers with a collective consciousness. There is among some Bangladeshi garment workers a strong sense of personal agency, an awareness of oppressive situations, and a capacity to engage in "everyday resistance" to egregious conditions. Furthermore, today garment workers in Bangladesh have a broad-based trade union organization. The Bangladesh Garment Workers Unity Council is an umbrella organization of garment workers federations, and it is actively demanding improved working conditions and resisting harassment and intimidation of workers. Through this and other organizations, women workers in the garment industry are joining with other advocacy groups working on behalf of women and social justice in Bangladesh. These are indeed significant changes for Bangladeshi women who have entered the waged labor work force. It is still, of course, a very small portion of all women in Bangladesh, a nation of 130 million.

How do we answer the "big" question for women? Does women's participation in labor markets, such as those found in the garment industries of Nicaragua, El Salvador, Bangladesh, Morocco, or many other countries, liberate them from patriarchal control with new kinds of opportunities and empowerment, or does it represent a new kind of oppression in bondage to the demands of foreign capital? Evidence suggests that both outcomes arise, and we must look at the specific situation and its economic, social, and cultural context to determine the nature of change in each case. One viewpoint claims, "Two cheers for sweatshops.

They're dirty and dangerous. They're also a major reason Asia is back on track."[45] While some may cheer, few debate the need for enforceable codes to improve employee working conditions and wages, in order to end the "race to the bottom." We know that much from observing women in Bangladesh at work in squalid sweatshops. We also know that despite the misery they engender, sweatshops can launch a precarious escape from severe poverty and that many countries, Bangladesh included, are hoping they will provide at least one path toward a foothold in the global economy.

Competing for the Nontraditional Agricultural Export (NTAE) Market

Roses, Thorns, and Valentine's Day

Cut flowers constitute Colombia's top nontraditional export, generating export revenues of $550.5 million in 1999, and providing employment for over 130,000 workers.[46] Colombia ranks second among international exporters of cut flowers; the Netherlands ranks first. Almost all of the nation's flowers (95 percent) are grown for export, with more than 80 percent of exported flowers going to the United States and the rest flown to dozens of countries around the world. More than 148,000 tons or between 2.5 billion and 6 billion flowers of more than fifty varieties leave Colombia per year.[47] Roses are the most desirable to buyers of Colombian flowers. Colombian roses alone constitute 48 percent of the roses in the U.S. flower market. In a recent year, florists in the United States alone bought roses worth $140.3 million, according to the Colombia National Department of Statistics.[48]

Thirty-five years ago, Colombia exported only twenty thousand dollars worth of flowers a year. Colombia's economy has been restructured from an import substitution strategy to an export-oriented approach with a variety of special measures designed to encourage and facilitate production for export. At the same time, low-cost transport and new communications technologies have enabled a number of Third World producers like Colombia — Ecuador and Kenya, for example — to enter the international flower market. The production of cut flowers for export is central to a neoliberal economic strategy and is also a component of efforts on the part of the U.S. and Colombian governments to find alternatives to coca production.

The economic restructuring has been accompanied by various demographic and social changes in Colombia that have led to cheap labor, an asset in the labor-intensive flower industry. These changes help explain why nearly 80 percent of the employees in the cut-flower industry are women. Surveys reveal that they find flower production preferable to the major alternative, domestic work, which has low pay, low status, and difficult working conditions.[49] Among other things, women are relatively well paid for the work in flower cultivation that demands precision and care. In the flower business, the vast majority of female employees are minimally skilled workers, but they perceive possibilities for increasing skills through technical training in order to obtain pay improvements and career advancement. They also enjoy the opportunity to work with others of similar background and interests. Moreover, the income is important, providing them with some measure of independence within their households.

Colombia's flower growing region is the savanna of Bogotá where over 450 farms produce a wide range of flowers from orchids to pom-poms. It is difficult to generalize about working conditions at Colombia flower farms because there is great variation. Some offer contracts with regular pay, overtime wages, transport to and from work, and reasonable services and infrastructure. Others do not. Most production cycles are labor intensive and planned to meet the quality standards and periodic high demand of the U.S. market. Work can be highly pressured with exhortation to maximize output and speed.

Probably the most serious problem encountered in flower production is the heavy use of pesticides and the consequent impacts on workers' health. In Colombia, a study of some eighty-nine hundred workers on flower plantations near Bogotá showed that they were exposed to 127 different types of pesticides, of which an estimated 20 percent were banned or unregistered in the United Kingdom or the United States.[50] These workers suffered a variety of acute effects from these pesticides. While there is little definitive research on this topic, informal queries suggest that these problems include dermatitis, impaired vision, asthma, conjunctivitis, nephritis, nausea, headaches, convulsions, and insomnia.[51] Worker safety is evidently not a priority on the vast majority of Colombia's flower farms.

Moreover, the environmental effects of the flower industry involve overuse of water, poor waste disposal, the potential contamination of the food chain and ground and surface water, as well as inadequate worker protection. The Colombia flower organization established an environmental program called "Florverde" to work with firms to reduce the negative social and environmental impacts of the production process. Some improvements have taken place in recent years, including the almost total disappearance of child labor. Such changes are laudable, but they fall far short of what is needed. The government is primarily interested in earning foreign exchange through sustaining its exports and finding strong alternatives to coca production. The foreign and domestic entrepreneurs are primarily interested in maximizing output and keeping labor costs low. The workers — concerned about the salaries they can obtain in this field — sustain the long-term risks to their health.

The Horticultural Market: French Beans and Other Veggies

Avocados from Kenya? Raspberries from Chile? Snow peas from Guatemala? American and European consumers have the luxury of purchasing year-round, fresh, nontraditional horticultural products from around the world. The international trade in such high-value, labor-intensive horticultural products has increased dramatically in the past two decades. Between 1989 and 1997 the value of exports of fresh vegetables from sub-Saharan Africa to the countries of the European Union increased by 150 percent.[52] In fact, export horticulture is considered one of the bright spots of African development with three countries, South Africa, Côte d'Ivoire, and Kenya, accounting for much of the success, though others are involved as well. In Kenya export of horticultural products has grown from a few items centered on Asian vegetables, such as chilies, during the 1960s to an extensive trade delivering approximately seventy-five products to dozens of overseas markets.[53]

Factors behind this success include European Union trade preferences that have favored African countries. What twenty years ago was typically an export sector dominated by a small number of family enterprises has today become an industry dominated by a few large-scale exporters geared to direct links with supermarkets in the West. This tendency toward concentration has meant that the smallholder share of production has declined as sourcing from large-scale production units increases. The demands for speedy and reliable delivery of fresh, high-quality produce a continent away make cargo space a priority. To be competitive in this arena requires a certain scale of operation. Thus, there is a tendency toward marginalization of smallholders.

What are the implications of this marginalization for some of the smallholders of Kenya's Meru or Murang'a districts? They have enthusiastically seized upon opportunities to engage in nontraditional cultivation — French beans, for example — in the face of declining profits from coffee and rising profits from horticultural activities. In both of these regions of Kenya, prior to the globalization of horticultural production, women have been responsible for the vegetables grown for household consumption and local sale in a time-honored system of allocation of plots of land by the head-of-household (male) to the women in the household for their use. Dolan notes that

> in response to pressure for agricultural diversification and the expanding European market for "gourmet" vegetables, horticulture, the historical domain of women, has been rapidly intensified, commoditized, and in many cases, appropriated by men. While there is widespread documentation of men's appropriation of cash crops (tobacco, coffee, and tea), there has been little evidence of men entering agricultural spheres conventionally regarded as female. Yet, for example, as French beans became increasingly lucrative, men began to usurp either the land allocated for, or the income derived from, export horticultural production.[54]

Findings in Gikarangu Sublocation in Murang'a are illustrative.[55] After a high point in the mid-1970s, coffee prices declined drastically, and only in spring 1994 did they start to build up again. In 1989, coffee was at its lowest price in forty years, bringing in returns below the cost of production. Smallholder residents in Gikarangu who relied on coffee as a sole income source desperately tried to abandon coffee altogether in order to reduce their dependence on a livelihood that was fast pushing them to bankruptcy.[56] Meanwhile, the government forbade farmers to uproot their coffee, in the persistent hope that prices would improve. With inadequate returns, many farmers chose to neglect their household's coffee stands, since they could not destroy them legally. Thus, smallholders were in effect underutilizing the most valuable and fertile land in the sublocation in order to comply with the law. Meanwhile, to compensate for loss of coffee income, men in some households gradually began to appropriate the women-controlled food crops, including bananas and surplus maize and beans. Crops that women traditionally control for domestic purposes were slowly becoming alternative sources of income to meet school fees and other customary, male responsibilities or cash needs.

In the early 1990s, the French bean started to gain popularity as a commercial crop in Gikarangu. Involvement in French bean cultivation has increased most vigorously among those who have the smallest land-holdings and who are looking for a strategy to improve their incomes. In Gikarangu sublocation, more than two-thirds of those involved in French bean cultivation and marketing have tiny landholdings and rent small additional plots suitable for French bean cultivation. They hoped to find a new and profitable way to supplement their incomes from a small piece of intensively cultivated, rented land.

Eventually contract farming emerged as the primary way in which smallholders have been integrated into horticultural production. This system, as is widely known, transfers the production costs and risks to the smallholder. The contracting firm provides the inputs and guarantees the price for a given unit of produce, but the farmer assumes the risks over land, weather, labor supply, and various and sundry other occurrences. With French beans, the men make the contract as they control land and labor, but the entire family does the work, and it is largely the women who are responsible for the cultivation of French beans. The French bean has, in fact, "restructured the household economy, altering women's time allocation and reshaping the form of their productive activities. The viability of contract horticulture rests on the application of women's unpaid labor to French bean production."[57] Thus, the globalization of horticultural production is shaping the essence of intrahousehold relations in a site distant from where those beans are consumed.

Far away from Kenya in another part of the world, contract farming is similarly creating economic and ideological struggles while it pits smallholders against the interests and pressures of the global market. In the Dominican Republic agriculture has been restructured by processes involving structural adjustment programs, international debt, and neoliberal policies. As the value of the Dominican Republic's traditional crops has declined, the government has encouraged horticultural production through the contract farming mechanism. In this context, given the state's declining capacity to provide agricultural services and credit for small-scale farmers, private firms have assumed these functions under contract-farming arrangements.

Tomatoes are one of the most important commodities for production by contract farmers in the Dominican Republic. According to a recent study, tomato processors procure over 90 percent of their tomatoes from sixty-five hundred small-scale growers in two regions, of whom four thousand are located in the southern valley of Azua, one of the poorest regions of the country.[58] Contracting allows the companies to have access to irrigated land for which they are not responsible as well as to flexible family labor that they do not need to manage. Because tomatoes are a labor-intensive crop demanding a lot of hand labor, these arrangements are a considerable bonus for the four contracting companies working in the area. They are reluctant to sign contracts with heads of household without significant family labor that they can control. Over 90 percent of the contracts are signed with men because they hold rights in the land and because they control the labor of the household. Women do the greater portion of the required labor.

The contractual nature of this relationship between company and smallholder has meant that the risks and the debt are assumed by the smallholder. One survey suggests that 60 percent of tomato growers in this region have become indebted to the company to whom they are contracted.[59] In a worst-case scenario, the companies have recently encouraged the use of increasing amounts of pesticides, triggering a whitefly outbreak and causing huge agricultural losses. The pest problems spread to subsistence crops such as beans and pigeon peas in adjacent fields. Increased pests and debts were joined by decreased yields, forcing many households into exceedingly precarious circumstances. With the appearance of the white fly outbreak, the processing firms cut their losses, reduced their contracted acreage in Azua, and relocated from the pest-infested areas to distant regions. By 1995 virtually all growers in Azua were in debt to powerful tomato-processing companies that had manipulated contracts and pushed losses onto marginal producers. If there was a positive side, it can be found in the fact that the farmers' land was not appropriated by the firms claiming the money owed to them. The farmers had received their land through agrarian reform, and that land could not be bought or sold. The larger reality for these farmers in the Dominican Republic and for those elsewhere is that contract farming of horticultural products for the international market is fraught with complex relations that often render the smallholder more precarious than he or she was at the outset.

Summary: Stretching Our Understanding of Distant Lives and Livelihoods

Most of the world's 3 billion poor are impoverished because their previous livelihood systems are no longer viable. New systems introduced from abroad or from capital cities such as Nairobi, Manila, Dhaka, or San Salvador have either created few new options for them or have done so in ways that are problematic or harmful. Some of the economic alternatives arising through globalization processes are linking them into broader livelihood systems in ways that are economically disadvantageous, such as contract farming observed in the Dominican Republic or coffee growing in Kenya. Some are alternatives harmful to their health, such as dynamite fishing in the Philippines or export flower production in Colombia. They may also provide potentially hazardous work situations such as those in many garment factories throughout the Global South. In many instances, one vulnerability is traded for another. The vulnerability to drought, hurricane, or flood is diminished but the vulnerability to international coffee prices, trade policies of distant lands, and preferences of consumers halfway around the world is vastly increased. Indeed they may cling to the economic opportunities that such work might provide, but there is no doubt that the terms on which it is offered need reexamination. This examination must take place in cross-national settings that include not only the financially powerful and well situated but the organizations representing ordinary workers.

This chapter has introduced several local communities in which the lives of women and men are changing dramatically as larger economic and political systems continue to transform them. Impoverished households and communities around the world are in a constant process of balancing competing needs and limited resources in order to preserve, insofar as possible, livelihood options, consumption patterns, health, and social relations. The fragmented families of rural Machakos in Kenya whose men leave home to seek whatever kinds of employment can provide some cash income have something in common with the fragmented families of Bangladesh whose young women flock to jobs in garment factories. The subsistence farmers of Nepal are not so very different from those of Honduras or Bolivia, given their precarious perches on the edges of survival. Whether smallholders, contract farmers, wage laborers, or factory workers, all these men and women struggle to find the economic, political, social, and environmental re-sources to assure their basic livelihoods. They need and want to deal more effectively with the changes resulting from the impinging global economy, and to attain a more certain and a more generous future.

Part Three

Critical Issues:
Population Dynamics,
Food Security, and
Environmental Degradation

Chapter 7

The Dynamics of Population, Development, and Environment

At the beginning of the twenty-first century, human activities — relating to the environment through resource use, consumption, pollution, and waste — occur on a scale and with a complexity unimaginable at the beginning of the last century. Whether we are taking an airplane trip from Boston to San Francisco to visit Aunt Susie, a quick trip in the car to the local grocer to pick up some milk for the household, or spending a late night reading the most recent novel of a favorite author, our use of energy and other resources has been transformed in recent decades.

The purposes of chapter 7 are to

- identify some of the key issues linking population, development, and environment today;
- clarify approaches, concepts, and terms used for analyzing population changes and impacts on the environment;
- investigate the relationship between people and renewable resources with particular attention to the need for sufficient clean water;
- examine the empowerment, education, and health of women as critical factors in addressing both human welfare and environmental issues; and
- identify three policy concerns for the new century: the impact of extractive industries on indigenous peoples in various parts of the world; the continuing spread of AIDS in Africa and elsewhere; and the intense pressures for migration within and across national boundaries.

The underlying perspective from which all these topics are addressed is that, around the globe, we need environmental sustainability, and we also need sustainable livelihoods for everyone.

The impact of population upon environment is embedded in social relations and the specifics of culture and behavior. Therefore, we propose two analytical frameworks for analyzing it. The first is a *political ecology perspective*. Political ecologists emphasize decision-making processes and the social, political, and economic context that shapes environmental policies and practices. Political ecologists focus on the uneven distribution of access to and control over resources. They are particularly concerned about differentiation on the basis of class and ethnicity. We add to this a feminist perspective that treats gender as a critical variable in shaping resource access and control, interacting not only with class and ethnicity, but also with caste, race, and culture. These are mutually embedded hierarchies shaping the struggles of men and women to sustain ecologically viable livelihoods, as well as the prospects of any community for sustainable development. Thus, we link an ecological perspective with analysis of economic and political power and with policies and actions at all scales: global, national, regional, and local.

The second is a *user's perspective* on the environment. We make no assumptions about who is performing a specific task — farming, managing the animals, running the shop, or seeking a job in the city. Despite its obvious practicality and common sense, such an approach must take into account that access to and use of resources are often contested terrain and therefore involve the exercise of power and resistance to it. Struggles routinely occur within households or between them. Moreover, in many parts of the world, management of resources and environmental activism involve struggles against expropriation by outsiders as well as resistance to exploitation by local elites.

For the most part, people are concerned about their environment and want to know how it can be protected. There are, however, different perceptions as to what that means. Whether decisions are being made by a local community of five thousand people, a nation of many millions, or our global society, viewpoints vary. Do we need different policies, different economic systems, new technologies, or changes in lifestyles? What problems should we focus on: land degradation, deforestation, pollution, loss of biological diversity, or a host of other conditions harmful to human welfare? Whether the conversation begins with people or the environment, many questions must be asked. Implicit in these questions are the values of a society. For example, what levels of material well-being and technology do we consider desirable, and for what portion of the local, national — or global — population? What degrees of inequity

Figure 7.1. Life Expectancy, Fertility Rates, and Literacy Rates for the Global Six Billion

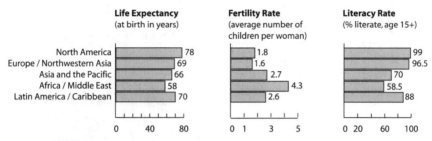

Source: The World Bank, *World Development Report and World Development Indicators* (New York: Oxford University Press, 2002).

among peoples are acceptable? Exactly how clean do we want our water and air to be, and for whom? What levels of carbon dioxide emissions are acceptable? How much loss of biodiversity are we prepared to tolerate? All are important questions pertaining to people and our planet.

Who Is Here at the Beginning of the Twenty-First Century?

The Current Situation

The world's population has passed 6 billion. The annual global increment — the number added to the world's population each year — is believed to have peaked about a dozen years ago at approximately 87 million per year. In most of the more developed countries, populations are stable or even declining, though the world continues to add about 80 million new people per year.[1] In the developing countries, absolute numbers continue to grow, but in many, the rate of increase has declined. However, more than 90 percent of world population growth today is occurring in less developed regions.[2] Figure 7.1 provides some glimpses into key human development indicators across the globe for today's 6 billion people.

Rapid population growth is a recent phenomenon. For centuries population figures hardly changed at all. Rapid progress in socioeconomic development, particularly in education, nutrition, and health, has helped to accelerate the rate of population growth by decreasing infant and child mortality, increasing the life span, and improving health conditions for untold numbers. These changes have been caused, in part,

Figure 7.2. Recent and Projected World Population Growth

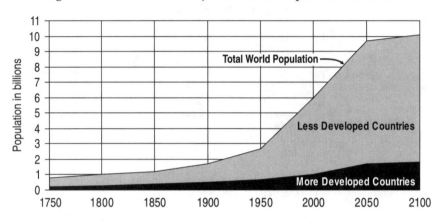

Source: United Nations, *World Population Prospects: The 2000 Revision,* vol. 1: *Comprehensive Tables,* 2001; Thomas W. Merrick, *World Population in Transition,* Washington, D.C., Population Reference Bureau, *Population Bulletin* 41, no. 2 (1991).

by a medical revolution following World War II in which the use of newly available antibiotics has saved countless lives and DDT's attack on malaria-bearing mosquitoes has set back one of the most debilitating scourges of tropical countries. The medical revolution, more than any single factor, accounts for the spike in population growth during the last half of the twentieth century. Figure 7.2 captures the differences in growth rates between the industrialized North and the developing South, between 1750 and the present. The graph projects growth through 2100, when the world's population is expected to reach just over 10 billion.

This projection relies on three assumptions: (a) fertility rates will continue to decline; (b) life expectancy will continue to increase; (c) developing countries will broadly follow the demographic transition to low population growth rates already experienced in the industrialized world.[3]

Why Should We Be Interested?

There are probably many reasons that all global citizens should be concerned about the world's population growth rates and specifically about the relationships between population and the environment. Four stand out.

- Consequences in terms of global climate change, loss of vital renewable resources, and increase in toxic pollution are likely to be severe. The industrialized world, and particularly the United States, shows little interest in reducing consumption and establishing a less wasteful way of life.

- Rapid growth is taking place in the developing world. As the populations of less developed countries begin to attain the living standards of the industrialized world, per capita consumption of energy and other goods will grow accordingly. This growth will have a substantial impact on the environment. Some problems may be assuaged but others, such as sanitation, waste disposal, or CO_2 emissions, may increase dramatically.

- Conflicting objectives exist. When we examine the relationships among population, development, and the environment, we can observe major objectives that are in conflict with one another. For example, the extraordinary accomplishments in medicine, eliminating the scourge of smallpox or diminishing the impacts of polio or measles, have brought increased health and longevity to millions. The benefits of medical advances cannot be denied; they have, at the same time, increased the challenge of economic development and placed great burdens on states for meeting a range of needs in health, education, employment, infrastructure, and general welfare for burgeoning populations.

- These environmental/population issues must be addressed at varying scales by the very smallest local communities, national governments, and the global community. Environmental and population concerns do not reside calmly within well-defined borders. They spill over in the form of drifting smoke, acid rain, or migrants fleeing lands devastated by soil erosion, drought, or flood.

The world has come together in UN conferences on a number of occasions starting in 1974, to focus on population, development, and environment concerns. Two UN-sponsored conferences were held in the early 1990s — one in Rio de Janeiro, Brazil, in 1992, on Environment and Development, and the second in Cairo, Egypt, in 1994, on Population and Development. At the former there was widespread concern on the part of Northern industrialized countries about rapid population growth in the South and, conversely, the developing nations of the South expressed alarm over the escalating consumption and pollution patterns of the North. At the latter, the agenda focused on population and environment, health, family well-being, reproductive rights, and reproductive health. The most recent UN conference pertaining to development, population, and environment, the World Summit on Sustainable Development (WSSD), was held in Johannesburg, South Africa, in August 2002. The WSSD made some important commitments to halve the proportion of people without access to sanitation and to safe drinking water by 2015, but overall, there was dissatisfaction over a lack of progress on policy initiatives promised in Rio and Cairo.

Tools, Concepts, and Terms for Considering Population and Environment Relationships

How do we go about understanding the relationship between population and environment? We must take into account not only the population and environment, but two additional variables: organization and technology.[4] In a practical application, one might use these categories to ask: What attributes of the human *population* might help us to understand this issue? For *organization,* how do existing policies and regulations affect human behavior on this issue? What are the characteristics of the *environment* that need to be considered? And, how has *technology* affected this issue? Is it a cause of the problem? What options for different technologies exist?

Take, for example, the severe loss of the Louisiana wetlands over the last several decades. For thousands of years, the Mississippi River has deposited about 400 million tons of riverine nutrients and sediment in the Gulf of Mexico annually, creating the Louisiana Delta, a vast wetlands, that is a tremendous source of fish species, and, as it turns out, also a source of oil. Nowadays it is losing between twenty-five and thirty-five square miles a year, a chunk approximately as big as Manhattan. The first settlers in New Orleans began a process of building levees to prevent flooding, and now these levees extend over two thousand miles along the Mississippi. This work was completed between the 1930s and the 1970s by the U.S. Army Corps of Engineers, which built a massive complex of dams, reservoirs, and pumping plants to secure the land against floodwaters. Meanwhile, major oil companies operative in the region have constructed oil rigs and a complex set of pipes and canals through which they supply about 18 percent of the nation's oil and gas. Now, no longer receiving the generous annual gift of mud, the Louisiana wetlands are literally dropping into the Gulf waters to the dismay not only of ecologists and environmentalists, but also of fishermen who see the fisheries diminishing, and oil companies as well as other businesses and their investors.

This approach — examining population, organization, environment, and technology — helps us focus on critical elements of this situation. Populations include, at the very least, consumers, residents, fishermen, and oil companies. In terms of organization, we must consider activities of the U.S. Army Corps of Engineers and various state and federal regulatory bodies on wetlands and on energy. The environmental resources include diminishing wetlands and diminishing species of fish. The technology has changed over time, of course, but the capacities to construct major waterworks and mechanisms for moving fuel would be part of an analysis. All of these components would be central to examining the issues surrounding the languishing Louisiana wetlands.

Another way to think about the population-environment connection is to examine the ways in which three variables relate to each other. Thus, the impact (I) of any group or nation on the environment is the product of its population's size (P) multiplied by per capita affluence (A) as measured by consumption, in turn multiplied by a measure of technologies involved in supporting each unit of consumption.[5] How do these three variables relate to one another. The consumption (A) variable measures how many goods each person uses and how much waste each creates. Technology (T) determines how much in the way of resources are needed to produce each unit of goods and how much waste is emitted into the environment after consumption.[6] Population (P) indicates the number of people involved. So (I) = (P) x (A) x (T). Thinking about population and consumption is straightforward as increases in both generally mean an increase in environmental impact. Changes in technology may increase environmental impacts or may decrease them, depending on the new technology being employed. For example, the use of plastic bags may have decreased the need for paper and, therefore, the pressures on forests for wood, but increased the damage done by nonrecyclable products. Today we are dealing with complex and difficult environmental impacts that have come about through widespread adoption of new technologies. Demand density pertains to the demand for particular resources, and impact density pertains to pollution density with waste output. For example, chemical fertilizers, chlorofluorocarbons, the automobile with its carbon emissions, and sulphur dioxide emissions are all environmental consequences of growing importance as people increase their consumption of these goods.

Concepts and Terms

Carrying Capacity

An important concept linking environment and population is the notion of carrying capacity. Here we ask about the level of resource use or waste output that can be sustained indefinitely, without long-term deterioration to the resource base. Carrying capacity has two aspects. The productive carrying capacity is the ability to provide resources such as food or minerals. The waste carrying capacity is the ability to absorb a certain level of pollution or degradation without significant damage.[7] Indeed, the two are linked. For example, attempts to increase productive carrying capacity by such measures as using chemical fertilizer or building irrigation schemes have led to problems with waste carrying capacity in the form of salinization or excessive minerals in the soils.

Analyzing Demographic Change

Two widely used concepts for analyzing processes of demographic change and their impacts are the theory of demographic transition and the theory of the demographic trap. According to the theory of demographic transition, population changes have moved through a sequence of three stages. In the first stage, approximating conditions through the eighteenth century, there are high birth rates and high death rates with a consequent slow population growth. In the second stage, living conditions improve. Public health measures are introduced. Mass immunizations take place and overall sanitation improves. In addition, there is expanding food production. These conditions characterize the latter part of the nineteenth century and all of the twentieth century. However, they reach a peak around World War II with a tremendous wartime effort in the public health arena. These features characterize the second stage, in which there are low death rates while high birth rates continue. The third stage is one in which many industrialized countries now find themselves with low birth rates and low death rates. The social and economic gains have led to an equilibrium in which the life span is extended, infant and child mortality rates are low, and family size is small.

The demographic trap occurs when a nation does not manage to get to stage three. It moves into stage two with low death rates and high birth rates, but it gets stuck there. Rapid population growth continues, and along with it comes escalating ecological and economic problems. In fact, many nations may remain stuck for some time in the second stage and even return to the first under conditions in which the local ecological and economic systems are overwhelmed.

Key Terms

Familiarity with several terms that appear frequently in discussions of population issues is helpful.

The *population growth rate* is determined by three processes: birth, death, and migration. Births minus deaths are shown as natural increase. The immigrants minus the emigrants are shown as net migration. Together they compose the population growth rate of any community.

Population momentum is the tendency for population growth to continue beyond the time that replacement-level fertility has been achieved. This occurs because for a period of time the previously high birth rates lead to a relatively high concentration of people in the childbearing years.

Replacement-level fertility has been reached when a nation's average fertility rate is 2.1 births per woman.

The *infant mortality rate* is the number of deaths of infants under one year of age per thousand live births in a given year.

The *dependency ratio* measures the proportion of children under fifteen and elders unable to contribute labor in relation to the working population.

Findings from North and South

Scholars have explored the relations between population and environment in a variety of situations and have documented remarkably diverse results. In Kenya, one team has carried out long-term research in Machakos District drawing on data between 1930 and 1990.[8] Their findings support the assertion that increased population has improved per capita productivity and the condition of the environment. Photos of hillsides that were denuded and full of gullies in 1937 revealed woodlots, terraces, trees, and fodder grasses in 1989. Another researcher makes a similar point in his descriptions of the lower valley of the Hudson River in New York state that, in the last century, has tripled both its forested areas and its population as the need for timber to make charcoal has diminished and small farms have collapsed.[9]

Conversely, Paul Harrison, among many other analysts, focuses on the "destructive forces of the present" in examining deforestation in Madagascar, Indonesia, Brazil, and the Congo with rapid population growth and stagnant technology leading to the "grinding of the ax" through the world's forests.[10] The forests are under multiple attacks from loggers, ranchers, landless poor farmers, and governments that may stand to profit from policies encouraging easy access to logging rights and extensive sales of timber, both nationally and internationally.

Nowhere has this kind of activity been documented more extensively than in the Philippines under the Marcos regime beginning with his declaration of martial law after seven years as president and ending with his overthrow in 1986. Connections between loggers and the top levels of government reinforced the export-oriented development strategy. A ban on log exports, intended for implementation in 1976 in order to conserve forests and build the wood processing industry, was shelved as government officials and business saw ways to profit from extensive logging, including illegal logging primarily for export to Japan and Taiwan. Government officials were widely involved (even the Bureau of Forestry Development, which was nicknamed the "Bureau of Forest Destruction"); there was known to be protection and ownership of logging companies by high-level military officials as well as politicians.[11]

According to several analysts, deforestation in the Philippines relates less to population growth than to governments that represent elite interests rather than those of the public. They assert that increases in population are not important in explaining the variation in deforestation across provinces of the Philippines. In fact, the order of sequence is the following: first, the primary forest is converted to secondary forest through logging, and second, human settlements, primarily composed of poor farmers, then encroach upon the secondary forest. "Implicit in this scenario is elite control of access to the primary forest and a development process which has created millions of poor people who have no place to go other than the forest."[12]

We return to the political ecology perspective and the social, political, and economic context that shape environmental policies and practices. The devastation of forests in the Philippines provides ample evidence for the utility of this perspective that incorporates analysis of political and economic power with regard to the environment at local, regional, national, and global scales. Whether in the Philippines or Ethiopia, Somalia or Kenya, the United States or Brazil, or many other countries, substantial evidence links deforestation with soil degradation and erosion, demonstrating the processes of deterioration of the land's productivity as heavy rainfall, wind erosion, and inadequate soil conservation take their toll. Loss of topsoil, loss of fertility, reduced moisture retention, and reduction in soil flora and fauna all lead to a decline in productivity, particularly in low-resource agricultural systems.[13]

This scenario need not be the case. One example illustrates the difference appropriate policies can make. This optimistic analysis of population-environment-development interactions focuses on Mauritius, an island nation in the Indian Ocean.[14] Forty years ago rapid population growth, extreme poverty, and poor economic prospects characterized Mauritius. Various development scenarios were produced for Mauritius, and from them investment in human resources emerged, along with a recognition that water availability was the key environmental constraint to growth in that setting. Significant investments were made in both water and human resources. By 1990 the economy was flourishing, unemployment was low, fertility had declined to replacement levels, and life expectancy equaled levels found in developed countries. Today Mauritius ranks in the "high" human development category with adult literacy at 84 percent. It ranks in the top sixty on a gender empowerment measure, and only 11 percent of the population is below the poverty line.[15] The tale of Mauritius suggests not only the value of forging policy and program links among social, economic, and ecological objectives, but also the usefulness of the political ecology perspective.

Lessons from China and India

Perhaps China and India are the most instructive countries to observe when considering the implications of various policies related to population growth and environment. These two countries have long been paired for this purpose as they together account for more than one-third of the people on earth, with China's population at 1.2 billion and India at 1 billion.[16] Both face a mismatch between population and resources. At independence in August 1947, India made a commitment to parliamentary democracy, while at just about the same time China completed a long revolutionary struggle pursuing communism under the leadership of Mao Tse-tung.

During the next decades China's top-down approach led the nation through an array of changes from collective farming in the Great Leap Forward to the cultural revolution's "reeducation" of intellectuals in hard work thousands of miles from home. In the 1970s new strategies led to economic liberalization under Deng Xiaoping with transformations in agriculture, changes in rural land ownership and a limited opening to foreign investment and trade in special enterprise zones along the coast. China's well-known one-child policy, decreeing that families could have only one child, was implemented most strictly in the late 1970s and early 1980s. China undoubtedly had the strictest approach to family planning in the world. The government required late marriage, limited couples to one child, and had government community workers and employers supervise and enforce the single-child target. The consequences were reported to be high levels of sterilization, abortion, and female infanticide. Finally, the government eased up in the face of great resentment and lack of compliance in the rural areas.

India has seventeen states functioning quite independently, with eighteen major languages, a multiparty system, six major religions, twenty-five distinct ethnic identities, a caste hierarchy, great gaps between rich and poor, and incredible diversity along just about every dimension. Despite all these characteristics, it has maintained a functioning democracy, and it has not divided into numerous parts as some predicted it would. While India has not delivered a substantially better life for most of its citizens, it has built a powerful and technologically sophisticated military establishment and an impressive system of higher education, reflecting its large middle class and inegalitarian social structure. Birth rates continue to be high, and the one attempt at enforced family planning and a sterilization program in the 1970s engendered sharp public hostility toward the prime minister, Indira Gandhi.

Comparisons between China and India can be illuminating. In China about 10 percent of the men and 25 percent of the women are illiterate, whereas in India fully one-third of the men and nearly two-thirds of the women are illiterate.[17] In China one-sixth of the children are malnourished; in India the figure is just over half. In India nearly half the population lives on less than one dollar a day, whereas in China approximately 20 percent are in that category. Fertility rates (births per woman) are 1.9 in China and 3.3 in India.[18] The costs in Chinese human rights through enforcement of the one-child-per-family policies of the 1970s and 1980s are clear, but their other accomplishments are also evident. Some ask whether India might have been able to achieve more success, even in its loosely structured democracy, with better leadership at the top. Others ask why amid the poverty of India, political leaders live in luxury, and they raise key questions about India's social structure and politics. It seems we cannot turn to either India or China for answers to the population dilemma. China's draconian measures violating human rights are unpalatable to most countries. The violence of poverty still widespread in India is also unpalatable.

Nevertheless, both countries must confront the dilemma of vast populations and inadequate resources. If China has one-fifth of the earth's population, it has only 7 percent of its farmland and its population density is three times the world average. Both China and India face the complex tasks of increasing food output, moving their economies into manufacturing and services, building infrastructure, assuring energy supplies, and absorbing the vast numbers of new entrants into the work force. Yet, as Paul Kennedy emphasizes in *Preparing for the Twenty-first Century,* "The greatest problem is social and political: how to transform ancient societies sufficiently to meet the challenges of the high-tech revolution of 'the borderless world' without social strains, resentments, political unrest, and regional chaos — and that in countries already finding it hard to handle their population explosion."[19] Further, he elaborates, both China and India are in a race against time. If population increases erode gains in agriculture, industry, and manufacturing, putting those peoples into the demographic trap, then a vast portion of the world's population will continue living in poverty and deprivation. On the other hand, if these vast populations do increase their standard of living significantly, there are implications for the local environment and the atmosphere.

What Links Population, Environment, and Development?

Family and Household Decision Making

While representatives of governments, the UN, and NGOs meet periodically to make decisions at the global level on population, resources, and environment, at the household level critical decisions about family size are made — which, when combined, create the trends that policymakers discuss. What circumstances and attitudes shape decisions within the household about family size? There are many, and they seem to differ widely by culture, class, and socioeconomic and environmental setting. Children are valued for many reasons. In addition to the nearly universal desire to have a child to love, care for, and teach, as well as to carry on the family line, there are many practical reasons for wanting children.

These reasons vary substantially between a poor rural household and one established in an urban setting. In many rural communities, children constitute part of a family labor pool, essential for carrying water, supervising livestock, or gathering fuelwood. They also provide future family security, caring for parents in their old age and maintaining continuity on the land. In the cities, most children become an economic responsibility as opposed to an economic asset. Food and clothing must be purchased to sustain the family; children may be required to attend school; and rent must be paid. The cost of supporting these children is far greater than the cost of supporting their rural cousins, and the long-term security to be found in a large family is far less. Thus, families are likely to have fewer children as they become more expensive or as their economic value decreases, and this is more likely to occur in an urban than in a rural setting.

In sum, children in poor societies are often an economic and social asset (as opposed to an economic responsibility) with an expected return in the form of economic contributions to the household and financial or other support of parents in old age. In addition, children often provide symbolic adult status for both their fathers and their mothers, but particularly for the latter. In many societies only when the woman has produced her first child is she regarded as fully adult. Also at that time her status in the household shifts and her value is more fully recognized. In many instances, her improved status may be granted more readily if she has produced a son, rather than a daughter. As income and socioeconomic status of the household increases, family members may perceive new choices in the ways they allocate their time and money, and this fact may incline them toward smaller families.

The most rapid fertility declines have occurred so far in countries that have achieved major improvements in child survival rates, have increased male and female educational levels, and have also implemented family planning programs. These changes have also been associated with improved reproductive rights, new employment patterns, and changes in labor force participation rates. Examples include Bangladesh, Thailand, Singapore, and Korea. Among the twenty poorest countries in the world, Bangladesh has achieved a significant, sustained fertility decline over the last two decades. The figures for Bangladesh (a decline in average number of births per woman from 7 to 3.2) are still well above replacement level in a land that is already the second most densely populated territory on earth after Hong Kong; nevertheless, the accomplishment is extraordinary.[20] Despite the strides in reducing family size, the challenges for Bangladesh remain managing the basic needs and economic opportunities required by a vast number of people living in a small space. In most African countries, fertility rates continue to be high, although they have declined, on average, from nearly seven children per woman to just under six.

Population Decisions in a Household in Kenya

Perhaps a glimpse into the lives of two women who live in Western Kenya will help clarify the dilemmas they face vis-à-vis choices about family size and child mortality. South Kamwango is a community in western Kenya quite near Lake Victoria.[21] Health problems, infant mortality, and low levels of productivity affect everyone. Serafina and Salima are co-wives in a typical extended family in this generally polygamous community. Each manages her own household within the larger family compound. Neither is sure of her age; Serafina knows that she was married in 1968; Salima is not sure when her marriage took place. Currently living in the household are their husband, the two co-wives themselves, five sons, four daughters-in-law and twelve grandchildren. Three daughters are married and living elsewhere; two sons work outside the district. Of the eleven children Serafina has borne, six have died. Of the ten Salima has borne, five have died. All deaths occurred before the age of three. They attribute the deaths to kwashiorkor, tetanus, malaria, measles, and witchcraft. It is evident that the grandchildren are suffering from malnutrition and respiratory infections. The family has an unprotected well on its land. The water is not boiled despite its muddy color. They do not associate the deaths of the children with possible contamination of the water. Given this record of child mortality, Serafina and Salima and the younger women in their household are a long way from embracing the idea of small family size.

In the district of Kenya, Migori, in which South Kamwango is located, the population is young. Those age fifteen years and younger constitute about 50 percent of the entire population. As a result, the dependency ratio is high. Although there is considerable awareness of family planning, and 85 percent of the adult population is familiar with the concept, a decade ago, the acceptance rate was only 5 percent.[22] The overall effects of population increase on resources are well understood, yet this understanding, under present circumstances, does not necessarily influence household decisions on family size.

South Kamwango is beginning to experience pressures on resources related to rapid population growth. It is commonplace to find households with two or three wives each with four or five living children. Some people recognize and can articulate the impact of these statistics on their own families. They recognize the troubles their children will have in obtaining sufficient land for cultivation; they lament their inability to provide secondary education for their own children. At a public meeting, several women and older men spoke in favor of family planning and limiting family size. Yet, several younger men opposed it. "How," one asked, "can we have family planning when so many of our children die?"

Questions of population growth can be examined only in the context of South Kamwango's health and its extraordinarily high infant mortality rates. Eighty percent of households interviewed had lost a child before the age of five; many households had lost half the children born, and several had lost more than half. How representative are these circumstances? Like Serafina and Salima, many people face critical shortfalls of essentials needed for health and well-being. Worldwide approximately 1.3 billion live in absolute poverty; 840 million are undernourished; 1.4 billion lack safe drinking water, and about 900 million are illiterate.[23] Of the latter, two-thirds are females. For all these people, limiting family size is unlikely to be in their best interests at the present time.

Access to Renewable Resources: Water, People, and Health

In a world in which two-thirds of the world's surface is covered with water, it is hard to imagine that water shortages could become a significant problem of this new century. Yet it is projected that within twenty-five years, up to 3 billion people could be dealing with chronic water shortages. In fact, Population Action International (PAI) projects that by the middle of the twenty-first century, more than half of the world's population might live in countries with chronic or recurring water shortages.[24] Some suggest that conflicts of the future are likely to be "water wars." That is, rapid population growth, drought, and enormous demand on rivers and aquifers used jointly by several nations may lead to issues surrounding fair and appropriate allocation of water.

The problem resides in the fact that only 2.5 percent of the water on earth is fresh; the rest is found in the oceans and seas.[25] Of this, less than 1 percent is available for human use; the rest is locked away in glaciers and polar ice caps or is contaminated by wastes. Moreover, human requirements continue to expand because of increasing population and often wasteful water management. At the present time 70 percent of the world's fresh water is used for agriculture. Rapid drainage of aquifers, plummeting water tables, leaking pipes, unlined irrigation canals, and inefficient water pumps are all part and parcel of the problems leading to water shortage. Surface water shortages are causing more and more nations to tap their supplies of groundwater, with the consequence that water tables are dropping.

At present over 2 billion people lack access to safe drinking water, and many communities are struggling with specific problems of water quality. Raw sewage, toxic metals, and other industrial wastes are causing water-borne diseases such as cholera, typhoid fever, and dysentery. Contaminated water, whether from mercury along the Tapajos River in Brazil or hog refuse in the flooded farms of North Carolina in the United States, makes water quality is an important issue. Industrial and household effluent can often overwhelm treatment capacities, and untreated waste from paper, textile, and food industries in many developing countries contaminate the water sources of millions of people. Dam construction has also increased infection rates for schistosomiasis in some parts of Africa. Other water-borne diseases affect large portions of the world's population.

Returning to South Kamwango provides us with another opportunity to consider the population, environment, health, and development issues particularly as they are affected by water. The continuing presence of severe, environmentally related health problems is one of the most significant issues for South Kamwango. The widespread and commonplace assortment of diseases can be attributed to several factors. The water is sufficient, but the quality is poor. Rare is the family that has a protected well or boils its drinking water. The Kira River that runs through the sublocation, and that is used by many households to provide drinking water, is seriously polluted. Furthermore, there are low levels of sanitation. Fewer than half the households have a latrine; groundwater levels are high, and opportunities for spread of disease are evident. It is widely known that the incidence of diarrheal and other diseases is greatly increased by the use of contaminated water for drinking and bathing. These problems are compounded by insufficient education on environmental sanitation and hygiene. South Kamwango households provide clear evidence.

The poor health status of the community, especially among children, is caused largely by preventable factors. Malnutrition in the form of marasmius, kwashiorkor, and various vitamin deficiencies has reached epidemic levels, but most mothers do not associate conditions caused by malnutrition with poor diet. Similarly, they do not relate increasing numbers of stomach ailments and skin infections to the quality of water. Nor do people link these problems to general health status and levels of sanitation. Measures that would improve family health, such as boiling drinking water, are not undertaken because the women have no basis for understanding a cause-effect relationship between water quality and health and because, in some instances, firewood is in short supply.

Child rearing and childcare are the exclusive domain of the women. The status of children in the sublocation reflects the nature of women's knowledge regarding nutrition and disease. The household interviews revealed that most mothers have some knowledge of the nature of diseases, but have difficulty in conceptualizing the cause-and-effect relationship of the children's health problems. There is very low awareness of hygiene, nutrition, and sanitation in general, and their relationship to clean environment. The World Resources Institute reminds us of the importance of women's knowledge on these and other issues. "Where rapid gains in reducing mortality have been achieved, improvement in the educational and social status of women has been a key. The mother is the basic health worker in all societies."[26]

Thus, there is an urgent need to increase women's understanding of the nature and origins of many illnesses and thereby to improve both their willingness and capacity to address the root causes of these problems. Knowledge about matters of health, sanitation, and nutrition should be central to the lives of women in South Kamwango. At present, trends in these areas are negative. If sustainable development is to take place in South Kamwango, reversing these trends in health, nutrition, and sanitation is essential.

The Central Place of Women's Empowerment, Education, and Health in the Population/Environment Discussions

The preceding comments on health, environment, and women's responsibilities in a small community in Kenya reveal the roles of women in shaping family, household, and community linkages with the environment. We can explore these implications not only in Kenya, but throughout the world. In many societies children are both a social and an economic necessity for women, essential for survival, security, status, and prestige. Many of the factors that encourage large families are associated with the limited roles and opportunities for women. In many parts of the world women continue to be dependent on men for essential resources and on their children for immediate economic assistance and for long-term economic security. In fact, if a rural woman's survival, old age security, and status are dependent on her family and on agriculture, rationality will assure that she does not reduce her fertility.

What is the relationship between women's education and completed family size? Education is widely regarded as the single most important variable affecting fertility. There is an inverse relationship between the level of female education and completed family size. That is, statistically, world over, the more highly educated a woman is, the smaller her completed family size is likely to be. Conversely, less educated women are more likely to have large families. Causation may relate to specific information or knowledge including knowledge about child health and child care as well as contraceptive protection. It may relate to the greater opportunities available to women as they climb the educational ladder. Sorting out the effects of education on women's aspirations and on the opportunity costs they encounter by having to care for a large family is difficult.

There is also a significant relationship between education and the age of marriage. The more highly educated a woman is, the more she is likely to delay the age of marriage and thus delay beginning her family. In the short term, women with only a few years of primary education are unlikely to show a decline in fertility levels. The positive relationship between education and family size is more likely to occur with secondary or postsecondary education. Several studies from developing countries have shown that where few females are enrolled in secondary schools, the average woman has seven children. As enrollment in secondary school increases, completed family size decreases. The relationship between employment and fertility is not quite so clear-cut. There seems to be a mutually reinforcing pattern that links increased female labor force participation with a decline in family size. Certainly a small family makes working easier. However, it may be the need to support a large family that propels a woman into the labor force in the first place. In this case employment and family size correlate positively rather than inversely. In terms of employment, the concept of role compatibility is important. If roles are compatible, there may be little relation between employment and fertility. For example, if a woman can take her baby with her while she picks tea, her roles as mother and wage laborer do not conflict. On the other hand, she cannot take the baby to an office where she will be working on a computer. Here there is no role compatibility. In general, a negative employment-fertility relationship is strong in modern-sector employment and weak or nonexistent in informal-sector and agricultural employment. Where young women are gaining access to employment in export zones or other modern-sector avenues, a negative employment-fertility relationship is emerging, as noted in the cases of Thailand and Bangladesh.

Usually there are big differences in role compatibility between rural and urban areas and between those kinds of jobs demanding little or significant skills. A well-educated woman who has found satisfying, well-remunerated employment will have an incentive to limit family size and to engage in a variety of activities outside child care. The reality for most women, however, is that they are likely to be seeking a job because of children whom they must support. Most rural paid employment of a high status is oriented toward men. Rarely, therefore, is high-status, well-paid employment a viable option for a woman. Child bearing today remains the way most rural women can demonstrate importance and value. It is unrealistic to expect a woman to limit the size of her family if her sense of self-worth and the community's assessment of her worth are determined by the number of children she bears. Moreover, in many societies, women do not have control over their own fertility. Husbands, or possibly a mother-in-law, are likely to make decisions about family size. If men judge their status simply by the number of children rather than the well-being and quality of life of their children, the pressure for having large families is likely to remain high.

Many suggest that the most critical global population challenge is elevating the status of women. There is, after all, a relevant lesson from India pertaining to women's empowerment, population growth, family size, and environment. India now has a population of 1 billion, increasing by 16 million every year. The most optimistic UN projection foresees India's population stabilizing when it is nearly double, at 1.8 billion, a despairing thought given the teeming poverty that characterizes that nation. A bright spot, however, in this otherwise gloomy picture is Kerala, a state on the southwest coast where there is a zero population growth rate in marked contrast to the rest of the nation. The question is why?

In Kerala, literacy, including women's literacy, is 90 percent, in contrast to the overall figure for India of 54 percent. Education is compulsory; health care is free; and infant mortality rates are twelve per thousand compared with eighty-five per thousand in Uttar Pradesh to the north.[27] Moreover, Kerala has a vigorous democratically elected state government, a strong mix of religious identities, and a lively economy based on rubber, cashews, coir (a fibre made from coconut husks), and tourists. Increasingly Kerala's citizens are working abroad, particularly in the Gulf States, and sending remittances home. It is not easy to discern what among this mix of factors is making the difference in Kerala, but the empowerment of women is a good place to begin.

Kerala's experience leads us to rethink some old assumptions. For over three decades the international family planning movement has been based on the strategy of legitimizing the idea of small families and providing the means to reduce fertility. There is no doubt that opportunities for family planning do contribute to women's empowerment and to improving women's status. Enabling women to space the births of children can improve the health of both mother and child. Kerala's experience suggests that securing access to new resources and providing new kinds of opportunities for women begins a process of changing perceptions. The opportunity costs of large families begin to look different. Slowly, the linkages among women's health, economic opportunities, and reduced fertility emerge. People are beginning to recognize that programs that improve women's health, status, and well-being are central to reducing birthrates. The issue is not simply the impact of population growth on economic development. Evidence suggests that improving the status of women not only helps development but also helps to reduce fertility, emphasizing the connection between a woman's productive and reproductive roles. Improvements in women's health, education, and economic opportunity lead to empowerment. They are also basic human rights.

Individuals and women's organizations have worked over several decades to bring a gender perspective and a focus on reproductive rights to population issues. Indeed, no one has spoken on the topic with more eloquence and more commitment than Betsy Hartmann in her 1987 *Reproductive Rights and Wrongs: The Global Politics of Population Control and Contraceptive Choice.*[28] She affirms that the central issue is giving women the economic resources and the social and political power that would enable them to control their reproductive lives. Circling back to the beginning of this chapter, we can see the feminist insights that draw on a political ecology perspective and include gender in the analysis of population, environment, and development issues. These insights can offer a compelling critique of approaches that emphasize population control to the exclusion of poverty alleviation or women's roles. To do so neglects the social and structural roots of women's subordination. It also limits capacities to generate creative approaches to the dilemmas linking population and resources in the development process.

Three Policy Concerns for the Global South in the New Century

Resource Extraction and Devastated Populations

Raw materials are traded globally, but must be extracted locally and the costs — environmental, social, and economic — are borne locally. People and their habitat may be exploited and destroyed, particularly around mineral extraction efforts. Often governments of the South have difficulty regulating production and sale of raw materials. They face resistance from a variety of economic and political forces, including the external markets, externally controlled capital and technology, and various domestic interests. The state may also be in collusion with the outside commercial interests to take advantage of the resource with little concern for the well-being of the local population.

From the Arctic to the Amazon our dependence on fossil fuels has been detrimental to the peoples living in areas of mineral extraction. Two sites illustrate the problem well. In the western part of Ecuador in the provinces of Orellana and Succumbios, the local people have seen little benefit from thirty years of oil extraction. On another continent, nowhere is this problem more evident than in Nigeria among the Ogoni people, a small tribe living on the coastal plains of the Niger River Delta. We consider these two sites in turn.

The Ecuadorian Amazon contains among the most biologically diverse forests of the globe. It also has rich deposits of heavy-grade crude oil, an attractive item for the government of Ecuador facing large international debt obligations. Since the late 1960s several American oil companies, led by Texaco, have pumped oil from that region in a complex involving several hundred drill sites as well as hundreds of miles of roads and pipelines.[29] For years, indigenous groups and environmental organizations have been concerned about the practices of Texaco and Occidental

Petroleum in this region, about 30 percent of which is open to oil activities while also the home to nearly a hundred thousand indigenous peoples of eight different cultural groups. Ecuadorans filed a class action lawsuit against Texaco in federal court in New York in 1993. In 2002 the suit remains "pending"; the devastation remains overwhelming. Perhaps a quote from a publication of the Natural Resources Defense Council clarifies the picture:

> Past the petroleum camp, a large river, recently burned, still ran black, its banks charred and devoid of vegetation. Oil wastes streamed from the broken berm of a nearby production pit. On the horizon dense plumes of inky smoke rose from burning production pits and gas flares linked by dirt roads stained with oil, sprayed to subdue the dust. Along these roads (still within the reserve), colonists' homes of cane and thatch stood amidst fields of coffee, plantains, and fallen trees.... When they burn their pits, smoke falls in pieces from the sky, then we have black rains and the particles drop on our crops and animals.[30]

Environmental devastation in the form of oil waste pits with a witch's brew of toxic chemicals and contamination of lakes, rivers, and streams brings harm to fragile ecosystems, causing irreparable harm to aquatic life. It has health and economic consequences as well. One doctor describes 70 percent malnutrition in young children whereas in areas nearby without oil production there are no cases of malnutrition. Bioaccumulation of petroleum and other heavy metals in the food chain can cause serious human health problems. Cancer, birth defects, sores, and other skin problems can also be a consequence of contact with toxic wastes. These problems have inspired *campesino* communities to organize in protest of a new OCP pipeline and related plans to double oil production in the region. The OCP consortium includes oil companies from Canada, the United States, Italy, Spain, and Argentina. U.S. and German banks along with the World Bank and the IMF are supporting the plan.

Thus, the lines are drawn between the concerns of environmentalists, advocacy groups, and indigenous communities vis-à-vis those of big business, Northern consumers, and profiting elites both North and South. At risk is the possibility of an irreversible loss of the region's renewable and nonrenewable resources and continuing harm to the health and livelihoods of the local residents.

On another continent we find a very similar situation. Oil exploration by international oil companies, especially Shell, has turned the Ogoni homeland in Nigeria into a wasteland of pollution with a poisoned atmosphere and widespread devastation caused by acid rain, oil spillages, and oil blowouts.[31] Lands, stream, and creeks are totally and continually polluted; the atmosphere has been poisoned, charged as it is with hydrocarbon, vapors, methane, carbon monoxide, carbon dioxide, and soot emitted by gas which has been flared twenty-four hours a day for thirty-three years in very close proximity to human habitation. Neither the Nigerian State nor Shell Oil has been committed to containing pollution. Impoverished and inconsequential in Nigeria's political context, the Ogoni have little leverage for demanding pollution control or any of the benefits of oil profits in the form of development efforts.

In 1990 the Ogoni people (numbering about five hundred thousand) presented an Ogoni Bill of Rights to the Nigerian government. In this document, they described their past experience of both internal and British colonialism. They specified that oil had been mined on their land since 1958 in seven oil fields and that in over thirty years the Ogoni people have provided an estimated $30 billion in revenue for the Nigerian government for which they have received nothing. The Ogoni people have "(i) No representation whatsoever in ALL institutions of the Federal government of Nigeria. (ii) No pipe-borne water. (iii) No electricity. (iv) No job opportunities for the citizens in Federal, state, public sector or private sector companies. (v) No social or economic project of the Federal government." Further, they link oil exploitation to ethnic politics suggesting that the federal and state governments are "gradually pushing the Ogoni people to slavery and possible extinction."[32]

The Ogoni people of Nigeria, as well as the Ecuadoran *campesinos*, are far from the sites in which key decisions about technological choices, government and corporate strategies, resource access, and resource depletion are made. Their needs and concerns must be brought into the discussion. Their troubling and very similar situations involve extraordinary environmental devastation, continuing human rights violations, overwhelming health problems, and marginal economic viability brought about by the production of oil in their homeland for the benefit of people elsewhere.

AIDS in Africa

Infectious diseases remain a serious worldwide threat in the twenty-first century despite enormous progress in dealing with some of them in the last century. Among the most urgent concerns is that of Acquired Immune Deficiency Syndrome (AIDS), which by 2000 had infected 36 million people worldwide, of whom 22 million had died. HIV/AIDS causes mortality primarily among adults, decreasing adult life expectancy. It has direct health costs as well as indirect economic and social impacts caused by the disease. There are also significant implications from the changing demographic structure and decreasing life span for many.

At the present time the AIDS epidemic is growing most rapidly in Eastern Europe and Central Asia. It also looms as an increasing problem in China which, for the first time, is openly acknowledging its AIDS problem and is seeking international support from the Global Fund to Fight AIDS, Tuberculosis and Malaria. Ninety-four of every hundred HIV-infected people live in developing nations where currently available drug therapies are largely unaffordable. More than half of all new HIV infections are among women.[33] Three million people died of AIDS in 2000. All these figures are staggering and of enormous import to all global citizens.

Despite these new frontiers on which the AIDS battles must be fought, Africa remains the most significant arena for the struggle against AIDS. One analyst suggests that Africa, already beset by problems of regime transition and poor levels of institutionalization, faces serious human resource loss and strained capacities associated with the HIV/AIDS pandemic and he asserts, "we can be grimly confident that HIV/AIDS and its impact are Africa's biggest problem."[34] According to UNAIDS, since the start of the AIDS epidemic, an estimated 34 million people living in sub-Saharan Africa have been infected with HIV and 17 million of those people have already died, a quarter of them children.[35] One in five deaths in sub-Saharan Africa is caused by AIDS, and life expectancy is plummeting. Some suggest that by 2010 the disease will decrease life expectancy on the continent to levels found at the beginning of the last century.[36] UNAIDS and the World Health Organization (WHO) claim that seven out of ten people in sub-Saharan Africa are infected with HIV. Sub-Saharan Africa is the only part of the world where many more girls are infected than boys.

In Africa AIDS is not only causing untold human suffering, it is jeopardizing economic growth, political stability, and civil society. Africa has a growing number of children living in AIDS-affected households or attempting to survive after the death of their mother, or both parents, to

AIDS. UNAIDS estimates there are over 12 million AIDS orphans in Africa.[37] According to the Office of National AIDS Policy, during this decade, more than 40 million children will be orphaned by AIDS, and this number is not expected to peak until 2030. The AIDS-orphan emergency is causing unprecedented threats to child welfare. The orphans become vulnerable due to malnutrition and decreased access to education, health care, housing, and clothing. In addition, they suffer from psychological and social distress brought on by the death of a parent, isolation, and stigma.

The epidemic is shattering families and placing a new burden on the extended family and village systems. AIDS and the need to care for orphans have overwhelmed the capacities of the extended family, which is central to African culture. According to the Southern African Institute for Security Studies, there are linkages between the growing number of children orphaned by AIDS and increases in crime and civil unrest.[38] As the number of homeless, disaffected, troubled, and undereducated young people increases, many sub-Saharan countries may face serious threats to their social stability. Certainly the spread of HIV/AIDS and increases in violent conflict are dominant features in sub-Saharan Africa. There are no doubt complex crosscutting connections between these two phenomena. In fact, HIV/AIDS simply may undermine processes leading to the demographic transition, economic development, and functioning states, instead abetting poverty, civil war, and state collapse.

The Ugandan Model: An Approach to AIDS

Uganda was one of the first countries to recognize AIDS cases (1982), to report its AIDS problem to the WHO, and to open its doors to international AIDS researchers.[39] In 1986, in collaboration with the World Health Organization, an AIDS Control Program (ACP) was set up in Uganda. In 1992 the government of Uganda established a national oversight agency, the Uganda AIDS Commission, to supervise activities related to formulating policy, disseminating information, raising awareness, and mobilizing resources. For more than a decade Ugandan president Yoweri Museveni has waged a prolonged campaign of public education, condom distribution, voluntary testing, counseling, and support services. He has been credited with spurring public awareness, fighting the stigma often serving as a barrier to effective HIV/AIDS prevention, and securing the involvement of Ugandans at all levels of society.

As a consequence, Uganda has reduced rates of HIV prevalence from 15 percent in 1991 to 5 percent in 2001.[40] The most dramatic decline in HIV prevalence is seen among youths aged fifteen to twenty-four; Uganda's challenge now is to maintain these declining levels. While Uganda has benefited from international support for its HIV/AIDS prevention efforts, its program provides an example of an initiative that does not take an exorbitant amount of resources while giving rapid results. Uganda's success at curbing HIV infections could, therefore, serve as a model for other African countries.

Recent Initiatives on AIDS

The World Health Organization is focusing on three aspects of the epidemic: caring for the more than 30 million people currently living with HIV/AIDS, reducing the number of mother-to-child transmissions, and accessing HIV/AIDS-related drugs. The latter is a significant problem worldwide with a titanic struggle between pharmaceutical companies and public health advocates including governments of the South. In the face of devastation from the AIDS epidemic, Third World countries say they need to manufacture or import generic drugs that are cheaper than the patented drugs currently produced by major pharmaceutical companies of the North. At the center of the debate is the 1994 Agreement on Trade-Related Aspects of Intellectual Property Rights (TRIPS) that protects patents of inventors and manufacturers for twenty years. The TRIPS agreement permits governments to use compulsory licensing in crisis situations involving public safety, war, health, or environmental disasters. The Western pharmaceutical companies have been opposed to compulsory licensing and "parallel importing" that lets a country's drug buyers seek the cheapest price anywhere in the world. The issues remain unresolved and must be addressed in order to provide access to medications for poor AIDS patients around the world.

Philanthropists, such as Microsoft's founder, Bill Gates, have committed funds for research for vaccine development and AIDS prevention.[41] The U.S. government has promised an American increase to help fight the disease in Africa.[42] A broad cross-section of African NGOs is involved with the International Partnership against AIDS in Africa intending to promote and protect human rights, reduce new HIV infections, and provide a continuum of care for those infected and affected. In addition, UNAIDS hopes to assist African governments to implement more effective and sustained national responses to HIV and AIDS. Most Africans believe that the institutions in place are not the answer to addressing the impacts of AIDS. Many believe that new solutions must be found in the community itself. Increasingly, Africans are joining their modest resources at the local level to care for the sick, raise the orphans, and prevent the virus from claiming more lives from their communities. At all scales — local, regional, national, and international — AIDS must be challenged.

Poverty, Growing Inequality, Migration

Finally, the third policy concern links the growing global economic inequalities — a recurring theme of this book — with population movements. One of the most alarming trends to emerge in the past several decades is the growing gap between rich and poor. Disparities have widened internally with the poorest 20 percent of the world's population now receiving 1.1 percent of global income, while the richest 20 percent claim 86 percent. Between 1960 and 1994 the ratio of the income of the richest 20 percent to the poorest 20 percent increased from 30:1 to 78:1.[43]

Not only are these disparities indicative of the hardships endured by many, but they are associated with social instability and increasing conflict. Whether we examine the Zapatista rebellion in Mexico's Chiapas state, where small farmers face inequitable patterns of land tenure and small, degraded land holdings; the farmers and unemployed young people in Indonesia; or the youth on the streets of Cairo, the tensions arising from grossly unfair allocation of resources, deprivation, and unemployment are apparent. Technical solutions may ameliorate these problems but will not solve them. They may respond to better pricing policies, to erosion control measures, to new agricultural techniques, to improved health or greater educational opportunities, but the root causes remain. The fundamental issues are not technical but are found in the socioeconomic and political environment in which the fairness of access to resources and access to the benefits of a given social system is determined.

As we know well from the history of this last century, poverty and inequalities have a significant effect on patterns of migration that in turn shape environmental impacts. Land scarcity, environmental degradation, and population growth are underlying causes of emigration from rural communities to other areas by people who hope they will find new agricultural opportunities or urban jobs. For example, the young men and women living on Siquijor Island in the Philippines may journey to Mindanao, another island, in the hope they might obtain work on a coffee or pineapple plantation, saving some money and eventually renting or buying their own land. In some instances these rural residents follow timber concessions into the uplands cultivating areas ill suited to agricultural purposes, and thus often contributing to the degradation of the environment. The restless young people from Siquijor may not choose a rural destination. They may head to Cebu City or to Manila or beyond to seek their fortunes in an urban environment, usually in the informal sector. Urban growth has its own sets of problems, namely the expansion of services and infrastructure to keep up with the needs of the population. Education, health, transportation, housing, water, electricity — all pose challenges to rapidly growing urban communities.

International migration includes both voluntary migration, usually for economic reasons, and the involuntary movement of refugees. The United Nations estimates that at least 120 million people (excluding refugees) lived or worked outside of their own country in 1990, an increase from about 75 million in 1965.[44] Approximately half of all international migration takes place within the developing world. For example, in recent decades perhaps as many as 17 million people have moved from Bangladesh to the adjacent Indian states of Assam, Tripura, and West Bengal.[45] For Assam, this has meant that migrants from Bangladesh represent about one-third of the state's residents; for Tripura ethnic imbalances related to migration led to violence and unrest throughout most of the 1980s and into the 1990s. Such unrest is not uncommon in other parts of the world where spillover from one rural community to another has precipitated competition over scarce resources, sometimes ending in tense and violent relations. In the industrialized world, between 1990 and 1995, 45 percent of overall population growth was due to immigration.[46] These visitors, seeking economic opportunity and a new life, often face a restless set of host nations whose people are not entirely welcoming to the newcomers. We are only at the beginning of new flows of people across national boundaries, migrants intent on finding new opportunities despite the heavy risks involved. Addressing poverty and its attendant violence and injustice so that people are not propelled out of their homes to distant places to secure the most basic livelihoods is incumbent upon all of us.

Concluding Observations:
Poverty, Environment, and Population

In this chapter we have considered the relationships among development, poverty, population, and environment. The political ecology perspective introduced at the outset provides a view in which the focus is not specifically on either economics or the environment. From this perspective, poverty and the unequal access to resources are the root causes of both environmental degradation and population growth. This line of argument suggests that addressing poverty, reducing inequalities, and providing a more equitable distribution of resources will have a beneficial impact on population growth and hence on the environment and human welfare. The UNDP's *Human Development Report* for 1994, assessing the last fifty years, emphasizes an arresting picture of unprecedented human progress and unspeakable human misery, of rich and poor nations alike afflicted by growing human distress.[47] A political ecology perspective, aided by a feminist critique of development processes that are sometimes mindlessly growth-oriented and technology driven, can contribute to our understanding of population and environment linkages. It can also contribute to the definition of alternative paradigms of social change in order to address the economic and political barriers to environmental sustainability and social justice.

We have examined the household logic of large families, and we have explored fundamental development issues around water and health. We have identified the demographic transition and the demographic trap. We have observed that there is a growing consensus that both family planning (access to information and contraceptive technology) and social and economic development have strong independent effects on fertility. We have observed the critical roles of women in these processes, and the importance of empowering women in the arenas of health, education, and economic and political opportunity.

There is a practical question: where should governments and non-governmental organizations invest limited resources to cope with the consequences of high rates of population growth? Much evidence now suggests that investing in human resources, particularly in terms of education and health, provides the strongest base for economic growth. This investment in basic social services appears to bring strong returns. However, in recent decades structural adjustment policies, military budgets, and declining economies have not led to increased public spending in this area. Evidence presented in this chapter suggests that we must invest more in human capital in sub-Saharan Africa, as well as in parts of South Asia and Latin America, if we are to reverse the downward spiral of poverty, underemployment, and resource degradation.

In the coming decades, we can anticipate global increases in both the numbers of people trying to secure their livelihoods and welfare and in the environmental problems caused by these efforts. Even if we have the projected "best possible scenario" of approximately 8 billion people on earth by 2050, there will still be tremendous pressures on global resources and on our environment. Some of these pressures can be addressed by local and national measures, but many will require international collaboration on environmental and resource management policies. The destruction of inland fisheries or forests may be amenable to national action, but ozone depletion, diminishing biodiversity, decimated ocean fisheries, and global air pollution will require action by responsible policymakers and global citizens who understand the relationship between sustainability of our environment and the sustainability of all peoples.

Chapter 8

Food Security, Rural Change, and Global Politics

In a world of unprecedented wealth and abundance, it seems inconceivable that hunger is widespread, malnutrition a continuing curse, and food security merely a hope or dream for many. This chapter moves across local, national, and global scales to consider food issues and food security in the Global South in the context of global politics. First, we provide a twenty-first-century update on global food production and explore current trends in two widely differing food systems: East and Southeast Asia composing one, and sub-Saharan Africa the other. We then identify three kinds of constraints on food production: land and water resources, agricultural institutions, and levels and nature of technology. We next move to the local level to examine the responsibilities of women for food production in three different national and cultural settings: Kenya, the Philippines, and Honduras. These glimpses help us to recognize the roles that women play in assuring food security in rural households around the world. Finally, we consider several broad issues that need to be part of a global agenda for transforming agriculture in the twenty-first century.

The World's Changing Food Systems

A Twenty-First-Century Update

The last half of the twentieth century saw incredible growth in global food production with a nearly 50 percent increase per capita. However, this statistic conceals wide variations in the output of different regions and countries. Great differences also exist in the distribution of food and the access of different social groups and classes to the food they need. Thus, there is cause for both pessimism and optimism about the prospects of achieving global food security. The Green Revolution

247

with its significant advances in agricultural biotechnology, new varieties of seeds, expansion of irrigation, and broad use of fertilizers encourages optimism. The world's expanding population, along with relatively slow growth in the productivity of food grains in the 1990s, is cause for pessimism. Africa's specific situation with its rain-fed agriculture, low levels of technology, and challenging climate and landscape adds to this pessimism.

We obtain food from both land and the seas with three types of land-based food production systems. One is industrial agriculture with its intensive and large-scale use of capital and inputs largely in temperate climates. The second might be considered "Green Revolution" agriculture with irrigated conditions and carefully managed inputs, usually in the tropics. The third is low-yielding, resource-poor agriculture largely in developing countries. This last is rain-fed, vulnerable, and widespread in sub-Saharan Africa as well as in parts of Asia and Latin America. Although the world's agricultural systems have made significant gains, some suggest that we have reached a yield plateau or yield stagnation in many major food crops.[1] Yield growth rates have been declining for wheat and corn while remaining stable for rice over the past twenty years, yet the demand for all cereals is expected to rise substantially during the early part of the twenty-first century. Unfortunately, most of the high-quality agricultural land is in use. The benefits of converting remaining lands to agricultural uses have to be weighed against the costs of diminishing forest and grasslands and the possibility that these lands have fragile and relatively unproductive soil. Crop intensification, which has occurred with the technologies of the Green Revolution, enabling farmers to grow two or even three crops where they once grew only one, places great strain on soils. Crops such as sorghum and millet commonly grown by small farmers in drought-prone areas (widespread in Africa) have experienced low or declining yields per hectare, partly because of the capital and labor limitations of these farmers. An additional concern is the problem of postharvest loss through insects, rotting, or rodents.

To increase agricultural output it is necessary either to increase the amount of land cultivated or to increase the productivity of the land already under cultivation. In many countries there is already pressure on high-quality agricultural lands, and bringing more land under cultivation poses difficulties. Investing in new forms of land management and new technologies to intensify agricultural production is, therefore, an important alternative to bringing new lands into cultivation. With much of the Global South producing food with low levels of technology on rain-fed fields, there is much that could be done to increase productivity. The challenge is to increase production, improve distribution, and reduce the environmental and health costs.

In the least developed countries these challenges are most acute. Of the 3 billion people in low income countries, approximately 65 percent live in rural areas. In these countries agriculture accounts for 28 percent of the GDP.[2] According to several recent UNCTAD reports, the least developed countries have, on average, 73 percent of the labor force in agriculture.[3] Over the last several decades per capita food production has declined in twenty-six of these countries.[4] Thus, one may safely conclude that large numbers of people are working very hard but producing relatively little.

The reasons, in addition to soils and climate, are numerous. Governments have tried to use agriculture to help build industry and to keep city populations happy with low prices for food. Often returns for farmers have not met the expenses of fertilizer, high-yielding seeds, and other inputs. Thus only the wealthiest farmers have been able to utilize new technologies. Policies have been extractive toward agriculture with negative consequences for rural populations. Rural people have found it difficult to support themselves with traditional agriculture; they have lacked the inputs needed for intensive agriculture, and they have had few alternatives to an agricultural livelihood. As a consequence, they have frequently headed to the cities to seek employment. In many instances this strategy has been carried out in a way that divides the family, leaving women, children, and old men on the farm while young male adults, and sometimes young women, head to the cities.

Figure 8.1 demonstrates the variation of the world's food distribution. Food security is improving; matching supply with need is not always possible. There are many who are inadequately nourished; the challenge remains to enable people either to produce sufficient food or to make it available to all at prices they can afford. In Asia and Latin America both total and per capita food production have risen markedly. In Africa, food production on a per capita basis has declined, as it has also in the former Soviet Union. Even if, as the FAO projects, the proportion of the world's population that is undernourished were to decrease over the next decade, that still leaves nearly 700 million people with inadequate food, of whom more than 250 million are located in Africa.

Figure 8.1. Progress in Feeding the World:
Trends in Per Capita Food Production

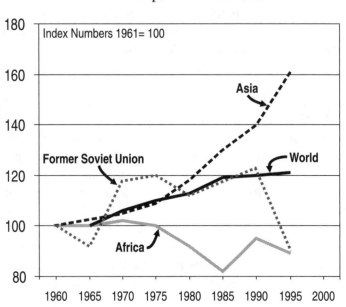

Source: Information from the Food and Agriculture Organization of the United Nations (FAO), *FAOSTAT Statistical Database, apps.fao.org,* and based on Figure FW.2, 154, in the *1998–99 World Resources: A Guide to the Global Environment* from World Resources Institute. Note figures are indexed to 1961 production levels.

The concept of food security is thus broader than that of national food self-sufficiency; it is also a problem of income and access. Poverty is a key cause of hunger and malnutrition. People lack money to buy food or the land and other resources to grow it. Food security and poverty are distinct problems. People can achieve food security if they have access to income outside agriculture for buying food. Conversely, increases in food production may benefit only a few people, leaving many without adequate food. Figure 8.2 reveals regional trends in undernourishment in developing countries.

Other factors are relevant to a discussion of food security. Drought has been linked to hunger from time immemorial. For the most part, massive starvation caused by prolonged drought is a thing of the past. A devastating famine, such as the famous Bengal famine of 1947, for example, did not recur in the last part of the twentieth century, in large part because early warning systems and capacities for deployment of food aid

Figure 8.2. Trends in Undernourishment in Developing Countries

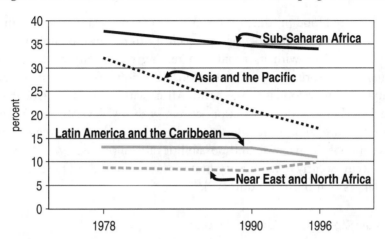

Source: Food and Agriculture Organization of the United Nations (FAO), *The State of Food and Agriculture, 2001* (Rome: FAO, 2001), Table 4.

have become more effective. For example, in Southern Africa drought and the complications of AIDS created a situation in which 14 million people across seven states would have faced starvation in mid-2002 were it not for massive assistance from organizations such as the World Food Program. In addition, human beings have no shortage of ways to induce hunger. War, upheaval, the flight of refugees, or prolonged civil war bring about conditions of starvation and malnutrition and encourage the use of food and hunger as political weapons.

In sum, we must examine the social and structural, as well as the biological and physical, causes of a world food supply problem and consequent malnutrition. It is not simply a matter of insufficient food production; it is also a matter of access and distribution. Poverty is a root cause of chronic malnutrition. A household must be able to produce or purchase its food, but poor families rarely have the resources to do so adequately. Food insecurity thus may relate to land scarcity or degradation, to low wages, lack of work, or underemployment. In addition, inefficient pricing, disincentives for small farmers, skewed land distribution, and inadequate extension services are among the factors that may operate to produce agricultural stagnation and food insecurity. Strife, conflict, and adverse climatic conditions frequently aggravate an already fragile food situation.

An Exploration of Two Food Production Systems

Two regional food production systems are of particular interest in an examination of food production and security trends in the Global South. The first is Asia with its rapidly increasing globalization of agrofood systems and reorganization of relations of regional production and consumption. The second is sub-Saharan Africa with its continuing problems in a land-based food production system with low levels of technology, infrastructure, and productivity. Consideration of these two regions clarifies some of the promise and possibilities for improved agriculture and food security early in the twenty-first century, and some of the continuing challenges that must be addressed.

Reorganizing the Food Economy in Asia

Three trends characterize a changing pattern of food production and consumption in Asia.[5] First, led by Japan's dependency on imported foodstuffs, there is a regional organization of agriculture around an increasing number of agricultural exports and imports. The reliance on tropical unprocessed exports is changing, and is being supplemented with nontraditional and processed agroindustrial exports. The intensification of regional food trade has involved such activities as Japanese or Thai companies investing in the Asia-Pacific region to build a productive capacity in China, Malaysia, Indonesia, or elsewhere. Thus financial, banking, and other commercial penetration of one Asian country by another is enhancing financial integration and coordination of food production and marketing.

To illustrate, Thailand, for example, is the world's leading exporter of rice and a major exporter of poultry, canned fruit and vegetables, and animal feed, with agriculture accounting for 25 percent of the value of exports. Thailand has established itself as a major exporter of value-added and processed agrofoods, particularly through shrimp aquaculture, but it is also a major exporter of poultry products to Japan. In fact, a leading Thai firm, the CP Group that started in the 1920s in animal feed production, is today a transnational corporation with operations ranging from agrochemicals to baby foods in Thailand, more than seventy-five feedmills in China, Kentucky Fried Chicken franchises in several countries, and poultry operations in Vietnam, Cambodia, Malaysia, and Indonesia among others.[6]

Thus, there is a movement away from the postwar food regime. This regime has been based in the political management of food surpluses in a bilateral system centered around U.S. food surpluses. The movement is toward multilateral food trade based on agricultural liberalization and the World Trade Organization. One of the trends that has sparked this restructuring away from the post–World War II food regime has been the affluence of the Japanese consumer and need of Japan to import foodstuffs. These changes in the agrofood complex are altering organizational and geopolitical relations. Increasingly the United States is not the global breadbasket and the East Asian food system is a central node in a global regime forming around private, rather than state-driven, agrofood markets.[7]

As a consequence, some countries are shifting from a policy and strategic focus on national food self-sufficiency to regional and global export and import of agricultural products. In fact, no longer is there simply talk about the NICs, the newly industrializing countries; there are now newly agroindustrializing countries (NACs) that are involved in the transnational integration of agricultural production chains.[8] Thailand, the Philippines, and Taiwan are in this category. India, Indonesia, and Malaysia, along with some other countries, are committed — to varying degrees — to policies of national food self-sufficiency. Such policies become more complex as agrofood transnationals challenge the national systems with their transfers of capital, agrotechnology, and organization in a process of restructuring and globalization.

India has made significant improvements in the country's food system with increases in wheat and rice production. (It is the world's second largest producer of rice and is tied with the United States as the world's second largest producer of wheat, but the yields are low and the yields of rice are half that of China's.)[9] The sheer magnitude of food needed to meet India's future requirements suggests that India may be unable to do so from domestic resources. India has already benefited substantially from the Green Revolution technologies, and it is unlikely that India's arable land can be expanded much beyond its present extent.[10]

Long-term questions pertain particularly to both India and China with their overwhelming portions of the world's population. China is expected to have significant shortfalls of grain within the next two or three decades as ecological deterioration occurs, croplands shrink, and productivity slows. If Chinese society becomes more affluent, and, therefore, more able to import foods, and if China's relationship with the global economy expands through its increased involvement with the WTO, significant pressures from China on global food supplies may emerge.

In sum, transnational food production, distribution, and organizational processes in Asia are changing significantly. Agriculture is becoming increasingly globalized, not along North-South dimensions, but regionally, and is reshaping the region's food economy.

Food Production in a Troubled Region: Africa

Across the continent people of sub-Saharan Africa's fifty-three nations have experienced low levels of economic productivity, environmental degradation, a variety of natural catastrophes, inadequate physical and social infrastructure, rapid population growth, famine, civil war, massive unemployment, a growing refugee crisis, and the spread of diseases such as AIDS and the Ebola virus. Moreover, in too many African countries people have endured governments that are corrupt and that even cripple their own economies, subjecting the populace to a wide range of hardships. In some instances, political turmoil, exacerbated by ethnic and class rivalries, has led to violence and to military conflict. All of these circumstances are deeply affected by the exigencies of structural adjustment and the battering of commodity prices in the global market. In sum, the last two decades have been particularly difficult ones for many African countries struggling with a wide range of political, economic, social, and ecological issues.

While there are major differences among African nations and the perspectives of people across the continent, significant commonalities exist. One of the most important is simply the narrow margin of survival that characterizes the lives of many in all African countries. These narrow margins provide the context in which issues of food security, rural change, and global politics are situated. Millions of smallholders, dependent on rudimentary technology in semiarid lands, are raising staple crops unsuited to their environment but promoted by national policy and demanded by urban markets. In many countries, this smallholder agriculture is based primarily on women's labor using simple tools in rain-fed agricultural systems with few inputs and services. In fact, agricultural policies have generally ignored the responsibilities of rural women. Virtually nowhere in Africa have decision makers made a policy linkage between women's roles as food producers, women's roles in managing the environment, and national food security. In effect, governments have not even tried to enable women to achieve effective participation and performance in national development. No wonder that the household producing its own food in this manner does not readily provide the agricultural surplus to feed nations whose populations are growing at 3.1 percent a year and urbanizing, according to World Bank statistics, at the rate of an 8 percent increase per year.[11]

Although Africa had been producing enough food to feed itself as recently as 1970, by 1984 food imports for the continent took approximately 20 percent of foreign exchange earnings. Africa was feeding the equivalent of the continent's entire urban population on imported grain. While agricultural production since then has increased, this gain was below the rate of population increase. According to FAO data, thirty-two African nations experienced a significant decrease in per capita agricultural production in the 1980s.[12]

No doubt this slippage in agricultural production has been affected by the HIV/AIDS pandemic that is widely regarded as a problem of critical importance to African development, not simply a health issue (see chapter 7). It intensifies existing bottlenecks in agricultural labor, increases widespread malnutrition and food insecurity, and aggravates the problems faced by rural women arising from the gender division of labor and entitlements to land and other resources. It also adds significantly to the numbers of orphans who must be cared for by their extended families or by public services. The effects of HIV/AIDS are felt on a critical farm production factor: household labor quality and quantity are reduced both initially through the illness and long term through the death of the adult. Often more than one adult in a family is infected and, given Africa's labor-intensive farming systems with low levels of mechanization and agricultural inputs, the farming household is extremely vulnerable to the impact of the disease. Such impacts may include reduction in the area of land under cultivation; delay in farming operations such as tillage, planting, and weeding; reduction in the ability to control crop pests; decline in crop yields and livestock production; and loss of agricultural knowledge and management skills.[13] Thus AIDS has clearly had a serious and complex impact on agricultural production and household food security.

Today, despite political independence, most African nations continue to be involved with the global economy on less than favorable terms, as discussed in chapter 5. Despite their efforts to produce for the international market, the value of African exports is declining. Over the past seventeen years, many African nations have faced deteriorating terms of trade vis-à-vis the industrialized nations. This relates in part to energy prices, high debt servicing, and major trade deficits. It also relates to the fact that most of the value added comes from processing, of which African countries do very little. Sub-Saharan Africa's share of global trade has fallen to between 2 and 3 percent in the 1990s from nearly 5 percent in the mid-1960s.[14]

In 1992, developing countries received from the North $60 billion in foreign aid and another $102 billion in private capital, but only 6 percent went to sub-Saharan Africa.[15] Meanwhile, Africa has faced staggering foreign debt problems since the oil crisis in the early 1970s. In 1980 debt stood at $55 billion with debt servicing costs absorbing 8 percent of foreign exchange earnings. In 1998, it was $226 billion. Debt servicing alone accounted for 25 percent of the continent's exports of goods and services.[16] In a world of falling commodity prices over which African nations have no control, these countries have great difficulty repaying the debt. The debt crisis reinforces the economic crisis by absorbing a substantial proportion of crucially needed scarce foreign exchange in debt service payments. It simply is very difficult to find the resources to invest in improving agricultural production.

Constraints on Food Production

Turning now to some of the specific constraints on food production that affect all continents, we identify, first, resources and specifically the availability of land and water; second, agrarian institutions; and third, technology.

Land, Water, and the Three D's: Deforestation, Desertification, Degradation

Deforestation

Forests have a variety of economic, social, and environmental functions, many of which pertain to food security. In subsistence economies, they may provide diverse foods ranging from mushrooms to various kinds of roots. They also provide habitat for small animals and fodder for livestock, with direct use values related to harvesting forest plants and animals. Other direct uses of forest products range from *tendu* leaves used in India for cigarette paper, *romblon* leaves and *nipa* fronds for mats and roofing shingles in the Philippines to medicinal herbs in Kenya. There are also indirect use values resulting from forest ecosystem processes. Forests provide vital environmental functions related to the hydrological cycles and to conservation of biodiversity.

The threat to forests comes from several quarters. One is extensive agriculture. Whether in the United States, Brazil, the Philippines, or elsewhere, forests have been regarded as a resource "frontier" with widespread forest clearance for agricultural purposes. Logging and timber extraction constitute a second major threat to forest cover. In some instances timber interests have dominated decisions about forest use. Predatory enterprises have taken advantage of national policies encouraging timber extraction. The consequence has been the demise of some forests, and the degradation and loss of resilience of others. A third threat to forests, particularly near population centers, is destruction for fuelwood. Fuelwood and charcoal account for approximately 80 percent of wood consumption in developing countries because most people use biomass as their primary source of energy.[17]

At issue is the conflict between those who wish to convert forest capital to immediate cash and those who wish to preserve forests for the long-term ecological, economic, and social values. Forests provide the ecological basis for long-term food security, a value not always recognized when immediate production increases through new agricultural lands can be obtained. If forestry policies are developed only in light of immediate economic and strategic needs, they are likely to lead to deforestation with long-term consequences for food security.

Desertification

This term refers to the degradation of soil and vegetation within the arid, semiarid, and subhumid zones caused largely by harmful human activities.[18] Thus, it does not refer to creeping deserts. In fact, the concern is not rainfall variability, but rather dryland degradation where human and livestock populations are putting pressure on the available resources. In Africa, for example, increasing demands on resources, conflict among different resource users, and growing numbers of political conflicts as well as refugee populations have created new constraints and vulnerabilities for the dryland areas.

One of the causes of desertification is the increasing sedentarization of most African populations. Traditional resource management systems encouraged movement of people and livestock between areas of deficit and areas of surplus in regard to both fodder and water. With privatization of lands such movement has become much more difficult. Households that two generations ago kept one or two hundred head of cattle may now keep only a handful as they seek new ways to diversify their incomes under quite altered systems of resource access and use. With Africa's increased population has come migration of people into marginal farmlands where farming households try to eke out a living on land that is unproductive and cannot support them adequately. Pressure on the land — whether from natural increase in numbers, inadequate economic alternatives, or strife and conflict — continues to challenge the management of drylands.

Degradation

Soil degradation has both immediate and long-term causes. Soil erosion is usually caused by water or wind action washing or blowing away topsoil. Repeated cropping without adequate fallow periods and without replacement of nutrients can deplete the soil, and excessive use of chemicals can kill beneficial organisms in the soil. Water logging and salinization can take place on irrigated croplands. If salt levels build up to toxic levels, the land ceases to be productive. Much effort is going into the development of management practices that can improve soil quality. Various techniques such as intercropping and agroforestry, contour farming, terracing, and other improved land-use practices at the farm level and the watershed level are offering new options to allay soil degradation.

Agrarian Institutions

Land tenure systems vary widely around the world. For Africa, some scholars have argued that traditional systems of land tenure, whereby "ownership of the land" is with the tribe and not with individuals, do not provide sufficient security to farmers. They believe that individual title is necessary before farmers will make investments in their land to increase productivity. Others suggest that indigenous tenure systems do not seem to be a constraint on productivity as long as farmers and herders believe their rights will be enforced in cases of conflict.[19] Among pastoralists there may be various forms of shared management of common property resources such as grazing areas and water sources. These involve control and decision making by the community, as opposed to open access regimes where there is no community regulation and where degradation often occurs.

Agrarian reform has been attempted in many countries but has been successful in relatively few. Obstacles to successful reform are numerous. They include landlord or owner resistance varying from numerous ways to circumvent reform, such as placing title in the names of relatives, to extreme measures of intimidation and violence. In many regions of the world, landlords have been known to hire goons to assure that their sharecroppers and field hands do not get out of line. Then there are assorted legal, policy, and administrative issues that can stall agrarian reforms. These range from attempts to influence the legal system, to measures to affect land valuation, to subterfuges around identification of owners and/or beneficiaries. In those countries where agrarian reform has been introduced successfully, it has often been accompanied by radical upheaval in the form of war or revolution, as illustrated by the experiences of South Korea, Japan, Taiwan, and China, all of which have implemented successful smallholder agricultural reforms. The Philippines offers an example of an ongoing agrarian reform effort, the Comprehensive Agrarian Reform Program (CARP) introduced in 1988, which is proceeding slowly and at least partially effectively.[20] Galvanized by the fatal shooting of nineteen farmer-protestors in front of the president's office in 1987, the church, the media, a committed group of non-governmental organizations, and a strong people's organization joined in an effort to mount this broad advocacy campaign.

CARP limits the total number of farms and farm size per household and addresses sharecropping arrangements, land transfer, and beneficiary selection, among other issues. More than a land-to-the-tiller program, its purpose is to enable farmers to become productive and self-reliant, achieving household food security. It has made progress despite funding constraints, bureaucratic tangles, lethargy, and conflicting policies. While the agricultural reform program covers more than 50 percent of its target area, some difficult questions remain regarding the poorest farming households (about 18 million people) cultivating erosion-prone uplands.

Security of tenure has somewhat improved the lives of beneficiaries, but data suggest that most of the beneficiaries still live in conditions of poverty.[21] There is a continuing need to strengthen people's organizations and their links with broad advocacy groups that can monitor the progress of the agrarian reform. It is also important to strengthen support services around credit, infrastructure, marketing, and all the backward and forward linkages related to agriculture, and to keep at front and center issues of productivity, gender equity, environmental management, poverty alleviation, and sustainability.

In contrast to the Philippines, Zimbabwe provides an example of a nation greatly in need of land reform, but proceeding with it in a highly politicized and chaotic manner. (See chapter 3 for a discussion of Zimbabwe.) The injustices are clear; the issues are real. Until recently, well-to-do white farmers owned the best agricultural lands. Figures indicate that, even twenty years after independence, forty-five hundred white commercial farmers owned 31 million acres of prime agricultural land, or about 20.7 percent of the country's total surface area. Most rural blacks subsist on marginal communal lands accounting for 41 percent of the country.[22] The dispossessed and unemployed black population is desperate for good land. Although Great Britain has provided some $70 million to finance land reform since 1980, the money has been used to resettle a mere seventy thousand families. It has been suggested that much of the acquired land has gone to friends of the president. The issue became highly politicized by the Mugabe government before the elections in early 2002 when it encouraged the black African population to seize and occupy the white-owned land. The High Court was brought into the picture, first in 2000 declaring land seizures illegal, then a year later reversing the decision. With Mugabe's electoral victory, some of the land seized remains in the hands of poor black farmers; some has been returned to owners. The issue has receded amid stalemate and promises of future action. The severe poverty and grave injustices remain. The combination of politicization and ineffective action on reform has occurred at a time when food security throughout Southern Africa, and especially in Zimbabwe, is a serious concern.

The Technology Gap

The Green Revolution, as it is widely known, has involved research in agricultural technologies related to food grains and has led to increases in grain production through the use of new high-yield varieties of seeds, pesticides, fertilizers, and improved management practices. These technologies were originally designed for Asia where land is short but labor and water are abundant. The Green Revolution has had an enormous impact on many countries, for example on India, enabling that country to become food self-sufficient, or on Thailand, enabling it to become a leading exporter of rice.

There has, however, been a downside to the technologies of the Green Revolution. One is that only the wealthier farmers can afford it, and thus it has been inaccessible to large numbers of people and has increased inequities in some parts of the world. Another is the environmental degradation that has resulted from use of agricultural chemicals, inorganic fertilizers, or extensive irrigation. These costs are leading to a decline in the rate of increase of yields. Some suggest that agricultural technologies require a new look for approaches that are less environmentally harmful.

The Green Revolution technologies have not worked well, if at all, in regions characterized by shortage of labor and water and abundant (if not necessarily high-quality) land. To date, the Green Revolution or any similar sort of research effort has bypassed those crops most widely used in Africa — sorghum, millet, cassava — all good dryland crops. Yet the research is sorely needed. For example, there are viruses that regularly destroy sweet potato harvests in Africa, and developing a more virus-resistant sweet potato would be a great benefit to African farmers.

Many small farming households around the world have little access to agricultural inputs, to improved seeds, to credit, fertilizers, or to infra-structure for marketing. Whether they are in the highlands of Peru, the uplands of the Philippines, the savannas of Tanzania, or the river deltas of Bangladesh, the technological improvements and the support services are minimal. It is instructive to consider farming households in three re-gions in order to examine in somewhat closer detail women's roles in struggling to achieve food security.

Women and Food Security: Views from the South

Gender is a key determinant of the claims that individuals or groups can make on their society, and the realities they face achieving livelihood and food security. In many instances, changes in property rights, increased linkages with the cash economy, and the erosion of various traditional rights and patronage systems have either weakened or erased formal entitlements for women in poor households. To sustain themselves and their families, many women have had to rely on their own skills and efforts and on the social relations of responsibility and reciprocity that persist outside of formal structures.

Women's coping strategies often focus on food production, prepara-tion, and distribution, as well as the use of common property resources.

The situation for many women has declined in the face of a growing commercialization that has strengthened opportunities for men in the broader market economy. In Northern India, for example, in a region of the Himalayas, men are increasingly involved in off-farm employment while women, as agriculturalists, are left behind in a world that does not offer them the resources, information, and tools to carry out their work effectively.[23]

Asymmetrical entitlements to resources — based on gender — are commonplace. Access to resources — whether by *de facto* or *de jure* rights, exclusive or shared rights, primary or secondary rights, ownership or use rights — proves to be an important issue for women virtually everywhere. In Kenya most rural women's livelihoods depend on the land as a resource base for food, energy, and income, yet women lack legal rights and control over land and their tenure is insecure. In the Indian Himalayas, the gender-based asymmetries result in women's exclusion from certain kinds of property rights. For example, men own and control tools based on animal energy. Women depend on men both to initiate the agricultural season by plowing and also to market the product of their efforts. In some regions with increasing specialization, out-migration, and dependence on the market, gender entitlements to resources are becoming more asymmetrical than ever.

Analysts of resource access and tenure in the Philippines also observe this asymmetry, even though they begin with a more egalitarian ownership, and inheritance structure.[24] In one region, the gender-based specialization of the market economy and the prioritization of men's earning ability is sharpening the gender differences in resource tenure, and creating an atmosphere of competition among residents for scarce productive resources. Similarly in the Dominican Republic, the introduction of a timber tree as a men's cash crop contributes to the asymmetries in access, ownership and control over resources.[25] Everywhere women have a disproportionate share of responsibilities for procuring resources for the household, and for maintaining the environment, with very limited formal rights.

Privatization of land has had enormous implications for women around the world, especially poor, rural women, who have lost access to commonly held resources and who often have a contingent relationship to property through their relations with males. In Kenya, bestowing title deeds to men implies that men are the heads of households and major decision-makers. Women's roles in decision making, as well as their contribution to the production, reproduction, and maintenance of the families, are ignored. Legally, women may not be prohibited from land ownership in Kenya, but only 4 to 5 percent own land.[26] The traditional system with its customary laws and religious beliefs has been replicated through the new system in terms of the continuing subordination of women in property ownership. It follows that since women are not legal owners of land, their access to productive agricultural resources such as credit is limited.

In addition to privatization, consolidation and the development of strictly defined boundaries, as well as the reduction of common lands, have reduced the flexibility and diversity of farming systems. The reduction of open-access lands has affected women all over the world, particularly poor women, as they are often highly dependent on forest and grazing resources for meeting their daily needs and responsibilities. In Kenya, women note the distances they must travel for fuelwood. In the Philippines, women lament the loss of sources of fiber and vines for weaving mats or making materials for roofing. In the rural communities in the Saklana valley of the Himalayas, women must walk to increasingly distant forests for fodder for the buffaloes that they now keep for both milk and fertilizer.

In many countries, not only is landlessness increasing among the rural poor but the numbers of women and women-headed households among the poorest are rising as well. There is a growing awareness that the burdens of natural resource destruction may fall most heavily on women in poor households. The inextricable link between land resources and rural livelihoods, along with the increasing role of women as household providers in declining rural economies, stresses the need to consider the gendered terms of access and control of the resource base, particularly in ecologically vulnerable regions.

In sum, poverty and environmental degradation significantly affect and are affected by gender relations in the countryside. Rural families may reformulate gender relations in order to take advantage of a market economy with differential structuring of men's and women's roles in production, distribution, and consumption. In the context of the struggle to secure livelihoods, rural women and men make difficult choices about roles and responsibilities. They are often forced to make logical short-term decisions about managing resources, decisions that are not necessarily appropriate for the long-term sustainability of the resource base or of their families. We can effectively illustrate these points by considering the lives of women from three countries: Wanjeri from Kenya, Corazon from the Philippines, and Argelia from Honduras.

Wanjeri from Kenya

Wanjeri is a robust, energetic woman of forty-five years with the equivalent of a sixth-grade education. She is married and is the mother of seven children, three seeking work in Nairobi, one employed as a bus conductor, and three still in school nearby. As with most rural women in Kenya, Wanjeri has primary responsibility for meeting the family's basic needs for food, water, and fuel. Her husband's responsibility is to provide the home and to generate sufficient income to pay for school fees and major capital expenditures. He has six acres of land, of which two are planted in coffee. Wanjeri helps with care of the coffee and manages two acres of maize and beans. She also attends to the traditional tasks of caring for the children, housekeeping, fetching water, and gathering fuelwood. Her agricultural responsibilities are complicated by the fact that the six acres are divided into four parcels. This is an important strategy for diversifying risk, yet the time spent to reach these parcels has a negative impact on labor allocation for food production. One of them is a sixty-minute walk from the homestead. In Wanjeri's case, there is not sufficient land to afford leaving a portion fallow, but she does rotate crops to improve productivity. She uses animal fertilizers, although she has access to relatively little. Commercial fertilizer is purchased from the coffee cooperative primarily for coffee trees, not food crops. The household does not produce enough food to sustain the family fully, and it must purchase food for some portion of the year. Coffee returns are limited, and only occasionally is there income sent by the son with the job. As with many rural folks who have small, scattered holdings, insufficient agricultural yields for the family, and poor returns on coffee, Wanjeri seeks occasional employment as a casual laborer on a nearby coffee plantation that belongs to a member of Parliament. She is also an active member of a women's group that sometimes hires out for work digging bench terraces or picking coffee, according to season.

Wanjeri's livelihood and that of her family depend on the land, yet insecure land tenure and lack of entitlements, including rights and control of land, characterize her legal relationship to the land. Historically, Kenyan women have had use rights guaranteed to them by community tradition, but with the privatization of land and the introduction of registration and land titles, these informal arrangements have no legal binding. Land is held in the name of the head of the household, and in all but a few cases this is the husband. In fact, the state has institutionalized men's more privileged access to capital and land. Thus Wanjeri, like most women in Kenya, is in the position of providing the bulk of household agricultural labor but is dependent on the family member who controls the land. Without ownership, she is unable to obtain credit for tools, equipment, and other inputs necessary to increase food production. Moreover, Wanjeri is worried that the small amount of land that the family has will eventually have to be subdivided, according to custom, among her three sons. It barely provides a livelihood for the existing family and will certainly not do so for an extended family and household.

Corazon from the Philippines

Corazon and her husband, Leandro, have three small parcels of unplowable, degraded land, virtually volcanic rubble, in Napo, on the island of Siquijor. These three plots amount to no more than one and one-half acres. They struggle to grow maize and cassava, intercropping the two with one planting per year. Ordinarily they also plant a small amount of beans, sweet potatoes and other vegetables in the same fields and use them for home consumption. Cassava is dried for food and pig fodder. The harvest feeds them and their five young children for only two months. Both Corazon and Leandro therefore engage in a variety of income-generating activities to supplement their income. Leandro alternates fishing and farming. He occasionally sells his labor to saw lumber, and he also sells tuba, wine made from the sap of the coconut trees along the edge of his land. Corazon makes mats, gathers seaweed, raises pigs by arrangement with a wealthier neighbor, and sells fish for her husband at the outdoor markets by the cockfights on Sundays.

Fish are traditionally caught from small, paddled outriggers using nets. The only property (aside from the land) is Leandro's outrigger that saves them from renting one and having to divide the catch with the owner. Competition for the fish is great. Large trawlers come from other islands and from Japan and Taiwan, dragging nets through the shallow waters around the islands. Their small-gauge nets and proximity to the coast anger local fishermen and officials.

Pressed for their livelihoods, some local fishermen use cyanide and dynamite when they fish alone. Leandro does not engage in dynamite fishing because of the danger, but he is tempted when he observes the increased catch of some of the other fishermen. Although illegal, *moro-ami* (dynamite fishing) continues to be used, effectively unchecked. Corazon's situation is legally quite different from that of Wanjeri. Philippine law affords both men and women equal chances to own and/or inherit land and other parental properties. She is also as well educated as her husband; both have completed schooling through the tenth grade. Moreover, there is some fluidity in the ways in which their family and others allocate roles and responsibilities for their members. Within the range of household responsibilities, there is considerable crossing over and sharing both between women and men and between the old and young.

Corazon contributes to the family well-being by participating in several income-generating activities. Through a social exchange system called *alima,* she contracts to raise and breed another family's pigs. She is responsible for the expenses of maintaining the animal, and eventually she divides the offspring and the selling price of the original animal with the owner. Corazon's work with pigs makes an important contribution to the household, but she is worried because the government is trying to popularize a high-breed imported hog and she knows she cannot afford the medicines and special feed for these hogs. In addition, Corazon negotiates with the owners of rice paddies for access to the sago palm, or *nipa* growing along the edges of their fields. With the *nipa* she makes shingles, securing the *nipa* fronds to bamboo rods with vines. This small-scale business adds to the household income. It is becoming more difficult, however, as natural resource degradation and privatization are diminishing the availability of *nipa*. In fact, the social exchange networks and social capital historically characteristic of the Philippines countryside are under assault from increasing commercialization. Privatization, degradation, and capitalization have created an atmosphere of competition among people for scarce productive resources. As a consequence, Corazon's opportunities for sustaining gender-based informal livelihood schemes have declined.

Argelia from Honduras[27]

Argelia, age twenty-nine, lives in Linaca with her husband, Ramon, and three children. They are among the 20 percent of landless households in the community in Southern Honduras. They work as sharecroppers on a neighbor's parcel in exchange for a third of the harvest. The land, however, is hilly and stony, and drought is increasingly common.

Crops include corn, sorghum, red beans, yuca, and camote. With land shortages, a decrease in fallow land, and a subsequent decline in production and soil fertility, few farmers, including Argelia and Ramon, harvest enough food for their families. They are, therefore, dependent on wage earnings and seek employment in agriculture and semiskilled manual labor.

Ramon migrates for three to four months during the dry season looking for seasonal work, while Argelia stays behind to care for children, small livestock, and the household. The newest and most accessible source of temporary employment for Ramon is in melon production. There are five melon plantations/packing plants in Southern Honduras owned by investors from the United States, Israel, and Honduras. Sur-Agro, a U.S.-Honduran–owned company established in 1984, employs many workers from Linaca. Ramon heads there for work, collecting and transporting the fruit between December and March. Occasionally he stays on and seeks work with a sugar cane plantation through April. This migration pattern is reshaping the social fabric of the upland community where they live. Ramon and his friends continue to seek work in the export agricultural sector. Migration is a central component of Ramon and Argelia's household survival strategy.

Argelia's daily responsibilities include preparing food, fetching water, washing, cleaning, caring for their young children, caring for small domestic animals, maintaining a household garden, and, above all, grinding corn and making tortillas, an important and time-consuming activity. There are few opportunities for Argelia to establish a small business for herself. Sometimes she bakes items to sell, and she is able to earn some income from unprocessed foodstuffs such as eggs or fruit.

As families strive to secure their sustenance, roles and responsibilities for many women have multiplied, but their access to and control over both natural and financial resources have remained disproportionately low. The principal sources of income generation remain predominantly in the hands of male household members. By and large, men inherit, purchase, and rent land, while women manage it and other natural resources when the men migrate. Increasingly men such as Ramon are being drawn into a wage labor force that functions seasonally or permanently beyond the community's borders. Conditions are difficult; returns often minimal; and these migrants are joining the broader economy on disadvantageous terms. The large melon plantations or shrimp farms favor the landed oligarchy; existing economic, social, and legal patterns are biased against these poor rural households. Ramon and Argelia, and others like them, need secure livelihoods but instead struggle to maintain a very precarious existence.

Some Common Observations

What emerges from this discussion of three different households are the complex and often negative impacts on both women and men as family members are drawn into the modern cash economy. The cash may be desperately needed, but it is not only inadequate, it comes at great cost. In most cases, the households continue to rely on social exchange networks and "safety nets" that are central to household and family sustenance. These resilient traditional groups are normally community-based and structured around gendered and class interests. They give shape and texture to the complex livelihood system wavering between economic promise and ecological stress in places even as small and remote as the villages of Wanjeri, Corazon, and Argelia.

Perhaps most important is the integral role of male migration in the livelihood systems of the rural communities investigated. Migration is a key strategy as more and more households face resource degradation, landlessness or fragmentation of land holdings into minuscule pieces, inadequate employment opportunities in rural communities, and few incentives for remaining on the land. The gendered consequences of these circumstances are evident as increasing numbers of men, and some women as well, leave rural communities to seek new and better opportunities, leaving the struggling household behind them. The low and marginal productivity of these farming households is readily apparent. The coping strategies at the household and community level are diverse. What policy and program options might offer improved economic and social opportunities for these households and communities? What could begin to address the most acute food security problems faced by rural communities in the South?

Critical Issues in Achieving Food Security in the Global South

Building on Local Knowledge, Processes, and Systems

Surely Wanjeri, Corazon, and Argelia — and the other members of their households and communities — would benefit from efforts to strengthen local knowledge and agricultural processes and systems. Over the last twenty years, discussions about agriculture and food security have been joined by supporters of low-external-input technologies to conserve soil, manage water, recycle wastes, deter pests, and use local resources efficiently.[28] The objective is to enable farmers to choose technologies appropriate to local livelihoods. This approach is distinctly different from that of the Green Revolution in which scientists bred new varieties of maize, rice, and potatoes that matured quickly and produced more and sturdier grain using inorganic fertilizers, pesticides, machinery, credit, and irrigation. The modern varieties tend to require a package of necessary inputs that must be available at the appropriate times. There are many hidden costs related to the greater use of inputs and the overall increased dependency on external resources. The Green Revolution technologies with their emphasis on high inputs, irrigation, and fertilizer are widely regarded as unsuitable for Africa, as well as for some other parts of the world, where the enabling infrastructure to permit high-input, irrigation-based technology simply is not present and may not be for several decades, if ever.[29]

The approach involving low external inputs builds on local knowledge and local organization and management systems. Pest management strategies, for example, emphasize the natural enemies of pests, using locally available insecticides, increasing ecosystem diversity to reduce pests, and using integrated pest management (IPM) to devise pest control strategies that minimize their harmful effects. Soil nutrients are improved through livestock manure, composting, green material, and household wastes. Various nitrogen-fixing legumes can be intercropped with cereals to improve soil structure and yields. In addition, water harvesting systems can take advantage of runoff and conserve water for farm and household use. Local residents worldwide build small-scale low dams to block gullies, slow the flow of water, and permit its use through terracing mechanisms.

Returning specifically to Africa's food security, this thinking in regard to low-external-input agriculture is particularly relevant. Useful technologies and appropriate infrastructure continue to be major concerns. Hunger is a chronic part of the landscape, and food, environmental, and economic crises are persistent. Farmers are resource-poor; soils are fragile and the climate unpredictable. A dependence on imported foods is growing, a situation that many precarious economies can ill afford. Some analysts have suggested that the combination of declining per capita output, environmental degradation, and rising population growth, against a background of an adverse international economic environment, is setting the stage for a human tragedy of vast proportions in which the first acts of this tragedy have already been performed.[30]

Thus, the work of research organizations such as the Consultative Group on International Agricultural Research (CGIAR), the world's largest international agricultural research institution, is vitally important as they search for new ways to address Africa's food security problems. CGIAR researchers believe that Africa's fragile and variable soils, unpredictable rainfall, scarce irrigation, and impoverished farmers will not permit adoption of the approach used in Asia. The largest share of its research funding — around 38 percent of an annual average of $280 million in the 1993 to 1998 period — is for technologies that are adapted to the sub-Saharan environment.[31] The CGIAR centers in West Africa, for example, are concentrating on grain varieties that are more resistant to drought, take less time to produce, and perform reasonably well with low inputs. The CGIAR centers are expanding their work in regard to key food staples, such as yams and sorghum, used by a majority of the population. Increased rural-based processing of Africa's main cereals, legumes, roots, and tubers would raise the value of these products to the benefit of local residents. This agroindustrialization must extend not only to downstream processing of farm produce but also to upstream activities in the production of seeds, planting materials, farm implements, and tools as part of a broad strategy for reducing rural poverty.[32] Such measures will begin to address food security as well as the root causes of hunger and malnutrition embodied in structures of poverty.

Seeds and Genetic Manipulation

In sharp contrast to the specifics of the preceding approach that emphasizes low inputs and drought-resistant, locally selected varieties of seeds is an approach that calls for genetic modification of seeds, along with large-scale, global corporate initiatives and control over research and its distribution. Genetic modification (GM) of foods has been around for a number of years and is being hailed as the solution to the world's food problems. At Bio2000, a record-setting biotechnology conference held in Boston, Massachusetts, in March 2000, seven thousand participants gathered to share the latest information on promising drugs and technologies. In preparation, two thousand scientists signed a "Declaration in Support of Agricultural Biotechnology" affirming that biotech crops allow farmers to grow more food on less land with less synthetic pesticides and herbicides.[33]

Companies such as Monsanto, a leading producer of Genetically Modified Organisms (GMOs), claim that genetically engineered foods are safe and environmentally friendly, reduce the need for chemicals in agriculture while still helping to feed the world's hungry. Furthermore, Monsanto's latest genetic technique, Technology Protection System (TPS) — labeled "terminator technology" or the suicide seed by its opponents — offers the prospect of opening worldwide seed markets to the sale of seeds by Monsanto and other large corporations. The Technology Protection System would prevent the germination of seeds from genetically improved plants after one or two years. The use of the terminator gene would mean that seeds harvested at the end of a growing season could not be saved and replanted the following year as farmers around the world currently do. Monsanto believes that TPS is needed to make sure the yields on agricultural lands are as high as they can be. With biotechnology, they claim that there is the right genetic information in the plant from the outset, fewer pesticides are wasted in the soil from spraying, and productivity is increased.[34]

However, several public interest groups paint a different picture. According to Friends of the Earth UK, there are major concerns about GMOs that might escape into the environment and pose a threat to wild plants, increase outbreaks of allergic reactions in humans, and become resistant to antibiotics.[35] They also claim that GMOs involve unsustainable, intensive agriculture that requires high-quality soils, enormous investment in machinery, and an increased use of chemicals. If current trends continue, Friends of the Earth and other organizations warn that farmers will be perpetually dependent on Monsanto's seeds, using the TPS technique and chemicals for survival. According to the Consultative Group on International Agricultural Research (CGIAR), the TT technique for preventing plants from producing viable seeds could have significant implications for farming systems, biodiversity, and food security in developing countries. Farmers would have to abandon the age-old practice of using this year's seed for next year's harvest.[36]

Furthermore, critics raise concerns about the control of companies such as Monsanto that are buying up genetic engineering companies, seed suppliers, and grain merchants. They use patent laws to "own" every genetically engineered plant grown from their seed. According to Friends of the Earth UK, some companies are producing contracts for farmers that force them to pay a technology fee, require the farmer to use the company's own chemicals, prevent them from saving seed, and even allow the company to inspect the farm. If this technology becomes widely adopted, control of seed production will ultimately move from the farmer's field to corporate headquarters, and farmers will become wholly dependent upon corporations for seeds.

It seems unlikely that genetic modification of foods is the answer to the poorest countries' food problems. Over 1 billion of the world's poorest people rely on farm-saved seed and seeds exchanged with farm neighbors as their primary seed source. A technology that threatens to extinguish farmer expertise in selecting seed and developing locally adapted strains is a threat to food security and agricultural biodiversity, especially for the poor. Genetic engineering companies argue that their technology is the only realistic solution to the shortfall in food supplies that will "inevitably" arise from world population growth. They claim that nearly 40 percent of the world's food production is lost to weed growth, pests, and diseases; that desertification and urbanization are diminishing the amount of available agricultural land; and that the need for their technology is inevitable. In contrast, public interest groups believe that the terminator technology has nothing to do with feeding the hungry, cleaning up the environment, or improving nutrition. They believe that this is a patented, proprietary technology that gives the few multinational corporations who own the patent exclusive rights to determine who will get access to it and how much they will pay for it.

I conclude that the issue should not be framed in terms of "up or down" on genetically modified foods but rather how it is to be done and who controls the outcome. Scientists in Kenya are working on developing varieties of cassava, maize, and sweet potato that would be resistant to several viruses that are widespread in Africa. It would seem that biotechnology targeted to increasing Africa's harvests could only be beneficial if developed and controlled by Africans for widespread domestic benefit. Control of seeds by corporations headquartered in a distant part of the world that have patents on their production and use is clearly a legitimate concern. This discussion of GMOs leads explicitly to the third issue under consideration in regard to food security in the Global South. This is the question of biodiversity and intellectual property rights and the form the issue is taking under the Trade-Related Intellectual Property Rights (TRIPS) Agreement.

Biodiversity and Intellectual Property Rights

Less-developed countries are some of the world's richest in terms of biological diversity, and this diversity is now under threat from genetic erosion and genetic piracy. There are two opposing paradigms of biodiversity conservation. The first is held by communities whose survival and sustenance is linked to local biodiversity utilization and conservation. The second is held by commercial interests whose profits are linked to utilization of global biodiversity for production of pharmaceuticals or other substances. For local indigenous communities, conserving biodiversity means to conserve the integrity of ecosystems and species, the right to these resources and knowledge. For commercial interests, biodiversity itself has no value; it is merely "raw material" for the production of commodities and for the maximization of profits.[37]

Underlying this debate is the expansion of patents and intellectual property rights (IPR) into the domain of biodiversity via the Trade-Related Intellectual Property Rights Agreement (TRIPS) of the World Trade Organization. Some suggest that TRIPS has been shaped by the objectives and interests of trade and transnational corporations; it is not intended to protect and conserve biodiversity, nor is its purpose the protection of indigenous intellectual heritage and social creativity.[38]

Under the TRIPS agreement, it is no longer possible to manufacture a drug or buy it abroad without the permission (granted in return for payment of royalties) of the owner of the invention, who holds this power for twenty years. As a result of pressure from countries like Spain and Canada, the TRIPS Agreement does contain exception clauses. For example, in the event of a medical emergency, a government may resort to "compulsory licenses" and "parallel imports." Compulsory licenses allow a product to be manufactured without the inventor's consent, while parallel imports allow it to be bought wherever it is sold the cheapest.[39]

WTO rules regarding price controls and the production of generic medicines do not prevent extreme pressures from being put on developing countries to relinquish rights over biological resources. In fact, the pharmaceutical lobbies are hoping to use the WTO to get all exceptions to patent rights abolished. At the same time, the companies want greater access, without cost and without constraint, to the plant life of the developing countries, since knowledge of their genomes is one of the keys to future medicines. In other words, they want complete control over the raw materials and ever-tighter protection for the discoveries made from those plants, making them inaccessible to the countries they came from.[40]

Through patents, genetic engineering, and mergers, giant chemical companies are repositioning themselves as "life sciences" companies. There is concern that they seek to control agriculture in lesser developed countries. Seed patent laws, enforced by WTO rules, would be one way that the resources of the Third World poor could be reaped to generate profits for giant corporations, as noted earlier under the discussion of seeds and genetic manipulation. Some have termed this activity "biopiracy," a phrase representing the newest threat to biodiversity, whereby industrialized nations and transnational corporations are claiming intellectual property rights by usurping traditional knowledge systems and genetic resources from the domain of commons. Vandana Shiva, a world-renowned environmental thinker and activist from India, asserts, "as farmers are transformed from producers into consumers of corporate-patented agricultural products, as markets are destroyed locally and nationally but expanded globally, the myth of 'free trade' and the global economy becomes a means for the rich to rob the poor of their right to food and even their right to life."[41] Free exchange of seed among farmers has been the basis of maintaining biodiversity as well as food security. But new intellectual-property rights laws that are being universalized through the Trade Related Intellectual Property Rights Agreement of the WTO allow corporations to usurp the knowledge of the seed and monopolize it by claiming it as their private property. Today, ten corporations control 32 percent of the commercial-seed market, valued at $23 billion, and 100 percent of the market for genetically engineered or transgenic seeds.[42]

In sum, vigorous arguments are presented both in favor of and in opposition to intellectual property rights (IPRs) in regard to biological resources. In favor are those (largely transnational corporations and governments of industrialized nations) who argue that IPRs will benefit all parties involved. They will lead to technological improvements; they will provide financial incentives for explorations (bioprospecting); they will prevent a "tragedy of the Commons" because resources will be depleted much more quickly without proper introduction of IPR laws.[43]

In opposition to the IPRs are those who believe that a few will benefit at the expense of many. The protection of IPRs does little for economic development in the poor countries that are unlikely to benefit from the current and proposed IPR regime. These issues and this controversy may seem far from the lives, households, and communities of Wanjeri, Corazon, and Argelia, yet their outcomes promise to affect the livelihood potentials of people just like them around the world. Their interests — not just those of Monsanto, Cargill, Microsoft, or Wal-Mart — must be represented in the discussions of the WTO and the TRIPS agreement. To date, power and leverage in global economics and politics remain with large corporate interests.

Concluding Observations:
Toward Sustainable Agriculture and Food Security

According to World Bank estimates, global food supplies will need to double over the next thirty-five years because of population (and economic) growth.[44] While food supplies have actually doubled since 1975, the next doubling is expected to be difficult and will have to take place at a time when 800 million people worldwide are malnourished, 25 billion tons of topsoil are lost annually, and nearly three-quarters of the ocean's fish stocks are overexploited.[45] The pessimists may be right. The world could be moving into a new era of scarcity. We note the prospect of rising food prices, the wide disparities of income among countries, the large number of grain-importing countries, the limited number of grain-exporting countries, the decline in ocean fish stocks, and the continuing troubles of Africa. This is not a hopeful picture. Are we, as some have suggested, embarking upon the politics of scarcity?

In this chapter, the emphasis is on food security and rural change in the Global South, with particular attention on Africa. The discussion is embedded within the context of several global and highly political issues pertaining to food security. We recognize, however, that hunger may also have an urban face and a refugee's face. The latter may or may not be rural. These "faces" are, of course, closely related to the questions of food security and livelihoods arising in rural communities, for from impoverished rural communities urban migrants come; unsettling economic and political conditions in rural communities can precipitate the exodus of refugees.

In the course of this past century there has been a twentyfold increase in the numbers of people living in cities.[46] In 1900 there were 160 million or approximately one-tenth of the world's population. Today there are over 3 billion. The majority of these are in the Global South. In 1900 the world's ten largest cities were all in the industrial North. In 2000 eight of the largest cities in the world are in the Global South.

People come to urban areas because the countryside is not providing an adequate living and because they seek opportunities not available to them in rural communities. They crowd into tenements and shantytowns hoping to find employment and a new life, sometimes individually, and sometimes with families. Many engage in a form of circular migration, keeping a foot planted firmly in the city and one in the countryside. They manage to create a bifurcated household with two branches, one urban and one rural. We have seen this pattern in the discussions of Wanjeri's family in Kenya and Argelia's in Honduras.

The tremendous increases in urban dwellers create new pressures on food availability. No longer producing their own food, these urbanites need to be able to purchase food. The questions then become: (1) Is food available from domestic sources? Can the rural residents feed the urbanites? If not, can food be purchased from abroad or donated through some form of aid mechanism? (2) Do people have the financial resources with which to buy food? Here the vulnerability of vast numbers of urban dwellers in the Global South is apparent. Competition for employment is severe; many jobs are temporary or seasonal or occasional. Securing the means for adequate food, water, shelter, and other services can be very difficult. In the tenements of Bangladesh's Old Dhaka, for example, one can see hundreds of urban dwellers just barely surviving. They feel fortunate to have one rice meal a day, and fortunate, as well, to be able to rent out a bit of corridor space in an office building on which to put down a straw mat to sleep at night. Hunger for them is not an occasional circumstance. It is a daily companion.

Other people for whom hunger can be a traveling companion are refugees. The end of this last century has seen the movement of vast numbers of people within and across national borders seeking safety and refuge (see chapter 4). Refugees are found in all parts of the world: Tibetans to India, Kosovars to Macedonia, Cambodians to Thailand, Eritreans to Sudan, Guatemalans to Mexico, Afghans to Pakistan. Support for those in a crisis situation is, of course, essential. Many organizations, including UN agencies and non-governmental organizations, have the capacity to mount urgent relief efforts in the face of natural or human-made catastrophe. The World Food Program of the United Nations has been established to coordinate and monitor food security around the world and pays particular attention to refugee needs. In a world that sees increasing numbers of refugees, the links between relief and development, and the links between development and long-term food security cannot be ignored. Emergency responses must be linked to effective development policy. Issues of food security, long-term development, and refugee relief must be linked. Ignoring that linkage has long-term consequences for the social landscape in many parts of the world. At the beginning of the twenty-first century these concerns seem to be growing rather than receding.

With these caveats, there are promising steps to take as we try to figure out what agriculture must do around the globe. What are these steps? First, we need to strengthen our efforts to research and invest in agricultural systems in those countries and those regions currently struggling with low productivity and food insecurity. In this regard, the CGIAR network of research institutions seems to be on the right track as it conducts research on crops suitable for more arid climates focusing particularly on African food commodities. Second, local agriculture must meet increasing demands for food in ways that provide the farmers an acceptable return for their investments and labor, and must do so without damaging the ecosystem. This objective requires public policies carefully crafted to meet the interests of rural communities.

In this chapter we suggest that the nations with low productivity face near overwhelming challenges related to infrastructure, technology, and social concerns such as HIV/AIDS. It is difficult for small farming households to keep pace with fast-growing demand. Steps clearly must include investment in new forms of high-yield, low-input agricultural technology. There must also be a fresh look at the biases in development policies; at possibilities for new forms of agricultural organization and management; and at equity concerns in land ownership, resource access and income distribution, as well as environmental sustainability. Gains in some parts of the world have been extraordinary. The global research and development community must now turn its attention to the regions where food security remains a paramount and urgent concern.

Part Four

Designing Our Future: Local Action and Global Change

Chapter 9

New Voices and New Agendas

Chapter 9 has three objectives. First, it reviews and summarizes the way our world looks at the beginning of the twenty-first century especially from the perspective of the Global South in a rapidly changing world system. Second, it suggests that key voices from the South are, either independently or in consort with those in the North, addressing critical issues facing all of us today. These voices are gaining significance and credibility on issues concerning the environment, indigenous peoples and land rights, gender equity, workers' rights, and humanitarian concerns. Last, this chapter asks some broad questions about global ethics and global society and identifies several emerging challenges and unfinished agendas for twenty-first-century reflection and activism.

The World We Are Creating

What is this new world we are in the process of creating? There is no doubt that a fundamentally new global system is being formed. It is markedly different from the system of the last half of the twentieth century, perpetuated by the Cold War until the fall of the Berlin Wall in 1989. In this new world, the bipolar power structure dominated by the Soviet Union and the United States is being replaced by an evolving multipolar world. The European Union, China, Brazil, India, and Japan are all new and emerging global entities in a world in which the economic and military strength of the United States still towers over all others. One Oxford scholar has declared the beginning of the twenty-first century as a time of transition of American global power from informal to formal imperialism.[1] However, in this economically and ecologically interdependent global system, even enormous strength can be vulnerable.

Along with new major state actors and the collapse of the bipolar world, what else characterizes this new world? Several small nations or city states have achieved prominence as NICs, the newly industrializing countries: Korea, Thailand, Singapore, and Hong Kong, the latter now part of China. While their economic progress may have been uneven, they have demonstrated a strong, trade-oriented path to development. In the economic arena, the rise of the multinational corporations has been one of the most significant characteristics of the last half century, and their power shows signs of increasing well into this next one. Even now the worth of the ten highest earning corporations in the world individually exceeds the gross national income of all but twenty-nine countries.[2] Along with the multinationals have emerged the international financial centers with money whizzing around the globe at the click of a computer key twenty-four hours a day. This dazzling movement of money by stock, bond, and currency traders is facilitated by the global communications revolution. The pen, telephone, and telegraph have been supplemented by the World Wide Web, e-mail, teleconference calls, and instant messaging.

These changes have been accompanied by the emergence of civil society organizations onto a global stage. These organizations range from trade organizations to churches, non-governmental organizations, special-interest groups, women's organizations, and more. They constitute a third set of actors in the global arena: the state, the market, and civil society groups. The organizations of civil society have grown in both advocacy and implementation roles. In some instances they have assumed some of the responsibilities formerly regarded as belonging to the state. That is, non-governmental organizations (NGOs) have assumed, in a limited way, such responsibilities as agricultural extension work in some African countries, or some of the urban social welfare activities relinquished by state and federal governments in the United States.

This new world is characterized by a variety of cultural and ideological changes. A decline in support for Marxist ideologies has accompanied the unprecedented emphasis in the North on a neoliberal orthodoxy sometimes called the "Washington Consensus." This perspective casts development in terms of macroeconomic stability, liberalized trade, and getting the prices right. States pursuing a Marxist ideology are few, and those for whom Marxism may be official dogma, as in the case of China, behave increasingly like enthusiastic capitalists. There are also changing conceptions of the Third World. No longer is it possible to "lump" all the countries perceived as impoverished and subjected to colonialism in one box. The variation among these countries from military powerhouse (India) to tiny Burundi, or the seven thousand islands of the Philippines to the ecologically devastated half of an island (Haiti) is enormous. In many ways, recognizing this diversity is a principal philosophical change in this new century.

In other ways cultural changes have been dramatic. One of the most important is the transformation of women's roles. In the course of this past century women's roles have evolved from primarily domestic concerns, albeit with critical responsibilities in agricultural production in many parts of the world, to participation in the industrial workforce as well as in positions of professional responsibility. Moreover, there is a growing awareness — if reluctantly conceded in some corners of the globe — that educating women and providing them with access to resources is essential for securing strong families, livelihoods, and communities.

Probably the cultural arena receiving the most attention at the beginning of the twenty-first century is the suddenly perceived confrontation between Western and Islamic worlds. Some have chosen to regard this confrontation as a new (or perhaps renewed) clash of civilizations, but others perceive the world not so neatly divided, choosing to see pluralities of identities rather than a homogenous Islam and an equally homogenous West. We have — all of us — many attributes as political, economic, and religious beings, as citizens, family members, workers, men, and women. Appreciating this complex and interesting diversity is indeed a challenge for the twenty-first century.[3]

With all this, we have an economically and ecologically interdependent global system. Rapidly changing technologies from fiber optic cables to cell phones and instant messaging facilitate this interdependence along with corporate restructuring and changing work strategies. An individual company can organize worldwide production systems based on satellite communication, sharing information on design, production, marketing, and financial accounting across many borders in a far-flung system. Time and space are compressed; speed and proximity are defining attributes of our daily experience. Some fear that the results are a kind of cultural homogenization — a blue-jean or Coke culture emerging worldwide.

Globalization is an elusive concept. The term "globalization" may be the catchword of the decade. Its key features involve, in sum, integration of cultures and economies, technological change, capital moving rapidly around the world with increased market liberalization and deregulation, and an unprecedented degree of economic specialization. It has led to an enormous increase in concentration of wealth and a concomitant growth in poverty. The process elicits two diametrically opposed and strongly held viewpoints.

On the one hand, some specify that "the economic gains that are achieved through trade liberalization, with decisions based on rational market principles, are uncontested and well documented." They believe, "There is no doubt that in the aggregate the benefits of trade liberalization largely outweigh the costs."[4] Such supporters say that intensification of contacts around the world ultimately benefits everyone and creates global cooperation and cohesion. Moreover the process is unstoppable. In this camp are a wide range of analysts including Thomas Friedman of the *New York Times,* who asserts in *The Lexus and the Olive Tree,* "if you want a higher standard of living in a world without walls, the free market is the only alternative left — one road, different speeds, but one road. When a country recognizes the rules of the free market in to-day's global economy and decides to abide by them, it puts on the golden straitjacket. To fit into this golden straitjacket it must make the private sector the engine of economic growth, maintain low inflation and price stability, shrink the state's bureaucracy, and all the other familiar criteria of neoliberalization models of development."[5] Such enthusiasts recount "the blessings and challenges of globalization," asserting that globalization offers the best hope to the world's poorest and that the economy of Adam Smith's invisible hand does lead to greater general prosperity.[6]

Others differ sharply. Jeremy Brecher, noted U.S. author on labor and social movements, describes globalization as a "race to the bottom promoting a destructive competition, not just between developing and industrialized countries but also among the countries of the Third World."[7] Vandana Shiva, director of the Research Foundation for Science, Technology and Ecology in New Delhi, emphatically agrees: "We are in the midst of war, a war unleashed by the global market on the life of the planet and the life of people. This war is an everyday war — a war carried out in the name of economic competition, a war of corporations against the people. It is an organized theft of the survival resources of the poorest in order to increase the profits of the most powerful corporations."[8] The global competition to lower labor, environmental, and social costs is devastating for the poor, as is the power of highly mobile capital to pour into a country, create an economic bubble, and then withdraw.

To those in the latter camp, globalization has rendered millions of people displaced, dispossessed, and marginalized. In short, what is being globalized is poverty. To the supporters of globalization the growth of financial markets is laudable, whereas the skeptics say that those capital flows are largely short-term speculative investments. Supporters believe that global communication is building collaboration and goodwill; critics see enormous disparities in access to these communication opportunities. How "global" is global communication, they ask, when in 1997 some 62 percent of the world's main telephone lines are in just twenty-three affluent countries accounting for only 15 percent of the world's population?[9]

To many, including this author, the issues are not quite so clear cut. The question is not "whether" to proceed with globalization, but "how" the process is occurring. We must ask who is benefiting, who is being hurt, and whether the pace is appropriate. Many want to democratize globalizing processes. Perhaps this could be called an alternative globalization movement, seeking to diminish inequalities between rich and poor and between those with power and those who are powerless. Most of the thousands of demonstrators in Seattle at the WTO meetings or in Genoa, at the G-7 meetings and elsewhere, are not unalterably opposed to globalization. They question whether the "self regulation" of Adam Smith works, and demand regulation of financial and labor markets so that the world is not pushed ever closer to the edge of economic and social disaster. They are opposed to the ways in which capitalist globalization is taking place. Said one observer at Genoa, "The levers of power around the world are controlled by political leaders who meet in cloistered summits, by free trade organizations that care little about poor or developing countries and by corporations whose principle goal is to fatten the bottom line."[10]

There really is no question of opting out of globalization — the process has a momentum all its own — but there is opportunity to implement policies that will provide it with a more human face. Increasingly ordinary citizens are thinking about these questions and are unwilling simply to leave power and control to CEOs or political authorities.

New Voices: Grassroots Movements for Global Change, South and North

A global revolution in civil society associations is a significant phenomenon of the last part of the twentieth century. There is a vast array and diversity of organizations and networks including NGOs, social movements, foundations, media, churches, consumer organizations, and many more. These civil society organizations and networks have become a force for challenging existing policies and institutions. Slowly they are reshaping the rules of the game. What seems to be emerging are loosely coordinated social movements composed of relatively autonomous groupings. A movement is an organized attempt by a group or groups to bring about change in society through collective mobilization based on common principles and strategies. The movements often are networks of organizations formed for advocacy purposes and characterized by voluntary, reciprocal, and horizontal patterns of communication and exchange. They are informally linked and nonhierarchal. Each entity has its own program, but these coalesce around national and international campaigns, sometimes into a powerful whole.

Many of these organizations are redefining poverty eradication as sitting squarely within the context of citizens' rights. That is, combating poverty is not a matter of charity. Citizens have rights and entitlements. People living in poverty are citizens who have a right to the benefits of development. This is, in fact, a rights-based approach to poverty and, by extension, to the processes of globalization. Organizations such as Oxfam America have shifted their analysis from a primarily moral or ethical argument to include one that is founded on the rights and entitlements of individuals. For Oxfam America, this rights-based approach to combating poverty includes the right to livelihood, services, security, participation, and diversity. This new philosophical stance toward poverty, emanating as it does from the work of civil society organizations and networks, is having a profound impact on the ways in which poverty is both perceived and addressed. These groups are working not only to modify patterns of exclusion and intolerance, but also to bring into the public arena groups that have been marginalized because of rigid hierarchies, social attitudes, and discriminatory practices.

These organizations and networks face many challenges. Enabling people from North and South to work together and breaking down the North-South barriers are among them. Such organizations of both South and North are struggling to share strategies and build solidarities. In the North, it is a challenge to quell isolationism or a kind of unilateralism. In the United States, for example, the concept of "preemptive military power" or a "we'll-go-it-alone" attitude often pervades our view of politics. To counter such attitudes, these organizations seek ways to deepen the knowledge that they bring to their analysis of problems, by research and by information exchange. They are engaged in an increasing amount of advocacy work vis-à-vis the World Trade Organization, the North American Free Trade Agreement, the International Monetary Fund, and other international institutions. Following are several examples of these new forms of cross-national, cross-regional, cross-cultural social action.[11]

Campaigns Focused on Particular Legislation or Agreement: The Coalition in Opposition to the Multilateral Agreement on Investment (MAI)

MAI negotiations started in 1995 as an effort on the part of twenty-nine industrialized countries to establish an international investment agreement that would, in effect, empower foreign corporations to challenge policies of local governments as well as existing environmental laws. Advocates believe that the MAI will enhance the globalized marketplace by producing advancements in both trade and technology. The MAI would require national governments to grant foreign corporations the same rights and opportunities as local companies, while at the same time they would lose the right to regulate these investments. The agreement would give corporations the right to sue national governments for compensation for lost profits due to local laws or regulations that did not conform with MAI provisions. It would also forbid governments to require foreign corporations to transfer technology, thus cutting off an avenue for access to upgraded technologies for host countries.

Over 650 civil society organizations from seventy countries joined this global campaign using a variety of instruments — media, advocacy, alternative investment politics, and a range of collectively agreed-upon strategies. Included were various Southern and Northern civil society organizations and movements including environmental, development, human rights, and church-based organizations, and non-governmental organizations (both religious and nonsectarian). The Council of Canadians, Canada's preeminent citizens watchdog organization with over a hundred thousand members and numerous chapters across the country, played a key role in the fight to defeat the Multilateral Agreement on Investment. Campaigns were organized in more than half the OECD member countries. OECD member governments were surprised by the scale, strength, and speed with which the opposition appeared and developed. One of the conveners noted, "For the first time one is seeing the emergence of a global civil society represented by non-governmental organizations that are based in several states and communicate beyond their frontiers. This evolution is doubtless irreversible."[12] Negotiations on the Multilateral Agreement on Investment were suspended in 1998, an undeniable victory for the campaign that some suggest marked a turning point in the struggle by ordinary citizens around the world to democratize globalization processes.

International Movements with Multiple Agendas: The People's Global Action (PGA)

Over three hundred representatives of people's movements from more than sixty countries met in February 1998 in Geneva to initiate an international popular movement against various aspects of globalization. Members include the National Alliance of People's Movements (India), the National Zapatista Liberation Front (Mexico), the Landless Peasant Movement (Brazil), the Peasant Movement of the Philippines, and the Canadian Postal Union. The meeting resulted in a manifesto against global corporate rule. Subsequent meetings have taken place in Bangalore, India, and in Cochabamba, Bolivia. This coalition rejects capitalism and all trade agreements, institutions, and governments that promote destructive globalization. It advocates direct action and civil disobedience, not simply lobbying. Its organizational philosophy is based on decentralization and autonomy as well as the construction of local alternatives to global capitalism.

Ongoing International Research and Monitoring Committees: Human Rights Watch

Human Rights Watch is an independent, non-governmental organization that conducts fact-finding investigations into human rights abuses by governments and nonstate actors in all regions of the world. Founded as the "Helsinki Watch" in 1978 to support citizens' groups forming throughout the Eastern bloc to monitor their governments' compliance with the 1975 Helsinki Accords, its headquarters are now in New York and it maintains offices in ten other countries. Its procedures include visiting sites of abuses to interview victims, witnesses, and others; publishing findings; generating extensive coverage in local and international media; and exposing the violations. The organization's intentions are to document abuses and thereby shame the abusers and help to put pressure on them to reform their conduct. By investigating and exposing past human rights violations and holding their perpetrators accountable both politically and judicially, Human Rights Watch believes it is engaging in a preventive strategy. Human Rights Watch is the largest international human rights organization based in the United States. It has nearly two hundred employees and a budget just under $20 million.

Civil Society Networks with Focused Agendas: The Structural Adjustment Participatory Research Initiative Network (SAPRIN)[13]

This worldwide network of civil society organizations examines the impact of structural adjustment requirements on the poor. The network is linked with citizen's groups in more than twelve countries to organize public processes to determine the real impact of World Bank– and IMF-supported economic reform programs and to make recommendations for the future. Launched in 1997, SAPRIN brings together organizations of civil society, their governments, and the World Bank in a joint review of structural adjustment programs and, particularly, to explore new policy options. It seeks to legitimize local knowledge in the analysis of economic-reform programs and to make space for and to institutionalize grassroots involvement in macroeconomic decision making. In all the countries where the Network is active, including Bangladesh, Ecuador, El Salvador, Ghana, Hungary, Mali, Uganda, and Zimbabwe, high-profile public discussions of the controversial SAP policies have taken place in an Opening National Forum.[14] Many organizations in each country have participated both in the forum and in ongoing research on the local impacts of structural adjustment measures. A Global Forum held in April 2002 in Washington, D.C., was entitled "From Engagement to Protest: A Public Forum on Citizens' Challenges to the World Bank." Participants included representatives from a wide variety of organizations, as well as SAPRIN members from at least seven nations who presented reports on the impacts of structural adjustment policies in their home countries.

International Umbrella Networks and Conferences of Civil Society Organizations: Hague Appeal for Peace[15]

The Hague Appeal for Peace Organizing and Coordinating Committees focuses on the need to create a culture of peace, to implement human rights laws, to prevent violent conflict, and to achieve disarmament and human security. In the spring of 1999, civil society organizations held the largest international peace conference in history to launch the Hague Appeal for Peace and Justice for the 21st Century. The conference brought together nearly ten thousand activists, government representatives, and community leaders from over a hundred countries. The Hague Appeal Conference was significant because unlike the UN global summits of the past decade, this conference was organized entirely by civil society organizations, not governments.

The citizens' Agenda for Peace and Justice for the 21st Century is intended to build strategies and action toward common goals. These include campaigns aimed at eradicating land mines, reducing the traffic of small arms, alleviating Third World debt, ending violence against women, abolishing nuclear weapons, protecting the rights of children, stopping the use of child soldiers, and building an independent International Criminal Court. These grassroots efforts mobilize ordinary people; integrate different sectors such as human rights, the environment, humanitarian assistance, disarmament, and sustainable development; and are inclusive, inviting the full participation of women, youth, indigenous peoples, minorities, the disabled, and other marginalized groups. Campaigns take on their own identity such as The International Action Network on Small Arms (IANSA), a global network of NGOs dedicated to preventing the proliferation and unlawful use of small arms.

Key Voices from the South

Across the regions of the Global South new voices are being heard in regard to environmental concerns, workers and women's issues, the rights of indigenous peoples, and more broadly, human rights of all peoples. Here we identify these arenas of activism with an illustration or two from each category that exemplifies some of the extraordinary changes taking place in the mobilization of people around public issues.

The Environment

Rising ecological and human rights awareness has led to increasing criticism of large-scale development projects.[16] Highlighted is the growing opposition to centrally planned, large-scale development projects that are devoid of public input. At stake is a challenge to fundamental structures of power and processes of decision making that discriminate against the primary victims of economic development. People are questioning the concept of large dam building as a favored mode of developmental intervention, either for irrigation or for power. The concern about large-scale dislocation is leading to reassessment of a number of large-scale projects.[17]

One of the most controversial development projects of the last fifty years has been the Narmada dam project in Gujarat, India, and particularly the largest of the proposed dams, the Sardar Sarovar. The Narmada complex, started in 1987, is intended to become the single largest river development scheme in India and one of the largest hydroelectric projects in the world. It will displace an estimated 1.5 million people from their land. The environmental costs of such a project, which involves the construction of 30 large, 135 medium and 3,000 small dams, are immense. There are two issues central to the debate over Sardar Sarovar and sustainable development: environmental degradation and the interests of project-affected people.[18] The Sardar Sarovar Project (SSP) has come under scrutiny at a time when there are growing concerns about environmental degradation and about the rights of indigenous people.

The government claims that the multipurpose Sardar Sarovar Project would provide water to 40 million people, irrigate more than 1.8 million hectares (mostly in Gujarat State, some in Rajasthan State) and generate about 1450 megawatts of power. Proponents insist that sustainable development is compatible with large-scale, ambitious, centrally controlled schemes and that the Narmada Development Project will meet the increasing needs of a growing economy for food, water, and energy. Furthermore, they claim that the project is designed to alleviate severe drought and irrigation problems. The opponents of the dam counter that these benefits are grossly exaggerated and would never accrue to the extent suggested by the government. They see it as another project that will exploit the available resources to the detriment of the poor and the benefit of the rich. They argue that the project is unsustainable and unjust and that large-scale, centrally controlled schemes are incompatible with sustainable development.[19] Furthermore, they believe that the project would displace more than what the government estimated and will affect the livelihood of thousands of others. Moreover, the project will inundate thousands of acres of forests and agricultural land, devastating human lives and biodiversity.

The controversy over large dams on the River Narmada has become a symbol of the struggle for a just and equitable society in India, indeed, a symbol for the struggle for local autonomy against forced displacement associated with a state-directed and internationally funded project.[20] Opponents of the damming of the Narmada struggle over issues of displacement, resettlement, and indigenous peoples' rights and participation within the development process. Many people have already been displaced and others will be in the future. In addition, the resettlement processes for the thousands displaced are inequitable. Most indigenous peoples are resettled in areas with less fertile land and are receiving little or no compensation. In addition, most of the indigenous people do not own land; they gain their livelihoods from the river. Yet, because they are landless, they do not qualify as project-affected and are not eligible for rehabilitation.

As a consequence, the struggle over indigenous rights and participation in the development process is at the forefront of this controversy. Most indigenous peoples and others living in the submergence area were never contacted for their opinions on whether they needed a dam and more irrigated lands. Tens of thousands of *adivasis* (India's indigenous people) could be thrown off their traditional land to make way for a wildlife sanctuary supposed to "mitigate" the loss of wildlife to the SSP reservoir. Since most *adivasis* have no formal title to their land, they cannot claim compensation anyway.[21] In sum, critics believe that the project will alter the ecology of the entire river basin of one of India's biggest rivers. It will affect the lives of 25 million people who live in the valley and submerge and destroy four thousand square kilometers of natural deciduous forests.

The opposition to the Sardar Sarovar Project has been conducted through the organized efforts of a people's organization, the Narmada Bachao Andolan (Save the Narmada Movement, or NBA). The movement has crossed international boundaries from the Narmada Valley to non-governmental organizations in Washington, D.C., and Tokyo and has been strong and well coordinated since the mid-1980s when the World Bank committed funds to its construction. The public pressure of the Narmada Movement forced the Japanese to withdraw its commitment to provide a loan for the project. Because of the substantial organized pressure, local, national, and international, the World Bank president commissioned an independent review of the Sardar Sarovar Project in 1991 leading to a final withdrawal of World Bank monies in 1993. Nevertheless, many *adivasis* have been moved off the land, and the government of India continues with implementation of its plans without international support. Despite efforts of the NBA, the *adivasis* have not yet succeeded in receiving just compensation for their land.

Public pressure and collaboration of various groups succeeded in generating a debate across the subcontinent and, indeed across the world,

that encapsulated the conflict between two opposing styles of development: one massively destructive of people and the environment in the
quest for large-scale industrialization; the other consisting of replicable
small-scale activities harmoniously integrated with both local communities and nature.[22] The challenges that are posed are certainly not confined
to the dams on the Narmada River.

Indigenous Peoples and Land Rights

Closely linked to environmental concerns as they relate to development
policy, but still distinctly separate, are the rights of indigenous people.
This is another arena in which there are key voices from the Global
South. Of particular importance have been their claims to the land and
resources indigenous peoples have historically used to support themselves, a struggle common to most indigenous peoples across nations.
Defining the term "indigenous" presents a challenge. There is a UN
Working Definition of Indigenous Peoples adopted in 1982.[23] Central
elements of a definition include the assertions that indigenous peoples
meet the following characteristics:[24]

- are descendants of the original inhabitants of a territory that has
  been overcome by conquest;

- are nomadic and seminomadic peoples, such as shifting cultivators,
  herders and hunters and gatherers, and/or practice a labor-intensive
  form of agriculture that produces little surplus and have low
  energy needs;

- do not have centralized political institutions, organize at the level
  of the community, and make decisions on a consensus basis;

- have all the characteristics of a national minority in that they
  share a common language, religion, culture, and other identifying
  characteristics and a relationship to a particular territory, but are
  subjugated by a dominant culture and society;

- have a different worldview, consisting of a custodial and nonmate-
  rialistic attitude to land and natural resources, and want to pursue
  a separate development to that preferred by the dominant society.

It is sometimes difficult to determine who is indigenous and who is a
member of an ethnic or cultural minority. In general, however, indigenous peoples claim their lands because they were there first and have
occupied them from time immemorial. They have often been conquered

and subordinated by peoples different from themselves and treated as inferior by them. The salient characteristic of indigenous peoples, states Maybury-Lewis of Cultural Survival, an organization dedicated to promoting multiethnic solutions to otherwise conflictive situations, is that "they are marginal to, or dominated by, the states that claim jurisdiction over them."[25] They are often called "tribal" and are usually characterized by a small-scale, isolated lifestyle and a lack of centralized authority; they are also among the world's most underprivileged minorities.

Indigenous peoples constitute approximately 5 percent of the world's population and total about 300 million. There are nearly 32 million in the Americas, largely in Central and South America. The former Soviet Union contains approximately 28 million indigenous peoples; while Southeast Asia and the Philippines have approximately 26 million; China has 91 million, and smaller numbers are scattered throughout the world. In many instances indigenous peoples have been treated harshly by conquerors, colonial powers, expanding empires, or developing states that have sought their land and their resources. Usually they have been driven off their land, exterminated, or confined to less desirable regions; often they have been vulnerable to diseases that the outsiders brought with them and to the debilitating consequences of deprivation and cruelty. We associate this marauding with the history of exploration, but the truth is that today indigenous populations worldwide are vulnerable to the advancement of the development-oriented state and the individuals and groups in control of them.

Today indigenous peoples in many parts of the world are organizing to protect their rights. We consider two situations where this is the case: Peru, Bolivia, and Ecuador, involving both the Andean Highlands and the Amazon Basin; and on the other side of the world, the Philippines.

In the three countries of South America there are nearly 16 million indigenous people. These three countries constitute a major concentration of poverty, having the lowest per capita incomes of the region. The landscape is characterized by extensive deforestation, erosion, soil loss, overgrazing, contamination of water sources by mines, and desertification and salinization in some areas. In all three countries, legislation recognizes indigenous organizations and territories and the right to seek title to traditional community lands. Yet these organizations confront a new issue: the growing number of extractive industries on indigenous lands. The rights to the land involve only the land surface and do not represent exclusive access to and control over either what grows on this land surface (such as the forests) or what lies underneath (such as oil and mineral reserves), both of which are the property of the state.[26] Thus, there may be competing claimants for three distinct but scarcely separable sets of rights involving the same land area. The indigenous people may have permanent land titles while timber, oil, and mining companies may only have concessions. The reality, however, when interests conflict, is that the parties are dramatically unequal in their power and resources.

All three countries now have organizations of indigenous peoples with federations working at the local, regional, and national levels. The Confederation of Indigenous Nationalities of Ecuador (CONAIE) has become an important political actor at the national level. A federation of the nine countries within the Amazon Basin, the Coordinator of the Indigenous Organizations of the Amazon Basin (COICA) based in Quito, has been a powerful factor in bringing international attention to issues concerning the Amazonian rain forest and its peoples. COICA is linked with the Washington, D.C.–based Amazon Coalition, an organization of Amazonian indigenous organizations and Northern environmental and human rights organizations. There is no comparable coordinating body for the Andean highlands indigenous peoples, but their institutions are slowly being strengthened. Thus, there is a current resurgence of indigenous peoples and their organizations. Despite the challenges and difficulties, these organizations are increasing their capacities to defend the rights and manage the resources while strengthening the cultural identities of indigenous peoples and improving their livelihoods.

On the other side of the world in the Philippines, the indigenous people's struggle for land rights has lasted for decades. In 1997, the Philippines president signed into law the Indigenous Peoples Rights Act (IPRA) to recognize, protect, and promote the rights of the indigenous cultural communities for whom we must "accelerate emancipation from the bondage of inequity, poverty, deprivation, and alienation from the mainstream."[27] This legislation provides for the delineation and recognition of ancestral domains by indigenous peoples. Palawan, an island located west of the main chain of the Philippines and known as "the last frontier," mainly because of its geographical isolation, is the Philippines' largest province, but has a population of only one-half million. There has been extensive deforestation caused by commercial logging and settlement by impoverished lowlanders and migrants from other islands. The threatened condition of the frontier lands in Palawan and the conflicts over resource use drew much attention in the 1980s and 1990s thanks, in part, to a book entitled *Plundering Paradise,* which revealed that one of the biggest logging companies in the country had been operating since the early 1970s on Palawan. And that was not the only one: timber barons were prospering; the local people were not; and the provincial coffers were minimal.[28]

The United Tribes of Palawan Federation (NATRIPAL) was formed in 1989 with support from the Catholic Church and several NGOs. NATRIPAL has served as a channel for communication from local community groups to policymakers, bureaucrats, and donor agencies as well as a horizontal link with non-governmental organizations working in the province. Since its inception it has expanded to a province-wide federation of fifty-seven community-based indigenous peoples' organizations (IPOs), each representing forty to fifty member-households. It has gained access to government information, programs, and services, and has played an important role in advocating for indigenous peoples' rights. NATRIPAL has been instrumental in enabling indigenous communities to obtain approval for Certificates for Ancestral Domain Claims (CADCs), which assure the local people of the use of forest resources for traditional sustainable activities. NATRIPAL has also played a key role in building the capacities of local communities for long-term sustainable management of ancestral domains. Its efforts, however, require vigilance and political savvy in the face of economic interests that wish to encroach on the island and that are insistent and powerful.

Gender Equity

At the beginning of the twentieth century there was little participation of women in public affairs and in civil society organizations. Domestic responsibilities occupied most of their time. In fact, women did not gain the right to vote in most parts of the world until after World War I. It was in the 1960s that a much more engaged and transformative approach to women's responsibilities, opportunities, and rights emerged. Those in the development field tend to mark it with the publication in 1970 of Ester Boserup's book *Woman's Role in Economic Development,* but there are many other markers that can also be used: publication of *The Feminine Mystique* by Betty Friedan; the changes wrought by World War II when Rosie the riveter came to symbolize women assuming new tasks in a modern world; Eleanor Roosevelt, who as a former First Lady in the United States assumed a prominent international role on humanitarian concerns; or Indira Gandhi, who became a formidable prime minister of India. Such accomplishments have been punctuated by the 1979 Convention on the Elimination of All Forms of Discrimination Against Women, and the UN-sponsored women's conferences in Mexico City (1975), Nairobi (1985), and Beijing (1995). Today, at the beginning of the twenty-first century, women almost everywhere have won countless improvements in their status. These are reflected in indicators for life expectancy, literacy, and child (under five) mortality shown in Table 1.1 for the nine countries selected in chapter 1 as representative of low, medium, and high income groups. Yet the barriers to women's efforts to achieve equal rights and opportunities continue to be enormous. The Gender Empowerment Measure (GEM) is indicated in three ways: political participation and decision making, as measured by women's and men's percentage shares of parliamentary seats; economic participation and decision making as measured by women's percentage shares in political and professional and technical positions; power over economic resources as measured by estimated earned income. On the GEM scale Norway ranks first, Canada fifth, and Australia ninth. The middle income countries — Malaysia, Egypt, and Ecuador — rank thirty-eighth, sixty-fourth, and forty-third, while the poorest countries do not provide data for this measure, either because it is of no concern or because there is little to report.[29]

Women around the world have engaged in debates about women's roles and rights, and many women from the South have entered into these debates, focusing in particular on the intersecting histories of gender, race, colonialism, and capitalism. They see the marginality and oppression of women as grounded in a broader set of struggles to survive against imperialism, racism, caste, and other forms of domination. They want to focus on the day-to-day experience and struggles of women within the context of other forms of subordination. The varying theoretical perspectives on women's issues and gender roles have led to the emergence of two strands of practical and organizational response.

First, there are broad coalitions of women from both South and North who are examining the global forces affecting women. One of the most prominent among these is the Women's Eyes on the World Bank campaign. This campaign emerged from the 1995 Fourth World Conference on Women in Beijing in order to monitor the World Bank's progress toward implementing commitments World Bank president James Wolfensohn made to women at that time. The campaign intends to:

- increase participation of grassroots women in the Bank's economic policymaking;
- institutionalize a gender perspective in all World Bank policies and programs;
- increase World Bank investments in social and financial services for women;
- increase the number and racial diversity of women in senior management positions within the World Bank.

Members of the coalition working on the campaign are concerned about the explicit or implicit gender-specific division of labor, the differential access to resources, and the host of legal, cultural, and political constraints that keep women in subordinate roles within households and within society. They argue that in many settings women continue to be an underclass facing obstacles in terms of access to resources and opportunities. Moreover, there is a documented global trend toward the "feminization of poverty."[30] They suggest that this trend has been aggravated by policies of the World Bank, especially structural adjustment programs that have at best sustained the status quo of unequal gender relations, and at worst have, in many cases, deepened gender disparities.

The campaign also helps activate women's organizations worldwide to participate in monitoring Bank projects and policies. Both Southern and Northern groups are involved in this effort. A recent report of several chapters working across continents on the Women's Eyes on the World Bank Campaign provides a comprehensive review and analysis of how the Bank has performed in implementing commitments made at the Beijing Conference in 1995 to place women at the center of the development process. The campaign's central finding was that the "increased will on the part of Bank leadership to address gender issues had not been backed by commitment to the systematic changes necessary to translate this commitment into a reality."[31]

Second, there are women's movements and organizations with a highly focused political mission or cultural identity. Women's movements are associated with a broad range of struggles from the well-known Chipko environmental movement undertaken by women in India to Chile's Mothers of the Plaza de Mayo seeking the return of and information about their "disappeared" relatives. The underlying goal of these movements is to promote gender equality and to advance the particular interests and concerns of a given group of women. They take place in many parts of the world and are strengthened by the networks and communications possible today, sometimes linking activists in the South with those sharing a common objective in the North.

One such example comes from Burma where conflict on the Burma-Thai border is endemic and has caused much suffering among the hill peoples. In 1984, the first refugee camp in Thailand at the Burma-Thai border was set up for people, especially the Karens, fleeing military repression in Burma. To help solve some of the problems of the Burmese refugees, the women in the camps began to organize. With the assistance of EarthRights International, a nonprofit, non-governmental organization, the women organized training on women's rights and violence against women. Those who attended the training began to realize their own abilities and to share the information with their families and neighbors. They also began to participate in camp affairs as part of the camp leadership, in order to stop the violence against women, and to help promote peace in their community. All these efforts have increased their organizing, development work, and international networking.[32] By 1994, there were seven documented indigenous women's groups on the Thai-Burmese border. Today, women's groups on the border have organized themselves into an association called the Women's Federation of Burma, which, with support from EarthRights International, is documenting the situation of women in Burma for a report to be submitted to the Convention on the Elimination of All Forms of Discrimination against Women (CEDAW).[33] This linkage between the Women's Federation of Burma, its constituent groups, and ERI with its network and resources illustrates the interconnectedness of all efforts to achieve environmental and social justice.

Women's voices have usually been omitted from traditional state-centered analyses of war, conflict, and refugee movements. Their absence has wide-ranging implications for what and how we see (or do not see), and for which issues are rendered visible or invisible. "Where are the women?" asks feminist scholar Cynthia Enloe. "Most historical accounts are written as though the principals concerned never had gender on their minds...."[34] Such omissions suggest that the human experience in politics, war, and refugee movements is largely male. Nothing could be further from the truth. These Burmese groups and their federation believe that the violent impact of war on women must be revealed. No doubt they would have strong support from the women of Afghanistan, Kosovo, Rwanda, and elsewhere.

Workers' Rights

For workers and their rights the implications of global transformation are staggering. In the last twenty years there have been vast changes in systems of production and the ways in which labor is reproduced, mobilized, used, and controlled. One cause of these changes derives from the neoliberal market forces shaping economic activity. A second relates to the flexible production systems with their patterns of decentralization, outsourcing, employing temporary workers, maintaining low inventories, and increasing short-term adaptability. All of these elements of global production systems have weakened the bargaining power of labor. Moreover, conditions of high unemployment are a powerful impediment to a strong labor movement. Thus, in many countries of the South, labor's organizational strength and its potential for collective bargaining have been limited or even nonexistent. Despite the political and economic constraints, there are cases of labor activism, some of them strengthened by emerging North-South alliances around workers' rights, globalization, and justice.

Several examples of effective activism relate to the garment industry. For example, Wendy Diaz, a garment worker from Honduras, gave personal testimony at the age of fifteen to members of the U.S. Congress, which led to the founding of an anti-sweatshop group, the Apparel Industry Partnership. In another instance a Vietnamese-American businessman established the Vietnam Labor Watch through which he spotlights labor abuses in Vietnamese factories making athletic shoes for export. Such activities have been going on since the mid-1990s. In 1997 students at several universities in the United States founded the United Students Against Sweatshops that is active at over a hundred U.S. and Canadian universities. These students are now linked with several AFL-CIO unions in an effort to combat sweatshops. They demonstrate solidarity with increasing numbers of activists from the South. One, Dita Sari, a young Indonesian law student who spent three years in prison because of her activism, has established the Indonesian National Front for Labor Struggles. She credits her release from prison, not to the government's generosity, but to the strong international pressure mounted by allies abroad.[35]

One analyst suggests that two sets of kindred people and organizations, one fledgling and the other mature, both struggling against mighty odds, are laying the foundation of something like a global solidarity movement.[36] These include new gadfly-style organizations such as the Vietnam Labor Watch, and experienced organizations such as the Brussels-based International Textile, Garment, and Leather Workers Federation with affiliates in 135 countries. The emerging movement, aided by media exposures of the downside of globalization, has succeeded in elevating worker rights to a serious issue among global policymakers.

These efforts do not yet affect the countless women and men working under inhumane conditions in every nook and cranny of the globalized labor market. The April 2001 Chowdhury Knitwears garment factory fire in Bangladesh is illustrative. The fire broke out on the fourth floor of a multistory building amid boxes of polo shirts. It was night and workers rushing to leave found the gate below locked, the electricity not functioning, and the dark stairwells packed with terrified stampeding workers. Of the twelve hundred workers, fifty-two died, most of them young women.[37] The factory now possesses new safety equipment, but otherwise, it is business as usual. The textile associations offer neither guidelines nor inspections; the government enforces no standards; and the labor unions are powerless. In most factories, as at Chowdhury Knitwear, safety equipment is introduced only under duress.

In the last fifteen years Bangladesh has attracted a now $4.3 billion apparel industry that provides 1.5 million jobs, two-thirds of them to women who provide cheap and abundant labor to the more than three thousand inadequately regulated garment factories (see chapter 6). Workers earn on the order of ten cents an hour. There is little incentive for improvement or reform because of the incredible poverty in this land of 131 million people. One new source of reform, however, is the large retailer — a Gap or Wal-Mart, Tommy Hilfiger or JCPenney — which is beginning to take an interest in the conditions under which its garments are produced because of bad publicity among its present and future customers. If the United Students Against Sweatshops and similar organizations can keep the pressure on the firms, the companies may make some demands on their contractors. This, however, is likely to be a slow process; it needs the added clout of global institutional and governmental support.

Pressure, publicity, social movements, and the expanded awareness of new voices of both North and South are beginning to make a difference in the attention firms are willing to give to labor issues and the efforts they are willing to make to improve conditions. For example, in Geneva in June 2001 Chiquita (the largest employer of unionized banana workers in Latin America), the IUF (International Union of Food and Agricultural Workers Associations), and COLSIBA (the Latin American Coordinating Committee of Banana Workers' Unions) signed an agreement reaffirming Chiquita's commitment to respect the core labor Conventions of the ILO, including the Convention on freedom of association. The agreement was described as providing a historic opportunity for workers and employers to solve problems in an industry that has throughout its history been highly confrontational.[38]

At the same time that relations seem to be improving in the banana industry, the pressure of publicity and the courts is being brought by unions against Coke and Panamerican Beverages, the primary bottler of Coke products in Latin America. SINALTRAINAL, the trade union that represents workers at the Coke facilities in Colombia, asserts that "Coke is among the most notorious employers in Colombia, maintaining open relations with murderous death squads as part of a program to intimidate trade union leaders. The case is extremely important for trade union and human rights activists. If we cannot get Coke, one of the most well known companies in the world, to protect the lives and human rights of the workers at its world-wide bottling facilities, then we certainly have a long way to go in making the global economy safe for trade unionists."[39] The case is being filed in a U.S. District Court in Miami under the alien Tort Claims Act, a law passed by Congress in 1789 to protect the new nation's international reputation by enabling noncitizens to use federal courts to hold Americans accountable for violations of international law. The United Steel Workers Union and the International Labor Rights Fund have joined SINALTRAINAL to show their solidarity with Colombian workers. Such legal procedures can send a message to more firms than just Coke. In mid-2002, the District Court began to hear arguments on this case.

If there is a groundswell of concern around workers' rights and the global economy, this issue became more than just a groundswell at the meetings in Genoa of the leaders of the G-8, the leading industrialized countries, in July 2001. Over a hundred thousand protesters amassed to convey their concerns to the gathered presidents and prime ministers.

While a handful of anarchists became violent and destructive, the unusually large number of concerned and peaceful citizens gave pause to the leaders and to the general public. It was clear that they heard the messages: there is an emerging world citizenship suspicious of the ways in which the global economy is being organized, its lack of transparency and the absence of fair labor standards, and who wish to democratize the global economic system.

Human Rights

Human rights issues pertain not just to the forces of economic globalization, but also to violations of human safety and security, as well as economic, social, and cultural rights. The International Campaign to Ban Landmines (ICBL) demonstrates how civil society can bring together numerous NGOs, mobilize widespread public support, and enlist responsive governments in support of their objectives. It is a clear example of the power of civil society to change expectations and law on an international level.

About twenty-six thousand people are killed or maimed worldwide each year by antipersonnel (AP) land mines.[40] Most of these people are in Third World countries that have been caught up in Cold War conflicts (Vietnam, Laos, Cambodia, and Angola) or ethnic conflicts and internal strife. Over a hundred thousand U.S. citizens were killed or injured by AP mines in the twentieth century. The continuing threat created by live land mines can prevent civilians from living in their homes and using their fields and can seriously threaten the ability of an entire country to rebuild long after the war has ended. Antipersonnel mines are notable for the particularly egregious nature of the injuries they cause. The majority of land mine explosions that do not cause death often result in traumatic or surgical amputations. As reported in the *British Medical Journal* in 1991 about victims in Angola, "Land mines . . . have ruinous effects on the human body; they drive dirt, bacteria, clothing and metal and plastic fragments into the tissue, causing secondary infections. The shock wave from an exploding mine can destroy blood vessels well up the leg, causing surgeons to amputate much higher than the site of the primary wound."[41]

From 1969 to 1992, the United States exported 4.4 million AP mines to at least thirty-eight countries. U.S.-made or -supplied AP mines have been found in countries including Afghanistan, Angola, Cambodia,

Iraq, Laos, Lebanon, Mozambique, Nicaragua, Rwanda, Somalia, and Vietnam. From 1985 to 1996, the United States produced more than 10 million new AP mines, adding to a stockpile of an estimated 12 to 18 million AP mines.

The struggle against land mines has arisen in both the South and the North. In 1991, the International Committee of the Red Cross and several nongovernmental organizations and individuals began to discuss the necessity for coordinating initiatives to bring the global land mine crisis to the attention of the public and governments and to call for a ban on antipersonnel land mines.[42] Six NGOs, Handicap International, Human Rights Watch, Medico International, Mines Advisory Group, Physicians for Human Rights, and the Vietnam Veterans of America Foundation came together in October 1992 to formalize the ICBL. The movement grew out of a desire by those working in postconflict areas to stop the damage being done by antipersonnel mines. They began by writing a definition for an antipersonnel mine based on its effect rather than its design, and they campaigned for an end to any weapon that fell within that definition.[43] The movement quickly grew beyond just the NGOs and was endorsed by various international agencies as well as by influential media, such as *The Economist* and the *Daily Telegraph*.

In the beginning, the campaign defined itself as a flexible network of organizations that share common objectives. The campaign calls for an international ban on the use, production, stockpiling, and transfer of antipersonnel land mines, and for increased international resources for humanitarian mine clearance and mine victim assistance programs. By 1993, the campaign steering committee was formalized, dozens of national campaigns formed around the world, and hundreds of organizations joined the campaign. Currently, the campaign brings together over thirteen hundred human rights, humanitarian, children's, peace, disability, veterans, medical, humanitarian mine action, development, arms control, religious, environmental, and women's groups in over seventy-five countries who work locally, nationally, regionally, and internationally to ban antipersonnel mines.[44] A senior UNICEF official has said the ICBL is "the single most effective exercise of civil society since the Second World War."[45]

The work of the International Campaign to Ban Landmines has brought about tremendous change in a short period of time. In Ottawa,

in December 1997, 122 countries signed a treaty that bans the use, production, stockpiling, and transfer of antipersonnel mines. In addition,
in 1997, the Nobel Peace Prize was awarded to the ICBL and its then
coordinator, Jody Williams. In its announcement, the Norwegian Nobel
Committee said the Campaign had changed a ban from "a vision to a
feasible reality." It also noted that by working with small and medium-
sized countries, "this work has grown into a convincing example of an
effective policy for peace that could prove of decisive importance to the
international effort for disarmament...."[46]

The Ottawa ban treaty is unique because of the speed with which it
was negotiated and the extent of NGO involvement in the negotiations.
By March 1, 1999, 135 states had signed and ratified the treaty, and
sixty-seven of these had gone one step further and officially ratified it.
Among the countries that have already ratified are former major producers and exporters of mines although the treaty has suffered because
several major governments still refuse to renounce the use of land mines
completely. (The United States has not signed on.)

In 1999, several core groups (Human Rights Watch, Handicap International, Kenya Coalition Against Landmines, Mines Action Canada,
and Norwegian People's Aid) established a civil society–based reporting network for monitoring state compliance. Landmine Monitor is an
unprecedented initiative by ICBL to monitor implementation of and
compliance with the 1997 Mine Ban Treaty, and more generally to as-
sess the efforts of the international community to resolve the land mines
crisis. It is the first time that non-governmental organizations are coming together in a coordinated, systematic, and sustained way to monitor
a humanitarian law or disarmament treaty, and to regularly document
progress and problems.[47] While the Landmine Monitor will have no official status under the treaty, it is likely to be taken seriously by states
because the treaty provides for no official verification organization to
be established. The absence of such a structure results from the lack
of agreement among the negotiating states on what verification was
required or feasible.[48] In the United States alone, forty-seven companies have been involved in the manufacture of AP mines. Seventeen of
these companies have agreed to renounce future involvement, including Motorola Corp. Nevertheless, Human Rights Watch reports that
"Washington is one of the largest producers and exporters of mines in
the past, and one of the largest stockpilers today. In 2001, the United
States had the third largest stockpile of antipersonnel mines in the world,

more than 11 million, including stocks in twelve foreign countries, five of which have signed the Mine Ban Treaty."[49] The *Landmine Monitor Report 2002* published by the International Campaign to Ban Landmines cites accomplishments — more than 34 million antipersonnel mines that have been destroyed by sixty-one states since the 1997 Mine Ban Treaty, and fewer victims each year. It registered enormous concern, however, not only about the U.S. stockpiles, but also about the massive new mine-laying operations by India and Pakistan along their border.

New Agendas

Global Ethics and Global Society: Which Way and Where Are We Going?

The globalization of the world economy, well begun by the end of the twentieth century, is going to be the story of the twenty-first century. It has political, social, and cultural ramifications we do not begin to understand. New communication and transportation technologies along with the restructuring of production, accelerating migration of peoples, and, indeed, high levels of cultural exchange make it quite clear that globalization is taking place. At stake, however, is *how* we are globalizing. The world is shrinking whether we like it or not. The question we pose here is not whether we globalize, but how we globalize.

It is evident that globalization processes are creating inequalities in the form of a gulf that separates rich from poor. We have a world in which, according to UN calculations in the mid-1990s, the 358 richest individuals in the world controlled economic assets equal to the combined annual incomes of poor countries with 45 percent of the world's population.[50] In chapter 1, we referred to this phenomenon as a "poverty curtain" dividing North and South that is replacing the "iron curtain" that divided East and West in the post–World War II years. Evidence suggests that the inequalities and the poverty being generated are not simply the result of markets sorting themselves out eventually to bring — via some trickle-down process — the benefits of capitalism to all. Rather there are explicit policies and public choices providing the political underpinnings of these economic trends. Hans Küng, the German theologian, philosopher, and author noted in chapter 1, asks us to address the policies that create many more losers than winners in this global economy and to begin a formal process of identifying common values, shared commitments, and what he calls a global ethic.

What, in our view, must underlie efforts to develop a global ethic for a global society? First, we must listen to voices from the margins. Is the world marching toward a colonial, affluent West and a non-Western, formerly colonized, impoverished *Other*? This seems to be the perception of many in South Asia, Africa, and Central America. History looks different through many non-Western eyes, and we cannot assume that the forces of modernization, Westernization, and global economic interdependence are creating a more just world or a more desirable one.

Second, we would do well to heed the words of Brecher and others who caution us about the centralizing processes of globalization from above and encourage us to foster globalization from below.[51] They urge us to assure rights of participation in global decision-making processes and to hold leaders accountable. We need to proceed in a systematic way to develop avenues for dialogue, reflection, criticism, and negotiation. Such efforts must link states and civil society, promoting inclusiveness in decision making.

Third, we must establish a link between global decision making and human rights, based, as they are, on principles of equality, self-determination, nondiscrimination, and rights to political participation. Embedded in a focus on human rights are the principles by which we can evaluate the forces of globalization. Together a focus on human rights and on development can be complementary and mutually reinforcing in a move toward greater social justice. A new global ethic demands focus on questions of distribution and sustainability. Governance in a global context requires us to reconcile distributional challenges between rich and poor, haves and have-nots, with concerns about sustainability of our economy and environment. One good place to begin is an examination of ways to link human development, economic growth, and poverty reduction.

Linking Human Development, Economic Growth, and Poverty Reduction

A priority for the global community is to halt the worsening conditions experienced by many and shaped by the growing disparities of wealth. Whether they are caused by the forces of economic globalization or by unjust policies pursued by various governments, or both, they must be addressed. There is what *The Oxfam Poverty Report* calls "a silent emergency of poverty."[52] Today, one in four of the world's people lives in a state of absolute want, unable to meet their basic needs, while millions more live close to this perilous condition on the very margins of survival. The UN's Poverty Report 2000, *Overcoming Human Poverty,* confirms the need to focus poverty reduction resources, to mount a new global strategy, and to set "time-bound goals and targets for the substantial reduction of overall poverty and the eradication of extreme poverty."[53]

Arguments for poverty reduction can be framed theoretically and practically. The theoretical grounds constitute (1) a moral imperative and (2) a matter of human rights and entitlements. Amartya Sen, economist and theorist discussed in chapter 1, helps us frame these ideas around concepts of capabilities and freedom, not simply economic inequality. The World Summit for Social Development that met in Copenhagen in 1995 promoted a consensus that poverty is a denial of human rights, not just a plight or condition. "The notion of poverty eradication as a fundamental obligation of nation-states and the global community as a whole is an important reconceptualization of the way we define poverty."[54] Trickle-down approaches or "noblesse oblige" attitudes will not do in addressing this injustice.

The case can also be made on practical grounds. One often heard could be termed enlightened self-interest — the poor of today are the markets of tomorrow. A compelling analysis has been offered by Morris Morris, who focuses on the physical quality of life index (PQLI) composed of infant mortality, life expectancy at age one, and basic literacy.[55] He argues that it is possible to have improvements in PQLI *without* first having substantial economic growth. There is enough experience from countries around the world to suggest that a more direct focus on the improvement of social indicators may prove to be the most humane and socially responsible development strategy. The southern state of Kerala in India is one example of a government focusing on health, education, and women's rights with marked success in improving those indicators despite a comparatively low per capita income. In fact, improvements that raise the PQLI may actively drive per capita income growth, as many believe has been the case in countries of East Asia. China, for example, exhibited formidable PQLI improvement from 1960 through 1980, and this appears to have provided the social underpinning for subsequent sustained economic growth. By contrast India's PQLI improvement has been much slower, as have its economic growth rates. Morris suggests that we reduce our "current single-minded commitment to rapid growth of the GNP [GNI, see p. 315, note 3] and pay attention to social indicators and local capacities for organizational innovation to improve the well-being of their people."[56]

Economic growth by itself does not reduce absolute poverty, as has been demonstrated time and again. Attention must also be given to increasing employment, raising the productivity of the poor, meeting basic needs, and reducing inequalities in income and wealth. Most countries follow a "two-track" approach to poverty reduction: growth on one track and human development on the other.[57] Economic policies are not designed to be "pro-poor." Social services are administered in ways unrelated to opportunities for enhancing productivity and growth. The tracks run parallel rather than intersecting in ways that enable synergetic improvements to arise. Interactive processes of human development, economic growth, and poverty reduction are required; strategic policies and programs are needed to enable them to happen. Perhaps then we shall be able to lift the "poverty curtain" increasingly dividing North and South.

Emerging Choices and Challenges for the Twenty-First Century

Rethinking the Roles of States and Their Relations with Civil Society

Globalization is an integrative process in which the whole is greater than the sum of the parts. These "parts" are sovereign states with profound crosscutting linkages and influences. The state is both buffeted by these pressures and enhanced by the opportunities they can present. At the same time, many states face strategic internal challenges of state and nation building as described in chapter 4. Political fragility occurs around the world whether in Sri Lanka, Rwanda, Nigeria, Colombia, or Eritrea. Some face a remarkable set of challenges trying to move from war to peace (Rwanda or East Timor), from strong man to democracy (Nigeria or Indonesia), from failed state to institution building (Afghanistan or Congo), and from controlled to open economies (Mexico and India). Many states at once face several of these challenges, and it can be difficult to do so without slipping into cycles of violence, repression, poverty, and displacement.

One new challenge for the state is to recast the concept of civil society within the context of globalization. Rajni Kothari, Indian political scientist introduced in chapter 1, hopes that civil society will be restructured by movements led by the excluded, the exploited, and the disenfranchised, and that they will serve as catalysts for change. As the first part of this chapter suggests, slowly such changes are beginning to happen. The international media, churches with their international structures, and organizations such as Amnesty International or Human Rights Watch support the "staying power" of those who are trying to lead the way toward a more democratic, just, and egalitarian society.

At present both collaboration and confrontation between governments and civil society organizations are increasing. Organizations vary widely in the ways they work, in their objectives, and their capacities. Yet, civil society organizations are linked both conceptually and practically to the promotion of democracy, to good governance, and ultimately to sustainable development.[58] A strong civil society characterized by trends toward decentralization and local governance requires an enabling environment that encourages both the creation and autonomy of voluntary association. One analyst goes so far as to say that non-governmental organizations may provide the only possible long-term approach for undermining power monopolies. Power creation from below enables groups to collaborate with each other and to work with government to assure both sustainable development and accountability.[59]

What organizations have the potential to bring new voice to the poor and disenfranchised? How can communities mobilize to alter the terms of exchange by which they relate to the world beyond? These are important questions for all peoples to ask, and many states do not do so willingly. When a government closes off avenues for encompassing diversity, for constructive participation in the polity, and for assuring its own accountability, frustration is likely to grow and give voice to despair. Thus, a challenge for analysts and activists in this new century is to explore ways to strengthen both state and civil society and the accountability of each to all of us. One avenue that this exploration might take is to figure out how to make decisions as close to the appropriate activity as possible. Social scientists have labeled this approach the "subsidiarity principle."[60] Democratic involvement is maximized in policymaking, implementation, and enforcement because decisions are taken at the most local level suitable to the topic at hand. Thus, locality, region, nation, and global society are linked in a network designed to fit the decision-making functions and arena to the scope of the task. In this way we might begin to build a somewhat different kind of governance, one that is more inclusive and more suited to objectives of participation and democratization.

Reforming the Financial and Social Global Architecture

There are few mechanisms at the present time that can manage globalization processes. We live in a world economy, but we lack institutions that can stabilize and regulate it. For example, the sorts of regulatory commissions that we have nationally, such as the U.S. Securities and Exchange Commission that oversees domestic trade of stocks and bonds, do not exist on a worldwide basis. Financial concerns are not the only ones. Across the board, we need to examine ways in which our global society functions and what institutions we need for its equitable and creative management. The global competition to lower labor, environmental, and social costs creates what some have called the global race to the bottom. The mobility of capital that can pour into a country and then, in a flash, depart equally quickly, leaving financial devastation in its wake, is another source of global financial turmoil. Mechanisms and strategies to address such concerns are essential.

Many questions arise for global citizens and international organizations. How can we improve power-sharing among the international institutions deriving from the end of World War II, the United Nations, the World Bank, the International Monetary Fund, and the World Trade Organization? In what ways can we create strategic partnerships among myriads of non-governmental and governmental organizations, partnerships that will benefit broad cross sections of the globe's people? Is it possible to put aid on a predictable long-term basis in ways that it actually reaches the intended recipients, has a pro–poverty reduction orientation, and does not serve as an incentive for politicians to cling to power and pocket the benefits? Already there are efforts to explore some of these topics. Campaigns and social movements are emerging that seek to build a viable form of global democracy in which all people have rights to be well represented in global decision-making processes and in which leaders are held accountable to ordinary citizens as well as to affluent elites. In the long run, such movements promote democratization of state-society relations.

Creating New Strategies for Cooperation between Rich and Poor

Global citizens need new strategies for cooperation between rich and poor peoples. At the global level, we need to find effective and generous ways to deal with the debt owed by the poorest countries. The HIPC Initiative (debt repayment relief for heavily indebted poor countries) has been helpful, but the requirements for a poor country to qualify are stringent, and thus far, relief through this program has been too limited.

Another avenue for exploration is a more formal global effort to mobilize science and technology to address critical problems. There are many areas for which such mobilization is keenly needed: an AIDS vaccine, malaria eradication, food security in sub-Saharan Africa, research on biotechnology and drought-resistant food crops, to name a few. In 2001, the secretary general of the United Nations, Kofi Annan, launched a global campaign to raise funds for AIDS research and medications for poor countries. It is one of the first initiatives of this kind, but, as yet, falls far short of the funding required to make a substantial difference in the fight against AIDS.

At the national level, affluent nations need to address squarely the ways in which the free-market ideology offers false promises to many nations of the Global South and to the poorer citizens within them. There are harsh lessons emerging from the lost decades of structural adjustment and onerous debts. The North, in imposing its perceptions of neoliberal market values on states around the globe, has benefited from the imposition of this system at the expense of many of the poorest nations. It is time to reevaluate these philosophical and policy positions. A good place to begin would be an assessment of protectionist policies and enormous subsidies of agricultural commodities on the part of the North.

Our world is changing, not simply because of a newfound concern about terrorism, our inability to understand the Global South, or our uncertainty about the role of the United States in a new global order. It is changing for all the reasons noted at the outset of this volume in chapter 1: porous boundaries, new technologies, the information age, communal conflicts, the poverty curtain — to mention a few. The pathways forward may appear hazy and unclear. At the individual level we must be keenly aware of the linkages and the connections between our lives and the policies of our governments. Those of us who live in the industrialized North are linked inextricably with laborers on the sugar plantations in the Philippines, women in the sweatshops of Bangladesh, Colombians cultivating flowers for the U.S. market, and even the child soldiers in distant Sierra Leone. We as individuals must begin to understand that we are global citizens, not merely citizens of a given nation, and that the well-being of each and every one of us is a widely shared responsibility. Then we must develop the political will, energy, and commitment to address the tough questions of equity and social justice between South and North that this new century, the twenty-first, poses.

Notes

Chapter 1: Understanding the "Global South"

1. Anthony Lewis, "The Inescapable World," *New York Times*, October 20, 2001.

2. Alan Schwartz, "Getting at the Roots of Arab Poverty," *New York Times*, December 1, 2001.

3. According to the World Bank's *Building Institutions for Markets: World Development Report 2000*, "Gross national income (GNI — formerly gross national product or GNP) is the broadest measure of national income, measures total value added from domestic and foreign sources claimed by residents. GNI comprises gross domestic product (GDP) plus net receipts of primary income from foreign sources," 244.

4. World Bank, *Knowledge for Development: World Development Report 1999* (New York: Oxford University Press, 1999), 196–97; and the World Resources Institute, UNEP, UNDP, and the World Bank, *World Resources 1998–99, A Guide to the Global Environment* (Oxford: Oxford University Press, 1998), 248–49; and UNDP, *Overcoming Human Poverty* (New York: UNDP, 1998).

5. World Bank, *World Development Report 2002*, selected world development indicators.

6. Denis Goulet, *The Cruel Choice: A New Concept in the Theory of Development* (New York: Atheneum, 1971); Denis Goulet, *Incentives for Development: The Key to Equity* (New York: New Horizons Press, 1989).

7. Amartya Sen, *Inequality Reexamined* (Cambridge, Mass.: Harvard University Press, 1992); Sen, *Development as Freedom* (New York: Random House, 1999).

8. Sen, *Development as Freedom*, 3.

9. See Charles K. Wilber and Kenneth Jameson, "Paradigms of Economic Development and Beyond," *The Political Economy of Development and Underdevelopment*, ed. Charles K. Wilber, 3d ed. (New York: Random House, 1984), for an excellent overview of these two approaches to development.

10. Adam Smith, *An Inquiry into the Nature and Causes of the Wealth of Nations*, first published in 1776 (New York: Modern Library, 1937).

11. W. W. Rostow, *The Stages of Economic Growth: A Non-Communist Manifesto*, 2d ed. (Cambridge: Cambridge University Press, 1971).

12. Samir Amin, *Unequal Development: An Essay on the Social Formation of Peripheral Capitalism* (New York: Monthly Review Press, 1977); Amin, *Delinking: Toward a Polycentric World* (New York: Zed Books, 1990); Amin, *Maldevelopment: Anatomy of a Global Failure* (New York: United Nations University Press, 1990).

13. Andre Gunder Frank, "The Development of Underdevelopment," in Wilber, ed., *The Political Economy of Development and Underdevelopment*, 100.

14. Ibid., 103.

15. Wolfgang Sachs, ed. *The Development Dictionary: A Guide to Knowledge as Power* (London: Zed Books, 1993), 1.

16. Michael Foucault, *Power/Knowledge: Selected Interviews and Other Writings, 1972–1977*, ed. C. Gordon (New York: Pantheon Books, 1980).

17. C. Douglas Lummis, "Equality" in Sachs, *The Development Dictionary*, 47.

18. Ester Boserup, *Woman's Role in Economic Development* (New York: St. Martin's Press, 1970).

19. See, for example, Chandra Mohanty, "Under Western Eyes," in *Third World Women and the Politics of Feminism*, ed. Chandra Mohanty, Ann Russo, and Lourdes Torres (Bloomington: Indiana University Press, 1991); Amrita Basu, *Women's Movements in Global Perspective* (Boulder, Colo.: Westview Press, 1995).

20. Rajni Kothari, *Poverty, Human Consciousness, and the Amnesia of Development* (London: Zed Books, 1993); Hans Küng, *A Global Ethic for Global Politics and Economics* (Oxford: Oxford University Press, 1998).

21. Source: *www.walmartstores.com*, October 13, 2001.

22. Source: *www.homedepot.com*, October 10, 2002.

23. Craig Smith, "Globalization Puts a Starbucks into the Forbidden City in Beijing," *New York Times*, November 25, 2000.

24. Fareed Zakaria, "Globalization Grows Up and Gets Political," *New York Times*, December 31, 2000.

25. Source: Goldman Sachs, *www.gs.com*, October 20, 2002.

26. World Bank, *Building Institutions for Markets: World Development Report 2002*, 232–33.

27. UNDP, *Overcoming Human Poverty* (New York: UNDP Poverty Report, 1998), 49.

28. International Monetary Fund. "Debt Relief for Poor Countries (HIPC): What Has Been Achieved — A Fact Sheet," November 2001; *www.imf.org*, October 2002.

29. UNDP, *Overcoming*, 46.

30. Michael Harris, *Lament for an Ocean* (Toronto: McClelland and Stewart, 1998).

31. Stockholm International Peace Research Institute, *SIPRI Yearbook 2001 — Armaments, Disarmament, and International Security* (London: Oxford University Press, 2001).

32. Derick Z. Jackson, "Clinton's Promise to Africa Should Be a Farewell to Arms," *Boston Globe*, March 25, 1998.

33. Isabella Asamba and Barbara Thomas-Slayter, "From Cattle to Coffee: Transformation in Rural Machakos," in Barbara P. Thomas-Slayter and Dianne Rocheleau, *Gender, Environment, and Development in Kenya: A Grassroots Perspective* (Boulder, Colo.: Lynne Rienner, 1995).

34. Dale Shields and Barbara Thomas-Slayter, "Gender, Class, Ecological Decline, and Livelihood Strategies: A Case Study of Siquijor Island, The Philippines" (Worcester, Mass.: Clark University ECOGEN case study, 1993).

35. Barbara Thomas-Slayter, Nina Bhatt, Indira Koirala, and Laju Shrestha, *Managing Resources in a Nepalese Village: Changing Dynamics of Gender, Caste, and Ethnicity* (Worcester, Mass.: Clark University, ECOGEN Publication, 1994).

36. Nicholas Kristof and Edward Wyatt, "Who Went Under in the World's Sea of Cash," *New York Times*, February 15, 1999. The profile of Salamet and his family's struggles is presented in this article.

Chapter 2: Exploring North-South Relationships

1. R. R. Palmer, *A History of the Modern World*, 2d ed. (New York: Alfred A. Knopf, 1956), 90.

2. Ibid., 91.

3. Ibid., 94.

4. Bill Rau, *From Feast to Famine: Official Cures and Grassroots Remedies to Africa's Food Crisis* (London: Zed Books, 1991), 16.

5. William Murdoch, *The Poverty of Nations: The Political Economy of Hunger and Population* (Baltimore: Johns Hopkins University Press, 1980), 205.

6. John Isbister, *Promises Not Kept: The Betrayal of Social Change in the Third World*, 4th ed. (West Hartford, Conn.: Kumarian Press, 1998), 75.

7. Murdoch, *Poverty*, 213.

8. H. A. Reitsma and J. M. G. Kleinpenning, *The Third World in Perspective* (Assen, The Netherlands: Rowman & Allanheld, 1985), 216.

9. Christopher Clapham, *Third World Politics: An Introduction* (Madison: University of Wisconsin Press, 1985), 21.

10. Peter Uvin, *Aiding Violence: The Development Enterprise in Rwanda* (West Hartford, Conn.: Kumarian Press, 1998), 19.

11. Ngugi wa Thiong'o, *Decolonising the Mind: The Politics of Language in African Literature* (London: Heinemann Books), 16.

12. Ngugi wa Thiong'o, *The River Between* (London: Heinemann, 1965).

13. Gita Sen and Caren Grown, *Development, Crises, and Alternative Visions* (New York: Monthly Review Press, 1987), 80.

14. V. Spike Peterson and Anne Sisson Runyan, *Global Gender Issues* (Boulder, Colo.: Westview Press, 1999), 172.

15. Martha Brill Olcott, *Revisiting the Twelve Myths of Central Asia* (Carnegie Endowment for International Peace, Working Paper No. 23, September 2001), 19.

16. "A Model of Nation-Building?" *The Economist* (April 18, 2002).

17. Peter Schraeder, *African Politics and Society* (Boston and New York: Bedford/St. Martins, 2000), 157.

18. Ahmed Rashid, "The Taliban: Exporting Extremism," *Foreign Affairs* 87, no. 6 (November/December 1999): 2.

19. Ahmed Rashid, *Taliban* (New Haven, Conn.: Yale University Press, 2001), 105.

20. H. D. S. Greenway, "As British Know, Pashtuns Have History of Fanaticism," *Boston Globe*, November 19, 2001.

21. Barnett R. Rubin, Aashraf Ghani, William Maley, Ahmed Rashid, Olivier Roy, *Afghanistan: Reconstruction and Peace-Building in a Regional Framework*, Koff Peacebuilding Reports (Bern: Swiss Peace Foundation, KOFF Center for Peacebuilding, 2001).

22. Frantz Fanon, *The Wretched of the Earth* (New York: Grove Press, 1968).

23. Walter Rodney, *How Europe Underdeveloped Africa*, trans. Constance Farrington (Dar es Salaam: Tanzania Publishing House, 1972).

24. Ngugi wa Thiong'o, *The River Between;* and *Weep Not, Child* (London: Heinemann, 1964).

25. Ngugi wa Thiong'o, *Decolonising,* 3.

26. V. S. Naipaul, *A Bend in the River* (New York: Random House, 1979); *Half a Life* (New York: Knopf, 2001).

27. J. M. Coetzee, *Disgrace* (New York: Viking, 1999).

28. Kamala Markandaya, *Nectar in a Sieve* (New York: John Day, 1954); and Michael Ondaatje, *Running in the Family* (New York: Knopf Publishing Group, 1993).

29. Vandana Shiva, "Resources," in *The Development Dictionary: A Guide to Knowledge as Power,* ed. Wolfgang Sachs (London: Zed Books, 1993).

30. Asoka Bandarage, *Women, Population and Global Crisis* (London: Zed Books, 1997), 272.

31. Priscilla Weeks, "Post-Colonial Challenges to Grand Theory," *Human Organization* 49, no. 3 (1990): 238.

32. Ibid., 242.

Chapter 3: Politics and the State

1. A. Douglas Kincaid and Alejandro Portes, "Sociology and Development in the 1990s: Critical Challenges and Empirical Trends," in *Comparative National Development: Society and Economy in the New Global Order,* ed. A. Douglas Kincaid and Alejandro Portes (Chapel Hill: University of North Carolina, 1994), 9.

2. Liah Greenfeld, *Nationalism: Five Roads to Modernity* (Cambridge, Mass.: Harvard University Press, 1992), 21.

3. John Isbister, *Promises Not Kept: The Betrayal of Social Change in the Third World,* 4th ed. (West Hartford, Conn.: Kumarian Press, 1998).

4. Bruce J. Berman, "Ethnicity, Patronage, and the African State: The Politics of Uncivil Nationalism," *African Affairs* 97, no. 388 (1998): 305.

5. There is a large literature on ethnicity particularly, but not exclusively, in Africa. See Berman, "Ethnicity, Patronage, and the African State"; Patrick Chabal and Jean-Pascal Daloz, *Africa Works: Disorder as Political Instrument* (Oxford, UK, and Bloomington: The International African Institute with James Currey [Oxford] and Indiana University Press, 1999); Robert Fatton, "Civil Society Revisited: Africa in the New Millennium," paper prepared for the Hesburgh International Center, University of Notre Dame conference "The Crisis of Development in Africa: Contexts, Connections, and Consequences of International Aid and NGOs"; Howard Handelman, *The Challenge of Third World Development* (Upper Saddle River, N.J.: Prentice-Hall, 1996); Robert D. Kaplan, *The Ends of the Earth: From Togo to Turkmenistan, from Iran to Cambodia, a Journey to the Frontiers of Anarchy* (New York: Vintage Books, 1997); Nelson Kasfir, ed., *State and Class in Africa* (London: Frank Cass, 1984); James Mayall and Mark Simpson, "Ethnicity Is Not Enough: Reflections on Protracted Secessionism in the Third World," *International Journal of Comparative Sociology* 33, nos. 1–2 (1992); Donald Rothchild and Victor A. Olorunsola, eds., *State versus Ethnic Claims* (Boulder, Colo.: Westview Press, 1983); Barbara P. Thomas-Slayter, "Class, Ethnicity, and the Kenyan State: Community Mobilization in the Context of Global Politics," *International Journal of Politics, Culture, and Society* 4, no. 3 (Spring 1991): 301–21.

6. Peter Mwangi Kagwanja, "Facing Mount Kenya or Facing Mecca? The Mungiki, Ethnic Violence and the Politics of the Moi Succession in Kenya, 1987–2002," *African Affairs* 102, no. 406 (2003): 27.

7. Philip Jenkins, "The Next Christianity," *Atlantic Monthly* 290, no. 3 (October 2002): 55.

8. Kagwanja, "Facing," 29.

9. David Maybury-Lewis, *Indigenous Peoples, Ethnic Groups, and the State*, 2d ed. (Boston: Allyn and Bacon, 2002), 78.

10. UNDP, *Human Development Report 2000* (New York: Oxford University Press, 2000); World Bank, *Entering the Twenty-first Century: World Development Report 1999/2000* (New York: Oxford University Press, 2000).

11. H. A. Reitsma and J. M. G. Kleinpenning, *The Third World in Perspective* (Assen, The Netherlands: Rowman and Allanheld, 1985); Edmond J. Keller, *Revolutionary Ethiopia: From Empire to People's Republic*, 2d ed. (Bloomington: Indiana University Press, 1991).

12. Ruth Iyob, "The Ethiopian-Eritrean Conflict: Diasporic vs. Hegemonic States in the Horn of Africa, 1991–2000," *Journal of Modern African Studies* 38, no. 4 (2000): 660.

13. World Bank, *www.worldbank.org/data/databytype*, October 9, 2001.

14. David Martin and Phyllis Johnson, *The Struggle for Zimbabwe* (New York: Monthly Review Press, 1981).

15. From the "Southern Rhodesia Elections, Report of the Commonwealth Observer Group," February 1980, documented by Martin and Johnson, *Struggle*, 334.

16. Donald McNeil, "Zimbabwe Squatters: Land Claims on White Farms," *New York Times*, June 22, 1998.

17. Rachel Swarns, "Chaos in Zimbabwe, Land Redistribution Ravages Economy," *International Herald Tribune*, December 27, 2002, 2.

18. Kurt Shillinger, "Zimbabwe's Turmoil Over Land Finds an Echo across Africa," *Boston Globe*, May 16, 2000.

19. "UN Study Says Armies Leave Corrupt Networks in Congo," *New York Times*, October 22, 2002.

20. Reitsma and Kleinpenning, *Third World*, 332.

21. John F. Burns, "Fifty Years Past Midnight," *New York Times*, August 14, 1997.

22. A. M. Rosenthal, "India, Mon Amour," *New York Times*, August 15, 1997.

23. Burns, "Fifty Years."

24. Reitsma and Kleinpenning, *Third World*, 316.

25. Pandit Jawaharlal Nehru, "A Tryst with Destiny," speech in the Constituent Assembly, India, August 14, 1947.

26. Kushwant Singh wrote a famous novel, *Mano Majra*, or *Train to Pakistan*, in which the horrors of this period are vividly portrayed. He remains an outspoken critic of ethnic and religious violence in India today.

27. Francine Frankel, *India's Political Economy, 1947–1977: The Gradual Revolution* (Princeton, N.J.: Princeton University Press, 1978). Quoting Jawaharlal Nehru.

28. Somini Sengupta, "India's Minefields Mean Bitter Harvest for Farmers," *New York Times*, January 4, 2002.

29. Celia Dugger, "India's Unwired Villages Mired in the Distant Past," *New York Times,* March 19, 2000.

30. World Bank, *The State in a Changing World: World Development Report, 1997* (New York: Oxford University Press, 1997), 15.

31. Patrick Chabal and Jean-Pascal Daloz, *Africa Works: Disorder as Political Instrument* (Oxford, UK, and Bloomington: The International African Institute with James Currey [Oxford] and Indiana University Press, 1999), 162.

32. Donald Rothchild and Naomi Chazan, eds., *The Precarious Balance: State and Society in Africa* (Boulder, Colo.: Westview Press, 1988); Barbara Thomas-Slayter, "Structural Change, Power Politics and Community Organizations in Africa: Challenging the Patterns, Puzzles and Paradoxes," *World Development* 22, no. 10 (1994): 1479–90; Fatton, "Civil Society Revisited."

Chapter 4: Conflict, Human Rights, and the Politics of Refugees

1. John Stremlau, *People in Peril: Human Rights, Humanitarian Action, and Preventing Deadly Conflict* (Washington, D.C.: Carnegie Commission on Preventing Deadly Conflict, 1998), 25.

2. Michael T. Klare, "The New Challenges to Global Security," in Robert Jackson, ed., *Global Issues, 1994/95,* 10th ed. (Guilford, Conn: Dushkin Publishing Group, 1994), 171.

3. John F. Burns, "Rajiv Gandhi's Widow Emerges as Party's Star," *New York Times,* February 6, 1998.

4. Stockholm International Peace Research Institute, *SIPRI Yearbook 2001 — Armaments, Disarmament, and International Security* (London: Oxford University Press, 2001); *http://editors.sipri.se,* October 20, 2002.

5. Derick Z. Jackson, "Clinton's Promise to Africa Should Be a Farewell to Arms," *Boston Globe,* March 25, 1998.

6. David Isenberg, "Arms Trade," in *Global Focus: A New Foreign Policy Agenda 1997–1998,* ed. Tom Barry and Martha Honey (Silver City, N.Mex.: Interhemispheric Resource Center, 1997), 93.

7. Donald McNeil, "South Africa Goes on a Shopping Trip Abroad for $5 Billion Worth of Arms," *New York Times,* November 19, 1998.

8. Isenberg, "Arms Trade," 93.

9. Graca Machel, *Impact of Armed Conflict on Children* (New York: United Nations Children's Fund, 1996), 136.

10. Cynthia Enloe, *The Morning After: Sexual Politics at the End of the Cold War* (Berkeley: University of California Press, 1993), 240.

11. Ibid., 128.

12. Francis Mading Deng, *War of Visions: Conflict of Identities in the Sudan* (Washington, D.C.: Brookings Institute, 1995), 99.

13. Celia Dugger, "In a Tinderbox, Sri Lanka President Turns Up the Heat," *New York Times,* December 5, 2001.

14. Celia Dugger, "After Ferocious Fighting, Sri Lanka Struggles with Peace," *New York Times,* April 9, 2002.

15. Ted Dagne, *Sudan: Humanitarian Crisis, Peace Talks, Terrorism, and U.S. Policy,* Congressional Research Service, the Library of Congress. Unpublished Report (2001), 9.

16. Deng, *War of Visions,* 11. Much of the discussion about Sudan is based on this volume of Frances Deng, former minister of state for foreign affairs; former ambassador from Sudan to Canada, the United States, and Scandinavia; and special representative of the United Nations secretary general for internally displaced persons.

17. Inez Andrews, personal conversation. Ms. Andrews worked in southern Sudan between 1994 and 1997 for the World Food Program's Operation Lifeline Sudan. 1998.

18. Deng, *War of Visions.*

19. Scott B. MacDonald, *Dancing on a Volcano: The Latin American Drug Trade* (New York: Praeger, 1988), 28.

20. Colombia Human Rights Committee, Action Alert from the US/Colombia Coordinating Office, Washington, D.C., 1999, online at *www.igc.colhrnet/newscont/ 599uscoalert.htm.*

21. Ibid.

22. Kirk Semple, "Accusations in Full Flower," *Boston Globe,* February 12, 1999.

23. MacDonald, *Dancing,* 46.

24. Aristide R. Zolberg, Astri Suhrke, and Sergio Aguayo, *Escape from Violence: Conflict and the Refugee Crisis in the Developing World* (New York: Oxford University Press, 1989), 33.

25. UNHCR, *The State of the World's Refugees: In Search of Solutions* (New York: Oxford University Press, 1995), 19.

26. Source: *www.unhcr.org,* October 20, 2002.

27. UNHCR, *The State of the World's Refugees,* 188.

28. Zolberg, *Escape,* 277.

29. Stremlau, *People,* 21.

30. Ibid., 24.

31. Risho Sapano, Inez Andrews, and Kim Roberson, "International Assistance in Sudan," *ID News and Views* (Worcester, Mass.: Clark University International Development Program, 1998).

32. Stremlau, *People,* 24.

33. Mary B. Anderson, *Do No Harm: Supporting Local Capacities for Peace through Aid* (Cambridge, Mass.: Collaborative for Development Action, 1996), 3.

34. UNDP, *Human Development Report, 1998* (New York: Oxford University Press, 1998).

35. UNHCR, *The State of the World's Refugees,* 58. All quotes in this paragraph are from page 58 in this UNHCR document.

36. Machel, *Impact,* 29.

37. Jan Goodwin, "Sierra Leone Is No Place to Be Young," *New York Times Magazine,* February 14, 1999, 48.

38. Pamela Constable, "Small Steps for Afghan Women," *Washington Post,* May 11, 1999.

39. World Bank, *World Development Indicators 1997* (Oxford: Oxford University Press, 1997).

40. These comments about Rwanda are drawn largely from the Final Report of the Carnegie Commission, *Preventing Deadly Conflict: Final Report* (Washington,

D.C.: Carnegie Commission, 1997). The commission gathered data from the International Federation of Human Rights, Africa Watch, and used materials from the Copenhagen Steering Committee on the Joint Evaluation of Emergency Assistance to Rwanda, *Humanitarian Aid and Effects, The International Response to Conflict and Genocide: Lessons from the Rwanda Experience,* Study 3 (1996); and from Peter Uvin, *Aiding Violence: The Development Enterprise in Rwanda* (West Hartford, Conn.: Kumarian Press, 1998).

41. Carnegie Commission, *Preventing,* 7.

42. Greg Bischak, "Military Modernization and Budget," in *Global Focus: A New Foreign Policy Agenda 1997–1998,* ed. Tom Barry and Martha Honey (Silver City, N.Mex.: Interhemispheric Resource Center, 1997), 86.

43. Isenberg, "Arms Trade," 94.

44. Hans Küng, *A Global Ethic for Global Politics and Economics* (Oxford: Oxford University Press, 1998), 165, 215.

Chapter 5: The Shape of the Global Economy

1. Edmund Andrews, "Deutsche Telekom: Lost More than Just Telecom Italia," *New York Times,* May 26, 1999.

2. "Global Internet Statistics," August 13, 2002, *www.glreach.com/globstats.*

3. Edward S. Herman, "Immiserating Growth in the Third World," in *Developing World, 1998/99,* ed. Robert Griffiths (Guilford, Conn.: Dushkin/McGraw-Hill, 1998), 52.

4. Julius O. Ihonvbere, "The Third World and the New World Order in the 1990s," in *Developing World,* ed. Griffiths, 8.

5. World Bank, *Entering the Twenty-first Century: World Development Report, 1999/2000* (New York: Oxford University Press, 2000), 231.

6. Allan Sloan, "Think Globally, Skip Tax Locally," *Newsweek,* June 3, 2002, 38. The company under discussion is PricewaterhouseCoopers.

7. Thomas L. Friedman, "The Real G-7s," *New York Times,* June 19, 1997.

8. Erik Leaver and John Cavanagh, "Controlling Transnational Corporations," in *Global Focus: A New Foreign Policy Agenda 1997–1998,* ed. Tom Barry and Martha Honey (Albuquerque, N.Mex.: Interhemispheric Resource Center Press, 1997), 65.

9. William Fisher, ed., *Toward Sustainable Development: Struggling over India's Narmada River* (Armonk, N.Y.: M. E. Sharpe, 1995).

10. Kevin Danaher, *Fifty Years Is Enough: The Case against the World Bank and the International Monetary Fund* (Boston: South End Press, 1994).

11. Lydia Williams, ed., *Gender Equity and the World Bank Group: A Post-Beijing Assessment* (Washington, D.C.: Women's Eyes on the World Bank, 1997).

12. Paul Lewis, "US May Try to Stop Loan Seen as Bad for Tibetans," *New York Times,* May 30, 1999.

13. Jo Marie Griesgraber, "Forgive Us Our Debts: The Third World's Financial Crisis," in *Developing World,* ed. Griffiths, 56.

14. Devesh Kapur, "The IMF: A Cure or a Curse?" in *Developing World,* ed. Griffiths, 55.

15. Oxfam International, *Rigged Rules and Double Standards: Trade, Globalization, and the Fight against Poverty* (Oxford: Oxfam International, 2002), 125.

16. Ibid., 251.

17. David Hunter and Brennan Van Dyke, "Trade and Environment," in *Global Focus,* ed. Barry and Honey, 20.

18. William Greider, *One World Ready or Not: The Manic Logic of Global Capitalism* (New York: Simon and Schuster, 1997), 22.

19. Leaver and Cavanagh, "Controlling," 41.

20. William Grimes, "Eyes on the Fries," *New York Times Magazine,* May 30, 1999.

21. *Panel of Experts* transcript of an IMF Economic Forum: "Foreign Direct Investment in China: What Do We Need to Know?" sponsored by the Asia and Pacific Department of the IMF, *www.IMF.org,* September 10, 2002.

22. James Sterngold, "The Awakening Chinese Consumer," *New York Times Magazine,* October 11, 1992.

23. *www.coca-cola.com,* October 20, 2002.

24. Sheryl WuDunn, "Booming China Is Dream Market for West," *New York Times,* February 15, 1993.

25. Glenn Collins, "How Venezuela Is Becoming Coca-Cola Country," *New York Times,* August 21, 1996.

26. David Cay Johnston, "Very Richest's Share of Wealth Grew Even Bigger, Data Show," *New York Times,* June 26, 2003. Article is reporting on data released June 25, 2003, by the United States Internal Revenue Service.

27. Philip Shenon, "Saipan Sweatshops Are No American Dream," *New York Times,* July 18, 1993.

28. "Frequently Asked Questions on Labor and Human Rights Abuses on the Island of Saipan," *www.globalexchange.org/economy/corporations/saipan,* August 19, 2002.

29. Ibid.

30. Diana Jean Schemo, "In Brazil Tobacco Country, Conglomerates Rule," *New York Times,* April 2, 1998.

31. Andrea Stape, "Online, All the Time," *Virtual Village* (May 1999).

32. Oxfam International, *Rigged Rules,* 150, quoting data from the World Bank's International Task Force on Commodity Risk Management, "Dealing with Commodity Price Volatility in Developing Countries" (Washington, D.C.: World Bank, 1999); and UNCTAD, "The World Commodity Economy: Recent Evolution, Financial Crises, and Changing Market Structures" (Geneva: UNCTAD, 1999).

33. Oxfam International, *Mugged: Poverty in Your Coffee Cup* (Brussels: Oxfam International, 2002), 10.

34. Oxfam International, *Rigged Rules,* 160.

35. UNCTAD, *The Least Developed Countries Report 2002: Escaping the Poverty Trap* (Geneva: UNCTAD, 2002), 147.

36. Joseph Stiglitz, "The Roaring Nineties," *Atlantic Monthly* 290, no. 3 (2002): 86.

37. Dani Rodrik, "Trading in Illusions," in *Developing World,* ed. Griffiths, 42.

38. "The Free Trade Accord: What's What in the Trade Pact," *New York Times,* November 14, 1993.

39. Sylvia Nasar, "A Primer: Why Economists Favor Free-Trade Agreement," *New York Times,* September 17, 1993.

40. Tina Rosenberg, "Why Mexico's Small Corn Farmers Go Hungry," *New York Times,* March 3, 2003.

41. Ibid.

42. Julius Nyerere, Address on the occasion of Mainland Tanzania's twentieth Anniversary of Independence, Dar es Salaam (December 1981), quoted in Paul Cammack, David Pool, and William Tordoff, *Third World Politics: A Comparative Introduction* (Baltimore: Johns Hopkins University Press, 1988), 262.

43. Griesgraber, "Forgive," 55.

44. Pedro-Pablo Kuczynski, "The Outlook for Latin American Debt," *Foreign Affairs* (Fall 1987): 129–49.

45. World Bank, *Building Institutions for Markets: World Development Report 2002* (New York: Oxford University Press, 2002).

46. Soren Ambrose and Ian Stewart, "Multilateral Debt," in *Global Focus,* ed. Barry and Honey, 69.

47. Griesgraber, "Forgive," 57.

48. Kuczynski, "The Outlook."

49. Ambrose and Stewart, "Multilateral Debt," 71.

50. Griesgraber, "Forgive," 60.

51. Pope John Paul II, The Apostolic Letter, Millennio Ineunte of His Holiness Pope John Paul II to the Bishops, Clergy, Lay Faithful of the Great Jubilee of the Year 2000, January 6, 2001. Paragraphs 14, 50–54.

52. Nicholas Kristof and Edward Wyatt, "Who Went Under in the World's Sea of Cash," *New York Times,* February 15, 1999.

53. Nicholas Kristof and David Sanger, "How US Wooed Asia to Let Cash Flow In," *New York Times,* February 16, 1999.

54. Nicholas Kristof and Sheryl WuDunn, "Of World Markets, None an Island," *New York Times,* February 17, 1999.

55. David E. Sanger, "US and IMF Made Asia Crisis Worse, World Bank Finds," *New York Times,* December 3, 1998.

56. Kristof and Wyatt, "Who Went Under."

57. Mark Landler, "Grim Assessment by UN of Economic Slide in Asia," *New York Times,* December 3, 1998.

58. Kristof and Wyatt, "Who Went Under."

59. Joseph Stiglitz, *Globalization and Its Discontents* (New York: W. W. Norton, 2002), 7.

60. UNCTAD, *The Least Developed Countries, 1998 Report,* 148.

Chapter 6: Economic Realities and Local Perspectives

1. World Bank, *Entering the Twenty-first Century: World Development Report 1999/2000* (New York: Oxford University Press, 2000). Comments on pages 182–84 above are adapted from Richard Ford and Barbara Thomas-Slayter, "Alternatives to Anarchy: Africa's Transition from Agricultural to Industrial Societies," in *Progress in Planning,* ed. D. Diamond and B. H. Massam (London: Pergamon, 2001), vol. 56, part 2, 66–68.

2. Idriss Jazairy, *The State of World Rural Poverty, an Inquiry into the Causes and Consequences,* International Fund for Agricultural Development (New York: New York University Press, 1992).

3. Aloys B. Ayako and Musambayi Katumanga, *Review of Poverty in Kenya* (Nairobi, Kenya: Institute of Policy Analysis and Research, 1997).

4. World Bank, *The State in a Changing World: World Development Report, 1997* (New York: Oxford University Press, 1997), 31.

5. UNDP, *Human Development Report, 1997* (New York: Oxford University Press, 1997), 3.

6. World Bank, *Global Economic Prospects and the Developing Countries 2001* (Washington, D.C.: IBRD, 2001); World Bank, *Global Economic Prospects 2000* (Washington, D.C.: IBRD, 2000).

7. UNDP, *Human Development Report, 1997*, 2.

8. This discussion of Mbusyani in Kenya is based upon Barbara Thomas-Slayter and Diane Rocheleau, *Gender, Environment, and Development in Kenya: A Grassroots Perspective* (Boulder, Colo.: Lynne Rienner, 1995), 105–31.

9. The discussion of Siquijor in the Philippines is drawn from Dale Shields and Barbara Thomas-Slayter, *Gender, Class, Ecological Decline and Livelihood Strategies: A Case Study of Siquijor Island, The Philippines* (Worcester, Mass.: Clark University ECOGEN Case Study, 1993). UNDP, *Human Development Report, 2002* (New York: Oxford University Press, 2002), 65.

10. Random DuBois, *Soil Erosion in a Coastal River Basin: A Case Study from the Philippines,* Geography Research Paper, No. 232 (Chicago: University of Chicago Press, 1990).

11. The discussion of Ghusel VDC in Nepal is based upon Barbara Thomas-Slayter and Nina Bhatt, "Land, Livestock, and Livelihoods: Changing Dynamics of Gender, Caste, and Ethnicity in a Nepalese Village," *Human Ecology* 22, no. 4 (1994): 467–94.

12. World Bank, *Building Institutions for Markets: World Development Report 2002* (New York: Oxford University Press, 2002), 233.

13. This discussion of Choluteca, Honduras, is based upon Anne-Marie Urban and Mary Hill Rojas, *Shifting Boundaries: Gender, Migration, and Community Resources in the Foothills of Choluteca, Honduras* (Worcester, Mass.: Clark University ECOGEN Case Study, 1994).

14. Susan Stonich, "Struggling with Honduran Poverty: The Environmental Consequences of Natural Resource-Based Development and Rural Transformation," *World Development* 20, no. 3 (1992).

15. Frank Ellis, "Household Strategies and Rural Livelihood Diversification," *Journal of Development Studies* 35, no. 1 (1998): 4.

16. Stefano Ponte, "Trapped in Decline? Reassessing Agrarian Change and Economic Diversification on the Uluguru Mountains, Tanzania," *Journal of Modern African Studies* 39, no. 1 (2001): 81–100; Alain De Janvry and Elisabeth Sadoulet, "Income Strategies among Rural Households in Mexico: The Role of Off-Farm Activities," *World Development* 29, no. 3 (2001): 467–80; Michael Carter and Julian May, "Poverty, Livelihood and Class in Rural South Africa," *World Development* 27, no. 1 (1998): 1–20.

17. Alayne Adams, Jindra Cekan, and Rainer Sauerborn, "Toward a Conceptual Framework of Household Coping: Reflections from Rural West Africa," in *Africa* 68, no. 2 (1998): 265.

18. Ibid., 268.

19. World Bank, *World Development Report, 2000,* 230.

20. Madeline Barbara Leons and Harry Sanabria, *Coca, Cocaine, and the Bolivian Reality* (Albany: State University of New York Press, 1997), 1.

21. U.S. Department of Justice, 1996, *www.usdoj.gov/dea/pubs/intel/cocaine.html,* October 28, 2002.

22. Nathaniel C. Nash, "US Anti-Drug Moves Irk Bolivians," *New York Times,* September 20, 1992.

23. Adrian Muniz, "Bolivia Coca Trade (BOLCOCA), 1996," *www.american.edu .ted/BOLCOCA.htm.* October 28, 2002.

24. Robert H. Jackson, *Coca and Agriculture in Cochabamba, Bolivia: Historical and Contemporary Perspectives,* unpublished report, 1998. *www.andes.missouri.edu/ Andes/especiales/rhjcoca/rhj_coca2.html,* October 29, 2002.

25. Kevin Healy, "The Coca-Cocaine Issue in Bolivia: A Political Resource for All Seasons," in Leons and Sanabria, *Coca, Cocaine, and the Bolivian Reality,* 227–52.

26. Food and Agriculture Organization, 2000. See *www.fao.org/NEWS/2000/ 000307-e.html,* October 30, 2002.

27. In the late 1990s, the Food and Agriculture Organization of the United Nations joined the Bolivian government efforts to raise the standard of living for farm families by introducing alternative forestry and agroforestry practices. The program focuses on the Cochabamba Tropics, a region in which much slash-and-burn cultivation has occurred in order to clear land for coca and other crops. It has two components: (1) developing forest management plans to allow for the sustainable production of wood and nonwood products, as well as local wood processing; and (2) the introduction of farming techniques that combine agriculture and forestry, interplanting trees and legume cover crops with annual and perennial crops. The intent is to diversify food production and reduce vulnerability.

28. Eduardo Gamarra, "Fighting Drugs in Bolivia: United States and Bolivian Perceptions at Odds," in Leons and Sanabria, *Coca, Cocaine, and the Bolivian Reality,* 243–52.

29. Clifford Krauss, "Bolivia, at Risk of Some Unrest, Is Making Big Gains in Eradicating Coca," *New York Times,* May 9, 1999.

30. Clifford Krauss, "Desperate Farmers Imperil Peru's Fight on Coca," *New York Times,* February 23, 2001.

31. U.S. Department of State, International Narcotics Control Strategy Report. March 2002. *www.megalink.com/usemblapaz/english/CertificacionBoliviae,* September 15, 2002.

32. United Nations Commission on Narcotic Drugs, *Economic and Social Consequences of Drug Abuse and Illicit Trafficking: An Interim Report* (March 1995): 26.

33. Karen Tranberg Hansen, "Second-Hand Clothing Encounters in Zambia; Global Discourses, Western Commodities, and Local Histories," *Africa* 69, no. 3 (1998): 347. Data on the secondhand clothing business in Africa is drawn largely from the work of Karen Tranberg Hansen. General comments on the popularity of purchasing secondhand clothing derive from personal observation and discussions with colleagues in Kenya.

34. Global Information Network, December 13, 1994, online at *web.lexis-nexis .com/univers,* October 29, 2002.

35. Hansen, "Second-Hand," 355.

36. Gary Gereffi, *The Transformation of the North American Apparel Industry: Is NAFTA a Curse or a Blessing?* (Santiago, Chile: United Nations Economic Commission for Latin America and the Caribbean, 2000), 11.

37. Steven Greenhouse, "Critics Calling US Supplier in Nicaragua a 'Sweatshop,'" *New York Times,* December 3, 2000.

38. Leslie Kaufman and David Gonzalez, "Labor Progress Clashes with Global Reality," *New York Times,* April 24, 2001.

39. Greenhouse, "Critics."

40. Jeremy Brecher, Tim Costello, and Brendan Smith, *Globalization from Below: The Power of Solidarity* (Cambridge, Mass.: South End Press, 2000), 6.

41. Bangladesh National Garment Workers Federation, *Activity Reports 1999–2002. www.nadir.org/nadir/initiativ/agp/s26/banglad/,* October 29, 2002.

42. Barry Bearak, "Lives Held Cheap in Bangladesh Sweatshops," *New York Times,* April 15, 2001.

43. Habiba Zaman, "Paid Work and Socio-Political Consciousness of Garment Workers in Bangladesh," *Journal of Contemporary Asia* 31, no. 2 (2001): 149.

44. Bearak, "Lives."

45. Nicholas D. Kristof and Sheryl WuDunn, "Two Cheers for Sweatshops," *New York Times Magazine,* September 24, 2000.

46. Asocolflores, *www.colombianflowers.com,* April 5, 2000.

47. Kirk Semple, "Accusations in Full Flower," *Boston Globe,* February 12, 1999.

48. Maria Isabel Garcia, "Trade-Colombia: War of the Roses," Global Information Network, Interpress Service, July 27, 1999, *web.lexis.com/univers,* RDS-ACC-No: 02085009.

49. V. Meier, "Cut-Flower Production in Colombia — A Major Development Success Story for Women?" *Environment and Planning* 31 (1999): 281.

50. World Resources Institute, UNEP, UNDP, and the World Bank, *World Resources, 1998–99: A Guide to the Global Environment* (Oxford: Oxford University Press, 1998).

51. Meier, "Cut-Flower," 284.

52. Catherine Dolan and John Humphrey, "Governance and Trade in Fresh Vegetables: The Impact of UK Supermarkets on the African Horticultural Industry," *Journal of Development Studies* 37, no. 2 (2000): 147.

53. Dolan and Humphrey, "Governance," 160.

54. Catherine Dolan, "The 'Good Wife': Struggles over Resources in the Kenyan Horticultural Sector," *Journal of Development Studies* 37 (2001): 41.

55. Barbara Thomas-Slayter and Dianne Rocheleau, *Gender, Environment and Development in Kenya: A Grassroots Perspective* (Boulder, Colo.: Lynne Rienner, 1995).

56. Focus group discussion, August 1993, as reported in Barbara Thomas-Slayter, Leah Wanjama, and Njoki Mbuthi, *Fragmentation, Fuelwood and French Beans: Old Problems, New Solutions, and Changing Gender Roles in Gikarangu* (Worcester, Mass.: Clark University, ECOGEN Case Study, 1993).

57. Dolan, "The Good Wife," 51.

58. Laura T. Raynolds, "Negotiating Contract Farming in the Dominican Republic," *Human Organization* 59, no. 4 (2000): 444.

59. Ibid., 448.

Chapter 7: The Dynamics of Population, Development, and Environment

1. Robert Livernash and Eric Rodenburg, *Population Change, Resources, and the Environment*, Population Bulletin 53, no. 1 (Washington, D.C.: Population Reference Bureau, 1998), 10.

2. Ibid., 11.

3. World Resources Institute, UNEP, UNDP, and the World Bank, *World Resources, 1998–99, A Guide to the Global Environment* (Oxford: Oxford University Press, 1998), 141.

4. This discussion of models draws on Carlyn Orians and Marina Skumanich, *The Population-Environment Connection: What Does It Mean for Environmental Policy?* U.S. Environmental Protection Agency document (Seattle: Battelle Seattle Research Center, 1995), 17–65.

5. Paul Harrison, *The Third Revolution: Population, Environment and a Sustainable World* (London: Penguin Books, 1993).

6. Ibid., 237.

7. Ibid., 243.

8. Mary Tiffen, Michael Mortimore, and Francis Gichuki, *Population Growth and Environmental Recovery: Policy Lessons from Kenya*, Gatekeeper Series, No. 45 (London: IIED, 1994), 8.

9. Charles C. Mann, "How Many Is Too Many?" *The Atlantic* 271, no. 2 (February 1993): 56.

10. Harrison, *The Third Revolution*, 88.

11. Gareth Porter with Delfin J. Ganapin Jr., *Resources, Population, and the Philippines' Future: A Case Study*, WRI Paper, No. 4 (Washington, D.C.: World Resources Institute, 1988), 28.

12. David M. Kummer, *Deforestation in the Postwar Philippines*, Geography Research Paper, No. 234 (Chicago: University of Chicago Press, 1991), 146.

13. Kevin M. Cleaver and Gotz A. Schreiber, *Reversing the Spiral: The Population, Agriculture, and Environment Nexus in Sub-Saharan Africa* (Washington, D.C.: World Bank, 1994), 22.

14. Livernash and Rodenburg, *Population Change, Resources, and the Environment*, 6.

15. UNDP, *Human Development Report, 2002* (New York: Oxford University Press, 2002).

16. Government of China, China Population Information and Research Center, National Bureau of Statistics using 2000 census data (*www.cpirc.org.cn*) and Government of India, Office of the Registrar General, using Provisional Population Totals, Census of India, 2001 (*www.censusindia.net/results*), October 20, 2002.

17. World Bank, *Entering the Twenty-first Century, World Development Report 1999/2000* (New York: Oxford University Press, 2000), 232.

18. World Bank, *World Development Report 2000*, 242; UNDP, *Human Development Report: Making New Technologies Work for Human Development* (New York: Oxford University Press, 2001), 155–56.

19. Paul Kennedy, *Preparing for the Twenty-first Century* (New York: Random House, 1993), 177.

20. World Bank, *World Development Report 1999/2000*, 242.

21. The discussion of South Kamwango is adapted from "A Pocket of Poverty: Linking Water, Health, and Gender-Based Responsibilities in South Kamwango," by Elizabeth Oduor-Noah and Barbara Thomas-Slayter, in Barbara Thomas-Slayter and Dianne Rocheleau, *Gender, Environment, and Development in Kenya* (Boulder, Colo.: Lynne Rienner, 1995), 161–88.

22. Pat Youri, *South Nyanza District Health Situation,* mimeograph (Nairobi, Kenya: African Medical Research Foundation, 1989).

23. World Resources Institute, *World Resources,* 143.

24. Jim Motavalli, "Contents Under Pressure," *Perspectives, World Politics* (Boulder, Colo.: Coursewise Publishing, 1998), 229.

25. Fen Montaigne, "Water Pressure," *National Geographic* 202, no. 3 (September 2002).

26. Robert Repetto, ed., *The Global Possible: Resources, Development, and the New Century* (New Haven and London: Yale University Press, 1985), 149.

27. Government of India, Office of the Registrar General, Census of India 2001, *www.censusindia.net;* Akash Kapur, "Poor but Prosperous," *Atlantic Monthly* 276, no. 9 (September 1998).

28. Betsy Hartmann, *Reproductive Rights and Wrongs: The Global Politics of Population Control and Contraceptive Choice* (New York: Harper and Row, 1987).

29. Jen Smith, "It's Not Accidental That Occidental Is in Ecuador," Special Report for the Native Forest Network, March 2002.

30. Judith Kimerling, *Amazon Crude* (New York: Natural Resources Defense Council, 1991), xii.

31. Ken Saro-wiwa, *A Month and a Day: A Detention Diary* (New York: Penguin Books, 1995), 96.

32. Ibid., 67 and 131.

33. Michael Klesius, "Amid the Unrelenting Spread of AIDS, Search for a Cure," *National Geographic* 201, no. 2 (2002): 32–43. U.S. Government, "Joining Forces in LIFE: Leadership and Investment in Fighting an Epidemic, A Global AIDS Initiative," Report on the Presidential Mission on Children Orphaned by AIDS in Sub-Saharan Africa: Finding and Plan of Action, *www.whitehouse.gov/ONAP/Africa,* July 1999.

34. Alex de Waal, "How Will HIV/AIDS Transform African Governance?" *African Affairs* 102, no. 406 (January 2003): 23.

35. UNAIDS, "AIDS in Africa," *www.unaids.org/publications,* November 30, 1998; and Stephanie Flanders, "In the Shadow of AIDS, a World of Other Problems," *New York Times,* June 24, 2001.

36. United States Institute of Peace, "AIDS and Violent Conflict in Africa," in *World Politics,* ed. Helen E. Purkitt (Guilford, Conn.: McGraw-Hill/Dushkin, 2001), 188.

37. Klesius, "Amid," 37.

38. Pieter Fourie and Martin Schonteich, "Africa's New Security Threat, HIV/ AIDS and Human Security in Southern Africa," *African Security Review* 10, no. 4 (2001).

39. UNAIDS, "AIDS in Africa," *http://unaids.org/publications,* November 30, 1998

40. Testimony of Dr. Anne Peterson, USAID Assistant Administrator for Global Health, before the Subcommittee on African Affairs, Committee on Foreign Relations, May 19, 2003, *www.usaid/gov/press/speeches/2003.* See also Matthew Green, "Bush Seen Talking AIDS in Uganda," *www.swissinfo.org,* July 11, 2003; "Combating HIV/AIDS in Africa," *www.worldbank.org,* July 13, 2003.

41. Jeffrey Bartholet, "The Plague Years," *Newsweek,* January 17, 2000, 32–37.

42. James Carroll, "Stopping Africa's AIDS Nightmare," Security Council: Meeting on the Situation in Africa — The Impact of AIDS on Peace and Security in Africa, 1/10/00, *www.un.org;* Bartholet, "The Plague Years."

43. UNDP, *Human Development Report, 1997* (New York: Oxford University Press, 1997), 9.

44. World Resources Institute, *World Resources,* 147.

45. Livernash and Rodenburg, *Population Change, Resources, and the Environment,* 15.

46. UN Population Division, "World Population Prospects: The 1996 Revision," *Population Newsletter,* no. 62 (December 1996): 9.

47. UNDP, *Human Development Report, 1994* (New York: Oxford University Press, 1994).

Chapter 8: Food Security, Rural Change, and Global Politics

1. World Resources Institute, UNEP, UNDP, and the World Bank, *World Resources, 1998–99, A Guide to the Global Environment* (Oxford: Oxford University Press, 1998), 152.

2. World Bank, *Building Institutions for Markets: World Development Report 2002* (New York: Oxford University Press, 2002).

3. United Nations Conference on Trade and Development (UNCTAD), *The Least Developed Countries, 1998 Report* (Geneva: UNCTAD, 1998), 175.

4. Ibid., 176.

5. This discussion of globalization of agrofood systems in Asia draws particularly on a special issue of *World Development, Changing Agro-Food and Fiber Systems in Asia* 28, no. 3 (March 2000), especially articles by Philip McMichael, "A Global Interpretation of the Rise of the East Asian Food Import Complex" (409–24); Susan Thompson and J. Tadlock Cowan, "Globalizing Agro-Food Systems in Asia: Introduction" (401–7); and Jasper Goss, David Burch, and Roy E. Rickson, "Agri-Food Restructuring and Third World Transnationals: Thailand, the CP Group, and the Global Shrimp Industry" (513–30).

6. Goss, Burch, and Rickson, "Agri-Food," 516.

7. McMichael, "A Global Interpretation of the Rise of the East Asian Food Import Complex," 421.

8. Goss, Burch, and Rickson, "Agri-Food," 514.

9. Gordon R. Hopper, "Changing Food Production and Quality of Diet in India, 1947–98," *Population and Development Review* 25, no. 3 (1999): 443–77.

10. Ibid., 473.

11. World Bank, *The Long-Term Perspective Study of Sub-Saharan Africa* (Washington, D.C.: IBRD, 1989), 3.

12. Jeffrey Herbst, "The Politics of Sustained Agricultural Reform in Africa," in *Hemmed In: Responses to Africa's Economic Decline,* ed. Thomas M. Callaghy and John Ravenhill (New York: Columbia University Press, 1993), 335.

13. Erich Baier, *The Impact of HIV/AIDS on Rural Households/Communities and the Need for Multisectoral Prevention and Mitigation Strategies to Combat the Epidemic in Rural Areas* (Rome: Food and Agriculture Organization, 1997).

14. C. Mgendi, "Official Tips on Agriculture." in *The Daily Nation,* Nairobi, Kenya, June 29, 1999, 3.

15. UNDP, *Human Development Report, 1994* (New York: Oxford University Press, 1994).

16. John Ravenhill, "A Second Decade of Adjustment: Greater Complexity, Greater Uncertainty," in *Hemmed In,* 18.

17. Caroline Sargent and Stephen Bass, "The Future Shape of Forests," in *Making Development Sustainable: Redefining Institutions, Policy, and Economics,* ed. Johan Holmberg (Washington, D.C.: Island Press, 1992), 207.

18. Camilla Toulmin, Ian Scoones, and Joshua Bishop, "The Future of Africa's Drylands: Is Local Resource Management the Answer?" in *Making Development Sustainable,* ed. Holmberg, 229.

19. Ibid., 243.

20. Rachel Polestico, Antonio B. Quizon, and Peter Hildemann, *Agrarian Reform in the Philippines: Status and Perspectives for 1998 and Beyond* (Cavite, Philippines: Deutsche Welthungerhilfe and International Institute of Rural Reconstruction, 1998).

21. Ibid., 134.

22. Kurt Shillinger, "Zimbabwe's Turmoil over Land Finds an Echo across Africa," *New York Times,* May 16, 2000.

23. Manjari Mehta, "Our Lives Are No Different from That of Our Buffaloes," in *Feminist Political Ecology: Global Issues and Local Experiences,* ed. Dianne Rocheleau, Barbara Thomas-Slayter, and Esther Wangari (London: Routledge, 1996), 180.

24. M. Dale Shields, Cornelia Butler Flora, Barbara Thomas-Slayter, and Gladys Buenavista, "Developing and Dismantling Social Capital," in *Feminist Political Ecology,* ed. Rocheleau, Thomas-Slayter, and Wangari, 155.

25. Diane Rocheleau, Laurie Ross, and Julio Morrobel, "From Forest Gardens to Tree Farms," in *Feminist Political Ecology,* ed. Rocheleau, Thomas-Slayter, and Wangari, 224.

26. Esther Wangari, Barbara Thomas-Slayter, and Dianne Rocheleau, "Gendered Visions for Survival," in *Feminist Political Ecology,* ed. Rocheleau, Thomas-Slayter, and Wangari, 130.

27. This discussion is adapted from Anne-Marie Urban and Mary Rojas, *Shifting Boundaries: Gender, Migration, and Community Resources in the Foothills of Choluteca, Honduras* (Worcester, Mass.: Clark University ECOGEN Case Study, 1994).

28. Jules Pretty, Irene Guijt, Ian Scoones, and John Thompson, "Regenerating Agriculture: The Agroecology of Low-External Input and Community-Based Development," in *Making Development Sustainable,* ed. Holmberg, 91.

29. Dunstan S. C. Spencer, *Infrastructure and Technology Constraints to Agricultural Development in the Humid and Subhumid Tropics of Africa*, EPTD Discussion Paper, No. 3 (Washington, D.C.: International Food Policy Research Institute, 1994).

30. M. S. Swaminathan, *Food 2000, Global Policies for Sustainable Agriculture*, A Report of the Advisory Panel on Food Security, Agriculture, Forestry and Environment to the World Commission on Environment and Development (London: Zed Books, 1987), 14.

31. Ernest Harsch, "Wanted: A Green Revolution of a Different Kind: Research Scientists Seek to Boost African Yields Using New and Adapted Technologies," in *Africa Recovery* (New York: United Nations) 11, no. 3 (1998).

32. African Development Bank, *African Development Report, 1998* (London: Oxford University Press, 1998), 40.

33. Carey Goldberg, "1,500 March in Boston to Protest Biotech Food," in *New York Times*, March 27, 2000.

34. "Monsanto Vows to Delay Commercialization," *Washington Post*, April 23, 1999; in *Monsanto Monitor, www.antenna.n./seed/monsanto/roundup1ee*. Robert B. Shapiro, "How Genetic Engineering Will Save Our Planet," *The Futurist*, April 1, 1999, *www.monsanto.com*.

35. Friends of the Earth UK, "Antibiotic Resistance Genes in GM Foods," *www.foe.co.uk/camps/foodbio/brief/gefood*, May 10, 2002. See also Alex Kirby, "GM Third World Warning," *BBC News*, May 9, 1999, *news2.thdo.bbc.co.uk/hi/english/sci*; Barnaby J. Feder, "Plant Sterility Research Inflames Debate on Biotechnology's Role in Farming," *New York Times*, April 19, 1999.

36. Rural Advancement Foundation International (RAFI), "Dead Seed Scrolls? The USDA's Terminator Defense," RAFI Translator, October 23, 1998.

37. Vandana Shiva, *Stolen Harvest: The Hijacking of the Global Food Supply* (Cambridge, Mass.: South End Press, 2000).

38. Rohini Acharya, *Intellectual Property, Biotechnology and Trade: The Impact of the Uruguay Round on Biodiversity* (Nairobi, Kenya: African Center for Technology Studies Press, 1992); Shuichi Kiyanagu, "Bioprospecting and Indigenous People: Further Exploitation or the Answer to Marginalization?" undergraduate thesis, Clark University, International Development Program, Worcester, Mass., 1998.

39. Kiyanagu, "Bioprospecting."

40. Shiva, *Stolen*.

41. Ibid. See also PBS film *Life and Debt* on how debt and corporate interests are destroying local agriculture and industry in developing countries, October 2002.

42. Shiva, *Stolen*.

43. Kiyanagu, "Bioprospecting."

44. World Bank, *Entering the Twenty-first Century: World Development Report 1999/2000* (New York: Oxford University Press, 2000), 28.

45. World Bank, *World Development Report 2000*, 28.

46. Molly O'Meara, "Exploring a New Vision for Cities," in *State of the World* (New York: W. W. Norton, 1999), 134.

Chapter 9: New Voices and New Agendas

1. Niall Ferguson, "2011, Ten Years From Now," *New York Times Magazine*, December 2, 2001, 79.

2. "Fortune's Global 500," *Fortune,* September 15, 2002.

3. For elaboration of this discussion, see Samuel Huntington's *The Clash of Civilizations and the Remaking of the World Order* (New York: Simon and Schuster, 1996) and various works by Amartya Sen including "A World Not Neatly Divided," *New York Times,* November 23, 2001, or Niall Ferguson, "2001."

4. Maarten Smeets, "Globalisation: Threat or Promise," *Global Dialogue: The Globalisation Phenomenon* 1, no. 1 (1999): 14.

5. Thomas L. Friedman, *The Lexus and the Olive Tree* (New York: Farrar, Straus and Giroux, 1999), 90.

6. Daniel T. Griswold, "The Blessings and Challenges of Globalization," in *Developing World 01/02,* ed. Robert J. Griffiths (Guilford, Conn.: McGraw-Hill/Dushkin, 2001), 54; Jay R. Mandle, "Trading Up, Why Globalization Aids the Poor," in Griffiths, *Developing World 01/02,* 59.

7. Jeremy Brecher, Tim Costello, and Brendan Smith, *Globalization from Below: The Power of Solidarity* (Cambridge, Mass.: South End Press, 2000), 5.

8. Vandana Shiva, "Diversity and Democracy: Resisting the Global Economy," *Global Dialogue: The Globalisation Phenomenon* 1, no. 1 (1999): 19.

9. Cees J. Hamelink, "The Elusive Concept of Globalisation," *Global Dialogue: The Globalisation Phenomenon* 1, no. 1 (1999): 3.

10. John Tagliabue, "Genoa Summit Meeting: Swelling Protest and Attention to Business," *New York Times,* July 22, 2001.

11. Miloon Kothari, "Globalisation, Social Action, and Human Rights," in *Development and Social Action,* ed. Deborah Eade (London: Oxfam GB, 1999), 17; Smitu Kothari, "Inclusive, Just, Plural, Dynamic: Building a 'Civil' Society in the Third World," in *Development and Social Action,* 34–53; Ignacio de Senillosa, "A New Age of Social Movements: A Fifth Generation Of Non-governmental Development Organisations in the Making?" in *Development and Social Action,* 87–103.

12. Kothari, "Globalisation," 16.

13. Caitlin Wiesen, Geoffrey Prewitt, and Babar Sobhan, "Civil Society and Poverty: Whose Rights Count?" CIVICUS, *Civil Society at the Millennium* (West Hartford, Conn: Kumarian Press, 1999), 142.

14. *www.sapring.org/overview.htm,* October 10, 2002.

15. *www.Haguepeace.org.* October 10, 2002.

16. Amita Bavbiskar, *In the Belly of the River: Tribal Conflicts over Development in the Narmada Valley* (Delhi: Oxford University Press, 1997); William Fisher, "Development and Resistance in the Narmada Valley," in *Toward Sustainable Development: Struggling over India's Narmada River,* ed. William Fisher (Armonk, New York: M. E. Sharpe, 1995); Patrick McCully, *Silenced Rivers: The Ecology and Politics of Large Dams* (Atlantic Highlands, N.J.: Zed Books, 1996); Arundhati Roy, *The Cost of Living* (New York: Modern Library, 1999); Himanshu Thakkar, "Displacement and Development: Construction of the Sardar Sarovar Dam," in "Going Under: Indigenous Peoples and the Struggle Against Large Dams," *Cultural Survival Quarterly* 23, no. 3 (1999). The discussion of the pros and cons of the Narmada Development Project derives from these sources.

17. Smitu Kothari, "Damming the Narmada and the Politics of Development," in *Toward Sustainable Development.*

18. Fisher, *Toward Sustainable Development,* 9.

19. Ibid.

20. Smitu Kothari, "Damming the Narmada and the Politics of Development," in *Toward Sustainable Development*, 421.

21. Roy, *Cost of Living*.

22. *www.rightlivelihood.se/recip1991_2.html*, September 14, 2002.

23. UN Economic and Social Council Commission on Human Rights, *Preliminary Report on the Problem of Discrimination Against Indigenous Populations*, UN Document E/CN.4/Sub.2/L5.66, chapter 11.

24. Eufemia Pinto, "Contesting Frontier Lands in Palawan, Philippines: Strategies of Indigenous Peoples for Community Development and Ancestral Domain Management," M.A. thesis, Clark University, Worcester, Mass., 1999, 2.

25. David Maybury-Lewis, *Indigenous Peoples, Ethnic Groups, and the State*, 2d ed. (Boston: Allyn and Bacon, 1997), 8.

26. Oxfam America, South America Regional Office, *South America Regional Program Paper*, unpublished document (Boston: Oxfam America, 1999), 10.

27. Pinto, "Contesting," 8.

28. Ibid., 54. See also Robin Broad and John Cavanaugh, *Plundering Paradise: The Struggle for the Environment in the Philippines* (Berkeley: University of California Press, 1993).

29. World Bank, *Building Institutions for Markets: World Development Report 2002* (New York: Oxford University Press, 2002).

30. Mayra Buvinic, "Women in Poverty: A New Global Underclass," in *Foreign Policy* 1998 (Fall 1997): 38–53

31. Lydia Williams, *Gender Equity and the World Bank Group: A Post-Beijing Assessment* (Washington, D.C.: Women's Eyes on the World Bank, 1997), 4.

32. Edith Mirante, "Update: Empowering Indigenous Women in Burma," in *Cultural Survival Quarterly* 19, no. 1 (Spring 1995).

33. *www.earthrights.org*, September 10, 2002.

34. Cynthia Enloe, *The Morning After: Sexual Politics at the End of the Cold War* (Berkeley: University of California Press, 1993), 106.

35. Robert Senser, "Workers of the World — Globalize!" Online: *www.senser.com/wr-wto.htm* (1999).

36. Ibid., 2.

37. Barry Bearak, "Lives Held Cheap in Bangladesh Sweatshops," *New York Times*, April 15, 2001.

38. IUF, COLSIBA, and Chiquita, 2001, *www.oif.org/iuf/press/010614.htm*.

39. *www.laborrights.org/press/coke071901.htm*.

40. "Facts about Land Mines," *www.vvaf.org/htdocs/library/index.html*, October 20, 2002.

41. Ibid.

42. Alex Vines and Henry Thompson, "Beyond the Landmine Ban: Eradicating a Lethal Legacy," *Conflict Studies*, unpublished paper, Research Institute for the Study of Conflict and Terrorism, March 1999.

43. Rae McGrath, "Clearing the Clusters" *Newsweek International*, August 2, 1999, 30.

44. International Campaign to Ban Landmines, ICBL, *www.icbl.org*, October 20, 2002.

45. Vines and Thompson, *Beyond,* 12.

46. (ICBL), *www.icbl.org,* October 20, 2002.

47. Human Rights Watch, "Landmine Monitor Report" (New York: Human Rights Watch, 1999).

48. Vines and Thompson, *Beyond.*

49. Human Rights Watch, "U.S. Also Bears Responsibility for Landmines Crisis," 2001, *www.hrw.org/press/2001/03/1mweek0305.htm,* October 20, 2002.

50. UNDP, *Human Development Report, 1996* (New York: Oxford University Press, 1996).

51. Brecher, Costello, and Smith, *Globalization from Below,* 63.

52. Kevin Watkins, *The Oxfam Poverty Report* (Oxford: Oxfam UK and Ireland, 1995), 2.

53. UNDP, *Human Development Report, 2002* (New York: Oxford University Press, 2002), 18.

54. Wiesen, Prewitt, and Sobhan, "Civil Society," 143.

55. Morris Morris, "The Changing Condition of the World's Poor, 1960–1990: Some Development Policy Implications," working paper, Center for the Comparative Study of Development, The Alan Shawn Feinstein World Hunger Program of the Thomas J. Watson Jr. Institute for International Studies, Brown University, 1996.

56. Ibid., 7.

57. UNDP, *Human Development Report 2000* (New York: Oxford University Press, 2000), 39.

58. Kumi Naidoo and Rajesh Tandon, "The Promise of Civil Society," CIVICUS, *Civil Society at the Millennium* (West Hartford, Conn.: Kumarian Press, 1999), 9.

59. Julie Fisher, *Nongovernments, NGOs, and the Political Development of the Third World* (West Hartford, Conn.: Kumarian Press, 1998), 19 and 159.

60. Brecher, Costello, and Smith, *Globalization from Below,* 42.

Selected Bibliography

Adams, Alayne, Jindra Cekan, and Rainer Sauerborn. "Toward a Conceptual Framework of Household Coping: Reflections from Rural West Africa." *Africa* 68, no. 2 (1998): 263–82.

Adelman, Irma, and Cynthia T. Morris. *Economic Growth and Social Equity in Developing Countries.* Stanford, Calif.: Stanford University Press, 1973.

African Development Bank. *African Development Report, 1998.* London: Oxford University Press, 1998.

Amin, Samir. *Delinking: Toward a Polycentric World.* New York: Zed Books, 1990.

———. *Maldevelopment: Anatomy of a Global Failure.* New York: United Nations University Press, 1990.

Anderson, Mary B. *Do No Harm: Supporting Local Capacities for Peace through Aid.* Cambridge, Mass.: The Collaborative for Development Action, 1996.

Arizpe, Lourdes, M. Priscilla Stone, and David C. Major, eds. *Population and Environment, Rethinking the Debate.* Boulder, Colo.: Westview Press, 1994.

Aseka, Eric Masinde, Julius Simiyu Nabende, Martha Wangari Musalia, Mildren Ndeda, eds. *The Political Economy of Transition: A Study of Issues and Social Movements in Kenya since 1945.* Nairobi, Kenya: Eight Publishers, 1999.

Ayako, Aloys B., and Musambayi Katumanga. *Review of Poverty in Kenya.* Nairobi, Kenya: Institute of Policy Analysis and Research, 1997.

Bandarage, Asoka. *Women, Population and Global Crisis.* London: Zed Books, 1997.

Barry, Tom, and Martha Honey, eds. *Global Focus: A New Foreign Policy Agenda 1997–1998.* Silver City, N.Mex.: Interhemispheric Resource Center, 1997.

Basu, Amrita. *Women's Movements in Global Perspective.* Boulder, Colo.: Westview Press, 1995.

Bello, Walden. *Brave New Third World? Strategies for Survival in the Global Economy.* San Francisco: The Institute for Food and Development Policy, 1989.

Beneria, Lourdes, and Catharine R. Stimpson, eds. *Women, Households, and the Economy.* New Brunswick, N.J.: Rutgers University Press, 1987.

Berman, Bruce J. "Ethnicity, Patronage, and the African State: The Politics of Uncivil Nationalism." *African Affairs* 97, no. 388 (1998): 305–41.

Berthelemy, Jean-Claude, and Ludvig Soderling. "The Role of Capital Accumulation, Adjustment and Structural Change for Economic Take-Off: Empirical Evidence from African Growth Episodes." *World Development* 29, no. 2 (2001): 323–43.

Black, Jan Knippers. *Inequity in the Global Village: Recycled Rhetoric and Disposable People.* West Hartford, Conn.: Kumarian Press, 1999.

Bond, George, and Joan Vincent. "AIDS in Uganda: The First Decade." In *AIDS in Africa and the Caribbean,* edited by George Bond et al. Boulder, Colo.: Westview Press, 1997.

Boone, Catherine. "State Building in the African Countryside: Structure and Politics at the Grassroots." *Journal of Development Studies* 34, no. 4 (1998): 1–31.

Boserup, Ester. *Woman's Role in Economic Development.* New York: St. Martin's Press, 1970.

Brecher, Jeremy, John Brown Childs, and Jill Cutler. *Global Visions Beyond the New World Order.* Boston: South End Press, 1993.

Brecher, Jeremy, Tim Costello, and Brendan Smith. *Globalization from Below: The Power of Solidarity.* Cambridge, Mass.: South End Press, 2000.

Broad, Robin, and John Cavanaugh. *Plundering Paradise: The Struggle for the Environment in the Philippines.* Berkeley: University of California Press, 1993.

Callaghy, Thomas M., and John Ravenhill, eds. *Hemmed In: Responses to Africa's Economic Decline.* New York: Columbia University Press, 1993.

Cammack, Paul, David Pool, and William Tordoff. *Third World Politics: A Comparative Introduction.* Baltimore: Johns Hopkins University Press, 1988.

Carnegie Commission on Preventing Deadly Conflict. *Preventing Deadly Conflict: Final Report.* Washington, D.C.: Carnegie Commission, 1997.

Carter, Michael, and Julian May. "Poverty, Livelihood and Class in Rural South Africa." *World Development* 27, no. 1 (1998): 1–20.

Chabal, Patrick, and Jean-Pascal Daloz. *Africa Works: Disorder as Political Instrument.* Oxford, UK, and Bloomington: The International African Institute with James Currey [Oxford] and Indiana University Press, 1999.

Chilcote, Ronald. *Theories of Comparative Politics: The Search for a Paradigm.* Boulder, Colo.: Westview Press, 1981.

Cincotta, Richard P., and Robert Engelman. *Economics and Rapid Change: The Influence of Population Growth.* Occasional Paper 3. Washington, D.C.: Population Action International, 1997.

Clapham, Christopher. *Third World Politics, An Introduction.* Madison: The University of Wisconsin Press, 1985.

Cleaver, Kevin M., and Gotz A. Schreiber. *Reversing the Spiral: The Population, Agriculture, and Environment Nexus in Sub-Saharan Africa.* Washington, D.C.: World Bank, 1994.

Coetzee, J. M. *Disgrace.* New York: Viking, 1999.

Danaher, Kevin, ed. *Fifty Years Is Enough: The Case against the World Bank and the International Monetary Fund.* Boston: South End Press, 1994.

De Janvry, Alain, and Elisabeth Sadoulet. "Income Strategies among Rural Households in Mexico: The Role of Off-Farm Activities." *World Development* 29, no. 3 (2001): 467–80.

Deng, Francis Mading. *War of Visions: Conflict of Identities in the Sudan.* Washington, D.C.: Brookings Institute, 1995.

De Waal, Alex. "How Will HIV/AIDS Transform African Governance?" *African Affairs* 102, no. 406 (2003): 1–23.

Dolan, Catherine. "The 'Good Wife': Struggles over Resources in the Kenyan Horticultural Sector." *Journal of Development Studies* 37, no. 3 (2001): 39–70.

Dolan, Catherine, and John Humphrey. "Governance and Trade in Fresh Vegetables: The Impact of UK Supermarkets on the African Horticultural Industry." *Journal of Development Studies* 37, no. 2 (2000): 147–76.

Dorraj, Manochehr. *The Changing Political Economy of the Third World.* Boulder, Colo.: Lynne Rienner, 1995.

Ellis, Frank. "Household Strategies and Rural Livelihood Diversification." *Journal of Development Studies* 35, no. 1 (1998): 1–38.

Enloe, Cynthia. *The Morning After: Sexual Politics at the End of the Cold War.* Berkeley: University of California Press, 1993.

Escobar, Arturo. "Discourse and Power in Development: Michel Foucault and the Relevance of His Work in the Third World." *Alternatives* 10 (1984): 377–400.

———. *Encountering Development.* Princeton, N.J.: Princeton University Press, 1995.

———. "Imagining a Post-Development Era: Critical Thought, Development and Social Movements." *Social Text* 32 (1992): 20–55.

Evans, Peter B. "Predatory, Developmental, and Other Apparatuses: A Comparative Political Economy Perspective on the Third World State." In *Comparative National Development: Society and Economy in the New Global Order,* edited by A. Douglas Kincaid and Alejandro Portes. Chapel Hill: University of North Carolina Press, 1994.

Falk, Richard. "The Monotheistic Religions in the Era of Globalisation." *Global Dialogue: The Globalisation Phenomenon* 1, no. 1 (1999): 139–48.

Fanon, Frantz. *The Wretched of the Earth.* Translated by Constance Farrington. New York: Grove Press, 1968.

Fatton, Robert. "Civil Society Revisited: Africa in the New Millennium." Paper prepared for the Hesburgh International center, University of Notre Dame Conference "The Crisis of Development in Africa: Contexts, Connections, and Consequences of International Aid and NGOs," 1999.

Fisher, William F., ed. *Toward Sustainable Development: Struggling over India's Narmada River.* Armonk, N.Y.: M. E. Sharpe, 1995.

Ford, Richard, and Barbara Thomas-Slayter. "Alternatives to Anarchy: Africa's Transition from Agricultural to Industrial Societies." *Progress in Planning* 56, part 2 (2001).

Frankel, Francine. *India's Political Economy, 1947–1977: The Gradual Revolution.* Princeton, N.J.: Princeton University Press, 1978.

Friedman, Thomas L. *The Lexus and the Olive Tree.* New York: Farrar, Straus and Giroux, 1999.

Gibbon, Peter. "Upgrading Primary Production: A Global Commodity Chain Approach." *World Development* 29, no. 2 (2001): 345–63.

Gordon, April A. *Transforming Capitalism and Patriarchy: Gender and Development in Africa.* Boulder, Colo.: Lynne Rienner, 1996.

Goss, Jasper, David Burch, and Roy E. Rickson. "Agri-Food Restructuring and Third World Transnationals: Thailand, the CP Group, and the Global Shrimp Industry." *World Development* special issue, *Changing Agro-Food and Fiber Systems in Asia* 28, no. 3 (2000): 513–30.

Goulet, Denis. *Incentives for Development: The Key to Equity.* New York: New Horizons Press, 1989.

———. *The Uncertain Promise: Value Conflicts in Technology Transfer.* New York: New Horizons Press, 1977.

Gourevitch, Philip. *We Wish to Inform You That Tomorrow We Will Be Killed With Our Families: Stories from Rwanda.* New York: Farrar, Straus and Giroux, 1998.

Greenfeld, Liah. *Nationalism: Five Roads to Modernity.* Cambridge, Mass.: Harvard University Press, 1992.

Greider, William. *One World Ready or Not: The Manic Logic of Global Capitalism.* New York: Simon and Schuster, 1997.

Griffiths, Robert J., ed. *Developing World 1998/99.* 8th ed. Guilford, Conn.: Dushkin/McGraw-Hill, 1998.

Hamelink, Cees J. "The Elusive Concept of Globalisation." *Global Dialogue: The Globalisation Phenomenon* 1, no. 1 (1999): 1–9.

Handelman, Howard. *The Challenge of Third World Development.* Upper Saddle River, N.J.: Prentice-Hall, 1996.

Hansen, Karen Tranberg. "Second-Hand Clothing Encounters in Zambia: Global Discourses, Western Commodities, and Local Histories." *Africa* 69, no. 3 (1998).

Harcourt, Wendy, ed. *Feminist Perspectives on Sustainable Development.* London: Zed Books, 1994.

Harris, Michael. *Lament for an Ocean.* Toronto: McClelland and Stewart, 1998.

Harrison, Paul. *The Third Revolution: Population, Environment and a Sustainable World.* London: Penguin Books, 1993.

Harsch, Ernest. "Wanted: A Green Revolution of a Different Kind: Research Scientists Seek to Boost African Yields Using New and Adapted Technologies." *Africa Recovery* (New York: United Nations) 11, no. 3 (1998).

Hartmann, Betsy. *Reproductive Rights and Wrongs: The Global Politics of Population Control and Contraceptive Choice.* New York: Harper and Row, 1987.

Hettne, Bjorn, ed. *International Political Economy: Understanding Global Disorder.* London: Zed Books, 1995.

Hoekman, Bernard, and Kym Anderson. "Developing-Country Agriculture and the New Trade Agenda." *Economic Development and Cultural Change* 49, no. 1 (2000): 171–80.

Hopper, Gordon R. "Changing Food Production and Quality of Diet in India, 1947–98." *Population and Development Review* 25, no. 3 (1999): 443–77.

Hoy, Paula. *Players and Issues in International Aid.* West Hartford, Conn.: Kumarian Press, 1998.

Isbister, John. *Promises Not Kept: The Betrayal of Social Change in the Third World.* 4th ed. West Hartford, Conn.: Kumarian Press, 1998.

Iyob, Ruth. "The Eritrean Experiment: A Cautious Pragmatism?" *Journal of Modern African Studies* 35, no. 4 (1997): 647–73.

———. "The Ethiopian-Eritrean Conflict: Diasporic vs. Hegemonic States in the Horn of Africa, 1991–2000." *Journal of Modern African Studies* 38, no. 4 (2000): 659–82.

Jackson, Robert, ed. *Global Issues 1994/95.* 10th ed. Guilford, Conn.: Dushkin Publishing Group, 1994.

Kagwanja, Peter Mwangi. "Facing Mount Kenya or Facing Mecca? The Mungiki, Ethnic Violence and the Politics of the Moi Succession in Kenya, 1987–2002." *Africa Affairs* 102, no. 406 (2003): 25–49.

Kamrava, Mehran. *Politics and Society in the Third World.* London: Routledge, 1993.

Kaplan, Robert D. *The Ends of the Earth: From Togo to Turkmenistan, from Iran to Cambodia, a Journey to the Frontiers of Anarchy.* New York: Vintage Books, 1997.

Kasfir, Nelson, ed. *State and Class in Africa.* London: Frank Cass, 1984.

Keller, Edmond J. *Revolutionary Ethiopia: From Empire to People's Republic.* 2d ed. Bloomington: Indiana University Press, 1991.

————. "Revolution and the Collapse of Traditional Monarchies." In *Revolution and Political Change in the Third World,* edited by Barry M. Schutz and Robert O. Slater, 81–98. Boulder, Colo.: Lynne Rienner, 1990.

Kennedy, Paul. *Preparing for the Twenty-first Century.* New York: Random House, 1993.

Klesius, Michael. "Amid the Unrelenting Spread of AIDS, Search for a Cure." *National Geographic* 201, no. 2 (2002).

Kohli, Atul, ed. *The State and Development in the Third World.* Princeton, N.J.: Princeton University Press, 1986.

Kothari, Miloon. "Globalisation, Social Action, and Human Rights." In *Development and Social Action,* edited by Deborah Eade, 9–33. London: Oxfam GB, 1999.

Kothari, Rajni. *Poverty, Human Consciousness, and the Amnesia of Development.* London: Zed Books, 1993.

Kothari, Smitu. "Inclusive, Just, Plural, Dynamic: Building a 'Civil' Society in the Third World." In *Development and Social Action,* edited by Deborah Eade, 34–53. London: Oxfam GB, 1999.

Kummer, David M. *Deforestation in the Postwar Philippines.* Geography Research Paper, No. 234. Chicago: University of Chicago, 1991.

Küng, Hans. *A Global Ethic for Global Politics and Economics.* Oxford: Oxford University Press, 1998.

Leons, Madeline Barbara, and Harry Sanabria. *Coca, Cocaine, and the Bolivian Reality.* Albany: State University of New York Press, 1997.

Lewellen, Ted C. *Dependency and Development: An Introduction to the Third World.* Westport, Conn.: Bergin and Garvey, 1995.

Lindsay, James M., ed. *Perspectives, World Politics.* Boulder, Colo.: Coursewise Publishing, 1998.

Livernash, Robert, and Eric Rodenburg. *Population Change, Resources, and the Environment.* Population Bulletin 53, no. 1. Washington, D.C.: Population Reference Bureau, 1998.

Lopez, Ramon, and Alberto Valdes. "Fighting Rural Poverty in Latin America: New Evidence of the Effects of Education, Demographics, and Access to Land." *Economic Development and Cultural Change* 49, no. 1 (2000): 197–211.

MacDonald, Scott B. *Dancing on a Volcano: The Latin American Drug Trade.* New York: Praeger, 1988.

Machel, Graca. *Impact of Armed Conflict on Children.* New York: United Nations Children's Fund, 1996.

Mann, Charles C. "How Many Is Too Many?" *The Atlantic* 271, no. 2 (1993): 47–67.

Markandaya, Kamala. *Nectar in a Sieve*. New York: John Day, 1954.

Martin, David, and Phyllis Johnson. *The Struggle for Zimbabwe*. New York: Monthly Review Press, 1981.

Mayall, James, and Mark Simpson. "Ethnicity Is Not Enough: Reflections on Protracted Secessionism in the Third World." *International Journal of Comparative Sociology* 33, nos. 1–2 (1992).

Maybury-Lewis, David. *Indigenous Peoples, Ethnic Groups, and the State*. 2d ed. Boston: Allyn and Bacon, 2002.

McKibben, Bill. "A Special Moment in History." *Atlantic Monthly* 281, no. 5 (1998).

McMichael, Philip. "A Global Interpretation of the Rise of the East Asian Food Import Complex." *World Development*, special issue, *Changing Agro-Food and Fiber Systems in Asia* 28, no. 3 (2000): 409–24.

Meier, V. "Cut-Flower Production in Colombia — A Major Development Success Story for Women?" *Environment and Planning* 31 (1999): 273–89.

Mengisteab, Kidane. *Globalization and Autocentricity in Africa's Development in the Twenty-first Century*. Trenton, N.J.: Africa World Press, 1996.

Merrick, Thomas W. *World Population in Transition*. Washington, D.C.: Population Reference Bureau. *Population Bulletin* 41, no. 2 (1991).

Mittelman, James H. *Out from Underdevelopment: Prospects for the Third World*. New York: St. Martin's Press, 1988.

Mittelman, James H., and Mustapha Kamal Pasha. *Out from Underdevelopment Revisited: Changing Global Structures and the Remaking of the Third World*. New York: St. Martin's Press, 1997.

Moffett, George D. *Critical Masses: The Global Population Challenge*. New York: Penguin Books, 1994.

Mohanty, Chandra, Ann Russo, and Lourdes Torres. *Third World Women and the Politics of Feminism*. Bloomington: Indiana University Press, 1991.

Morrissey, Oliver, and Igor Filatotchev. "Globalisation and Trade: The Implications for Exports from Marginalised Economies." *Journal of Development Studies* 37, no. 2 (2000): 1–45.

Murdoch, William. *The Poverty of Nations: The Political Economy of Hunger and Population*. Baltimore: Johns Hopkins University Press, 1980.

Naipaul, V. S. *A Bend in the River*. New York: Random House, 1979.

———. *Half a Life*. New York: Knopf, 2001.

Ndegwa, Stephen. *The Two Faces of Civil Society: NGOs and Politics in Africa*. West Hartford, Conn.: Kumarian Press, 1996.

Ngugi wa Thiong'o. *Decolonising the Mind: The Politics of Language in African Literature*. London: Heinemann Books, 1986.

———. *The River Between*. London: Heinemann, 1965.

Olcott, Martha Brill. *Revisiting the Twelve Myths of Central Asia*. New York: Carnegie Endowment for International Peace, Working Paper No. 23, September 2001.

Orians, Carlyn, and Marina Skumanich. *The Population-Environment Connection: What Does It Mean for Environmental Policy?* U.S. Environmental Protection Agency document. Seattle: Battelle Seattle Research Center, 1995.

Oxfam International. *Growth with Equity: An Agenda for Poverty Reduction*. Oxford: Oxfam International, 1997.

Palmer, R. R. *A History of the Modern World.* 2d ed. New York: Alfred A. Knopf, 1956.

Peterson, V. Spike, and Anne Sisson Runyan. *Global Gender Issues.* Boulder, Colo.: Westview Press, 1999.

Pettman, Ralph. *Understanding International Political Economy.* Boulder, Colo.: Lynne Rienner, 1996.

Pinkney, Robert. *Democracy in the Third World.* Boulder, Colo.: Lynne Rienner, 1994.

Phongpaichit, Sungsidh Piriyarangsan, and Nualnoi Treerat. *Guns, Girls, Gambling, and Ganja: Thailand's Illegal Economy and Public Policy.* Chiang Mai, Thailand: Silkworm Books, 1998.

Ponte, Stefano. "Trapped in Decline? Reassessing Agrarian Change and Economic Diversification on the Uluguru Mountains, Tanzania." *Journal of Modern African Studies* 39, no. 1 (2001): 81–100.

Porter, Gareth, with Delfin J. Ganapin Jr. *Resources, Population, and the Philippines' Future: A Case Study.* WRI Paper, No. 4. Washington, D.C.: World Resources Institute, 1988.

Pretty, Jules, Irene Guijt, Ian Scoones, and John Thompson. "Regenerating Agriculture: The Agroecology of Low-External Input and Community-Based Development." In *Making Development Sustainable: Redefining Institutions, Policy, and Economics,* edited by Johan Holmberg, 91–123. Washington, D.C.: Island Press, 1992.

Putnam, Robert D. *Making Democracy Work.* Princeton, N.J.: Princeton University Press, 1993.

Rashid, Ahmed. *Taliban.* New Haven, Conn.: Yale University Press, 2001.

———. "The Taliban: Exporting Extremism." *Foreign Affairs* 87, no. 6 (November/December 1999).

Rau, Bill. *From Feast to Famine: Official Cures and Grassroots Remedies to Africa's Food Crisis.* London: Zed Books, 1991.

Raynolds, Laura T. "Negotiating Contract Farming in the Dominican Republic." *Human Organization* 59, no. 4 (2000).

Reid, Elizabeth, ed. *HIV and AIDS, The Global Inter-Connection.* West Hartford, Conn.: Kumarian Press, 1995.

Reitsma, H. A., and J. M. G. Kleinpenning. *The Third World in Perspective.* Assen, The Netherlands: Rowman & Allanheld, 1985.

Repetto, Robert, ed. *The Global Possible: Resources, Development, and the New Century.* New Haven and London: Yale University, 1985.

Rich, Bruce. *Mortgaging the Earth: The World Bank, Environmental Impoverishment, and the Crisis of Development.* Boston: Beacon Press, 1994.

Rocheleau, Dianne, Barbara Thomas-Slayter, and Esther Wangari, eds. *Feminist Political Ecology: Global Issues and Local Experiences.* London: Routledge, 1996.

Rodan, Garry, Kevin Hewison, and Richard Robison. *The Political Economy of South-East Asia.* Oxford: Oxford University Press, 1997.

Rodney, Walter. *How Europe Underdeveloped Africa.* Dar es Salaam: Tanzania Publishing House, 1972.

Rostow, W. W. *The Stages of Economic Growth: A Non-Communist Manifesto.* 2d ed. Cambridge: Cambridge University Press, 1971.

Rothchild, Donald, and Naomi Chazan, eds. *The Precarious Balance: State and Society in Africa.* Boulder, Colo.: Westview Press, 1988.

Rothchild, Donald, and Victor A. Olorunsola, eds. *State versus Ethnic Claims.* Boulder, Colo.: Westview Press, 1983.

Rubin, Barnett R. "Who Are the Taliban?" *Current History* 98, no. 625 (1999): 79–91.

Rubin, Barnett R., Aashraf Ghani, William Maley, Ahmed Rashid, Olivier Roy. *Afghanistan: Reconstruction and Peace-Building in a Regional Framework.* Koff Peacebuilding Reports. Bern: Koff Center for Peacebuilding, Swiss Peace Foundation, 2001.

Sachs, Wolfgang, ed. *The Development Dictionary: A Guide to Knowledge as Power.* London: Zed Books, 1993.

Sargent, Caroline, and Stephen Bass. "The Future Shape of Forests." In *Making Development Sustainable: Redefining Institutions, Policy, and Economics,* edited by Johan Holmberg, 195–224. Washington, D.C.: Island Press, 1992.

Saro-wiwa, Ken. *A Month and a Day: A Detention Diary.* New York: Penguin Books, 1995.

Schraeder, Peter. *African Politics and Society.* Boston and New York: Bedford/St. Martins, 2000.

Schutz, Barry M., and Robert O. Slater. *Revolution and Political Change in the Third World.* Boulder, Colo.: Lynne Rienner, 1990.

Scott, James C. "Patron-Client Politics and Political Change in Southeast Asia." *American Political Science Review* 16, no. 1 (1972).

Sen, Amartya. *Development as Freedom.* New York: Random House, 1999.

———. *Inequality Reexamined.* Cambridge, Mass.: Harvard University Press, 1992.

Sen, Gita, and Caren Grown. *Development, Crises, and Alternative Visions.* New York: Monthly Review Press, 1987.

Senillosa, Ignacio de. "A New Age of Social Movements: a Fifth Generation of Nongovernmental Development Organisations in the Making?" In *Development in Action,* edited by Deborah Eade, 87–103. London: Oxfam GB, 1999.

Shiva, Vandana. "Diversity and Democracy: Resisting the Global Economy." *Global Dialogue: The Globalisation Phenomenon* 1, no. 1 (1999): 19–30.

Smeets, Maarten. "Globalisation: Threat or Promise." *Global Dialogue: The Globalisation Phenomenon* 1, no. 1 (1999): 10–18.

Spencer, Dunstan S. C. "Infrastructure and Technology Constraints to Agricultural Development in the Humid and Subhumid Tropics of Africa." EPTD Discussion Paper, No. 3 Washington, D.C.: International Food Policy Research Institute, August 1994.

Spradley, James, and David W. McCurdy. *Conformity and Conflict.* New York: Addison Wesley Longman, 1997.

Stamp, Patricia. *Technology, Gender and Power in Africa.* Ottawa, Ontario: International Development Research Center, 1989.

Stepanek, Joseph F. *Wringing Success from Failure in Late-Developing Countries: Lessons from the Field.* Westport, Conn.: Praeger, 1999.

Stiglitz, Joseph. *Globalization and Its Discontents.* New York: W. W. Norton, 2002.

Stockholm International Peace Research Institute. *SIPRI Yearbook 2001 — Armaments, Disarmament, and International Security.* London: Oxford University Press, 2001.

Stonich, Susan. "Struggling with Honduran Poverty: The Environmental Consequences of Natural Resource-Based Development and Rural Transformation." *World Development* 20, no. 3 (1992).

Stremlau, John. *People in Peril: Human Rights, Humanitarian Action, and Preventing Deadly Conflict.* Washington, D.C.: Carnegie Commission on Preventing Deadly Conflict, 1998.

Swaminathan, M. S. *Food 2000, Global Policies for Sustainable Agriculture.* A Report of the Advisory Panel on Food Security, Agriculture, Forestry and Environment to the World Commission on Environment and Development. London: Zed Books, 1987.

Teitelbaum, Michael S., and Myron Weiner, eds. *Threatened Peoples, Threatened Borders.* New York: W. W. Norton, 1995.

Thomas-Slayter, Barbara P. "Class, Ethnicity, and the Kenyan State: Community Mobilization in the Context of Global Politics." *International Journal of Politics, Culture, and Society* 4, no. 3 (Spring 1991): 301–21.

Thomas-Slayter, Barbara P., and Dianne Rocheleau. *Gender, Environment, and Development in Kenya: A Grassroots Perspective.* Boulder, Colo.: Lynne Rienner, 1995.

Thompson, Susan J., and J. Tadlock Cowan. "Globalizing Agro-Food Systems in Asia: Introduction." *World Development,* special issue, Changing Agro-Food and Fiber Systems in Asia, 28, no. 3 (2000): 401–7.

Thrupp, Lori Ann. *Bittersweet Harvests for Global Supermarkets: Challenges in Latin America's Agricultural Export Boom.* Washington, D.C. World Resources Institute, 1995.

Tiffin, Mary, Michael Mortimore, and Fancis Gichuki. *More People, Less Erosion: Environmental Recovery in Kenya.* London: Wiley and Sons, 1994.

———. *Population Growth and Environmental Recovery: Policy Lessons from Kenya.* London: IIED, Gatekeeper Series, No. 45, 1994.

Tinker, Irene. *Persistent Inequalities: Women and World Development.* Oxford: Oxford University Press, 1990.

Toulmin, Camilla, Ian Scoones, and Joshua Bishop. "The Future of Africa's Drylands: Is Local Resource Management the Answer?" In *Making Development Sustainable: Redefining Institutions, Policy, and Economics,* edited by Johan Holmberg, 225–57. Washington, D.C.: Island Press, 1992.

Topouzis, Daphne. "The Implications of HIV/AIDS for Rural Development Policy and Programming: Focus on Sub-Saharan Africa." FAO Report. Rome: FAO, 1998.

UNDP. *Human Development Report, 1994.* New York: Oxford University Press, 1994.

———. *Human Development Report: Making New Technologies Work for Human Development.* New York: Oxford University Press, 2001.

———. *Human Development Report, 2000.* New York: Oxford University Press, 2000.

———. *Human Development Report, 2002*. New York: Oxford University Press, 2002.

———. *Overcoming Human Poverty*. UNDP Poverty Report, 1998. New York: UNDP, 1998.

UNHCR. *The State of the World's Refugees: In Search of Solutions*. New York: Oxford University Press, 1995.

United Nations Commission on Narcotic Drugs. *Economic and Social Consequences of Drug Abuse and Illicit Trafficking*. An Interim Report March 1995.

United Nations Conference on Trade and Development (UNCTAD). *The Least Developed Countries, 1998 Report*. Geneva: UNCTAD, 1998.

Urban, Anne-Marie, and Mary Hill Rojas. *Shifting Boundaries: Gender, Migration, and Community Resources in the Foothills of Choluteca, Honduras*. Worcester, Mass.: Clark University, ECOGEN Case Study, 1994.

Uvin, Peter. *Aiding Violence: The Development Enterprise in Rwanda*. West Hartford, Conn.: Kumarian Press, 1998.

Watkins, Kevin. *The Oxfam Poverty Report*. Oxford: Oxfam UK and Ireland, 1995.

Weaver, James H., Michael T. Rock, and Kenneth Kusterer. *Achieving Broad-Based Sustainable Development*. West Hartford, Conn.: Kumarian Press, 1996.

Wilber, Charles K., ed. *The Political Economy of Development and Underdevelopment*. 3d ed. New York: Random House, 1984.

Williams, Lydia, ed. *Gender Equity and the World Bank Group: A Post-Beijing Assessment*. Washington, D.C.: Women's Eyes on the World Bank, 1997.

World Bank. *Entering the Twenty-first Century: World Development Report 1999/2000*. New York: Oxford University Press, 2000.

———. *The State in a Changing World: World Development Report 1997*. New York: Oxford University Press, 1997.

———. *Knowledge for Development: World Development Report 1999*. New York: Oxford University Press, 1999.

———. *World Development Report 2001 and World Development Indicators*. New York: Oxford University Press, 2001.

———. *Building Institutions for Markets: World Development Report 2002*. New York: Oxford University Press, 2002.

World Resources Institute, The United Nations Environment Program (UNEP) and the United Nations Development Program (UNDP), and the World Bank. *World Resources, 1998–99, A Guide to the Global Environment*. Oxford: Oxford University Press, 1998.

World Resources Institute, The United Nations Environment Program, and the United Nations Development Program. *World Resources, 1994–1995. People and the Environment*. Oxford: Oxford University Press, 1994.

Zaman, Habiba. "Paid Work and Socio-Political Consciousness of Garment Workers in Bangladesh." *Journal of Contemporary Asia* 31, no. 2 (2001): 145–60.

Zolberg, Aristide R., Astri Suhrke, and Sergio Aguayo. *Escape from Violence: Conflict and the Refugee Crisis in the Developing World*. New York: Oxford University Press, 1989.

Index

Afghanistan, 112, 116, 193
  colonialism's legacy for, 65, 69–71
  front line of Cold War, 70
  gender-based discrimination, 136, 137–38
Africa
  agricultural production, decrease per
    capita, 255
  AIDS in, 238–42
  carving up, 44–45, 67
  church's role in, 83
  debt problems, 256
  food assistance, 251
  food production in, 249, 250, 254–56
  food security, 269–70
  income disparity, 6
  inequitable land allocation in, 47–48
  international aid for diverted to Central
    Asia, 60–61
  land mines, 117
  narrow margin of survival, 254
  reduced share of global trade, 256
  secondhand clothing market, 199–201
  sedentarization of populations increasing,
    257–58
  taxation under colonialism, 47
Afwerki, Isaias, 88
agency, 81
agrarian reform, 29, 258–60
agrarian societies, neoclassical view of, 15
agriculture, 7–8. See also farming
  as dominant industry, 11
  liberalization of, 253
  low external input technologies, 269
  output, methods of increasing, 248–49
  policies, ignoring responsibilities of rural
    women, 254
  resources, gender-based entitlement to, 262
  types of, 248
agrofood markets, private, 253
AIDS, 238–42
  effect on African agricultural production,
    255
  recent initiatives, 241–42
  in Southern Africa, 89–90

AIDS Control Program (Uganda), 240
Albania, 130
Amin, Samir, 18
Angola, 25, 89, 117
Annan, Kofi, 29, 312
anti-sweatshop movement, 202–3, 300
apparel industry, contradictions within, 202.
    See also garment industry
Apparel Industry Partnership, 300
Argentina, 8, 116, 174
arms trade, 30, 116–18, 140–41
Asia
  beneficiary of Green Revolution, 260
  colonial settlements in, 46
  financial crisis (1990s), 11, 176–78
  food production in, 249, 250, 252–54
Asian Pacific Economic Cooperation group,
    171
Atlantic Charter, 57–58
Australia
  Gender Empowerment Measure ranking,
    297
  human development index, 5–6
authority, crisis of, 114–15
authority structures, loss of effectiveness
    under colonialism, 51–52
autonomy, 81

Bandarage, Asoka, 73–74
Bandaranaike, SWRD, 120
Bandung Conference (Indonesia, 1955), 4, 8,
    56, 98
Bangladesh, 8, 11
  colonialism's effect on, 46
  creation of, 98, 114
  emigration from, 243
  exports, 168
  fertility decline, 228–29
  garment industry, 203–4, 301
  hunger in, 276
  negative employment-fertility relationship,
    234
  resources of, 7, 16

347

About the Author

Barbara Thomas-Slayter is a professor in the Department of International Development, Community, and Environment at Clark University, Worcester, Massachusetts, where she has taught and directed the academic program in international development for over twenty years. A political scientist, she has written numerous articles and books pertaining to local institutions, gender, environment, politics, development, and rural livelihood systems in Africa and Asia. In addition to an accumulated ten years residence in Kenya, the Philippines, Sri Lanka, and Bangladesh, Professor Thomas-Slayter has carried out research in various other countries of East Asia, South Asia, and Eastern and Southern Africa. She is a founder of Oxfam America and has served a total of thirteen years on the Board of Directors of that organization. Professor Thomas-Slayter earned her Ph.D. from Brandeis University and subsequently was a visiting scholar at Boston University's African Studies Center, a Fulbright scholar in Zimbabwe, and a fellow at Radcliffe's Bunting Institute. Previous books include *Politics, Participation and Poverty: Development through Self-Help in Kenya; Gender, Environment, and Development in Kenya; Power, Process, and Participation: Tools for Change; A Manual for Socio-Economic and Gender Analysis;* and *Feminist Political Ecology, Global Issues, and Local Experiences.*

Also from Kumarian Press...

Global Issues

Confronting Globalization
Economic Integration and Popular Resistance in Mexico
Edited by Timothy A. Wise, Hilda Salazar and Laura Carlsen

Going Global: Transforming Relief and Development NGOs
Marc Lindenberg and Coralie Bryant

Inequity in the Global Village: Recycled Rhetoric and Disposable People
Jan Knippers Black

Running Out of Control: Dilemmas of Globalization
R. Alan Hedley

Sustainable Livelihoods: Building on the Wealth of the Poor
Kristin Helmore and Naresh Singh

Worlds Apart: Civil Society and the Battle for Ethical Globalization
John D. Clark

Where Corruption Lives
Edited by Gerald E. Caiden, O.P. Dwivedi and Joseph Jabbra

Conflict Resolution, Environment, Gender Studies, Globalization,
International Development, Microfinance, Political Economy

Advocacy for Social Justice: A Global Action and Reflection Guide
David Cohen, Rosa de la Vega, Gabrielle Watson for Oxfam America and the Advocacy Institute

Better Governance and Public Policy
Capacity Building and Democratic Renewal in Africa
Edited by Dele Olowu and Soumana Sako

The Humanitarian Enterprise: Dilemmas and Discoveries
Larry Minear

Pathways Out of Poverty: Innovations in Microfinance for the Poorest Families
Edited by Sam Daley-Harris

Protecting the Future: HIV Prevention, Care and Support Among Displaced
and War-Affected Populations
Wendy Holmes for The International Rescue Committee

War and Intervention: Issues for Contemporary Peace Operations
Michael V. Bhatia

Visit Kumarian Press at **www.kpbooks.com** or
call **toll-free 800.289.2664** for a complete catalog.

Kumarian Press, located in Bloomfield, Connecticut, is a forward-looking, scholarly press that promotes active international engagement and an awareness of global connectedness.